THE USE AND ABUSE OF INTELLECTUAL
PROPERTY RIGHTS IN E.C. LAW

AUSTRALIA
LBC Information Services
Sydney

CANADA and USA
Carswell
Toronto: Ontario

NEW ZEALAND
Brooker's
Auckland

SINGAPORE and MALAYSIA
Thomson Information (S.E. Asia)
Singapore

THE USE AND ABUSE OF INTELLECTUAL PROPERTY RIGHTS IN E.C. LAW

Including a case study of the E.C. spare parts debate

By

Dr INGE GOVAERE
Ph.D. (European University Institute, Florence)
Lecturer
Law Department
College of Europe
Bruges

With foreword by

Advocate General F. G. JACOBS
European Court of Justice

LONDON • SWEET & MAXWELL • 1996

Published in 1996 by
Sweet & Maxwell Limited
of South Quay Plaza
183 Marsh Wall, London E14 9FT
Typeset by MFK Information Services Ltd,
Hitchin, Herts.
Printed and bound in Great Britain
by Butler and Tanner Ltd, Frome and London

No natural forests were destroyed
to make this product only farmed
timber was used and replanted.

A CIP catalogue record for this book
is available from The British Library

ISBN 0 421 53930 5

To my husband Marco, and to Moesje and Ann.
In memory of my grandparents Maria and Albert.

Foreword

"The use and abuse of intellectual property rights", the somewhat provocative phrase which appears in the title of this book, epitomises the continuing debate about the proper scope of these rights in a liberal economy. We may no longer, it is true, think of the relationship between intellectual property rights and fair competition only in terms of conflict: we may instead recognise that such rights are an integral part of a competitive system. And we no longer think in simplistic terms of a conflict between intellectual property rights and free trade: as is illustrated by the incorporation of the TRIPS-Agreement into the World Trade Organisation Agreement, the protection of such rights should rather be regarded as an integral part of the world trading system. For practical purposes, nevertheless, it is the proper and improper use of intellectual property rights—patents, trade marks, industrial design, copyright and other rights, and each in the light of its own specific function—which the law must define, in every modern system, so as to reconcile conflicting objectives.

This book ambitiously seeks to determine the proper limits of intellectual property rights in E.C. law. That task has often had to be performed on a case-by-case basis by the European Court of Justice: as the author shows, the broad terms of the E.C. Treaty have imposed on the Court the task of tracing the limits of each form of intellectual property; in so doing the Court has, as she says, always endeavoured to strike a balance between intellectual property rights on the one hand and the Community objectives of creating a single market and maintaining workable competition on the other hand. Striking the right balance is no easy task, given the territoriality principle of rights which are for the most part still firmly anchored in the national law of each Member State. It could even be said that the Treaty, in requiring the Court by Articles 30 and 36 to decide in what circumstances restrictions on trade are "justified" on grounds of the protection of intellectual property, and in what circumstances such restrictions are not justified on those grounds, is asking the impossible. But answers had to be found. Most informed observers probably recognise that the answers have not been unreasonable. Occasionally perhaps there was excessive emphasis on market integration at the expense of trade marks, as in 1974 in the (wholly exceptional) situation of marks of common origin. But in the same year the *Centrafarm* judgments, defining the "specific subject-matter" of patents and trade marks, seemed to provide a sound basis for the interface between national intellectual property rights and the Common Market. More recently, some observers might say that the Court has gone too far in deferring to national rights, by failing in some cases to specify their proper limits and effectively leaving the solution to national law. Has the Court still got the balance right?

The reader of this book will be exceptionally well placed to answer that question and to grasp all its implications. The author's exposition of the issues is thorough and clear. She analyses the solutions adopted by the Court with a keen critical acumen. But her criticism is itself admirably balanced.

A further great advantage of the author's treatment of the subject is that she takes a case study to illuminate the subject, and has chosen a highly important and instructive one, the spare parts issue. The topic of the spare parts of cars provides an excellent basis for examining the place of intellectual property rights both in the context of the free movement of goods and in the context of antitrust. Again not uncritical of the case law, she uses it deftly to explore every aspect of this topic.

In paying tribute to this book, I would also pay tribute, as the author does, to the remarkable institutions for study and research in European law in which she was nurtured: the University of Ghent and the European University Institute in Florence. Like a number of other books from those institutions, this thoughtful work will be invaluable both for further academic study of the subject and for the practitioner—indeed, for all who seek a deeper understanding.

Advocate General F. G. Jacobs
European Court of Justice
Luxembourg,
September 1995

Acknowledgments

Writing this book would not have been possible without numerous discussions with colleagues and friends on the various topics raised. I am particularly grateful to the European University Institute in Florence (EUI), the European Institute at the University of Ghent (RUG) and the College of Europe in Bruges for having provided an excellent working environment. All three institutions have presented an important stimulus to my academic research. A special thanks goes to the EUI Publications Committee for the allocation of a grant to cover the editing cost of the manuscript.

Although it is impossible to mention everybody to whom I feel indebted individually, for which I hope they will accept my apologies, certain persons who were particularly helpful need to be named. I would first of all like to thank Advocate General F. Jacobs (ECJ), Judge K. Lenaerts (CFI), Professor C. Joerges (EUI), Professor M. Maresceau (RUG) and Professor J. Schwarze (University of Freiburg) for their valuable comments on the book. A special thanks goes to Professor C. Joerges who provided the initial impetus and encouraged me in my research all along. My former colleagues at the European Institute, Professor P. Eeckhout and Dr E. Montaguti, also need special mention for most interesting and fruitful exchanges of thoughts. I would further like to express my acknowledgment to Mr B. Posner of the E.C. Commission who has been extremely helpful in forwarding information on the elaboration of the proposals on the Community Design.

I also wish to express my thanks to Sweet & Maxwell and its staff for their practical help and support. I am very grateful for the delay they granted in order to allow me to incorporate the *Magill* appeal judgment into the book.

Inge Govaere
Bruges
August 21, 1995

Contents

Contents

Table of Cases

COURT OF FIRST INSTANCE

COMMISSION DECISIONS

Table of Legislation

PART I

INTRODUCTORY

1. General Introduction

1. INTELLECTUAL PROPERTY RIGHTS REVISITED

Intellectual property rights[1] have long been the subject of much legal dis-   1.01
cussion and writing due both to the complexity of the matter and to an
increasing awareness of the importance of the legal protection of innovative
and creative works for economic progress and development. Although in the
past controversies have arisen as to the necessity and purpose of these exclusive rights, nowadays the need for adequate protection is no longer seriously
contested. Instead, the main concern has become where to draw the line
between what constitutes a lawful use or an abuse of intellectual property
protection, as well as to clarify what these concepts entail. This may be

---

[1] The term "intellectual property rights" has two distinct meanings. It will be used in the book
principally in its broad sense to cover industrial, commercial and intellectual property rights. In
some cases it will be used, *stricto sensu*, to cover copyright and related rights. The latter
meaning may be inferred where intellectual property rights are distinguished from, or
compared with, industrial and/or commercial property rights.

explained by the conceptual change which has taken place in the perception of the role of intellectual property rights in international trade.[2]

1.02   Intellectual property rights, which confer temporary exclusive rights on the basis of the principle of territoriality, were traditionally regarded merely as non-tariff barriers to trade. This was due to the fact that they are particularly apt to jeopardise the movement of protected products and may, to a certain extent, be used to prohibit both inter-brand and intra-brand competition. Because of their apparently anti-competitive effects, the very existence of a system of intellectual property rights was initially challenged by some upon its necessity. Early studies mainly focused on establishing the need to maintain such a system in force and analysed the manner in which these exclusive rights were upheld in different legal systems. In other words, it was mainly illustrated that, and emphasised why, intellectual property rights were widely recognised to be *indispensable* barriers to trade.

1.03   In particular the so-called technological revolution marked a turning point in this line of thinking. The costly investments in research and development necessary to come to technological innovations, which were often all the more easy to copy, brought about an increasing awareness of the economic significance of intellectual property rights. This entailed a shift in the perception of the role of intellectual property rights by economic actors who were followed by the legislators. Rather than being perceived merely as barriers to trade, intellectual property rights thus became real trade assets and have proved to be an excellent means of obtaining market dominance not only on the home market but also abroad. In other words, the focus has shifted from emphasising the detrimental impact of the principle of territoriality towards emphasising the beneficial economic effects of exclusivity as conferred by intellectual property rights on trade. This conceptual change, from indispensable trade barriers to indispensable assets in furtherance of trade,[3] has not been confined to Europe. At the instigation of the industrialised countries the new perception of the role of intellectual property rights has also been endorsed in a worldwide context. The latter is best illustrated by the conclusion of the Agreement on Trade Related Aspects of Intellectual Property Rights (TRIPS-Agreement) as annexed to the Agreement on the World Trade Organisation (WTO-Agreement).

1.04   It is against this background of striving to extend the scope of protection offered by, and the enforcement of, exclusive rights in order to obtain market dominance that a renewed study of the place of intellectual property rights in Community law is highly relevant. Increasingly, the crucial issue has become whether conferring market power is merely incidental to, and may thus be

---

[2] For a detailed analysis of the conceptual change in the perception of the role of intellectual property rights in international trade, and in particular in so far as the E.C. is concerned, see I. Govaere, "Trade-related aspects of intellectual property rights: the E.C. dichotomy uncovered", in *La place de l'Europe dans le commerce mondial* (July Session 1994, Institut Universitaire International Luxembourg), pp. 161–215.

[3] On this issue, see also U. Joos and R. Moufang, "Report of the second Ringberg Symposium" in *GATT or WIPO?* (Beier and Schricker eds. 1989), (IIC Studies, VCH), Vol. 11, pp. 1–41. At p. 31 they point out that: "... the conceptual change is reflected by the fact that the existence of intellectual property rights was previously held to result in possible trade barriers whereas today a contrary view prevails, *i.e.* the lack and the deficiencies of legal protection are considered to endanger the international exchange of goods".

justified in terms of, safeguarding the protection of intangible property or whether, to the contrary, the system of intellectual property rights is diverted from its purpose in order to obtain market dominance. Rejecting offhand the hypothesis that intellectual property rights may be abused, and thus refusing to engage in the use-abuse debate, not only amounts to an "ostrich" attitude in the current context. It is tantamount to allowing the system of intellectual property rights to be reduced to an empty shell. In order to reinforce the long-term viability of the latter it is important to shield it from abuses, however few they are. In other words, nowadays more than ever before there is an urgent need to find adequate criteria to determine whether and when intellectual property rights are abusively used for purposes other than to safeguard the protection of "creations of the intellect". The importance of this issue is all the more apparent when, conversely, it is pointed out that it is on the basis of the same criteria that it will be decided that intellectual property rights should be fully upheld. In the absence of adequate criteria to distinguish between use and abuse, it may be that eventually the whole system of intellectual property rights is once again put at stake.

2. SCOPE, PURPOSE AND STRUCTURE

Even though the elaboration of clear and consistent guidelines on the use of intellectual property rights is essential to provide legal security in the market place, it seems to be particularly difficult to achieve this in the context of the European Union. This is perfectly illustrated by the controversies which surrounded the *Magill* cases from the outset and which are most likely to persist after, if they are not fuelled by, the judgment rendered by the European Court of Justice on appeal on April 6, 1995.[4] Not only do the laws of the Member States still differ in the absence of full harmonisation but the competence of the European Community, and especially of the European Court of Justice, to deal with substantive matters of intellectual property rights is still not fully acknowledged. This is due mainly to the fact that intellectual property rights are mentioned only in Article 36 of the E.C. Treaty which provides an exception to the fundamental principle of free movement of goods. It is important to note that this has not been altered by either the Single European Act or the Maastricht Treaty on a European Union. Obviously such rights have wider implications, for example for the application of Community rules on competition. Because intellectual property rights are inherently exclusive rights, the question recurrently arises as to how, and to what extent, they can be reconciled with the concept of workable competition in the European Community. **1.05**

The elaboration of coherent Community-wide guidelines as to what constitutes a lawful use or an abuse of intellectual property protection is dependent on the approach that will be taken in the future to several fundamental matters. Amongst these are the consequences of differing, and even conflicting, **1.06**

---

[4] Joined Cases C–241 and 242/91 P, *Radio Telefis Eireann (RTE) and Independent Television Publications Ltd (ITP) v. Commission*: [1995] E.C.R. I–743; [1995] 4 C.M.L.R. 718.

national laws; the importance attached to the scope and inherent functions of intellectual property rights; the delineation of competence between the E.C. and Member States; the application of general principles of Community law; and the implications of the so-called patent-antitrust debate. Even though all of these issues have already been raised in an E.C. context, to a large extent they still remain unresolved, or are subject to controversy, or appear to be open-ended.

1.07   The purpose of this book is to analyse the nature, and to examine the long-term feasibility, of the solutions so far adopted in relation to intellectual property rights under E.C. law, and also to pinpoint the major difficulties and shortcomings that urgently need to be remedied. Chapters 2 to 6 examine the current state of the application of E.C. law to patents, trade marks, copyright and related rights, as well as to industrial designs. It is important in this respect to look at not only E.C. harmonisation measures but also, perhaps even more so, at the case law of the Court on the application of the rules on the free movement of goods and services and the rules on competition. A detailed analysis of basic principles and concepts as introduced and in particular as further elaborated upon by the Court, such as the existence/exercise dichotomy, the principle of exhaustion, the specific subject-matter concept, etc., is crucial in order to try to understand on what basis intellectual property protection may be held to be abused under E.C. law. It should be emphasised in this respect that the Court has not yet elaborated a coherent approach to intellectual property rights but is still proceeding very much on a case-by-case basis. For instance, the concept of specific subject-matter is often redefined in order to justify the outcome of a case, whereas the principle of exhaustion[5] will not automatically be applied when the intellectual property owner consents to putting the protected products on the E.C. market. In other words, the meaning and importance of basic principles and essential concepts is often determined in the light of the circumstances specific to a case. This is the main cause of confusion when these principles and concepts are used in an abstract way. It therefore seems to be important, at least in the present state of E.C. law, to try to understand under what circumstances the Court might favour one approach over another, rather than merely to pin down abstract concepts.

1.08   One of the objectives of the book is to expose the subtleties and inconsistencies in the E.C. approach towards the use and abuse of intellectual property rights, and the variability of the concepts as currently used by the Court. This was particularly evident in the spare parts cases[6] which are dealt with by way of a case study in Chapters 7 to 9. A detailed analysis of the latter cases proved to be highly significant, in particular having regard to the fact that the Court expressly referred to the *Volvo* case in the subsequent *Magill* appeal judgment. It did so in spite of the apparently contradictory statements in both,

---

[5] In essence, the principle of exhaustion implies that the intellectual property owner may no longer invoke his intellectual property rights in Member States in order to prevent the importation of products which have been put on the Community market by himself or with his consent.

[6] Case 53/87, *Consorzio italiano della componentistica di ricambio per autoveivoli and Maxicar v. Régie nationale des usines Renault*, Judgment of October 5, 1988: [1988] E.C.R. 6039; [1990] 4 C.M.L.R. 265. Case 238/87, *AB Volvo v. Erik Veng (UK) Ltd*, Judgment of October 5, 1988: [1988] E.C.R. 6211; [1989] 4 C.M.L.R. 122.

and in spite of the fact that the practical results ensuing from the judgments are radically opposed. The case study of the spare parts cases and the recurrent comparison with *Magill* illustrate the variability of both the Court's approach and the basic concepts used. Furthermore, the case study addresses other issues that may arise in any given intellectual property case even though they are not specifically linked to the use-abuse controversy. A step-by-step analysis is given which covers both matters of general application of E.C. law, such as the scope of Articles 30–34, 85 and 86 E.C., and various arguments that may be put forward, for instance in terms of consumer protection. Chapters 7 to 9 are therefore complementary to, rather than merely a practical illustration of, the specific issues dealt with in Chapters 2 to 6. The following section gives an overview of the main issues raised in the various chapters of the book.

3. OVERVIEW OF THE MAIN ISSUES RAISED

(1) Intellectual property rights under community law

(a) Intellectual property rights in furtherance of competition

Chapter 2 gives a brief introduction to the functions and objectives of the different types of intellectual property rights in order to illustrate the specificity of patents, copyright, trade marks and design protection. A common characteristic is that they are all based on the principle of territoriality and confer exclusive rights. At first sight, they appear to have a detrimental impact on the free movement of goods and competition in the Community. The national character of intellectual property rights based on the territoriality principle is difficult to reconcile with the objective of creating a single market in which the free movement of goods prevails, whereas the conferring of exclusive rights might pose problems in terms of the rules on competition. It is important, however, to point out from the outset that intellectual property rights have an essential role to fulfil as a stimulus to innovation and development, and thus for economic growth. As such, it is generally acknowledged that the temporary restraints on competition are justified to ultimately further competition in the market.   **1.09**

The main question dealt with in Chapter 2 is whether all restraints on competition may be justified in terms of the need to safeguard intellectual property protection. It is submitted that, in order to provide an answer, regard must be had to the fact that different types of intellectual property rights respond to different objectives and thus have a specific function to fulfil. So far the attention of both lawyers and economists has mainly focused on the so-called patent-antitrust debate. This is mainly due to the fact that patents are most apt to confer monopoly power. May this debate simply be transposed to, for instance, design rights or trade marks? The specific function that each intellectual property right fulfils may justify different restrictions on competition. Conversely, this would also seem to imply that not all restraints on competition may be justified in terms of safeguarding the essential objective of any given intellectual property right. In other words, it is submitted that it is   **1.10** difficult to conceive of one unequivocal approach that satisfactorily covers the system of intellectual property protection in general. Instead, it seems that an appraisal needs to be made as to the balance between each type of intellectual property on the one hand and competition on the other.

1.11   Another important issue addressed in Chapter 2 is the relationship between E.C. law and international intellectual property conventions concluded *inter alia* by some or all Member States. In the absence of E.C. harmonisation measures, the latter often constitute the only factor of approximation of national intellectual property laws between Member States. The question therefore arises of when, and if, these intellectual property conventions may successfully be invoked in order to escape the application of the E.C. Treaty.

(b) The place of intellectual property rights in E.C. law

1.12   Chapter 3 examines the place that has been assigned to intellectual property rights in Community law. If one accepts the premise that intellectual property rights have a major impact on the market, and are an important stimulus to innovation and economic progress, then it is apparent that by their very nature and economic purpose they come within the ambit of the E.C. Treaty. However, from the wording of the E.C. Treaty it appears that the draftsmen were reluctant to subject national intellectual property law to E.C. rules and principles. The fact that the only express reference to intellectual property protection is to be found in Article 36 E.C. initially led to the question of whether the E.C. was at all competent to deal with matters of intellectual property protection. Although it can no longer be seriously contested that both the Member States and the E.C. have a concurrent competence in this matter, in the absence of harmonisation measures the question as to how to delineate between their respective competence still remains to a large extent unanswered. The purpose of Chapter 3 is to examine to what extent, and on what basis, the E.C. has appropriated the competence to deal with matters of intellectual property.

1.13   In principle, harmonisation transfers competence from the Member States to the Community. In particular, the Court has consistently held that Article 36 E.C. can no longer be invoked to justify derogations from the rules on the free movement of goods once harmonisation measures have been taken. The first question is whether this principle also unconditionally applies to intellectual property protection. At least three problems arise in this respect. First of all, the Single European Act introduced Article 100a(4) E.C. which potentially reinforces the exceptions laid down in Article 36 E.C. More importantly, harmonisation of intellectual property law leaves the principle of territoriality intact, which implies that Article 36 E.C. would not become totally redundant. Finally, whereas the replacement of national law by the unification of intellectual property law might be a solution, this meets with the reluctance of Member States which do not seem to be very eager to harmonise, let alone to unify, intellectual property law and, in so doing, transfer competence to the Community.

1.14   In the absence of the transfer of competence by virtue of harmonisation measures it is apparent that the Court's approach to intellectual property rights becomes even more important. The Court has always endeavoured to strike a balance between intellectual property rights on the one hand, and the Community objectives of creating a single market and maintaining workable competition on the other. The introduction of the existence/exercise dichotomy in the early cases whereby intellectual property rights were invoked was clearly meant to delineate between the competence of the E.C. and its Member States. The essence is that what constitutes the existence and normal use of the exclusive rights is to be left untouched by Community law, whereas what constitutes a misuse or an abuse may be curtailed by Community law. Chapter 3 examines the origin and meaning of these concepts as originally used in competition law cases. The main question here is whether the existence/exercise dichotomy is a workable criterion in practice, or whether additional criteria are needed for a consistent application of this basic idea. In particular, it is analysed whether or not the concepts of "normal use", and "misuse" or "abuse", are determined with reference to the function or objective of the exclusive right invoked.

(c) Movement of intellectual property protected products

The principle of free movement of goods does not always apply, and in some cases its application is conditional. Article 36 E.C. expressly provides exceptions to this rule relating, *inter alia*, to intellectual property rights and public health. Further exceptions, namely the so-called mandatory requirements such as consumer protection, have been introduced by virtue of case law. In order to prevent unjustified recourse to those exceptions the Court usually applies the justification and proportionality tests to the national measure concerned. On this basis it is established whether the measure is effectively meant to fulfil the higher objective invoked or whether, to the contrary, it amounts to an unjustified restriction on intra-Community trade. It is apparent that in the absence of such a control by the Court, the way would be paved for widespread abuses of those exceptions inspired by protectionist motives.

1.15

As is seen in Chapter 4 this is not, however, the approach adopted with regard to intellectual property rights. It is rather surprising to find that the Court has merely transposed the existence/exercise dichotomy, as introduced in the early competition cases, to the rules on the free movement of goods. Although Articles 30–36 E.C. are addressed to Member States, rather than to individuals, the Court has traditionally refrained from applying the usual justification and proportionality tests under Article 36 E.C. to the intellectual property measure concerned. Instead, the Court has expressly stated that it is the use made of an intellectual property right which is not in accordance with its specific subject-matter that is held to be contrary to Article 36 E.C. It is, for instance, on this basis that the principle of exhaustion of intellectual property rights was introduced in order to curtail the exercise made of his exclusive right by the intellectual property owner. Does the Court take the need to safeguard the function of the intellectual property right concerned into account in order to distinguish between normal use and misuse? Considering that each intellectual property right has a specific function to fulfil, the latter would imply that the concept of "specific subject-matter" is defined differently for

1.16

patents, copyright, trade marks and design rights. Chapter 4 therefore examines the concept of "specific subject-matter" as elaborated upon by the Court with respect to the different types of intellectual property rights.

(d) Exclusivity and the rules on competition

1.17   Chapter 5 analyses the approach taken to the application of the rules on competition to intellectual property rights, as well as the incidence of the evolution of the Court's traditional case law under the rules on free movement of goods. The main question is thereby whether or not intellectual property rights also occupy a special status under the rules on competition. In this respect the Court has consistently held that the rules on competition are, in principle, fully applicable but that the essence of intellectual property rights may not be curtailed. How does this apply in practice? The difficulties encountered in determining what constitutes the "essence" of the exclusive right, which does not fall foul of Article 85(1) E.C., is best illustrated by the Commission's radical shift in approach to patent licensing between the 1962 Christmas Message and the issuing of the block exemption on patent licensing agreements in 1984. Distinguishing between the normal use and the abuse of intellectual property rights seems to be even more difficult in relation to unilateral measures which are alleged to fall foul of Article 86 E.C. Here again reference is often made to the concept of "specific subject-matter". The main difference from the rules on the free movement of goods is that it is held that an additional element to the use of the exclusive right in accordance with its specific subject-matter is needed for Article 86 E.C. to apply. What constitutes this additional element? In particular, the question is once again posed as to whether this relates to the need to safeguard the function of intellectual property rights. The relevance of this question is illustrated by two cases dealt with by the Court of First Instance which were both challenged on appeal before the Court of Justice. In the *Hilti* case, the issue was raised as to whether a patent holder could eliminate competition in a related market in unprotected products,[7] whereas in the *Magill* cases the essential issue was to what extent a copyright holder could invoke his exclusive right to prevent the creation of a derivative market in a new product.[8] These questions are complementary to the main issue raised before the European Court of Justice in the spare parts cases, namely to what extent the owner of an industrial design could invoke his exclusive right to eliminate competition in the after-sales market of replacement parts. As mentioned before, the Court of Justice in its *Magill* appeal judgment expressly referred to its prior ruling in the *Volvo* case. It cannot go unnoticed, however, that the outcome of both cases is diametrically opposed. This apparently blatant contradiction has, more than ever before, made the crucial question of on what basis the Court differentiates between

---

[7] Case T–30/89, *Hilti AG v. Commission*, Judgment of December 12, 1991: [1991] E.C.R. II-1439; [1992] 4 C.M.L.R. 16.

[8] Case T–69/89, *Radio Telefis Eireann v. Commission*, Judgment of July 10, 1991: [1991] E.C.R. II-485; [1991] 4 C.M.L.R. 586. Case T–70/89, *The British Broadcasting Corporation and BBC Enterprises Limited v. Commission*, Judgment of July 10, 1991: [1991] E.C.R. II–535; [1991] 4 C.M.L.R. 669. Case T–76/89, *Independent Television Publications Limited v. Commission*, Judgment of July 10, 1991: [1991] E.C.R. II-575; [1991] 4 C.M.L.R. 745.

the use and abuse of intellectual property rights under Article 86 E.C. of great topical interest.

(e) (R)evolution in the case law on free movement of goods

Over the past seven to eight years there has been a subtle, though important, shift away from the traditional approach taken by the Court in its case law on the application of the rules on the free movement of goods to intellectual property rights. Even though in some cases the Court still holds on to the existence/exercise dichotomy, in other cases the Court seems to have put this basic principle aside through applying what resembles a justification test to the national measure granting the exclusive right. In still other cases, the Court has combined both approaches in that it only applies a justification test under the second sentence of Article 36 E.C. This shift in approach was most likely inspired by the newly-gained awareness about the fact that the exercise of intellectual property rights may be contrary to Community law simply because the exclusive right was abusively granted. **1.18**

It is apparent that if the legality or, in other words, the very existence of intellectual property rights is no longer to be taken for granted under Articles 30–36 E.C., this might have important repercussions on the current approach to the exercise of intellectual property rights under the rules on competition. The *Magill* appeal case seems foreboding in this respect. Although the Court formally upheld the intellectual property right concerned, in practice it was emptied of its substance. The purpose of Chapter 6 is to examine whether or not one can discern viable criteria to determine which approach the Court will in the future adopt to any given case under Articles 30–36 E.C.: the exercise/consent approach, the existence/justification approach, or an in-between approach which will be called the "marginal appraisal approach". First of all the question is posed as to whether the traditional application of the consent theory based on the existence/exercise dichotomy is coherent in view of the remaining discrepancies in national intellectual property legislation and the need to safeguard the inherent function of the various exclusive rights. Considering that the traditional approach continues to be applied in certain cases, the fundamental issue arises as to whether the recent cases in which the justification test was applied present particular features which explain the difference in approach or whether, to the contrary, the application of one or the other approach currently seems to be arbitrary. **1.19**

(2) A case study: the spare parts debate

(a) Articles 30–36 E.C.

Chapter 7 gives a detailed and step-by-step analysis of the issue, raised in the *Maxicar* case, of the compatibility of the enforcement of design rights in spare parts for cars with the rules on the free movement of goods. The *Maxicar* case was peculiar in at least two respects. It was the first time that the Court had to deal with the enforcement of intellectual property protection on components of complex products. Further, all previous cases brought before the Court **1.20** concerned the request of the owner of an exclusive right to obtain a legal injunction against third parties who manufacture, import and sell unauthorised products, or to prevent parallel importation. The national procedure in the *Maxicar* case, to the contrary, concerned a legal action brought by independent manufacturers claiming the annulment of certain design rights in bodywork components of cars. At first sight this seems to be a purely internal matter which does not affect intra-Community trade. The first question examined in Chapter 7 is, therefore, why the rules on the free movement of goods, and in particular Articles 30–34 E.C., apply to such a case.

1.21   Subsequently it is examined whether the exception laid down in Article 36 E.C. could be successfully invoked in this particular case in order to sustain the contested design rights. The issue at stake in the spare parts cases was clearly whether the grant and enforcement of design rights, which leads to the elimination of competition in the spare parts market, is at all covered by the term "industrial and commercial property" as mentioned in the first sentence of Article 36 E.C. This would apparently call for a justification test approach in order to establish whether or not the grant of design rights in spare parts for cars is in accordance with the functions and objectives of design law as understood under Community law. Seen from this perspective, it is rather surprising to find that the Court merely adopted the marginal appraisal approach. Even though the justification test was applied under the second sentence of Article 36 E.C., the Court resorted to its traditional approach under the first sentence of Article 36 E.C. through upholding the existence/exercise dichotomy. In other words, the Court impliedly rejected the hypothesis that the design rights concerned might have been abusively granted. Chapter 7 gives a critical analysis of the Court's approach both in view of its earlier case law and in terms of the function of design rights. Attention is thereby paid to how this all affects the consumer's interest.

(b) Article 86 E.C.

1.22   Since the Court upheld the national measures conferring design rights in bodywork components of cars in the *Maxicar* case, the other preliminary question posed in the same case became all the more relevant. Namely, could this exclusive right also be enforced to eliminate competition in the spare parts market without amounting to an abuse of a dominant position under Article 86 E.C.? In the *Volvo* case, the complementary question was posed of whether the refusal to grant licences upon reasonable terms constituted an infringement of Article 86 E.C. Chapter 8 gives a critical analysis of the Court's extremely brief response to those questions.

1.23   The first issue in this respect which is analysed, although it was not expressly dealt with by the Court, is the definition of the relevant product market. Whereas the car manufacturers invoked the so-called package theory to submit that the car and spare parts market is one and the same, the independent manufacturers maintained that the spare parts market is distinct from, though related to, the market in new motorvehicles. A related question that is dealt with is whether there is, or might be, a relationship between the existence of intellectual property protection and the finding of a dominant position on the relevant market.

Having established that the car manufacturers did occupy a dominant pos-   **1.24**
ition in the relevant market, the crucial issue next arises as to what extent
Article 86 E.C. might curtail the use made of the design rights in those bodywork components of cars. In other words, when might an intellectual property owner be held to have abused his dominant position? The question posed
in Chapter 8 is whether the finding of an abuse may be constituted by a use
which is not in conformity with the function of intellectual property rights.
However, this seems to deviate from the approach traditionally taken by the
Court. The latter has consistently adopted the premise that to come to the
finding of an abuse under Article 86 E.C. an additional element to the exercise
already covered by the specific subject-matter of an intellectual property right
is needed. The problem is to define precisely what this additional element is. In
the spare parts cases, contrary to the *Magill* appeal case, neither the elimination of competition nor the refusal to grant licences on reasonable terms
seemed to constitute the additional element in the view of the Court. The
Court merely gave the following examples of abusive behaviour: the arbitrary
refusal to sell spare parts to independent repairers, the charging of unfair
prices, or prematurely terminating production of spare parts if many cars are
still on the market. Chapter 8 gives a critical analysis of these examples in
terms of their practical applicability and examines to what extent intra-Community trade might be held to be affected by these kinds of abusive behaviour.
A comparison is made with the subsequent *Magill* appeal judgment wherever
relevant. With respect, the inconsistencies in the approach to intellectual
property rights, as currently adopted by the Court under Article 86 E.C. and
which are clearly exposed by the latter comparison, are striking.

(c) Competition policy objectives and remedies

A final question posed in Chapter 9, completing the spare parts picture under   **1.25**
Community law, is what is the potential impact of the Court's rulings in the
spare parts cases on the objectives of the block exemption for selective car
distribution? The unilateral enforcement of design rights on spare parts is not
contrary to Article 85 E.C. so it is obviously not prohibited by the block
exemption. It cannot go unnoticed, however, that the enforcement of design
rights in bodywork components of cars is particularly apt to change the competitive market structure on the basis of which the block exemption was
drafted. The rationale was that certain restrictions on intra-brand competition could be tolerated because inter-brand competition existed in the markets for both cars and spare parts. Yet the enforcement of design rights entails
the elimination of inter-brand competition in the market for bodywork components of cars. In this new context, is it still justified to exempt contractual
restrictions on intra-brand competition under Article 85(3) E.C.? This calls
for an analysis as to what extent the competition policy objectives, and in
particular those set forth in the block exemption, are jeopardised by the outcome of the spare parts cases.

A related question, which is dealt with in Chapter 9, is whether the E.C.   **1.26**
Commission could uphold or restore competition in the market in case the
latter is eliminated by virtue of the enforcement of intellectual property rights.

What is examined in particular is whether the rules on competition may be applied not so much to strike down, or curtail, the use made of intellectual property rights but rather to respond to their potentially detrimental consequences on competition policy objectives such as safeguarding a competitive market structure and consumers' interests. A controversial issue is whether the Commission may impose an affirmative action obligation on intellectual property owners. May the Commission, for instance, impose compulsory licences under Regulation 17? Even though the Court seemed to have impliedly rejected this possibility in the *Volvo* case, it was nonetheless expressly acknowledged in the subsequent *Magill* appeal case.

1.27 Chapter 9 also draws attention to the possibility of the E.C. Commission initiating legislative action in the field of intellectual property rights. In so doing it might be possible to strike a balance between intellectual property rights and competition at the source. In particular, an analysis is made of the current proposals on the Community Design in terms of the express objective of preventing monopolies in generic products from arising through the enforcement of design rights. The importance of the spare parts issue in an E.C. context is once again illustrated here. One of the most, if not the most, controversial issue the Commission had to deal with was precisely whether or not it should be possible to obtain design protection for spare parts of cars.

1.28 The question of possible remedies for anti-competitive effects arising from intellectual property protection is a fundamental issue which largely supersedes the current spare parts debate. As in the matter of determining what constitutes a normal use, as opposed to a misuse or abuse, of intellectual property rights under the E.C. rules on free movement of goods and competition, the spare parts issue essentially fulfils an amplifier function in this respect too.

PART II

ENFORCEMENT OF PATENTS, COPYRIGHT AND RELATED RIGHTS, TRADE MARKS AND INDUSTRIAL DESIGNS IN E.C. LAW

2. Introduction to Intellectual Property Protection

1. INTRODUCTION

The enforcement of intellectual property rights traditionally poses a problem **2.01**
within the context of E.C. law. This is due to the principles of territoriality and
exclusivity which are inherent in all intellectual property rights. These characteristics often raise questions concerning their compatibility with the E.C.
rules on the free movements of goods and competition. This is complicated
further by the fact that intellectual property rights are still, to a large extent,
granted nationally on the basis of criteria which are not necessarily equal, or
even similar to each other, between one Member State and another. Different
competitive conditions therefore may prevail in different Member States.

If the need for a coherent system providing protection for intellectual property can no longer be seriously contested,[1] there remains the pertinent question of how intellectual property rights should interact with the rules on competition. In this respect it is useful to recall briefly the functions those exclusive rights are meant to fulfil, or in other words why it is necessary to uphold intellectual property rights. At the same time it will be seen how the different systems of intellectual property rights can be reconciled with the principle of free, or rather workable, competition.[2]

2. CHARACTERISTICS OF INTELLECTUAL PROPERTY RIGHTS

(1) Exclusivity

(a) Principle

2.02   The principle of exclusivity inherent in all intellectual property rights implies that the right-owner is able to prohibit certain acts of third parties, for instance manufacturing and distribution, which would otherwise be lawful in the absence of intellectual property protection. Although in most cases the exclusive right entails a kind of monopoly right it in no way guarantees that the right-owner will also be able to exploit his competitive advantage on the market. This is mainly due to the fact that exclusive intellectual property rights are prohibitive rights. They do not automatically confer positive rights upon the right-owner, such as the right to market the protected product. Whether or not this exclusivity does extend to the marketing of the protected product will depend mainly on whether or not the intellectual property rights of another right-owner would be infringed by so doing.

(b) Impact on competition

2.03   The extent to which a right-owner can effectively prevent competition is largely dependent on the type of intellectual property right concerned and in particular on whether substitutable products are on, or may enter, the market which do not infringe the right. It is obvious that the exclusivity inherent in intellectual property rights must of necessity affect the competitive structure of a given market, because third parties are precluded from a part of the market to which they would otherwise have free access.

The differences in conditions and scope of protection offered in the various Member States create further distortions to competition in the Common Mar-

---

[1] For an overview of the most important "attacks" on the patent system in the past, see F.-K. Beier, "The significance of the patent system for technical, economic and social progress" [1980] I.I.C. 563 at 564–569.

[2] On this concept, see J. Clark, "Towards a concept of workable competition" [1940] *The American Economic Review* 241. At p. 241, he points out that "'perfect competition' does not and cannot exist and has presumably never existed...". At p. 246, he puts forward the view that "it seems probable that one of the criteria of workable competition is that there shall not be too gross discrepancies between the action of short-run pressures and long-run tendencies", whereas at p. 249 he states succinctly that "the most serious problems of imperfect competition seem [...] to center in the fact that the immediate short-run pressures are out of harmony with the conditions of long-run equilibrium".

ket. Moreover, as is seen below, by virtue of the principle of territoriality intellectual property protection can, in principle, be used to curtail both inter-brand and intra-brand competition from goods that have been lawfully marketed in another Member State.

(2) Territoriality

(a) Principle

Intellectual property rights are essentially temporary exclusive rights which are granted by law. Although E.C. harmonisation measures and international conventions concerning intellectual property rights exist,[3] it is still the national law that remains the principle source of the rights and obligations of the right-owner. This entails the scope of the intellectual property right being geographically limited to the territory of the Member State granting the protection. The conditions and scope of such protection may vary from one Member State to another.

    2.04

The principle of territoriality inherent in intellectual property rights thus means that the protection both begins and ends at the national border. This implies that one cannot invoke the intellectual property protection granted in Member State A to prohibit certain actions by third parties in Member State B, whereas in principle one can prohibit the importation of infringing goods, including one's own goods, into Member State A on the basis of the intellectual property right enjoyed there. It should be pointed out that the latter may be subject to the application of the exhaustion, or a similar, principle.[4]

(b) Impact on free movement of goods

The reason why the owner of an intellectual property right may want to prohibit the importation of goods which he himself put on the market in another Member State lies in the peculiarities of national markets, for instance, the supply/demand ratio, the need to invest in publicity and the existence of intellectual property protection.[5] Suppose a given product can be sold at 10 ECUs in Member State A and only at 5 ECUs in Member State B. It is obvious that the importation of the product from B to A would entail a decrease in price and profit margin for the right-owner in Member State A. He may therefore have an interest in invoking intellectual property protection in order to prevent intra-brand competition.

    2.05

    On the basis of his intellectual property right in Member State A the right-owner can, furthermore, prohibit the importation of goods that have been lawfully marketed in another Member State by a third party. This would be

---

[3] On the most important intellectual property conventions, see *infra*, at pt. 4. On E.C. harmonisation measures so far taken, see *infra*, Chap. 3, pt. 3(2).

[4] On the principle of exhaustion in E.C. law, see *infra*, Chap. 4, pt. 1.

[5] On the various reasons why one might want to prevent intra-brand competition, see also C. Baden Fuller, "Economic issues relating to property rights in trade marks: export bans, differential pricing, restrictions on resale and repackaging" (1981) 6 E.L.Rev. 162 at 170–173.

the case, for instance, if in that other state intellectual property protection could not be obtained, or had not been applied for, or had expired. In other words, inter-brand competition can also be prevented.

It is apparent that the principle of territoriality is difficult to reconcile with the Community principle of free movement of goods and runs contrary to the Community objective of creating a single market. It has been said, figuratively, that intellectual property protection allows for the creation of "islands" within the Community.[6]

3. FUNCTION OF INTELLECTUAL PROPERTY RIGHTS

(1) Intellectual property rights in general

2.06   Despite what are at first sight detrimental consequences, it should be emphasised that intellectual property rights fulfil an essential role in the market and should not be discarded easily. Generally speaking it could be said that their main function is to stimulate innovation and development, be it in the technical, aesthetical or cultural fields. Intellectual property rights provide an incentive, in the form of a temporary grant of exclusivity in the market, to invest time and money in research and development thereby putting the right-owner in a position to obtain a reward. These exclusive rights are therefore generally held to be pro-competitive, if not always in the short run then at least in the long term.[7]

Nonetheless, to accept that temporary restraints on competition may be indispensable to promote overall competition in the long term is not tantamount to accepting that in all circumstances all intellectual property rights should prevail over competition policy objectives. A balance needs to be sought between these two potentially conflicting objectives. It is submitted that this could be done on the basis of the following three-fold premise.[8] First, the stimulation of research and development through the grant of exclusive rights to individuals is ultimately in the public interest. Secondly, it is in the consumer's interest to safeguard a competitive market structure. Thirdly, when the first two premises cannot be reconciled in practice, criteria have to be sought to minimise injury to the public interest.[9]

2.07   It is especially in relation to patents, which are particularly apt to confer market power on the patent holder, that the so-called patent-antitrust debate has developed. Both economists and lawyers have endeavoured to find an equitable balance between maintaining the essential functions of patent pro-

---

[6] See G. Van Empel, *Bescherming van de intellectuele eigendom* (1987, Kluwer), p. 16.
[7] See for instance M. Lehmann, "Property and intellectual property – property rights as restrictions on competition in furtherance of competition" [1989] I.I.C. 1.
[8] Compare to J. Stedman, "Patents and antitrust – the impact of varying legal doctrines" [1973] *Utah Law Review* 588 at 594–595.
[9] Stedman holds that in that case, one has to seek rules "that will minimise the injury to each, and where such injury is unavoidable, rules should provide for a considered decision as to which goal should prevail", proposing seven possible but not equally desirable approaches. See J. Stedman, *op. cit.*, 595. However, it is submitted that it is difficult to justify either one of the approaches proposed if one does not set forth a fixed objective, such as reducing the injury to the public interest and ultimately the consumers.

tection and safeguarding the essential objectives of competition policy. It should be pointed out that not all intellectual property rights affect competition in the same way because each type of exclusive right has a different objective.[10] It is therefore submitted that it is necessary to determine the functions of each type of intellectual property right in order to establish which restrictions on competition should be permitted.

The need to fulfil the legitimate function of intellectual property rights has, in the past, been disputed by some lawyers as constituting a possible demarcation criterion in the patent-antitrust debate in the European Community.[11] They have pointed out that the laws of different nations may emphasise different objectives of the intellectual property protection they offer. This would imply that any approach based on the function of the intellectual property rights concerned would entail varying the application of the Community rules on competition between Member States. It is submitted that it is, nonetheless, possible to determine those functions that are generally invoked to justify the existence of the different systems of intellectual property rights. Although the importance of one or the other feature might be stressed, the functions that underlie the various national legal systems are not mutually exclusive but, rather, complementary. It should be possible, therefore, to supersede national interpretations through a commonly accepted approach.[12]

(2) Patents

(a) Principle

Patent protection confers a temporary exclusive right on the invention of a new industrial product or process that fulfils the stringent conditions for protectability. This means that once the patent is granted, the patent holder has the right to exclude the use of the protected product or process by third parties so that in principle market power is conferred. Because the patent merely confers a monopoly over the protected product or process, competition from substitute products is not necessarily, but may in exceptional cases be, excluded. Whether or not the patent also confers a legal monopoly with the possibility of charging monopoly prices thus depends on various factors, such as the

2.08

---

[10] See also W. Cornish, *Intellectual property: patents, copyright, trade marks and allied rights* (2nd ed., 1989, Sweet & Maxwell), pt. 1–016, where he points out that "patents, copyright and trade marks each have a different form of economic impact".

[11] See for instance H. Johannes, "*La propriété industrielle et le droit d'auteur dans le droit des communautés européennes*" [1973] R.T.D.E. 369 and 557, at 379–382; F. Gotzen, "*La libre circulation des produits couverts par un droit de propriété intellectuelle dans la jurisprudence de la Cour de Justice*" [1985] R.T.D.E. 467 at 472–473.

[12] By way of example, Gotzen points out that the reward function of patents is for instance not known in the U.K., because there they exclusively rely on the stimulation of progress function. See F. Gotzen, *op. cit.*, pp. 472–473. However, it is submitted below that it is exactly the possibility of obtaining a reward through the grant of exclusivity that constitutes the incentive to invest in R & D.

availability of non-infringing substitutable goods on the market and the importance of the invention as viewed by the consumers.[13]

(b) Economic justifications

2.09   The main justifications for the existence of the patent system are based on the reward, incentive and disclosure theories.[14] In this respect, Beier and Straus came to the following conclusions which illustrate the universal acceptance of these functions as the underlying objectives of the patent system in general:

> "to our surprise we discovered that these basic objectives of patent pro-tection [namely the reward-by-monopoly, monopoly-profit-incentive and exchange-for-secrets functions] are largely independent of the actual economic and social order and the development status of the respective countries, and that they, so to speak, belong to the basic structure of a legal and economic policy consensus with regard to the need for patent protection in East and West, North and South."[15]

2.10   Although a patent relates to an industrial product or process, there is a major difference with corporeal or tangible property. The protection is con-ferred on the intangible property, namely the invention, which may be incor-porated in an industrial product. So as to illustrate the specific features of this property, Arrow has equated the process of invention and research with the production of information.[16] On this premise, he has convincingly illustrated that if information is regarded as a commodity then the owner of the infor-mation naturally has a monopoly in the market. As soon as the latter discloses his information it can be reproduced by third parties at little or no cost with-out producing a benefit to the owner so that it does not provide an incentive for research. In the words of Subramanian, "if free appropriability is allowed *ex post*, there is little incentive *ex ante* to undertake knowledge-creating activities".[17] Arrow therefore concludes that it is necessary to introduce suit-able legal measures which render information an appropriable commodity in order to protect the owner against free-riders and to enable him to exert his

---

[13] See also J. Stedman, *op. cit.*, p. 588 and pp. 593–594, where he enumerates the following influencing factors: the nature of the invention, the environment in which the patent operates, the structure of the industry concerned, the identity of the patent holder, the use to which the patent is put. Kitch, to the contrary, maintains that a patent cannot be said to confer a monopoly right because of identifiable competitive market pressures, such as the expected entry of competing firms near the end of the patent life, see E. Kitch, "Patents: monopolies or property rights" in *The Economics of Patents and Copyright* (J. Palmer ed. 1986), pp. 31–49.

[14] See for instance S. Greif, "Patents and economic growth" [1987] I.I.C. 191; J. Markham, "Inventive activity: government controls and the legal environment" in *The rate and direction of inventive activity: economic and social factors* (1975, National Bureau of Economic Research), pp. 587–608 at p. 597; E. Goldstein, *Cases and materials on patents, trademarks and copyright law* (1959, The Foundation Press), p. 2.

[15] F.-K. Beier, J. Straus, "The patent system and its informational function – yesterday and today" [1977] I.I.C. 387 at 392 (inserts in brackets added).

[16] See K. Arrow, "Economic Welfare and the allocation of resources for invention" in *The rate and direction of inventive activity* (1975, National Bureau of Economic Research), pp. 609–626.

[17] A. Subramanian, "The international economics of intellectual property right protection: a welfare-theoretic trade policy analysis" [1991] *World Development* 945 at 946.

monopoly, although he points out that this will inevitably constitute a non-optimal allocation of resources.[18]

It is obvious from the reasoning of Arrow, who, of course, gives a much more detailed and profound analysis than that summarised above, that in the absence of legal protection the only way for the owner of valuable information to exploit it is to keep his invention as secret as possible. It is generally accepted, however, that secrecy in respect of industrial inventions goes against the public interest because it delays economic, technical and scientific progress.[19] Conferring an exclusive right to the contrary allows the technical knowledge to become a trade asset which is publicly known. The patent holder can share his assets with third parties, for instance through licensing contracts or assignments, so that technology can be transferred.[20] Also, third parties can use the disclosed information freely, not to produce infringing goods but as a basis for further innovation and progress.[21] As such, it is generally acknowledged that the patent system has an important information and disclosure function to fulfil which justifies temporary restraints on competition in order to further competition and innovation in the long term.[22] **2.11**

Patent protection in the form of exclusive rights is also widely acknowledged to have both a reward and an incentive, or stimulus, function. It is submitted that the reward and incentive functions are indissolubly linked.[23] The underlying idea, as illustrated by Machlup, is that it is the grant of the temporary monopoly that fulfils both the reward and the incentive function, although the emphasis is slightly different according to which is being stressed.[24] The reward-by-monopoly theory assumes that by granting a temporary monopoly, inventors will be rewarded in proportion to their usefulness to society. The monopoly-profit-incentive theory, on the other hand, emphasises the need to offer not just a reward but also an incentive for innovation.[25] The common denominator is that in each case it is held that the **2.12**

---

[18] K. Arrow, *op. cit.*, pp. 616–617, where he states that from a welfare point of view, information should be available free of charge, so that whatever the price, the demand for information will be less than optimal. For a critique of Arrow's theory, see for instance S. Cheung, "Property rights and innovation" in J. Palmer (ed.), *op. cit.*, pp. 5–18 at pp. 10–12.

[19] See for instance E. Goldstein, *op. cit.*, at p. 2.

[20] See for instance also F.-K. Beier, *op. cit.*, p. 582; D. Vincent, "The role of patents in the transfer of technology" in *Technology transfer practice of international firms* (F. Bradbury ed. 1978) (Alpen Aan den Rijn), pp. 40–43 at p. 43; A. Brown, "Impact of patents and licences on the transfer of technology" in *Technology transfer in industrialized countries* (Sherman Gee ed. 1979) (Sythoff & Noordhoff), pp. 311–324 at p. 313.

[21] See also S. Greif, *op. cit.*, at pp. 195–197.

[22] See especially the study made by F.-K. Beier, and J. Straus, *op. cit.*

[23] See for instance also R. Seymour, "Patents and the transfer of technology" in *Technology transfer practise of international firms* (F. Bradbury ed. 1978) (Alpen Aan den Rijn), pp. 35–39, at p. 37 where he writes that the incentive function of patents is "to permit the inventor a reasonable period of time in which he may control the use of his invention in order to obtain his reward".

[24] See F. Machlup, *An economic review of the patent system*, Study of the Committee on Patents, Trademarks, and Copyright Committee on the Judiciary, US Senate, 85th Congress, Study no. 15, Washington, 1958, pp. 20–24, as extensively cited by R. Joliet, "Patented articles and the free movement of goods within the EEC" [1975] *Current Legal Problems* 15.

[25] See for instance R. Seymour, *op. cit.*, p. 38, where he points out that: "...the existence of an adequate patent system will encourage investment, but will not *of itself* cause the investment to take place. However, the absence of an adequate patent system will have a definite negative impact and may *of itself* cause the investment and subsequent technology *not* to take place."

simplest, cheapest and most effective way to fulfil the envisaged function is by granting a temporary legal monopoly in the form of an exclusive patent right even if this might, in certain circumstances, lead to a monopoly position for the patent holder.

(c) Patent-antitrust debate

2.13 Monopolies are traditionally viewed as being anti-competitive and hence to be avoided. In Schumpterian terms of dynamic competition, however, the possibility of obtaining a patent monopoly with corresponding market power is a necessary prerequisite to economic progress and innovation. In turn, the latter is the fundamental impulse of the capitalist system based on the "creative destruction process".[26] It stimulates firms to innovate, whereas the threat of subsequently losing the acquired market power stimulates still further innovation.[27] Patent protection should therefore be seen as an essential element of a dynamic competition policy.[28] Although Scherer defines himself as a disciple of Schumpeter, he does not totally share the conviction that big monopolistic corporations are such an efficient engine of technological change.[29] He points out that substantial imitation lags, major competitive differentiation advantages from being the first in the market and oligopolistic market structures with non-patent barriers to entry may induce firms to invest in innovation without patent protection.[30] Nevertheless, on the basis of the results of the well-known study made by Taylor and Silberstone, which confirmed the advantages of patent protection,[31] he comes to the conclusion that patent protection is especially useful to smaller firms and independent inven-

---

[26] See J. Schumpeter, "Capitalism, socialism and democracy" (1976, George Allen & Unwin), p. 83, where he defines the "process of Creative Destruction", which he sees as the fundamental factor of capitalism, in the following terms: "...process of industrial mutation [...] that incessantly revolutionizes the economic structure *from within,* incessantly destroying the old one, incessantly creating a new one." In other words, innovation lies at the basis of capitalism. For an analysis of Schumpeter's theory in relation to patents, see R. Eisenberg, "Patents and the progress of science: exclusive rights and experimental use" [1989] *The University of Chicago Law Review* 1017 at 1038–1040. At p. 1038 she writes: "while Schumpeter does not focus exclusively on either technological innovation or the patent system, his analysis suggests how patent monopolies might promote technological innovation."

[27] J. Schumpeter, *op. cit.,* p. 96, where he writes that firms in a dominant position "...can and will fight progress itself".

[28] J. Schumpeter, *op. cit.,* p. 106, where he states: "It is not sufficient to argue that because perfect competition is impossible under modern industrial conditions [...] the large-scale establishment or unit of control must be accepted as a necessary evil inseparable from the economic progress which it is prevented from sabotaging by the forces inherent in its productive apparatus. What we have got to accept is that it has come to be the most powerful engine of that progress and in particular of the long-run expansion of total output not only in spite of, but to a considerable extent through, this strategy which looks so restrictive when viewed in the individual case and from the individual point of time."

[29] See F. Scherer, *Innovation and growth – Schumpetarian perspectives* (1984, Cambridge), at p. 198.

[30] See F. Scherer, *Industrial market structure and economic performance* (2nd ed., 1980, Chicago), pp. 444–447. Similarly, see W. Cornish, *op. cit.,* pt. 3–030, where he points out that these factors will be particularly relevant for major inventions, so that "it might well be that the incentive effect of patents is of more significance when it comes to marginal ideas – concepts that do not hold hope of more than minor improvements in the existing art".

[31] See C. Taylor, and Z. Silberstone, *The economic impact of the patent system* (1973, Cambridge). Their study, based on a questionnaire to undertakings, showed that the patent system is especially valuable in the pharmaceutical and chemicals sectors.

tors who lack the distribution channels and the market acceptance of their larger rivals.[32]

If the matter of whether or not a temporary monopoly should be given to an inventor is generally answered in the positive,[33] the difficult question still remains of the extent to which this monopoly position could, or should, be curtailed under the competition rules. This question is especially pertinent in view of the fact that patent exclusivity may amount to a legal monopoly which could be abused, for instance through failure to use the invention whilst stifling competition, defensive patenting or the use of patents to unduly restrict competition.[34] **2.14**

As Joliet pointed out, excessive pricing by a patent monopolist is considered to be abusive in most legal systems.[35] The ability to charge higher prices for the protected product is, however, precisely the corollary of both the reward and incentive functions of patent protection. In the words of Machlup:

> "Since it is the very essence of patents to restrict competition and permit output to be kept below, and price above, competitive levels, it is difficult to conceive economic criteria by which one could judge whether output is less than reasonably 'practicable' and price is 'unreasonably high'".[36]

For this reason, economists generally favour the reduction of the duration of patent protection for inventions which have a minor public interest over antitrust interferences in the pricing policies of dominant firms, although they recognise that determining the optimum patent life for each given invention is not workable in practice.[37]

---

[32] F. Scherer, *op. cit.* (1980), pp. 448–449. It should be noted that he distinguishes between competition and rivalry (see p. 10). He speaks of competition when no individual firm is able to appreciably alter a given commodity's price by varying the quantity of output it sells. Rivalry is used to denominate the situation whereby firms strive for a potentially incompatible position. He gives the following example of rivalry: if A sells 100 units of output to X, than B cannot satisfy that part of X's demand.

[33] However, in this respect it is interesting to take note of the remark made by G. Priest, "What economists can tell lawyers about intellectual property rights", in J. Palmer (ed.), *op. cit.*, pp. 19–24 at p. 22, where he points out that economists can tell lawyers whether patents will lead to more or less inventive activity, but not whether social welfare will thereby be enhanced.

[34] See also T. Hagan, S. Henry, "Is a compulsory licensing statute necessary? A study of the U.S. and foreign experience" [1976] *Patent Law Review* 285 at 285 and 288.

[35] R. Joliet, *op. cit.*, p. 32.

[36] F. Machlup, *op. cit.*, p. 12. Similarly, see R. Merkin, "The interface between anti-trust and intellectual property" [1985] E.C.L.R. 377 at 388, where he writes that whereas the use of patents not to exploit those rights, but to stifle competition, is inconsistent with the presumed intention of the statutory grant, "the same consideration cannot, however, apply to pricing policies, for it is difficult to see how a monopolist can extend or abuse his monopoly simply by exploiting it to the full".

[37] For an extensive analysis of this issue and an attempt to find a method to calculate the "just" reward, see for instance L. Kaplow, "The patent-antitrust intersection: a reappraisal" [1983–84] *Harvard Law Review* 1813–1892. At p. 1825, he determines the optimal patent life as "that length of time at which the marginal social cost of lengthening or shortening the patent life equals the marginal social benefit". See also F. Scherer, *op. cit.* (1980), p. 454, where he writes: "an ideal patent system would hand-tailor the life of each patent to the peculiar circumstances of the invention it covers, but this is administratively unfeasible". On the optimal patent life, see also Scherer's discussion of Nordhaus' theory, F. Scherer, *op. cit.* (1984), pp. 130–139; L. DeBrock, "Market structure, innovation, and optimal patent life" [1985] *The Journal of Law and Economics* 223. See also J. Markham, *op. cit.*, especially p. 602 where he pleads for a dual patent system, namely a long-term protection for major technological breakthroughs as opposed to a short-term protection for others.

2.15   It is generally acknowledged by both economists and lawyers that the patent monopoly may not be used to develop cartels in markets by inserting certain clauses in licensing agreements which exceed the scope of the patent or, with the exception of the Chicago school,[38] to tie-in related markets in unprotected products.[39] It is also commonly accepted that compulsory licences, or licences of right, have a role to fulfil in order to limit the market power of the patent owner in the public interest.[40] At present, the most common grounds for imposing obligatory licences are insufficient exploitation and abuse of monopoly power. Other grounds invoked include the need for development of dependent inventions, public interest/health, economic development, international trade and national defence.[41]

As such, it must be concluded that the patent-antitrust debate is not such an area of conflict as might at first be thought. Temporary restraints on competition in the form of monopoly rights (which are only granted if the stringent conditions for protectability are fulfilled) are considered to be necessary to stimulate innovation and competition in the long term. The counterpart is that possible abuses of the market power so conferred or, in other words, uses which cannot be justified in terms of public interest or dynamic competition, are struck down under the rules on competition.

(3) Copyright

(a) Principle

2.16   Essentially, copyright confers a temporary exclusive right on the original form in which ideas are expressed. This means that original ideas as such are not protectable and can be freely appropriated by others. The idea-expression dichotomy inherent in copyright law is based on the principle that ideas, information, and facts should be freely available. Only the original manner in which the author expresses these ideas or information is protected against

---

[38] See for instance R. Merkin, *op. cit.*, pp. 389–390. On the Chicago school approach to tie-ins in general, see R. Posner, "The Chicago School of antitrust analysis" [1979] *University of Pennsylvania Law Review* 925 at 934–936.

[39] See for instance Ky P. Ewing Jr., "Antitrust enforcement and the patent system: similarities in the European and American Approach" [1980] I.I.C. 279. On the application of the patent misuse defence in the USA to counter tie-ins of unprotected products, see also J. Wallace, "Proper use of the patent misuse doctrine – an antitrust defense to patent infringement actions in need of rational reform" [1976] *Patent Law Review* 357.

[40] For instance, the OECD study of industrial property law concludes that: "the statutory grant of compulsory licences should be made sufficiently broad to enable the competent authorities to deal effectively with the whole range of detrimental economic effects of market power obtained through patents": see *Market power and the law* (1970, OECD), p. 176. See also P. Kaufman, *Passing off and misappropriation* (1986, IIC Studies, VCH), Vol. 9, p. 78; F. Scherer, *op. cit.* (1980), at p. 456; M. Scott, "Compulsory licensing of intellectual property in international transactions" [1988] E.I.P.R. 319.

[41] On the various justifications for obligatory licences in different legal systems, see J.-M. Salamolard, *La licence obligatoire en matière de brevets d'invention* (1978, Genève). For a summary, see in particular pp. 40–46. For an analysis of the pros and cons of compulsory licences, see T. Hagan, S. Henry, *op. cit.*, pp. 290–300.

unauthorised reproduction.[42] A coherent application of this principle thus entails that if expression and ideas merge, because the manner of expression is merely incidental to the idea or facts so expressed, copyright protection cannot be enforced to prevent unauthorised copying.[43] Unlike patents, copyright is not usually dependent on registration and only offers protection against unauthorised reproduction.[44] If a third person comes to the same form of expression independently from the protected work, then in principle no copyright infringement should be established.[45]

(b) Copyright and market power

Although the term "monopoly" is often also used in relation to copyright, this obviously has a different meaning to its use in relation to patents. A third party may not use the protected invention to produce and market competing products under patent law. He may, however, use the unprotected ideas to produce and market competing products under copyright law provided he does not copy the original manner in which the ideas are expressed. For instance, if car engine X is patented, one may not rely on the invention to create a similar engine of, for example, a different shape because the patent holder has a monopoly on the exploitation of the invention. However, if an author writes a book about the functioning of car engine X he does not have a monopoly on books about car engine X. Any other person can write a similar book which will lawfully compete in the market, provided the original form of expression is not copied.[46] In this sense copyright does not confer a monopoly on a product in the same way as patents do.

2.17

In principle, copyright does not lead to the exclusion of potentially substitutable products on the market. Thus, an author will not usually behave as a monopolist. Nevertheless, in some rare cases where there are no perfectly substitutable products on the market, the copyright holder may take monopolistic advantages of his exclusive position in the market. This would be the case if the copyright work is perceived by the consumers as being unique because it is dictated by fashion, by reason of advertising and promotion, and consider-

---

[42] See also G. Dworkin, R. Taylor, *Blackstone's guide to the Copyright, Designs & Patents Act 1988* (1989, Blackstone Press), p. 4. For an economic analysis of the need to maintain the idea-expression dichotomy, see W. Landes, R. Posner, "An economic analysis of copyright law" [1989] *Journal of Legal Studies* 325, at 347–353. At p. 348, they point out that: "The traditional explanation for protecting only expression emphasises the welfare losses from monopoly of an idea. We emphasise the increase in cost of creating works and the reduction in the number of works rather than the higher price (per copy) that is normally associated with monopoly."

[43] See also W. Landes, R. Posner, *op. cit.*, pp. 350–353, where they give economic reasons for this solution, which has been adopted in the USA since the *Baker v. Selden* case ((1879) 101 U.S. 99) concerning unauthorised copies made of a book with blank bookkeeping forms.

[44] Imposing a registration requirement runs counter to Article 5(2) of the Berne Convention, which stipulates that "the enjoyment and the exercise of these rights shall not be subject to any formality". However, works which had not been duly registered in the USA before May 1989 (date of entry into force of the US Berne Convention Implementation Act) are nevertheless not granted copyright protection. On this issue, see A. Strowel, *Droit d'auteur et copyright: divergences et convergences* (1993, Bruylant), pp. 299–307.

[45] See also P. Hearn, *The business of industrial licensing* (1981, Gower), pp. 224–225.

[46] See also the example of the difference between tangible property and copyright given by S. Stewart, *International copyright and neighbouring rights* (1983, Butterworths), pt. 1.08.

ation of the author's reputation.[47] However, the level of reward the copyright holder may reap is determined by what consumers are willing to pay for the expression of the ideas in one form rather than in another.

(c) Economic justifications

2.18   Different economic justifications are put forward for the existence of the copyright system.[48] As for patents, it is generally recognised that copyright has both a reward and an incentive function which are closely linked. It is traditionally held that the exclusive right encourages creativity by ensuring that the author can make a livelihood from his work.[49] Nowadays, it is also commonly accepted that by providing the possibility of recouping the investment and making profits, the exclusivity provides the necessary incentive to invest time and money in the creation and exploitation of increasingly costly works which, due to new technologies, are also increasingly easier to copy.[50] Examples of this are works of architecture and films.[51] It is therefore generally acknowledged by both lawyers and economists that a temporary restraint on public access to the work is necessary to stimulate innovation in the creative or cultural fields.[52]

2.19   The main difference between the two prevailing law systems is whether the emphasis is on the need to grant protection to the author of the creative work, as in author's right systems of continental Europe, or to protect those who take the risk to exploit the creative work, as in the Anglo-Saxon copyright systems.[53] However, the current tendency is towards a merger of these two philosophies. This is illustrated by the growing awareness of the importance of neighbouring rights in continental European countries, and about the author's moral rights in Anglo-Saxon countries.[54]

---

[47] See W. Cornish, *op. cit.*, pts. 9–023 and 9–024. He gives the following examples of monopolistic behaviour under copyright: "the practice of publishing hard-back editions before paperbacks, [. . .], or that of showing films at expensive inner-city cinemas before allowing urban release and then television showing." Similarly, see W. Landes, R. Posner, *op. cit.*, p. 328.

[48] There are also non-economical justification, such as the principle of natural justice, the cultural argument and the social argument. See especially S. Stewart, *op. cit.*, pts. 1.02, 1.04 and 1.05.

[49] See for instance E. Goldstein, *op. cit.*, p. 10.

[50] On the relationship between copyright and technological evolution, see R. Adelstein, S. Peretz, "The competition of technologies in markets for ideas: copyright and fair use in evolutionary perspective" [1985] *International Review of Law and Economics* 209.

[51] See S. Stewart, *op. cit.*, pt. 1.03, where he writes that "these investments will not be made unless there is a reasonable expectation of recouping them and making a reasonable profit". See also G. Dworkin, D. Taylor, *op. cit.*, p. 3.

[52] See for instance P. Groves, *Copyright and designs law: a question of balance* (1991, Graham and Trotman), p. 1, where he writes: "The law of copyright is one big balancing trick. It exists to deal with an economic problem, to trade off the costs of limiting access to the works it protects against the benefits of providing incentives to create the work in the first place." For an economic viewpoint, see for instance W. Landes, R. Posner, *op. cit.*, p. 326, where they write: "Striking the correct balance between access and incentives is the central problem in copyright law."

[53] See for instance H. Cohen Jehoram, "Critical reflections on the economic importance of copyright" [1989] I.I.C. 485 at 496–497. For a more detailed account of the different philosophies, see S. Stewart, *op. cit.*, pts. 1.13–1.16; A. Strowel, *op. cit.*, pp. 17–34.

[54] See especially S. Stewart, *op. cit.*, pt. 1.16.; H. Cohen Jehoram, *op. cit.*, pp. 496–497; A. Strowel, *op. cit.*, pp. 149–156.

(4) Trade marks

(a) Principle

Trade marks are different again in that they merely confer exclusivity on a   2.20
distinctive brand name. This means that the proprietor of a trade mark has the
exclusive use of the distinctive mark and can prevent the unauthorised affixing of it, or of confusingly similar trade marks, to similar products. Similar
products may, however, be marketed under different brand names.

(b) Trade marks and market power

Trade marks do not relate to a product but merely to distinctive signs affixed   2.21
to a product in order to distinguish it from similar products made by others.[55]
This implies that they do not, as such, confer a monopoly position.[56] This
finding does not alter the fact that well-known brands may confer a certain
degree of market power[57] or that brand names can be exploited by a firm that
occupies a dominant position in the market. The latter could be done by, for
instance, enforcing differential pricing.[58]

(c) Economic justifications

The traditional and commonly accepted justification for trade marks is that   2.22
they provide an incentive to produce quality products of a constant level.[59]
The brand name is essentially an indication of the commercial origin of products.[60] The exclusivity inherent in trade marks allows the consumer to associate a given brand name with the quality of a certain product so that consumer
expectation and goodwill can be created.[61] This is important in as much as the
consumer is usually only in a position to evaluate a product after it has been

---

[55] See for instance E. Goldstein, *op. cit.*, p. 8.
[56] Similarly, see C. Baden Fuller, "Economic issues relating to property rights in trademarks:
export bans, differential pricing, restrictions on resale and repackaging" (1981) 6 E.L.Rev. 162
at 164–167, where he convincingly argues that neither the ownership of a brand name nor its
marketing activities are likely to give rise to a dominant position for the proprietor of the trade
mark.
[57] For an analysis of market power as conferred by strongly established brands, see for instance N.
Parr, M. Hughes, "The relevance of consumer brands and advertising in competition
enquiries" [1993] E.C.L.R. 157.
[58] See C. Baden Fuller, *op. cit.*, pp. 167–169.
[59] See for instance R. Higgins, P. Rubin, "Counterfeit goods" [1986] *Journal of Law &
Economics* 211, at 213. However, at p. 211, they point out that more recently, trade marks
have, in the eyes of certain consumers, also taken on the additional function of demonstrating
that they are consumers of a certain product. On p. 212, they write by way of illustration that
"in markets in which the purpose of the trade mark is to impress observers rather than to
guarantee quality to consumers, there is less effort at detection and avoidance of counterfeit
goods and therefore a relatively greater return from counterfeiting".
[60] See also W. Cornish, *op. cit.*, pt. 15–017.
[61] Franzosi defines "goodwill" in the following way: "Goodwill is the disposition of consumers to
purchase goods or services from a constant source. It is the favourable opinion of customers
that induces them to buy goods, either because they have experience with the source or because,
even if this is not so, it has their favourable consideration." See M. Franzosi, "Grey market—
parallel importation as a trade mark violation or an act of unfair competition" [1990] I.I.C.
194, at 197. Similarly, see J. Lowe, N. Crawford, *Innovation and technology transfer for the
growing firm* (1994, Oxford), p. 11; W. Cornish, *op. cit.*, pts. 15–013 and 15–014.

purchased. The trade mark does not guarantee that the product will be of a constant quality, but at least it prevents a third party undermining the goodwill created by a specific manufacturer. Because of the right of exclusivity, the trade mark proprietor will be solely responsible for the potential loss of goodwill due to any decline in the quality of his products.

(5) Industrial designs

(a) Principle

2.23   Although design legislation is far from being uniform, design rights in all legal systems essentially confer a temporary exclusive right on the new and/or original manner in which a technical or functional product is shaped. Wallace pointed out that there is no agreement internationally as to whether what he has called the "patents approach" or the "copyright approach" to design rights, or a mixture of both, should be applied.[62] In the "patents approach" he refers to those systems of design protection which require novelty and grant full exclusive rights.[63] In the "copyright approach" he refers to those systems of design protection which require originality and only grant protection against copying.[64]

The criteria for, and scope of, design protection is usually modelled on either patent or copyright law, or both. Nevertheless, the very existence of a separate system for design protection in most legal systems indicates that design rights fulfil a well-defined objective which is different from both patents or copyrights. The specificity of design rights has furthermore led to the development of a specific "design approach" by the Munich Max Planck Institute and the European Commission.[65]

[62] The concepts of the "patents approach" and the "copyright approach" to design rights were first introduced by William Wallace and are now commonly used. See W. Wallace, "Protection for designs in the United Kingdom" [1974] I.I.C. 421.

[63] W. Wallace, op. cit., p. 421: "By a 'patents approach' I mean a system like the patents system wherein the criterion for protection is that the design must be new: if it closely resembles a design which has already been made public, it is not protected; but if it is protected, the proprietor can stop anyone else marketing articles bearing that design, without having to prove that they were copied from him."

[64] W. Wallace, op. cit., p. 421: "... under a 'copyright approach' the criterion for protection is that the design must be original – the designer's own work and not something he has copied; even if virtually identical with someone else's design, he can claim protection if he can satisfy the Court that he did not copy, directly or indirectly, from that earlier design; but, as a corollary, his protection is only against copying, directly or indirectly, from him. In other words, he will not succeed against a defendant who satisfies the Court that the alleged infringing design was original and not copied."

[65] See the criteria and scope of design protection proposed in the Max Planck Draft for a European Design Law. For the full text, see The Green paper on the legal protection of industrial design (F. Gotzen ed. 1992) (Story Scientia), pp. 87–106. On the influence of the Max Planck proposal on the Commission's Green Paper on industrial designs, see also infra, Chap. 9, pt. 5(2). For a defense of a specific "design approach", see A. Kur, "The Green Paper's 'design approach' – what's wrong with it?" [1993] E.I.P.R. 374. At p. 376, she rejects Cohen Jehoram's view that designs are a subject of copyright protection in the following terms: "This statement reflects the unfortunate but common view that designs must belong either to the patent or the copyright side, tertium non datur. It is this view which has plagued designs ever since they entered the sphere of law, to the effect that they always have been denied a proper place of their own within the legal system." In defence of the "copyright approach", see H. Cohen Jehoram, "The E.C. Green Paper on the legal protection of industrial design. Halfway down the right track – a view from the Benelux" [1992] E.I.P.R. 75.

(b) Economic justifications

Like patents and copyright, design rights have a reward and incentive func- **2.24**
tion, but the objective is different. The objective of granting an exclusive right
in an industrial design can be defined as providing the possibility of obtaining
a return for investment made, and progress achieved, in the field of aesthetics
in order to stimulate overall research and development of the aesthetic features of technical or functional products.

(c) Industrial designs and market power

(i) Compared with patents

Unlike patents, the objective of design rights is not to create incentives to **2.25**
stimulate innovation or technical progress. Rather, it is to provide incentives
to stimulate the development of different aesthetic features of products or, in
other words, "the enrichment of the wealth of forms".[66] Patents relate to the
new functional device of an industrial product, or process, rather than to its
external features. In contrast, design rights relate to the external and visible
features of products rather than to the way in which they function, although a
particular design may enhance the proper functioning of a product. In other
words, unlike patent law, design protection relates to the form or appearance
rather than to the technical effects of a product.[67]

The exclusivity inherent in design protection is generally acknowledged to **2.26**
be pro-competitive because it encourages innovation in the aesthetic field and
leads to an increase in consumer choice through the stimulation of inter-brand
competition.[68] The reward and incentive for the creative effort is thus obviously dependent on the willingness of consumers to buy, and perhaps pay
more for, the product incorporating the protected design as compared to
another product. In other words, the level of reward is determined by the
willingness of consumers to pay for the added value the design confers on an
industrial or technical product. It is apparent in this respect that the fulfilment
of the objective of design law is subject to what Annette Kur has called "the
fundamental rule", namely that:

> " ... via design protection it should not be possible to obtain a monopoly
> for a technical effect. Only in those cases, where the outer appearance of a
> product is exclusively dictated by the function it performs – that is, if in
> order to make another product perform the same function, the manufac-
> turer has no choice but to give it the same appearance as the first one –
> eligibility for design protection must be denied."[69]

The underlying reason for the enforcement of this fundamental rule in most
legal systems is that design rights cannot be said to constitute a necessary

---

[66] See the most interesting article by A. Kur, "The Max Planck Draft for a European Design Law"
in *The Green Paper on the legal protection of industrial design* (F. Gotzen ed. 1992) (Story
Scientia), pp. 13–26 at 17.

[67] See A. Kur, *op. cit.*, p. 18.

[68] See for instance Confederation of British Industry, *Design right: designed wrong* (1988), pt. 1,
where it is held that "design protection is itself a vital driver of enterprise and competition,
encouraging innovation and thereby stimulating enterprising companies and increasing
consumer choice".

[69] A. Kur, *op. cit.*, p. 18.

restraint on competition in the short run in order to stimulate technical progress and competition in the long term. They should therefore not be allowed to confer a monopoly on a product as patents sometimes do. Contrary to patents, the design system is based on the premise that the diversification of the appearance of a given product can exist and should be enhanced in order to stimulate overall competition and ultimately increase consumers' choice.

(ii) Compared with copyright

2.27   The difference between design rights and copyright is less clear-cut because they both aim at enhancing innovation in the aesthetic or creative field. The differentiating factor lies in the fact that the purpose of design rights is essentially to enhance competition and to increase consumers' choice in relation to a functional or technical product. Its objective is not merely to stimulate innovation in the aesthetic field, for instance for cultural reasons, as copyright does. This means that under design rights the creative effort serves to compete better in the market and to sell a product, whereas under copyright the creative effort stands on its own. This "marketing function" of design rights is best illustrated by the following example given by Annette Kur:

> "It may sound exaggerated, but I believe there is a lot of truth in the statement that the design of a coffee machine serves to sell the coffee machine, while a painting certainly is not meant to serve the purpose of selling canvas."[70]

From this example, it is once again clear that design rights have an important role to fulfil as a factor of non-price competition. In the extreme hypothesis that consumers consider a coffee machine to be an indispensable instrument to make coffee, that no competition prevails and that entry barriers are high, there will be little or no incentive to invest time and money in developing an attractive design for the coffee machine. The obvious reason for this is that conferring an added value on the product will influence neither the amount nor the price at which the monopolist can sell his coffee machines. The issue of the fulfilment of the objectives of design protection is thus only posed once competitors enter, or may enter, the market or, in other words, in a situation of rivalry.

(iii) Compared with trade marks

2.28   It is obvious that design rights also have a different objective to trade marks. Trade marks are concerned with the indication of commercial origin and the incentive to produce quality products. Design rights essentially relate to the appearance of the product and not to its quality or commercial origin. Inasmuch as design rights are also an instrument of marketing, well-known designs may, in addition to the above-mentioned functions, also fulfil the same function as trade marks. This will be the case when consumers associate a particular design with the expected quality of the product incorporating the design. In this sense, design exclusivity might also prevent consumers being deceived about the qualities of the product they purchase.

---

[70] See A. Kur, *op. cit.*, p. 23.

(6) Intellectual property rights versus competition

All the systems of intellectual property rights are based on the premise that a restraint of competition is necessary to ultimately increase competition in the public interest. Seen from this perspective there is no real conflict between the rules on competition and intellectual property laws. It should, nevertheless, be kept in mind that although the different systems of intellectual property rights have a lot in common, in that they all relate to intangible property, are based on the principle of territoriality and confer exclusive rights, they each have a well-defined objective to fulfil. **2.29**

It was illustrated above that patents, copyrights, trade marks and design rights each have a different impact on the competitive market structure. This is dictated by the various economic functions the different types of intellectual property rights are meant to fulfil. On this basis, it is difficult to conceive a general approach to intellectual property rights which could sufficiently take these differences into account. It is therefore submitted that it should be considered in each particular case whether or not the function of the intellectual property right invoked has been respected. This is in order to establish whether or not an encroachment on the rules on competition can be justified in terms of the need to safeguard the protection of intellectual property rights, and *vice versa*. The answer could then only be positive if through the grant and enforcement of a specific type of exclusivity, overall competition is enhanced and the public interest is served.

4. INTERNATIONAL CONTEXT

Within the E.C. context, and especially in litigation, the question has repeatedly arisen as to what should be the relationship between E.C. law and the international harmonisation of intellectual property legislation. In other words, the issue is raised as to what extent the elaboration and interpretation of E.C. rules with regard to intellectual property rights should take account of intellectual property conventions concluded between some or all of the E.C. Member States and certain non-member countries. The same question will undoubtedly arise with regard to the Agreement on Trade-Related Aspects of Intellectual Property Rights (TRIPS-Agreement), recently concluded and annexed to the Agreement on the World Trade Organisation (WTO-Agreement). Although the tenor of the question may be the same, in so far as the answer is concerned a distinction needs to be made between the intellectual property conventions on the one hand, and the TRIPS-Agreement on the other. **2.30**

(1) Intellectual property conventions

Prior to the TRIPS-Agreement most of the international efforts made to harmonise intellectual property protection worldwide took place within the framework of the World Intellectual Property Organisation (WIPO). This is a specialised agency of the United Nations created in Stockholm on July 14, **2.31**

1967.[71] WIPO administers *inter alia* both the Paris and the Berne Conventions. These are the most important and universal intellectual property conventions dealing with the protection of industrial property and literary and artistic works respectively.[72]

(a) Scope

2.32　　The Paris Convention for the Protection of Industrial Property, originally signed in 1883 and last revised in Stockholm in 1967 (Stockholm Act), created the so-called Paris Union between the signatory countries. All the E.C. Member States are members of the Paris Union and all have acceded to the Stockholm Act.[73] Article 1(2) stipulates that the concept of "industrial property" covers patents, industrial designs and models, trade marks and trade names, indications of origin, as well as the rules on unfair competition. Article 5 *Quinquies* provides that industrial designs and models will be protected in all countries of the Paris Union, without, however, specifying how this should be done or what should be the criteria and conditions necessary to qualify for protection. It thus seems that industrial designs could just as well be protected through a specific design law, or through copyright or rules on unfair competition.[74]

2.33　　The Berne Convention for the Protection of Literary and Artistic Works, creating the Berne Union between the signatory countries, originally dates from 1886 and was last revised in 1971 (Paris Act). All E.C. Member States are parties to the Paris Act except Ireland and Belgium which are currently bound by the 1948 Brussels Act.[75] Article 2(1) stipulates that the expression "literary and artistic works" includes "every production in the literary, scientific and artistic domain, whatever may be the mode or form of its expression".[76] This is followed by a non-exhaustive list of works that are covered by this concept. Article 2(7) specifies that it is up to the countries of the Berne Union to decide whether or not to include works of applied art and industrial designs and models in the scope of copyright protection as well as to determine the conditions under which this protection will be granted.

2.34　　Two other conventions in the field of intellectual property rights need to be mentioned. First of all there is the Universal Copyright Convention (UCC) of September 6, 1952, as revised in Paris in 1971. However, the UCC does not apply between countries of the Berne Union with respect to the protection of works which have a Berne Union country as the country of origin.[77] Secondly,

---

[71] On the role and structure of WIPO, see J. Ekedi-Samnik, *L'Organisation Mondiale de la Propriété Intellectuelle (OMPI)* (1975, Bruylant).

[72] For an introduction to these and other intellectual property conventions, see WIPO, *Background reading material on intellectual property* (1988, WIPO Publication).

[73] Reference will therefore only be made to the current state of the Paris Convention without going into the changes which preceded the 1967 Stockholm Act.

[74] See A. Francon, "*Le droit international de la propriété intellectuelle*", in *La protection de la propriété intellectuelle: aspects juridiques européens et internationaux* (1989, Institut Universitaire Internationale Luxembourg), pp. 11–78 at p. 46.

[75] In view of their pending adherence (see *infra*, Chap. 3, pt. 3(2)(b)(iv)), reference will only be made to the Berne Convention as revised by the 1971 Paris Act.

[76] It may, however, be provided by legislation that certain works will not be protected unless they have been fixed in some material form (Article 2(2)).

[77] See the Appendix Declaration relating to Article XVII UCC. On this issue, see also E. Ulmer, *Intellectual property rights and the conflict of laws* (1978, Kluwer/E.C. Commission), p. 30.

there is the International Convention for the Protection of Performers, Producers of Phonograms and Broadcasting Organisations adopted in Rome on
October 26, 1961 (Rome Convention). Only parties to the Berne Convention
or the UCC may adhere to the Rome Convention. It essentially deals with the
protection of the so-called "neighbouring rights" and leaves the protection of
copyright in literary and artistic works in principle unaffected (Article 1).

A common feature of these intellectual property conventions is that they lay   **2.35**
down minimum standards of protection and introduce basic principles, such
as the principle of national treatment and independence of rights, in order to
enhance the protection of intellectual property rights worldwide. The objective of the intellectual property conventions is clearly to grant minimal,
though effective, protection to intellectual property owners worldwide; contracting countries may grant more, but not less, protection. It should be mentioned that this concern is, nevertheless, put in the balance against the need to
safeguard the public interest. As such, it is generally held that compulsory
licences may be provided for, and that certain rights may be subject to forfeiture, or free use, in the public interest. However, it may in turn be stipulated
that this will be subject to certain conditions in order to respect the rights of
the intellectual property owner to the fullest extent possible whilst safeguarding the public interest.[78]

(b) Basic principles

The *principle of national treatment*, which is often referred to as the corner-   **2.36**
stone of the intellectual property conventions, implies that the same intellectual property protection needs to be given to nationals of other contracting
countries as to one's own nationals. This principle may be extended to non-
nationals under well-specified conditions. Usually, this will be for those having their habitual residence in one of the contracting countries.[79] The nationality requirement may also be replaced by other criteria, such as the country of
first publication, in order to increase the intellectual property protection
offered to non-nationals.[80] The nationality requirement may, however, also
be supplemented by other criteria such as performance taking place in one of
the contracting countries. This can sometimes render it more difficult to
obtain intellectual property protection even for nationals of contracting
parties.[81]

Because the procedures and conditions under which intellectual property   **2.37**
protection is granted may vary greatly from one country to another, the *principle of independence of rights* is an important corollary of the principle of
national treatment. This principle means that an intellectual property right
that has been lawfully acquired in one country will not automatically be affected by decisions regarding that intellectual property right taken in other countries, including the country of origin, such as forfeiture or expiry of the right.[82]

[78] See for instance Article 5 Paris Convention; Articles 9(2), 10, 10bis, 11bis(2), 13(1) Berne
Convention; Article 15 Rome Convention.
[79] See for instance Articles 2 and 3 Paris Convention; Article 3(2) Berne Convention.
[80] See for instance Article 3(1)(b) Berne Convention.
[81] See for instance the criteria for eligibility laid down in Article 4 Rome Convention.
[82] See for instance Article 4bis (patents) and Article 6(3) (trade marks) Paris Convention; Article
5(2) Berne Convention.

2.38   In specific cases, certain intellectual property conventions allow for *reciprocity* as an exception to the general rule of national treatment. For instance, the Berne Convention contains, *inter alia,* a specific rule relating to works of applied art and industrial designs and models in Article 2(7). It takes into account the fact that in some countries they are protected under copyright law, in others under a specific design law, and in yet other countries under both.[83] Article 2(7) implies that in so far as copyright protection on industrial designs is concerned, a reciprocity requirement can be imposed. Namely, if in the country of origin the cumulation of protection is excluded, the host country can also limit protection to the application of its specific industrial design legislation.[84]

(c) Intellectual property conventions in E.C. law

2.39   It should be emphasised that it is individual E.C. Member States, and not the E.C. as such, that are the signatory parties to the various intellectual property conventions.[85] The question should therefore be posed as to whether, and to what extent, the E.C. has to take into account the international obligations which Member States have contracted when dealing with intellectual property rights. Community institutions often give due regard to relevant intellectual property conventions that all, or most, Member States have signed.[86] In cases where there is no manifest incompatibility between the E.C. Treaty and intellectual property conventions, the latter may prove to be highly relevant by giving guidance on matters of interpretation, or even to settle certain contested issues.[87] A problem clearly arises in cases of incompatibility between intellectual property conventions and the E.C. Treaty. A similar problem is

---

[83] See also Article 6, which stipulates that upon notification to WIPO, a Berne Union country of first publication of a work may restrict the protection given to authors who are not nationals and who are not habitually resident in a Union country, if the country of which they are nationals fails to protect the works of the authors of one of the Union countries in an adequate manner. Of more general application, with regard to the duration of protection, it is stipulated that in principle the term is governed by the legislation of the country where protection is claimed, but that "...unless the legislation of that country otherwise provides, the term shall not exceed the term fixed in the country of origin of the work" (Article 7(8)). On this issue, see P. Katzenberger, "General principles of the Berne and the Universal Copyright Conventions" in *GATT or WIPO?* (Beier and Schricker eds. 1988) (VCH), pp. 43–52.

[84] See also the analysis of the implications of the Berne Convention made by M.-A. Perot-Morel, *Les principes de protection des dessins et modèles dans les pays du Marché Commun* (1968, Editions Mouton), pp. 161–162. On the history of this Article, see S. Ladas, *Patents, Trademarks and Related Rights: national and international protection* (1975, Harvard University Press), Vol. II, Pt. IV, para. 485. Already before the *Phil Collins* judgment of the Court, the E.C. Commission was of the opinion that this was contrary to the principle of non-discrimination in E.C. law: see *infra*, Chap. 9, pt. 5(2).

[85] Though the E.C. Council has at least taken two decisions providing that the E.C. Commission could participate in negotiations in the framework of WIPO, see I. Govaere, "Intellectual property protection and commercial policy", in *The European Community's commercial policy after 1992: the legal dimension* (Maresceau ed. 1993) (Martinus Nijhoff Publishers), pp. 197–222 at 206.

[86] This is particularly obvious from the proposals for harmonisation of intellectual property legislation in which the Commission usually refers to the relevant existing intellectual property conventions concluded by most or all Member States.

[87] See for instance Case C–9/93, *Ideal-Standard*, Judgment of June 22, 1994: [1994] E.C.R. I-2789 at paras. 25–32; [1974] 3 C.M.L.R. 857, concerning the principle of independence of trade marks embodied in intellectual property conventions.

posed when Member States rely on enabling provisions of intellectual property conventions, such as those concerning compulsory licences, in order to oppose the application of the E.C. Treaty.

(i) Intellectual property conventions concluded before the E.C. Treaty

Most intellectual property conventions were concluded by Member States   2.40
before the E.C. Treaty entered into force, or before their accession to the E.C.
This means that Article 234 E.C., which the European Court of Justice has
held to be of general scope and applying to any international agreement irrespective of its subject-matter,[88] applies. Article 234 E.C. reads as follows:

> "The rights and obligations arising from agreements concluded before
> the entry into force of the Treaty between one or more Member States on
> the one hand, and one or more third countries on the other, shall not be
> affected by the provisions of this Treaty.
>
> To the extent that such agreements are not compatible with this
> Treaty, the Member State or States concerned shall take all appropriate
> steps to eliminate the incompatibilities established. Member States shall,
> where necessary, assist each other to this end and shall, where appropriate, adopt a common attitude.
>
> In applying the agreements referred to in the first paragraph, Member
> States shall take into account the fact that the advantages accorded under
> this Treaty by each Member State form an integral part of the establishment of the Community and are thereby inseparably linked with the creation of common institutions, the conferring of powers upon them and
> the granting of the same advantages by all the other Member States."

The Court has consistently held that the only purpose of Article 234, para. 1
E.C. is to safeguard the rights of non-member countries and cannot be
invoked in the relationship between Member States.[89] An intellectual property convention therefore cannot be invoked in an intra-Community context
to escape the application of rules laid down in the E.C. Treaty. Member States,
nevertheless, have to respect the rights of non-member countries under a prior
agreement and perform their obligations thereunder. Also Community institutions have the duty not to impede the performance of those obligations by
Member States, but this duty "does not bind the Community as regards the
non-member country in question".[90] Furthermore, concerning the relationship with non-member countries Member States have to endeavour to eliminate incompatibilities with the E.C. Treaty by virtue of Article 234, para. 2 E.C.
This would seem to imply that if incompatibilities were to be established,

[88] Case 812/79, *Attorney-General v. Burgoa*, Judgment of October 14, 1980: [1980] E.C.R.
2787; [1981] 2 C.M.L.R. 193, at para. 6.
[89] See for instance Case 812/79: [1980] E.C.R. 2787; [1981] 2 C.M.L.R. 193, at para. 8. Case
121/85, *Conegate Ltd v. HM Customs & Excise*, Judgment of March 11, 1986: [1986] E.C.R.
1007; [1986] 1 C.M.L.R. 739, at para. 25. Conversely, it seems that para. 3 calls for a restrictive
interpretation of those agreements in the sense that E.C. law should not simply be transposed to
non-member countries by virtue of certain clauses in agreements, such as the most favoured
nation clause. On this issue, see J. Groux, P. Manin, *The European Communities in the
international order* (1985, European Perspectives Series, E.C. Commission), pp. 105–106.
[90] Case 812/79: [1980] E.C.R. 2787; [1981] 2 C.M.L.R. 193, at para. 9.

Member States would, for instance, need to raise this issue and propose solutions during subsequent revisions of the intellectual property conventions.

2.41　　The fact that, in the relationship between Member States, the E.C. Treaty prevails over intellectual property conventions concluded prior to their accession to the E.C. was unequivocally clarified by the Court in the *Magill* appeal case.[91] In essence, the argument was raised that allowing for the E.C. Commission to impose compulsory licences would conflict with the normal exploitation of copyright on programme listings and would thus be contrary to Article 9(2) of the Berne Convention, as revised in Paris in 1971. The Court held:

> "...so far as the United Kingdom and Ireland are concerned, it is true that they were already parties to the Convention when they acceded to the Community and that Article 234 of the Treaty therefore applies to that Convention, in accordance with Article 5 of the Act of Accession. It is, however, settled case-law that the provisions of an agreement concluded prior to entry into force of the Treaty or prior to a Member State's accession cannot be relied on in intra-Community relations if, as in the present case, the rights of non-member countries are not involved (see, in particular, the judgment in Case 286/86, *Ministère Public v. Deserbais* [1988] E.C.R 4907, paragraph 18).
>
> Finally, the Paris Act, which amended Article 9(1) and (2) of the Convention (the provisions relied on by RTE), was ratified by the United Kingdom only after its accession to the Community and has still not been ratified by Ireland.
>
> The Court of First Instance was therefore correct to hold that Article 9 of the Convention cannot be relied on to limit the powers of the Community, as provided for in the EEC Treaty, since the Treaty can be amended only in accordance with the procedure laid down in Article 236."[92]

(ii) Intellectual property conventions concluded after the E.C. Treaty

2.42　　From the point of view of E.C. law, international agreements concluded by one or more Member States with third countries after the E.C. Treaty came into force, or after their accession to the E.C., have to be compatible with the E.C. Treaty by virtue of Article 5 E.C. This general provision provides that:

> "Member States shall take all the appropriate measures, whether general or particular, to ensure the fulfilment of obligations arising out of this Treaty or resulting from action taken by the institutions of the Community. They shall facilitate the achievement of the Community's tasks.
>
> They shall abstain from taking any measure which could jeopardise the attainment of the objectives of this Treaty."

Breach of Article 5 E.C. may be subject to judicial review by the European Court of Justice. It nonetheless remains up to the Member States to put an end

[91] Joined Cases C–241/91 P and C–242/91 P, *RTE and ITP*: [1995] E.C.R. I–743; [1995] 4 C.M.L.R. 718. On these cases, see also *infra*, Chap. 5, pt. 4(3).
[92] Joined Cases C–241/91 P and C–242/91 P, *op. cit.*, paras. 84–86.

to the infringement either through terminating or modifying the agreement which is held to be incompatible with E.C. law.[93]

It should be pointed out that sometimes different rules apply to the relation- **2.43** ship between Member States as compared with relations with third countries. For instance, the rules on the free movements of goods are in principle applicable only in an intra-Community context. This implies that the accession of a new Member State to the E.C. could have a direct consequence on the applicability of prior intellectual property conventions concluded between that state and Member States. This was unequivocally confirmed by the Court in the *Exportur* case.[94] A convention on denominations of origin was concluded between France and Spain in 1973. This was prior to the accession of Spain to the E.C. The issue at stake was whether this convention could be invoked after the accession of Spain with respect to the application of the E.C. rules on the free movement of goods. The Court unequivocally clarified that the provisions of a convention concluded after 1958 by a Member State and a non-member country can no longer be applied in the relation between those states as from the date of the accession of the latter to the European Community. Provided, of course, that these provisions are contrary to the rules applicable in intra-Community context as laid down in the E.C. Treaty,[95] which they were not in the case at issue.

(iii) Enabling provisions in intellectual property conventions

The general rule thus is that in relations between Member States, the E.C. **2.44** Treaty prevails over incompatible provisions in intellectual property conventions. It is not surprising, therefore, that this has also been held to be so when what were merely enabling provisions of intellectual property conventions were invoked by Member States to escape the application of the E.C. Treaty.[96] It is obvious that by virtue of Articles 5 and 234, para. 2 E.C., Member States are also bound to interpret the powers they retain under intellectual property conventions in accordance with the E.C. Treaty.[97]

(iv) Impact of the E.C. non-discrimination principle

Although the relationship between intellectual property conventions and E.C. **2.45** law may seem to be more or less clear-cut, it nevertheless raises essential questions as to which provisions and basic principles of the E.C. Treaty are applicable to intellectual property rights. The basic rule is that provisions in

---

[93] See also J. Groux and P. Manin, *op. cit.*, pp. 111–112. It is obvious, however, that E.C. law does not bind non-member countries.

[94] Case C–3/91, *Exportur v. LOR*, Judgment of November 10, 1992: [1992] E.C.R. I–5529.

[95] Case C–3/91: [1992] E.C.R. I-5529, para. 8.

[96] See, for instance, the grant of compulsory licences enabled by the Paris Convention but contrary to E.C. law: Cases C–235/89 and C–30/90, *Commission v. Italy* and *Commission v. U.K.* respectively, Judgments of February 18, 1992: [1992] E.C.R. I-777; [1992] 2 C.M.L.R. 709, at para. 27; and [1992] E.C.R. I-829; [1992] 2 C.M.L.R. 709, at para. 31 respectively. On these cases, see *infra*, Chap. 6, pt. 3(1)(a). For a critique of this approach, see N. Macfarlane, C. Wardle, J. Wilkinson, "The tension between national intellectual property rights and certain provisions of E.C. law" [1994] E.I.P.R. 525.

[97] See also the Opinion of Advocate General Van Gerven in Cases C–235/89 and C–30/90: [1992] E.C.R. I-777; [1992] 2 C.M.L.R. 709; and [1992] E.C.R. I-829; [1992] 2 C.M.L.R. 709, at pt. 14.

intellectual property conventions which are incompatible with the E.C. Treaty cannot be invoked between Member States. A prerequisite for the effective application of this rule is, therefore, certainty as to which E.C. Treaty rules the Member States have to comply with in relation to intellectual property rights. Unfortunately, uncertainty remains on this particular point, at least until the European Court of Justice has clarified the scope of the E.C. Treaty. It is, for instance, significant that it was only in 1993 that the Court clarified the relationship between intellectual property rights and the E.C. principle of non-discrimination. In so doing, it also indirectly ruled on the applicability of the principle of national treatment, which is also referred to as the cornerstone of the intellectual property conventions, in the relationship between Member States.

2.46   In the *Phil Collins* case of October 1993, the Court set an important precedent. It ruled that national copyright legislation, which discriminates against nationals of other Member States concerning the means of enforcing rights related to copyright, is contrary to the general principle of non-discrimination on the basis of nationality as laid down in Article 6 E.C. (formerly Article 7 E.C.).[98] The argument that this different treatment is not contrary to, or is expressly allowed for, or issues from the fact that not all Member States have adhered to relevant intellectual property conventions (*in casu* the Rome Convention), was therefore of no avail.

The Court clarified for the first time that intellectual property rights come within the scope of Article 6 E.C. without necessarily having to be linked to Articles 30, 36, 59 and 66 E.C., as was often thought previously.[99] Article 6 E.C. has direct effect and may thus be relied upon in its own right before national courts by intellectual property owners who are nationals of an E.C. Member State. On this basis they should obtain the same intellectual property protection as the Member State, where protection is sought, grants to its own nationals.

It is needless to point out that the impact of this judgment is far-reaching. The E.C. principle of non-discrimination will apply regardless of whether or not the imposition of additional criteria, or a reciprocity requirement, was allowed for in the relevant intellectual property conventions. National intellectual property legislation was, however, usually and in good faith drafted with the latter very much in mind.[1]

(2) TRIPS-Agreement

2.47   International harmonisation of intellectual property rights was also dealt with in the GATT Uruguay Round negotiations on trade-related aspects of intellectual property rights (TRIPS). This resulted in the TRIPS-Agreement

---

[98] Joined Cases C 92 and 326/92, *Phil Collins v. Imtrat Handelsgesellschaft mbh*, Judgment of October 20, 1993: [1993] E.C.R. I-5145; [1993] 3 C.M.L.R. 773.
[99] Joined Cases C 92 and 326/92: [1993] E.C.R. I-5145; [1993] 3 C.M.L.R. 773, at para. 27.
[1] On the practical implications, see also H. Cohen Jehoram, "The E.C. copyright directives, economics and author's rights" [1994] I.I.C. 821, at 825–826; G. Dworkin, J.A.L. Sterling, "Phil Collins and the term directive" [1994] E.I.P.R. 187.

which is annexed to and forms an integral part of the WTO-Agreement.[2] The linking of the issue of intellectual property protection with international trade is a relatively new phenomenon and is chiefly inspired by the growing awareness by the industrialised countries of the economic impact of intellectual property rights and their value as trade assets.[3] Existing intellectual property conventions were considered not to offer adequate protection against counterfeiting and piracy and the ensuing worldwide trade losses caused to economies. This is mainly due to the lack of enforcement mechanisms. The TRIPS-Agreement therefore provides a set of minimum standards of protection and enforcement of intellectual property rights, more elaborate and at a higher level than the intellectual property conventions, which has to be implemented by all WTO members (Article 1(1))[4] system. It also provides a system of dispute settlement.[5] It is rather surprising that the TRIPS-Agreement does not aim at liberalising trade in protected products by the insertion of a general principle of exhaustion of intellectual property rights. It expressly excludes this principle from the Agreement.[6] It is acknowledged, however, that appropriate measures consistent with the agreement may need to be taken to prevent the abuse of intellectual property rights which unduly restrict trade, or adversely affect the international transfer of technology (Article 8(2)).

(a) Basic GATT principles and their relationship to intellectual property conventions

In the preamble to the TRIPS-Agreement it is stated that WTO members desire to establish a mutually supportive relationship between, *inter alia*, the WTO and WIPO. The elaboration of such a relationship has resulted in a system of cross-references to relevant intellectual property conventions throughout the text of the TRIPS-Agreement. As such it is, for instance, stipulated that WTO members shall comply with the substantive provisions of the Paris and Berne Conventions.[7]

    The endeavour to safeguard the special features of the most important intellectual property conventions is especially evident in the way in which the basic GATT principles of national treatment (Article 3), and most-favoured-nation treatment (Article 4), have been formulated. Similarly, as for the principle of

2.48

---

[2] See Article 2(2) WTO-Agreement. Contrary to the previous GATT-practice of elaborating "codes" open to those willing to sign, the annexes to the WTO-Agreement are binding on all WTO members.

[3] On the conceptual change concerning intellectual property rights leading up to the TRIPS-Agreement, namely from trade barriers to trade assets, in both the GATT and E.C. context, see I. Govaere, "Trade-related aspects of intellectual property rights: the E.C. dichotomy uncovered" in *La place de l'Europe dans le commerce mondiale* (July Session 1994, Institut Universitaire International Luxembourg), pp. 161–215.

[4] For the transitional arrangements, see Articles 65 and 66.

[5] The Dispute Settlement Understanding also annexed to the WTO-Agreement will, in principle, also apply to TRIPS. For more details, see Article 64 TRIPS.

[6] WTO members are not obliged to adopt the principle of exhaustion. However, if they do adopt this principle then the principle of national treatment, and the most favoured nation clause, may be relied upon in dispute settlement (Article 6).

[7] See Articles 2 and 9 respectively. As concerns the Berne Convention, an exception is, however, made for Article 6bis which concerns the protection of moral rights.

national treatment in intellectual property conventions, it is expressly provided that these concepts refer to "nationals of the other members" instead of to products as is usually the case under GATT. It is significant that Article 1(3) refers to specified intellectual property conventions concerning the criteria for eligibility. The application of both principles is, furthermore, expressly subject to exceptions already provided for in certain intellectual property conventions, such as the reciprocity requirement in the Berne Convention. It should be recalled, however, that in respect of the relationship between E.C. Member States, it is the E.C. principle of non-discrimination that will prevail.[8]

(b) Scope

2.49   The TRIPS-Agreement extends beyond the intellectual property conventions in particular in so far as its scope is concerned.[9] Part II contains several detailed obligatory minimum standards concerning the availability, scope and use of copyright and related rights, trade marks, geographical indications, industrial designs, patents and lay-out designs of integrated circuits. It also contains rules for the protection of undisclosed information and the control of anti-competitive practices in contractual licences.[10] Part III lays down rather detailed rules concerning the enforcement of intellectual property rights, relating *inter alia* to fair and equitable procedures, evidence, injunctions, damages, remedies and provisional measures (Sections 2 and 3). It is also stipulated that specific border measures have to be adopted against the importation of counterfeit goods (Section 4) and that criminal procedures and penalties need to be applied, at least in cases of wilful counterfeiting or piracy on a commercial scale (Section 5). Furthermore, a system of dispute settlement and the establishment of a specific Council for TRIPS is provided for.[11]

(c) TRIPS-Agreement in E.C. law

(i) Nature of TRIPS-Agreement

2.50   Not in the least because the TRIPS-Agreement was negotiated within the framework of GATT, the E.C. Commission was of the opinion that the E.C. was competent to conclude the WTO-Agreement alone on the basis of its exclusive competence under the common commercial policy heading (Article 113 E.C.) or, alternatively, by virtue of the doctrine of implied powers.[12]

---

[8] See the *Phil Collins* judgment, *supra*, at pt. 4(c)(iv).

[9] For an overview of the most significant provisions, see J. Worthy, "Intellectual property protection after GATT" [1994] E.I.P.R. 195.

[10] Part II essentially deals with protectable subject matter, requirements for and duration of protection, rights conferred, etc. This often goes beyond what is provided for in intellectual property conventions. For instance, Article 27 TRIPS stipulates that patents should be granted for both products and processes in all fields, thus apparently also for pharmaceutical drugs, whereas Article 10 TRIPS explicitly holds that "computer programs, whether in source or object code, shall be protected as literary works under the Berne Convention".

[11] See Articles 68 and 64 TRIPS.

[12] This means, in essence, that even in the absence of an express Treaty provision, the E.C. may obtain competence, in external context, for matters for which it has internal competence. See Case 22/70, *Commission v. Council (AETR)*: [1971] E.C.R. 263; [1971] C.M.L.R. 335.

Because this view was not shared by the Member States, the European Court of Justice was asked to give an opinion pursuant to Article 228(6) E.C.[13] This resulted in Opinion 1/94[14] in which the Court held that the TRIPS-Agreement belongs to the shared competence of the E.C. and its Member States. In other words, the TRIPS-Agreement is, by its nature, a mixed agreement to be concluded jointly by both the E.C. and its Member States.[15] The Court, nevertheless, expressly qualified this approach. On the one hand, it was held that the E.C. is solely competent by virtue of Article 113 E.C. as concerns the adoption of border measures against the importation of counterfeit goods.[16] On the other hand, it was specified that the Member States do not retain an exclusive competence concerning the rules on enforcement of intellectual property rights.[17]

(ii) Agreements as acts of the Community

The Court has consistently held that, from the date they enter into force, agreements concluded by the E.C. by virtue of Article 228 E.C.,[18] including mixed agreements such as TRIPS, are acts of the Community within the meaning of Article 177, para. 1(b) E.C. and form integral part of E.C. law.[19] Article 228(7) E.C. provides that such agreements are binding not only on the Community institutions but also on the Member States. The Court has clarified that both the Community institutions and the Member States thus have a responsibility concerning the implementation of those agreements, not only in relation to non-member countries but also, and above all, in relation to the Community. The Court itself has the specific task of ensuring the uniform application of the agreements throughout the Community by interpreting the provisions of agreements within the framework of its jurisdiction.[20, 21]

2.51

---

[13] Not only the TRIPS-Agreement, but also the General Agreement on Trade in Services (GATS) annexed to the WTO-Agreement, posed similar problems.

[14] Court of Justice, Opinion 1/94 of November 15, 1994: [1994] E.C.R. I-5267.

[15] Although it should be recalled that the TRIPS-Agreement was not concluded separately from the WTO-Agreement but forms an integral part of it.

[16] Opinion 1/94, *op. cit.*, para. 55. This relates to Section 4, Part III TRIPS.

[17] Opinion 1/94, *op. cit.*, para. 104.

[18] Article 228 E.C. stipulates the procedure that has to be followed for the conclusion of agreements with third countries.

[19] See Case 181/73, *Haegeman v. Belgian State*, Judgment of April 30, 1974: [1974] E.C.R. 449; [1975] 1 C.M.L.R. 515, at paras. 4–5; Court of Justice, Opinion 1/91 of December 14, 1991, Agreement establishing the European Economic Area (EEA): [1991] E.C.R. I-6079, at paras. 37–38.

[20] See Case 104/81, *Kupferberg*, Judgment of October 26, 1982: [1982] E.C.R. 3641; [1983] 1 C.M.L.R. 1, at paras. 11–14. The same reasoning has also been extended to acts of organs created by such an agreement, see for instance Case C–192/89, *Sevince*, Judgment of September 20, 1990: [1990] E.C.R. I-3497; [1992] 2 C.M.L.R. 57.

[21] However, in the event that a provision in the TRIPS-Agreement was similar, if not identical, to the E.C. Treaty, this would not necessarily imply that it should also be interpreted in the light of the interpretation given by the Court of Justice to the E.C. Treaty. Rather, the Court has consistently held that regard must be had to the similarity, or dissimilarity, in objective, goal and context of the agreement concerned as compared to the E.C. Treaty. The outcome is not always easy to predict, for there are precedents both ways (compare, for instance, Case 270/80, *Polydor v. Harlequin*, Judgment of February 9, 1982: [1982] E.C.R. 329; [1982] 1 C.M.L.R. 677 with Case C–228/91, *Commission v. Italy*, Judgment of May 25, 1993: [1993] E.C.R. I-2701).

(iii) Primacy and direct effect

2.52 Being an act of the Community, and forming an integral part of E.C. law, agreements concluded with third countries, like all secondary E.C. legislation, should be compatible with the E.C. Treaty. This follows from points 5 and 6 of Article 228 E.C. The latter provides that, in case of incompatibility, the E.C. Treaty should first be amended in accordance with Article N TEU before the Council may conclude the agreement or, in case the Court has given an adverse opinion, before the agreement may enter into force. If by way of deduction the question of whether the E.C. Treaty has primacy over such agreements is generally answered in the positive,[22] it should be pointed out that agreements concluded with third countries do, in turn, take precedence over secondary E.C. legislation.[23]

2.53 The question of whether or not provisions of agreements concluded with third countries, and thus also the TRIPS-Agreement, also have direct effect is subject mainly to the same principles as are applied to the E.C.Treaty. The nature and structure of the agreement concerned must lend itself to direct effect and the invoked provision must be unconditional and sufficiently precise.[24] Prior to the WTO-Agreement the Court held that GATT was not unconditional in nature and therefore could not be invoked in order to contest the validity of secondary E.C. legislation. That is, unless either the Community intended to give effect to a particular obligation it contracted under GATT, or the Community act concerned expressly referred to precise provisions of GATT.[25] This approach was due mainly to the fact that GATT merely provided a dispute settlement mechanism based on negotiation.[26] It therefore remains to be seen whether the Court will take a different approach now that the system of dispute settlement has been elaborated upon in the WTO-Agreement.

---

[22] See for instance Manin, Groux, *op. cit.*, p. 117.
[23] See Joined Cases 21–24/72, *International Fruit Company*, Judgment of December 12, 1972: [1972] E.C.R. 1219; [1975] 2 C.M.L.R. 1.
[24] Case 104/81: [1982] E.C.R. 3641; [1983] 1 C.M.L.R. 1, at paras. 22–23.
[25] See for instance Case C–280/93, *Germany v. Council (Bananas)*: [1994] E.C.R. I–4973, at paras. 109–111. Here the Court extended this reasoning, which was previously elaborated with regard to claims made by individuals, to legal actions undertaken by Member States on the basis of Article 173 E.C.
[26] See Joined Cases 21–24/72: [1972] E.C.R. 1219; [1975] 2 C.M.L.R. 1, at paras. 19–28.

3. The Place of Intellectual Property Rights in E.C. Law

1. Objectives of the E.C. Treaty

The main objectives of the European Community are defined in Article 2 E.C. (as modified by the TEU) as follows:

    3.01

> "The Community shall have as its task, by establishing a common market and an economic and monetary Union and by implementing the common policies or activities referred to in Articles 3 and 3a, to promote throughout the Community a harmonious and balanced development of economic activities, sustainable and non-inflationary growth respecting the environment, a high degree of convergence of economic performance, a high level of employment and of social protection, the raising of the standard of living and quality of life, and economic and social cohesion and solidarity among Member States."

The Community objective of creating a common market stands in contrast to the view that intellectual property rights should remain within the national competence in order to stimulate national industrial and technological progress and economic growth. A consequence of a national-oriented approach is that intellectual property law is likely to be drafted in such a way as to protect national, or to attract foreign, industries. This might find its expression in a more or less protectionist system which could be to the detriment of the economic growth of other Member States.[1] A national-oriented approach to intellectual property rights would therefore seem to be incompatible with Article 2 E.C. which provides for the harmonious and balanced development of economic activities throughout the Community.

Article 3 E.C. lists, among the essential activities of the Community, attainment of the objectives mentioned in Article 2 E.C. by "the elimination, as between Member States, of customs duties and of quantitative restrictions on the import and export of goods, and of all other measures having equivalent effect" (Article 3(a) E.C.), and the institution of "a system ensuring that competition in the internal market is not distorted" (Article 3(g) E.C.). The crucial question is how this relates to intellectual property rights, which, by their very nature, have an effect on both intra-Community trade and the competitive market structure.

---

[1] It is significant that most national laws provide for a system of compulsory licences that applies in case the exclusive right is not worked on the national territory. On the compatibility of the latter with Community law, see *infra*, Chap. 6, pt. 3(1)(a).

41

2. THE RELEVANT PROVISIONS IN THE E.C. TREATY

(1) Introduction

3.02 Although it is obvious that national intellectual property rights impinge upon the objectives of the Community, the question had already arisen at an early stage as to whether, and to what extent, the E.C. is competent to remedy this situation. The main reason for this initial debate, which is still going on today, is to be found in the wording of the E.C. Treaty.

Intellectual property rights have a major impact on the economic market. As seen previously, an intellectual property owner has the right to exclude certain acts by potential competitors such as manufacturing and importing infringing products, as well as to impose certain obligations on contracting parties such as the payment of royalties. In other words, the enforcement of intellectual property rights has an effect both on competition and on the free movement of goods.[2] By their very nature and economic purpose intellectual property rights therefore fall within the ambit of the E.C. Treaty.[3] However, due to the importance of granting this type of exclusive protection for the stimulation of technical progress and economic growth the Member States have been reluctant to subject their national intellectual property laws to Community rules and principles. This already found its expression in the fact that intellectual property rights were expressly mentioned only in Article 36 of the Rome Treaty which provides exceptions to the free movement of goods. It is significant that this has not been altered by the Single European Act nor by the Maastricht Treaty on a European Union (TEU).

The very wording of the E.C. Treaty initially led to uncertainty about whether or not this implied that intellectual property rights are exempt from the application of the Treaty rules and thus whether or not they remain within the exclusive competence of the Member States. Nowadays, it is firmly established that intellectual property rights are not only subject to certain Treaty rules, such as the rules on the free movement of goods, services and competition, but also to the general principle of non-discrimination as laid down in Article 6 E.C.[4]

(2) Article 36 and the principle of free movement of goods

(a) Article 36: intellectual property exception or exclusion?

3.03 The wording of Article 36 E.C. can lead to two very different interpretations.[5] It reads as follows:

> "The provisions of Articles 30 to 34 shall not preclude prohibitions or restrictions on imports, exports or goods in transit justified on grounds of

---

[2] See *supra*, Chap. 2, pt. 2.

[3] This was expressly confirmed by the Court in the *Phil Collins* case. See Joined Cases C 92 and 326/92, Judgment of October 20, 1993: [1993] E.C.R. I-5154; [1993] 3 C.M.L.R. 773, at para. 22.

[4] On this issue, see the implications of the *Phil Collins* judgment, *supra*, Chap. 2, pt. 4(c)(iv).

[5] On the initial debate regarding the scope of Article 36 EEC, see G. Schrans, *Octrooien en octrooilicenties in het Europees mededingingsrecht* (1966, Story-Scientia), p. 162.

[. . .] the protection of industrial and commercial property. Such prohibitions and restrictions shall not, however, constitute a means of arbitrary discrimination or a disguised restriction on trade between Member States."

At first sight, the wording of Article 36 E.C. seems to suggest that intellectual property rights do not operate as quantitative restrictions or measures having an equivalent effect because they are exempted from the application of the rules concerning the free movement of goods. This argument was initially invoked to support the view that intellectual property rights remained within the Member States' exclusive competence.[6] It is, however, this express exemption from the application of the principle of free movement of goods, as well as the limitation to this exemption contained in the second sentence of Article 36 E.C., that has been invoked to prove the contrary and to maintain that intellectual property rights are, in principle, subject to Community law. The argument is that if industrial and commercial property rights were not considered by the draftsmen of the Treaty as, potentially, measures having an effect equivalent to quantitative restrictions,[7] then neither the reference to them in Article 36 E.C. nor the proviso contained in the second sentence would make any sense.[8]

(b) The rule: Article 36 directed to Member States

Although the European Court of Justice had already impliedly confirmed this second interpretation of Article 36 E.C. in relation to intellectual property rights,[9] in the *Simmenthal* case the Court expressly explained that: **3.04**

"Article 36 is not designed to reserve certain matters to the exclusive jurisdiction of Member States but permits national laws to derogate from the principle of free movement of goods to the extent to which such a derogation is and continues to be justified for the attainment of the objectives referred to in the article."[10]

This single phrase contains two important elements. The first one is the express confirmation that Article 36 E.C. in general does not reserve an exclusive competence to the Member States so that, in principle, Community law applies to the exceptions enumerated therein.[11] The rules on the free

---

[6] See especially M. Gotzen, "*La propriété industrielle et les Articles, 36 et 90 du Traité instituant la CEE*" [1958] R.T.D.C. 261 at 262–279.
[7] On intellectual property rights as "measures having equivalent effect to quantitative restrictions" within the meaning of Articles 30–34 E.C., see *infra*, Chap. 7, pt. 3.
[8] See, for instance, V. Korah, "The limitations of copyright and patents by the rules for the free movement of goods in the European Common Market" [1982] *Case Western Reserve Journal of International Law* 7, at 9–10; L. Gormley, *Prohibiting restrictions on trade within the EEC: the theory and application of Articles 30–36 of the EEC Treaty* (1985, North-Holland), p. 123.
[9] See *infra*, Chap. 4, pt. 1.
[10] Case 35/76, *Simmenthal SpA v. Italian Minister for Finance*, Judgment of December 15, 1976: [1976] E.C.R. 1871; [1977] 2 C.M.L.R. 1, at para. 14.
[11] As such, it is submitted that Bieber was wrong in using Article 36 to support the contention that the Treaty expressly refers to exclusive powers of Member States. See R. Bieber, "On the mutual completion of overlapping legal systems: the case of the European Communities and the national legal orders" (1988) 13 E.L.Rev. 147, at 151.

movement of goods are, in the first place, directed towards the Member States. The primary aim of those rules is to remedy the deflection of, or restrictions posed to, intra-Community trade which are caused by different national laws. The Court clarified that the exception to this general principle, as embodied in Article 36 E.C., is only meant to allow certain national laws in certain circumstances to derogate from the principle of free movement of goods.[12] The second important element is that the Court added a new limitation to the invokeability of Article 36, additional to the proviso contained in the second sentence. It clearly stated that national laws that derogate from the principle of free movement of goods have to be justified for the attainment of one of the objectives enumerated in that Article. In the *De Peijper* case, the Court had already made clear that the national measures concerned should also be proportional.[13] This means that no other measures should be available which can as effectively protect the higher interest invoked whilst having a less restrictive effect on intra-Community trade.

3.05   The proviso laid down in the second sentence of Article 36 E.C. may be seen as an additional "safety net" to ensure that the exceptions laid down in Article 36 E.C. are not unduly invoked. With regard to this prohibition, the Court has consistently held that it is:

> " ... designed to prevent restrictions on trade based on the grounds mentioned in the first sentence of Article 36 from being diverted from their proper purpose and used in such a way as either to create discrimination in respect of goods originating in other Member States or indirectly to protect national products."[14]

(c) The exception: Article 36 applied to the exercise of intellectual property rights

3.06   Thus the general rule is that in order to come under Article 36 E.C., national law has to be proportional and justifiable under the first sentence,[15] and may not run counter to the prohibition laid down in the second sentence, of Article 36 E.C.[16] The application of this rule to intellectual property rights is, how-

---

[12] See also J. Mertens de Wilmar, "The case-law of the Court of Justice in relation to the review of the legality of economic policy in mixed-economy systems" [1982] L.I.E.I. 1, at 4, where he points out that no discretionary power is conferred on Member States, whereas the concepts laid down in Article 36 "are susceptible of differing interpretations and, moreover, may vary in time and space".

[13] Case 104/75, *De Peijper*, Judgment of May 20, 1976: [1976] E.C.R. 613; [1976] 2 C.M.L.R. 271. See para. 17, where the Court held that "national rules or practices do not fall within the exception specified in Article 36 if the health and life of humans can as effectively be protected by measures which do not restrict intra-Community trade so much".

[14] Case 34/79, *R. v. Henn and Darby*, Judgment of December 14, 1979: [1979] E.C.R. 3795; [1980] 1 C.M.L.R. 246, at para. 21. Similarly, see for instance Case 40/82, *Commission v. UK (Newcastle Disease)*, Judgment of July 15, 1982: [1982] E.C.R. 2793: [1982] 3 C.M.L.R. 497, at para. 36.

[15] See also A. Mattera, "*La libre circulation des oeuvres d'art à l'intérieur de la Communauté et la protection des tresors nationaux ayant une valeur artistique, historique ou archéologique*" [1993] *Revue du Marché Unique Européen* 9, esp. at 16–17.

[16] See also L. Gormley, *op. cit.*, pp. 123–124, where he spells out the following three-step analysis that has to be fulfilled in the proper order: "(a) Does the contested measure in fact fall within the set of measures basically prohibited? If so, then: (b) does it qualify for the exemption under the first sentence of Article 36? If so, then: (c) does it nevertheless fail because of the second sentence of Article 36?"

ever, less obvious. Judging by the case law of the Court it is not so much the content of the national intellectual property law, but the way in which the intellectual property owner uses his exclusive rights that will determine whether Article 36 applies or whether the principle of free movement of goods should prevail.[17]

Specifically with regard to intellectual property rights, the Court has introduced the so-called existence/exercise dichotomy.[18] This implies that whereas the existence of the national intellectual property right will, in principle, not be affected by the provisions of the E.C. Treaty, the exercise of it by the right-owner may nevertheless be struck down. With respect to the exercise of intellectual property rights, the Court generally holds that Article 36 E.C. only admits derogation from the principle of free movement of goods to the extent to which such derogation is justified for the purpose of safeguarding rights which constitute the specific subject-matter of that property.[19]

(3) Article 36 transposed to services

(a) No intellectual property exception in Articles 59 et seq.

The Treaty rules on services, Articles 59 *et seq.* E.C., do not contain a provision similar to Article 36 E.C. relating to intellectual property rights although they have a similar objective to the rules on the free movement of goods. The text of Articles 59 *et seq.* E.C. would thus seem to imply that the rules on services are fully applicable to intellectual property law. As a consequence no restrictions could be imposed on the freedom to provide services within the Community on the basis of the need to protect intellectual property, with all the detrimental consequences this would entail for right-owners throughout the Community. In the first cases in which this issue was raised, however, Advocate General Warner convincingly argued that since the omission of an intellectual property exception in Articles 59 *et seq.* E.C. was probably due to an oversight, rather than the deliberate intention of the authors of the Treaty, Article 36 E.C. should be applied by analogy to services.[20] **3.07**

(b) Similar approach to goods and services

In the first case, *Coditel I*, the Court already implicitly followed the opinion of Advocate-General Warner.[21] However, it was only in the *Coditel II* case that the Court expressly applied the existence/exercise dichotomy to the context of services.[22] In the words of the Court: **3.08**

[17] See *infra*, Chap. 4. For the rare exceptions to this approach, see Chap. 6.
[18] On the existence/exercise dichotomy, see *infra*, pt. 4(2).
[19] See *infra*, Chap. 4, pt. 2.
[20] Opinion delivered on December 13, 1979, concerning both Case 52/79, *Procureur du Roi v. Debauve*, and Case 62/79, *Coditel v. Ciné Vog Films (Coditel I)*, Judgments of March 18, 1980, [1980] E.C.R. 860 at 878. He preferred this solution to extending the general exceptions provision of Article 56 E.C. to intellectual property protection.
[21] Case 62/79, *Coditel v. Ciné Vog Films (Coditel I)*, Judgment of March 18, 1980: [1980] E.C.R. 881; [1981] 2 C.M.L.R. 362.
[22] Case 262/81, *Coditel v. Ciné Vog Films (Coditel II)*, Judgment of October 6, 1982: [1982] E.C.R. 3381; [1983] 1 C.M.L.R. 49.

"The distinction, implicit in Article 36, between the existence of a right conferred by the legislation of a Member State in regard to the protection of artistic and intellectual property, which cannot be affected by the provisions of the Treaty, and the exercise of such right, which might constitute a disguised restriction on trade between Member States, also applies where that right is exercised in the context of the movement of services."[23]

The basic rule thus seems to be the same regardless of whether the issue of intellectual property rights is raised in the context of the application of the rules on the free movement of goods or services. It should be pointed out that the fact that it concerns services, rather than goods, may nonetheless have an impact on the definition of the specific subject-matter, and therefore also on the possibility of effectively using any given intellectual property right.[24]

(4) The incidence of Article 36 and Articles 85–86

(a) No intellectual property exception in rules on competition

3.09　Besides the question of the applicability of the Community principle of free movement of goods and services to national intellectual property rights, it is obvious that the matter of the applicability of the Community rules on competition to those exclusive rights is also of fundamental importance. It was shown in the previous section that the insertion of intellectual property rights in Article 36 E.C. points to the fact that they in principle come within the scope of the E.C. Treaty, but that under certain conditions Member States can derogate from Community principles. Article 36 E.C. expressly refers to the principle of free movement of goods whereas in the rules on competition no similar exception is to be found. This leads to the prima facie conclusion that the rules on competition, and especially Articles 85 and 86 E.C., fully apply to intellectual property rights.[25] However, the Court does seem to take Article 36 E.C. into account, be it indirectly, through holding that the "essence" or "normal use" of intellectual property rights may not be curtailed by virtue of the rules on competition.[26]

(b) Articles 85–86 directed to undertakings

3.10　The rules on competition are very different from the rules concerning the free movement of goods and services. The first are aimed at curtailing anti-competitive behaviour of economic actors which may affect intra-Community trade whereas the latter are mainly aimed at removing obstacles posed by

---

[23] Case 262/81: [1982] E.C.R. 3381; [1983] 1 C.M.L.R. 49, at para. 13.
[24] See *infra*, Chap. 4, pt. 2(2).
[25] See also P. Verloren van Themaat, *"Précisions sur la portée de l'Article 36 par rapport à l'Article 85 du Traité de la CEE concernant des contrats de licence de brevets"* [1964] S.E.W. 83.
[26] See *infra*, Chap. 5, pt. 2.

national law to intra-Community trade.[27] This implies that the rules on free movement of goods should in theory apply where it is intellectual property law that creates distortions to intra-Community trade. Conversely, the competition rules should apply if it is the intellectual property owner who uses his exclusive right to distort competition within the Community.[28] However, this distinction is not enforced in the case law concerning intellectual property rights.[29] National intellectual property law is hardly ever struck down under the rules on the free movement of goods, whereas both sets of rules are currently applied to curtail the alleged anti-competitive behaviour of economic actors who are right-owners, even though they may merely be enforcing their nationally granted rights.[30] This is largely due to the fact that intellectual property law is still considered to belong to the sphere of the national sovereignty, albeit it is acknowledged that it no longer belongs to the exclusive competence of Member States.

The question is whether the application of competition rules is adequate to counter the effect of possibly excessive exclusive rights granted by national intellectual property law. It may be possible, though not ideal, to use the rules on the free movement of goods to curtail the way in which a right-owner restricts intra-Community trade.[31] It seems less obvious to use competition rules to strike down national law that creates distortions to intra-Community trade. The best way to eliminate distortions posed to intra-Community trade by intellectual property law would be to harmonise, if not to make intellectual property law uniform. The next section will analyse whether this solution is feasible in the current Community context.

3.11

---

[27] See for instance Joined Cases 177–178/82, *Criminal proceedings against Jan van de Haar and Kaveka de Meern BV*, Judgment of April 5, 1984: [1984] E.C.R. 1797; [1985] 2 C.M.L.R. 566, where the Court ruled: "Article 30 of the EEC Treaty, which seeks to eliminate national measures capable of hindering trade between Member States, pursues an aim different from that of Article 85, which seeks to maintain effective competition between undertakings." The Court has reiterated this distinction in several other cases. See for instance Case 311/85, V.V.R., Judgment of October 1, 1987: [1987] E.C.R. 3801; [1989] 4 C.M.L.R. 213; Case 65/86, *Bayer*, Judgment of September 27, 1988: [1988] E.C.R. 5249; [1990] 4 C.M.L.R. 182.

[28] On this basic distinction between Articles 30–36 and 85–86 also see, for instance, M. Dauses, "*Mesures d'effet équivalent à des restrictions quantitatives à la lumière de la jurisprudence de la Cour de justice des Communautés européennes*" [1992] R.T.D.E. 607, at 611.

[29] See also E. White, "In search of the limits to Article 30 of the EEC Treaty" (1989) 26 C.M.L.Rev. 235 at 265.

[30] See *infra*, Chaps. 4 and 5. According to Koch, the Court's approach to intellectual property rights does not represent a change of interpretation of Article 30. He argues–rather unconvincingly–that because the exercise of intellectual property rights by the right-owner can resurrect obstacles to imports, "these obstacles are to be considered as state measures". See N. Koch, "Article 30 and the exercise of industrial property rights to block imports" [1986] Fordham Corp. L. Inst. 605 at 609–610.

[31] See M. Quinn, N. Macgowan, "Could Article 30 impose obligations on individuals?" (1987) 12 E.L.Rev. 163. At pp. 168–169 they argue that if Article 30 were applied to individuals, then Articles 85–86 would to a large extent become superfluous.

3. IMPACT OF E.C. HARMONISATION OF INTELLECTUAL PROPERTY LAW

(1) Establishment of the internal market

(a) Objective

3.12 The progressive establishment of the internal market logically implies that the principle of free movement of goods and services should be applied even more stringently than before. Although Article 36 E.C. was not in itself altered by the Single European Act or the TEU, a broad or flexible interpretation of its content would manifestly be contrary to the general aim and purpose of the internal market. The latter is defined in Article 7a E.C. (formerly Article 8a) as "an area without internal frontiers in which the free movement of goods, persons, services and capital is ensured".

(b) Article 36 versus Article 100 E.C.

3.13 In order to remove the barriers posed to intra-Community trade by the application of Article 36 E.C. harmonisation measures can be taken at Community level. This is possible because – as seen above – Article 36 E.C. does not confer an exclusive competence to the Member States so that the Community has concurrent competence in the fields covered by that provision.[32] Prior to the coming into force of the Single European Act, such harmonisation measures were taken on the basis of Article 100 E.C. by way of unanimous decision in the Council. The European Court of Justice held in the *Denkavit* case that the exception under Article 36 E.C. could no longer be invoked so as to rely on dissenting national law once a Council Directive on the basis of Article 100 E.C. was issued.[33] In other words, Article 100 E.C. could deprive Article 36 E.C. of its substance and render it inapplicable for the areas covered by harmonisation directives. Article 100 E.C. therefore formed an important potential legal basis to harmonise, or to approximate, the laws of Member States concerning intellectual property. In practice, however, this procedure proved to be unworkable because Member States proved not very eager to transfer to the Community their competence to legislate on matters of intellectual property.

(c) Article 36 versus Article 100a E.C.

3.14 The Single European Act introduced a new procedure for issuing harmonisation measures under Article 100a E.C. The main feature was that it intro-

---

[32] See *supra*, pt. 2(2)(a).

[33] Case 251/78, *Firma Denkavit Futtermittel GmbH v. Minister für Ernähring, Landwirtschaft und Forsten des Landes Nordrhein-Westfalen*, Judgment of November 8, 1979: [1979] E.C.R. 3369; [1980] 3 C.M.L.R. 513. At para. 14, it is held that "...when, in application of Article 100 of the Treaty, Community directives provide for the harmonisation of the measures necessary to guarantee the protection of animal and human health and when they establish procedures to check that they are observed, recourse to Article 36 is no longer justified and the appropriate checks must be carried out and the protective measures adopted within the framework outlined by the harmonisation directive".

duced qualified majority voting in the Council for matters which are enumerated in Article 7a, thus including free movement of goods and services. The rationale underlying this change was undoubtedly to pass harmonisation measures that could otherwise be blocked by the negative vote of one Member State and as such to accelerate the European integration process. It should be pointed out that nowadays the European Parliament may also prevent the adoption of harmonisation measures it does not agree with, as the TEU introduced the co-decision procedure of Article 189b with respect to Article 100a E.C. Since the coming into force of the TEU, the European Parliament has made use of this prerogative once in relation to intellectual property rights. It rejected the adoption of a directive on the legal protection of biotechnological inventions which had been approved in Council.[34]

The Single European Act compensated for the loss of the right of a veto of individual Member States in the Council by the introduction of Article 100a (4) E.C. The latter provides that: **3.15**

> "if, after the adoption of a harmonisation measure by the Council acting by a qualified majority, a Member State deems it necessary to apply national provisions on grounds of major needs referred to in Article 36, ... it shall notify the Commission of these provisions. The Commission shall confirm the provisions involved after having verified that they are not a means of arbitrary discrimination or a disguised restriction on trade between Member States."[35]

Article 100a(4) introduces a simplified procedure to challenge an "improper use" of the above-mentioned powers before the Court. Any other Member State, or the Commission, can bring the matter directly before the Court without resorting to the procedures of Articles 169 or 170 E.C.[36]

(d) Implications of Article 100a(4) E.C.

In other words, Article 100a(4) seems to eliminate the possibility of rendering Article 36 E.C. inapplicable through issuing Community harmonisation   **3.16**

---

[34] This concerned the amended proposal for a Council Directive on the legal protection of biotechnological inventions, see [1993] O.J. C44/36 and [1994] O.J. C101/65.

[35] See P. Verloren van Themaat, "The contribution to the establishment of the internal market by the case-law of the Court of Justice of the European Communities" in *1992: one European market? A critical analysis of the Commission's internal market strategy* (Bieber *et al.* eds. 1988) (Nomos Verlagsgesellschaft), pp. 109–126. At p. 117 he writes: "Although the new powers of supervision granted to the Commission in para. 4 may be satisfactory from a procedural point of view, they are not satisfactory in substance, because they only refer to the criteria of the second sentence of Article 36, and not to the requirement of justification under its first sentence."

[36] The general way in which the article is formulated raises uncertainty about its actual scope. See P. Verloren van Themaat, "*De Europese Akte*" [1986] S.E.W. 478 at 478–479; J. Mertens de Wilmar, "*Het Hof van Justitie van de Europese Gemeenschappen na de Europese Akte*" [1986] S.E.W. 615. This author is of the opinion that only those Member States that voted against the harmonisation measure should be allowed to invoke Article 100a(4). The view has also been expressed that Member States that "wish to apply divergent legislation should report this at the time of majority decision-making", see B. Van Voorst Tot Voorst, J. Van Dam, "Europe 1992: free movement of goods in the wider context of a changing Europe" (1988) 25 C.M.L.Rev. 693 at 703. See also H.-J. Glaesner, "*L'article 100A: un nouvel instrument pour la réalisation du Marché Commun*" [1989] Cah.Dr.Eur. 615; at pp. 621–622 he maintains that Article 100a(4) has to be read and applied in conformity with Article 5 EEC.

measures. Although access to the Court was simplified, the potential impact of its judgments has been severely limited. When Article 100a(4) E.C. is invoked the Court no longer has the power to put Article 36 E.C. aside in the light of the harmonisation measure, as it had done in the *Denkavit* case, but has to rule merely on the compliance of national provisions with the scope of the exception. From the first, and up till now only, case concerning Article 100a(4) E.C. the Court has had to deal with, it seems the Court will not easily accept recourse to this provision. The Court namely annulled a decision of the Commission confirming such a national derogation measure on the basis that the Commission did not sufficiently motivate why it held the conditions needed for the exception to be fulfilled.[37]

What is certain is that the Single European Act has, at least potentially, reinforced the exceptions to the principle of free movement of goods and services. Future developments will show whether or not it was worthwhile to do away with the only potential basis for harmonisation of national laws for the areas mentioned in Article 36 E.C. in order to accelerate overall harmonisation through a qualified majority decision procedure.[38] Looking only at intellectual property protection, it seems that the Single European Act is a step back from European integration to the era of supremacy of national protection. The European Court and Commission will, more than ever before, face the delicate task of striking a balance between national and Community objectives through the interpretation and application of the rules on free movement of goods, services and competition, now that the focus has potentially shifted from the decision making level to the enforcement level in so far as the exceptions embodied in Article 36 E.C. are concerned.[39]

(2) E.C. harmonisation of intellectual property law

(a) Introduction

(i) National versus Community interest

3.17 The negative impact of Article 100a(4) E.C. as described above has to be put into perspective in so far as intellectual property rights are concerned. Article 100a(4) E.C. can obviously only apply where the Member States are, in the first place, willing to harmonise their laws on the basis of Article 100a E.C. Similarly, Article 100a E.C. introduces an easier procedure to adopt harmonisation measures than the previously applicable Article 100 E.C., but it still implies that a majority of the Ministers in the Council have to agree upon the need and the conditions of harmonisation. In 1959, three working groups

---

[37] Case C–41/93, *France v. Commission*, Judgment of May 17, 1994: [1994] E.C.R. I-1829.

[38] Vignes asks whether it is not preferable to have a decision observed by 11 Member States rather than having no decision at all. See D. Vignes, "The harmonisation of national legislation and the EEC" (1990) 15 E.L.Rev. 358 at 367.

[39] See also F.-K. Beier, "Industrial property and the free movement of goods in the internal European market" [1990] I.I.C. 131. Concerning the fact that the Single European Act has not altered Article 36 EEC, he writes, at p. 142: "The Court cannot create a uniform territory without internal frontiers for intellectual property rights if the EEC Treaty continues to recognise them, and the legislative powers of the Member States in this field leaves them in principle untouched."

were established to study the feasibility of harmonising national patent, trade mark and industrial design law. More than 30 years later, these matters are still not harmonised, except for trade marks. This sustained pressure to keep intellectual property rights within the national competence is also noticeable with regard to traditional aspects of copyright protection.

The major problem with regard to intellectual property protection seems to be the lack of political willingness to put the Community interests above the national interests.[40] Any attempt to harmonise existing national intellectual property law meets with resistance from Member States who do not want to give up their sovereignty on the matter in favour of the Community. It is significant in this respect that Community harmonisation has up till now been achieved mainly for those new matters for which a solution had not yet been fully elaborated in national law.[41] This tendency seems difficult to reconcile with Article 3(h) E.C., which stipulates that the approximation of the laws of Member States is one of the means of achieving the objectives of the E.C. Treaty. The reluctance to harmonise also seems to be incompatible with Article 5 E.C. which provides that Member States "shall facilitate the achievement of the Community's tasks".[42]

(ii) Principle of subsidiarity

The formal introduction of the principle of subsidiarity by the Maastricht   **3.18**
Treaty, in Article 3b E.C., raises the question of whether harmonisation measures concerning intellectual property rights should be decided at E.C. level. Article 3b E.C. reads as follows:

> "The Community shall act within the limits of the powers conferred upon it by this Treaty and of the objectives assigned to it therein.
>
> In areas which do not fall within its exclusive competence, the Community shall take action, in accordance with the principle of subsidiarity, only if and in so far as the objectives of the proposed action cannot be sufficiently achieved by the Member States and can therefore, by reason of the scale or effects of the proposed action, be better achieved by the Community.
>
> Any action by the Community shall not go beyond what is necessary to achieve the objectives of this Treaty."

In this respect, it should be emphasised that the aim of E.C. harmonisation measures concerning intellectual property rights is to remove obstacles to the free movement of intellectual property protected products caused by divergent national intellectual property law. In other words, the purpose is to achieve an objective set forth in the E.C. Treaty, namely the establishment of the internal market. Furthermore, it is clear that this objective cannot be achieved sufficiently, if at all, on the basis of national intellectual property law

---

[40] See for instance "Harmonisation of industrial property and copyright law in the European Community", Report of a symposium held by the Max Planck Institute [1987] I.I.C. 303. At p. 306 it is reported that Schwartz held that "the substantive criticism of some plans for legal harmonisation is in many cases based on desires for national protectionism".
[41] See *infra*, at pt. (b)(v).
[42] For the full text of Article 5 E.C., see *supra*, Chap. 2, pt. 4(1)(c)(ii).

alone.[43] This would seem to imply that, in principle, E.C. harmonisation of intellectual property rights is not excluded by virtue of the principle of subsidiarity. But this finding does not alter the fact that whether or not a proposed harmonisation measure is proportional in the sense of Article 3b, para. 3, in so far as its content is concerned, will need to be settled on a case by case basis. It will thus need to be established in each specific case to what extent and in which aspects intellectual property law should be subject to harmonisation in order to fulfil the internal market objective.[44]

(b) E.C. harmonisation measures

(i) Patents

3.19 The working group on patents presided over by Mr K. Haertel[45] could be called the most successful, although it is submitted that it is only a partial success when considered from the point of view of the Community. Its proposals lay at the basis of 1973 Munich Convention on the European Patent,[46] and the 1975 Community Patent Convention.[47] The latter, which is more important because besides introducing a common application procedure it also harmonises more substantive matters and applies specifically to the E.C. Member States, still has not entered into force.[48] The Community Patent is a European patent, in the sense of the Munich Convention, and is granted for all the E.C. Member States. It is effective throughout, and may only be granted, transferred, revoked or allowed to lapse in respect of the whole E.C. territory.[49] National rules on compulsory licences may still be applied, and it is provided that national patents continue to co-exist with Community patents. This implies that barriers to intra-Community trade are not totally elimin-

---

[43] For a practical illustration see the evaluation made by the Commission under the subsidiarity principle of its proposal for a Regulation on the Community Design, COM (93) 243 of December 3, 1993, Explanatory Memorandum, pt. 1.

[44] For a practical illustration of the application of the proportionality test by the Commission, see its proposal for a Directive on the Legal Protection of Industrial Designs, COM (93) 344 of December 3, 1993, Explanatory Memorandum, specifically pt. 1.5.

[45] On the role of Kurt Haertel, who is considered to be "the founding father of European patent law", see F.-K. Beier, "The future of intellectual property in Europe: thoughts on the development of Patent, Utility Model and Industrial Design law" (1991) 22 I.I.C. 157.

[46] On the 1973 Munich Convention on the grant of the European Patent, see, *e.g.* P. Gori, "The European patent grant system and how it ties in with revocation procedures" [1990] I.I.C. 452; J. Staehelin, "The European Patent Organisation" [1981] I *Yearbook of European Law* 333.

[47] Convention for the European Patent for the Common Market [1976] O.J. L17/1. This convention was last amended in 1989. For the Luxembourg Agreement relating to Community patents of December 15, 1989 and the amended Community Patent Convention, see [1989] O.J. L401/1. On the 1975 Convention, see F. Savignon, "Luxembourg Conference on the Community Patent – A general report" [1976] I.I.C. 91.

[48] The Convention has finally been signed by all 12 Member States and is currently being submitted to the national parliaments for ratification.

[49] On the Community patent, see for instance J. Neukom, "What price the Community Patent?" (1992) 15 E.I.P.R. 111; V. Scordamaglia, "The Common Appeal Court and the future of the Community Patent following the Luxembourg conference" [1991] I.I.C. 334 and 458–474; A. Schäfers, "The Luxembourg Patent Convention, the best option for the internal market" (1987) 23 *Journal of Common Market Studies* 193; B. Scwhab, "*L'unification et l'harmonisation du droit des brevets*" in *La protection de la propriété intellectuelle* (July Session 1989, Institut Universitaire International Luxembourg), pp. 169–185.

ated. It is, however, more significant that this harmonisation of patent legislation has been negotiated as a convention between the Member States rather than by applying the harmonisation provisions of the E.C. Treaty.[50] This means that competence to legislate on this matter has not been transferred to the Community but remains with Member States who each have to ratify the Convention.[51] This is probably the best example of the reluctance of Member States to limit their sovereignty on the matter in favour of the Community.

The only E.C. harmonisation measure concerning patents so far adopted is a regulation concerning a supplementary protection certificate for pharmaceutical products.[52] It should, however, be pointed out with regard to the latter that a case is currently pending before the Court in which annulment of the regulation is sought.[53] In particular Spain, supported by Greece, maintains that the Community has no competence to act in the area of patent law. In the alternative it is held that the regulation could only be adopted on the basis of Article 235 E.C. which requires unanimity voting in the Council and not on the basis of Article 100a E.C. which allows qualified majority voting. It is expected that the Court will follow the opinion delivered by Advocate General Jacobs and will dismiss the application as being unfounded.

(ii) Trade marks

Unlike patents, the harmonisation of trade mark law has been dealt with in the Community context, but the outcome of efforts to this effect was long uncertain. The proposals presented by the working group on trade marks, presided over by Mr de Haan, lay at the basis of the current Council Regulation on the Community trade mark.[54] The objective is to render trade mark protection uniform through the introduction of a Community trade mark and specialised Community institutions such as the Community Trade Mark Office.[55] The Commission had justified this far-reaching objective *inter alia* through pointing to the need to eliminate obstacles posed to intra-Community trade by the principle of territoriality inherent in intellectual property rights. The problem is that the E.C. Treaty does not explicitly confer the competence that is needed to create Community intellectual property rights and thus does not provide a specific legal basis for this kind of initiative. Article 100a E.C. merely foresees harmonisation measures, not the creation of new Community procedures or institutions. The Commission therefore based its proposal on Article 235 E.C.

3.20

---

[50] Albrechtskirchinger emphasises the fact that it is an agreement under international public law, expressly leaving aside the question of whether it should have been based instead on the EEC Treaty. See G. Albrechtskirchinger, "The impact of the Luxembourg patent on the law of license agreements" [1976] I.I.C. 447 at 449–450.

[51] This was confirmed by the Court of Justice in its Opinion 1/94 of November 14, 1994: [1994] E.C.R. I–5267, at para. 103. See also L. Idot, "*Le rapprochement des législations en matière de propriété intellectuelle. Bilan provisoire des travaux*" [1989] D.P.C.I. 272 at 276–278.

[52] Regulation 1768/92 of June 17, 1992 [1992] O.J. L182/1. As mentioned before, the European Parliament rejected the adoption of a directive on the legal protection of biotechnological inventions.

[53] Case C–350/92, *Spain v. Council*, (judgment awaited).

[54] Council Regulation 40/94 on the Community Trade Mark [1994] O.J. L11/1, as amended by Regulation 3288/94 [1994] O.J. L349.

[55] See for instance, A. Brun, "*L'unification et l'harmonisation du droit des marques*", in *La protection de la propriété intellectuelle*, (July Session 1989, Institut Universitaire Internationale, Luxembourg), pp. 187–216.

which implied that unanimity was required in the Council.[56] It is significant that it was only by the end of 1993 that this proposal, which dates from 1980, has carried away the approval of the Council.[57]

The realisation of the objective to create one uniform system of trade mark protection in the E.C. is, nonetheless, weakened through the continuing con-current existence of national trade marks. To remedy the effect of the disparities in national trade mark law and to render the latter more compatible with the Regulation on the Community Trade Mark, a first Council Directive has been issued on the basis of Article 100a E.C. to approximate the laws of Member States relating to trade marks.[58] But as the wording suggests, it merely concerns the approximation of a limited number of national provisions and not a full harmonisation of national trade mark law.

(iii) Industrial designs

3.21   The working group on industrial designs, presided over by Mr Roscioni, was by far the least successful.[59] In a report presented in 1962, it had been submitted that the differences in the national design laws of the six original Member States were so fundamental that the possibility of harmonising these laws seemed unlikely. Nonetheless, it was suggested that a solution might be to create an independent Community system for the protection of industrial designs which would co-exist with the national systems.[60] It is only recently that the Commission has followed up this suggestion.[61] In 1991 the Commission issued the Green Paper on the Legal Protection of Industrial Designs which forms the basis for the current proposals for a Council Regulation on the Community Design, and a Council Directive on the approximation of national design law.[62] As for trade marks, the objective is not so much to harmonise existing law. Rather, the aim is to introduce a uniform Community system of industrial design protection on the basis of Article 100a E.C. alongside national systems of design protection which remain in effect, but in respect of which those provisions that are most important for the functioning

---

[56] Article 235 E.C. reads as follows: "If action by the Community should prove necessary to attain, in the course of the operation of the Common Market, one of the objectives of the Community and this Treaty has not provided the necessary powers, the Council shall, acting unanimously on a proposal from the Commission and after consulting the European Parliament, take the appropriate measures."

[57] Specific problems arose in the Council *inter alia* with regard to the location of the Trade Mark Office (Madrid) and the linguistic regime.

[58] First Council Directive 89/104 of December 21, 1988 to approximate the laws of the Member States relating to trade marks [1989] O.J. L40/1. See also Council Decision 92/10 of December 19, 1991 postponing the date on which the national provisions applying Directive 89/104 to approximate the laws of the Member States relating to trade marks are to be put into effect [1992] O.J. L6/35.

[59] For the history and the results of this working group, see the Commission's Green Paper on the legal protection of Industrial Design, III/F/5131/91, June 1991, at pp. 8–10.

[60] See "Harmonisation of industrial property and copyright law in the European Community" [1987] I.I.C. 303 at 331.

[61] The Commission explains this delay by pointing out that its attention initially focused on the problems posed by patents and trade mark law, whereas it is only recently that industrial designs have gained in importance as an essential element in the commercialisation of consumer goods. See the Commission's Green Paper on the Legal Protection of Industrial Design, III/F/5131/91, June 1991, pp. 8–9.

[62] [1993] O.J. C345/14 (proposal directive); [1994] O.J. C29/20 (proposal regulation).

of the internal market are to be approximated. It remains to be seen how the Council will react to these proposals. It is doubtful if the reaction will be more positive and more rapid than that concerning trade marks, especially as the spare parts controversy has proved to be a highly political issue.[63]

(iv) Copyright

It was initially thought that copyright protection did not directly interfere with the proper functioning of the internal market. This may explain why Article 36 E.C. only mentions industrial and commercial property and no working group was established in 1959 to study the feasibility of harmonising copyright legislation.[64] It soon became apparent that the exercise of the economic rights, as opposed to the moral rights, conferred by copyright had the same effect upon the Common Market as patents or trade marks. At an early stage, the Court clarified that copyright and akin rights come under the scope of the E.C. Treaty in so far as economic rights are concerned.[65] But it was not until 1988 that the Commission issued its Green Paper on Copyright and the Challenge of Technology, in which were identified those aspects of copyright legislation that needed most urgently to be harmonised at Community level.[66] This was thought to be the case in respect of the legal protection for relatively new technologies such as semi-conductors and computer programmes, and for specific rights such as distribution and rental rights.[67] For the more established matter of copyright protection, it was maintained that a sufficient level of harmonisation could be achieved within the framework of international intellectual property conventions negotiated by the Member States, in particular the Berne Convention for the Protection of Literary and Artistic Works.[68] It was therefore held that direct Community action in this field was not necessary.[69]

3.22

The problem with this approach was that this left copyright law to a large extent outside the Community competence, whereas it confirmed the competence of Member States to individually negotiate copyright law within the framework of WIPO. This disregarded the situation whereby all Member States except two, namely Belgium and Ireland, had adhered to the 1971 Paris Act of the Berne Convention.[70] To counter this lack of basic harmonisation,

3.23

---

[63] On the Commission's proposals, see *infra*, Chap. 9, pt. 5(2).

[64] On the early discussions in the legal doctrine concerning the applicability of the Rome Treaty to copyright, see L. Ubertazzi, "Copyright and the free movement of goods" [1985] I.I.C. 46, at 47–52.

[65] This was impliedly held in the *Deutsche Grammophon* case (Case 78/70, Judgment of June 8, 1971: [1971] E.C.R. 487; [1971] C.M.L.R. 631) and expressly clarified in the *Musik-Vertrieb Memban v. GEMA* case (Joint Cases 55 and 57/80, Judgment of January 20, 1981: [1981] E.C.R. 147; [1981] 2 C.M.L.R. 44); see *infra*, Chap. 4, pt. 2(2)(a)(i).

[66] Commission Green Paper on Copyright and the Challenge of Technology: Copyright Issues Requiring Immediate Action, COM (88) 172 final, of June 7, 1988. See also R. Strivens, "The E.C. Commission Green Paper on copyright" [1988] E.I.P.R. 275.

[67] On the implementation of the ideas expressed in the Green Paper, see *infra*, pt. (v). On this issue, see also D. Franzone, "*Droit d'auteur et droits voisins: bilan et perspectives de l'action communautaires*" [1993] *Revue du Marché Unique Européen* 143, at 149.

[68] On the most relevant intellectual property conventions, see *supra*, Chap. 2, pt. 4(1).

[69] See especially the Green Paper, *op. cit.*, at pp. 7–8. Dietz, to the contrary, convincingly demonstrated the need for harmonisation of copyright laws. See A. Dietz, "The harmonisation of copyright in the European Community" [1985] I.I.C. 379.

[70] See also *supra*, Chap. 2, pt. 4(1)(a).

and to remedy the discrepancies that arose between actions undertaken under the Community's exclusive competence in the field of commercial policy and the internal division of competence,[71] the Commission proposed in 1991 to issue a Council Decision concerning the accession of Member States to *inter alia* the Paris Act of the Berne Convention.[72] The Member States in principle agreed to the need to harmonise their copyright laws through adherence to the Convention. Nevertheless, they disagreed with the Commission on the point that this should be rendered obligatory through the use of a legally binding Community instrument, which would confer competence on the Community.[73] Instead of the proposed Council Decision, a Council Resolution was issued in which the Council merely "notes" that the Member States undertake to become parties to the Paris Act of the Berne Convention by January 1, 1995.[74]

However, in recent years the Commission has become aware that the basic harmonisation provided under the Berne Convention still gives rise to important discrepancies which affect the functioning of the internal market. The Berne Convention sets minimum standards of protection, leaving it to each Union country to enforce higher standards of protection. To remedy the distortions to intra-Community trade created by the different durations of copyright protection, the Berne Convention providing only a minimum term of 50 years *post mortem auctores*, the Commission proposed to issue a Council Directive to harmonise the term of protection according to the longest term of protection given in a Member State, namely in Germany.[75] This directive to extend the duration of copyright protection to 70 years *post mortem auctores* was adopted by the Council on October 29, 1993 and should be implemented by Member States by July 1, 1995 at the latest.[76]

(v) Relatively new areas of intellectual property protection

3.24 Except for trade marks, the internal market objective has so far virtually only led to Community harmonisation of border measures to prohibit the release into the Community of counterfeit and pirated products coming from third countries,[77] or with regard to relatively new areas of intellectual property pro-

---

[71] On the relationship between intellectual property rights and commercial policy, see I. Govaere, "Intellectual property protection and commercial policy" in *The European Community's commercial policy after 1992: the legal dimension* (Maresceau ed. 1993) (Kluwer Academic Publishers), pp. 197–222, especially at pp. 119–221.

[72] Proposal for a Council Decision concerning the accession of the Member States to the Berne Convention for the Protection of Literary and Artistic Works, as revised by the Paris Act of July 24, 1971, and the International Convention for the Protection of Performers, Producers of Phonograms and Broadcasting Organisations (Rome Convention) of October 26, 1961, COM (90) final of January 11, 1991.

[73] See also D. Franzone, *op. cit.*, pp. 156–157.

[74] Council Resolution [1992] O.J. C138/01 of May 14, 1992 on increased protection for copyright and neighbouring rights. A similar obligation has subsequently been written into the Agreement on the European Economic Area.

[75] Amended proposal for a Council Directive harmonising the term of protection of copyright and certain related rights [1993] O.J. C27/7.

[76] Council Directive 93/98 of October 29, 1993 harmonising the term of protection of copyright and certain related rights, [1993] O.J. L290/9. For a critical view, see G. Dworkin, "Authorship of films and the European Commission proposals for harmonising the term of copyright" [1993] E.I.P.R. 151.

[77] Council Regulation 3295/94, [1994] O.J. L341/8.

tection for which specific national laws had not yet been fully elaborated. The latter essentially concern new technologies such as topographies of semi-conductors and computer programs,[78] and rights which have recently gained in economic importance such as lending and renting rights which are akin to copyright.[79]

The rapid development of new technologies over the past decade has posed the problem of their legal protection all over the world. The investment made in research and development is considerable, whereas it was obvious that the absence of legal protection would lead to piracy on a large scale and thus reduce the possibility of a reasonable return and reward for the investment made. The main problem was that it proved to be difficult to protect these new technologies efficaciously on the basis of existing intellectual property law. For instance, computer programs were generally thought not to fulfil the requirements for patent protection, whilst merely interpreting the copyright definition of "artistic and literary works" so widely as to include computer programs would have entailed granting the (minimum) life plus 50 years protection against unauthorised reproduction.[80] This was generally thought to be both unreasonably long and inherently anti-competitive. This meant that existing law had to be adapted to modern needs or that new forms of intellectual property protection had to be devised to deal specifically with these new types of intellectual creations.[81]

It is against this background of the urgent need for fundamental legislative   **3.25**
change or innovation that the Community has been able to take initiatives, instead of the individual Member States, and issue harmonisation directives on the basis of Article 100a E.C.[82] A factor which is thereby taken into account is the need to create a favourable environment for the European technology industry in order to stimulate the Community's industrial development. Linked to this is the desire to uphold, or reinforce, the Community's competitive position *vis-à-vis* its trading partners, in particular the United States and

---

[78] Council Directive 87/54 of December 16, 1986 on the legal protection of topographies of semi-conductor products, [1987] O.J. L24/36 (see also the subsequent Council Decisions extending the protection to persons from certain countries and territories). Council Directive 91/250 of May 14, 1991 on the legal protection of computer programs, [1991] O.J. L122/42. See also Directive 93/83 on Copyright and neighbouring rights relating to satellite broadcasting and cable retransmissions ([1993] O.J. L248/15); and the amended proposal for a Council Directive on the legal protection of databases ([1993] O.J. C308/1).

[79] See Council Directive 92/100 of November 19, 1992 on rental right and lending right and on certain rights related to copyright in the field of intellectual property, [1992] O.J. L346/61. This was largely inspired by the judgment of the Court in the *Warner Brothers* case, see *infra*, Chap. 6, pt. 3(3).

[80] However, the TRIPS-Agreement stipulates that computer programs will be protected as literary works under the Berne Convention. See also *supra*, Chap. 2, at pt. 4(2)(b).

[81] See also L. Idot, *op. cit.*, p. 283.

[82] See, for instance, Council Directive 91/250 on the legal protection of computer programs, *op. cit.*, where it is held in the preamble that "computer programmes are presently not clearly protected in all Member States by existing legislation".

Japan.[83] However, Community harmonisation seems to be feasible only because it concerns the legal protection of specific and new issues rather than intellectual property law in general. It therefore has to be emphasised that, apart perhaps trade marks and these well-specified issues concerning mainly new technologies, the 1992 objective has not, so far, had a significant impact upon the division of competence between the E.C. and its Member States in the field of intellectual property rights.[84]

(3) Article 36 and harmonisation of intellectual property law

(a) The concepts "harmonisation" and "unification"

3.26 Although it is clear from the foregoing that Member States are not eager to harmonise their intellectual property law through the adoption of E.C. harmonisation measures, it is nevertheless important to analyse the effect harmonisation may have on the application and working of Article 36 E.C. The difference between harmonisation and approximation on the basis of Article 100a E.C. on the one hand, and unification on the basis of Article 235 E.C. on the other, is very important in so far as intellectual property rights are concerned.[85] The Court of Justice has consistently held that in the absence of harmonisation or approximation it is up to Member States to determine the conditions and procedures for obtaining intellectual property protection.[86] The *Phil Collins* judgment adds the important qualification that due regard should thereby be paid to the E.C. principle of non-discrimination.[87] However, the Court has also pointed out that, in the absence of unification, the principle of territoriality inherent in intellectual property protection is capable of jeopardising the objectives of the Treaty.[88]

(b) Harmonisation and the principle of territoriality

3.27 Mere harmonisation, or approximation, of intellectual property law, which is the Community approach to the new technologies and to some extend also to

---

[83] See, for instance, the first proposal on the legal protection of biotechnological inventions, COM (88) 496 final of October 17, 1988, Explanatory Memorandum, at p. 6, where it was held that "... establishing a harmonised system of patent law in this area will facilitate the development of Community industry in biotechnology, trade in biotechnological products and the establishment of a Common Market in this field. Moreover, it will enable Community industry to keep pace with leading nations in biotechnology and to close or narrow existing gaps". An amended version of this proposal was accepted by the Council. However, the E.P. made use of its new powers under the TEU and rejected its final adoption, despite the commercial arguments advanced in favour of it by the Commission. See also *supra*, pt. (1)(c).

[84] See also the analysis made by the Court in Opinion 1/94, *op. cit.*, esp. at paras. 102–105. The Court held that the current state of E.C. harmonisation of intellectual property law did not allow for the conclusion that the Community was solely competent to conclude the TRIPS-Agreement by virtue of the doctrine of implied powers.

[85] Vigner points out that, except for Article 113 EEC, no other Treaty provision expressly uses "words derived from the idea of unity, such as 'unification' or 'making uniform'". See D. Vignes, "The harmonisation of national legislation and the EEC" (1990) 15 E.L.Rev. 358 at 361.

[86] See for instance Case 341/87, *EMI Electrola v. Patricia Im– und Export*, Judgment of January 24, 1989: [1989] E.C.R. 79, at para. 11.

[87] See *supra*, Chap. 2, pt. 4(1)(c)(iv).

[88] See, for instance, Case 24/67, *Parke Davis v. Centrafarm*, Judgment of February 29, 1968: [1968] E.C.R. 55; [1968] C.M.L.R. 47, at para. 71.

trade marks and industrial design rights, creates a more uniform and transparent system of conditions and procedures for obtaining protection. However, it should be emphasised that harmonisation keeps the national territoriality principle intact. It therefore does not prevent the intellectual property owner from invoking his exclusive right in a given Member State in order to prohibit the importation of infringing goods which have been lawfully marketed in the Member State of exportation.[89] In other words, following the *Denkavit* approach, and disregarding a possible recourse to Article 100a(4) E.C.,[90] harmonisation or approximation would mean that Article 36 E.C. can no longer be invoked to rely on those national conditions and procedures for obtaining intellectual property protection which are incompatible with the harmonisation measure. Article 36 E.C. could, however, still be invoked by the intellectual property owner to enforce the exclusive nature of the right under the territoriality principle. As such, harmonisation of intellectual property law does not automatically safeguard the free movement of goods. This is a major difference from the other objectives mentioned in Article 36 E.C. as harmonisation with regard to the latter renders the application of Article 36 E.C. void.

(c) Unification and the principle of territoriality

Article 36 E.C. would only cease to apply to intellectual property rights if   **3.28**
national intellectual property law were subject to unification, in the sense of national intellectual property rights being replaced by Community intellectual property rights. The reason for this is that only the unification of intellectual property law would extend the principle of territoriality to the whole of the Community.[91] That this is not merely a theoretical construction is illustrated by the fact that on the basis of this argument the Commission currently proposes to create the Community Design, as was done previously for the Community Trade Mark.[92] However, the objective of the Commission's proposals, at least at present, is not to totally replace existing national intellectual property law but to create a concurrent legal system. This means that the application of Article 36 E.C. to trade marks and industrial designs will still not be totally eliminated because of the co-existence of national, albeit approximated, law.

(d) Impact of harmonisation measures

Thus it does not seem likely that the problems posed by intellectual property   **3.29**
rights to the functioning of the internal market will be solved by adequate legislative action in the near future. The Community legislative process is, in

---

[89] This will be important in cases where parallel protection has not been applied for, or has since expired, in the Member State of exportation. The exhaustion principle will only apply if the goods were marketed with the right-owner's consent. See *infra*, Chap. 4, pt. 2(b).

[90] See *supra*, at pt. 3(1).

[91] For a more detailed analysis, see I. Govaere, "Intellectual property protection and commercial policy" in Maresceau, *op. cit.*, especially pp. 215–220. This is confirmed by the Court in Case C–9/93, *Ideal-Standard*, Judgment of June 22, 1994: [1994] E.C.R. I-2789, at paras. 49–58.

[92] See *supra*, at pts. 3(2)(b)(ii) and (iii).

the first place, hampered by the reluctance of Member States to limit their sovereignty on the matter. Furthermore, the specific nature of intellectual property rights weakens the effect of those harmonisation measures that have been, or will be, agreed upon. To eliminate the application of Article 36 E.C., and thus to abolish restrictions to intra-Community trade, would require a complete transfer of competence to the Community and the abolition of national intellectual property protection altogether. It is clear that this will not readily be accepted by Member States. The result is that the case law of the Court on the application of Article 36 E.C. to intellectual property rights will remain of major importance even when harmonisation has been achieved.

On the other hand, it goes without saying that the case law on the application of the Articles 85–86 E.C. to intellectual property rights will always remain important, even in the hypothetical event of complete unification being achieved. It has been maintained above that the inclusion of intellectual property rights in the Article 36 E.C.-exception to the free movement of goods has no direct bearing on the application of E.C. competition rules to those exclusive rights.[93] This would *a fortiori* be so were the exception no longer to apply.

4. RULE-MAKING BY THE COURT OF JUSTICE

(1) National intellectual property rights and E.C. principles

(a) Importance of case law

3.30   In the absence of adequate harmonisation of intellectual property law, the relationship between national intellectual property rights and Community principles has almost exclusively been determined by the case law of the European Court of Justice. The Court has always rejected the view that the matters mentioned in Article 36 E.C. belong to the exclusive competence of Member States and therefore are not subject to scrutiny under E.C. Treaty provisions.[94] Consequently, the Court has in its case law gradually elaborated general principles which give guidance on the extent to which Community rules, in particular the rules on the free movement of goods, services and competition, and most recently also the E.C. non-discrimination principle,[95] impinge upon national intellectual property rights in order to safeguard the objectives of the E.C. Treaty.

(b) Sustaining competition in the market

3.31   As seen previously, intellectual property rights are exclusive rights confined territorially to a Member State, although parallel intellectual property protection may be obtained in other Member States.[96] This implies that on the basis

---

[93] See *supra*, at pt. 2(4).
[94] See *supra*, at pt. 2(2).
[95] On the applicability of Article 6 E.C. to intellectual property rights, see *supra*, Chap. 2, pt. 4(1)(c)(iv).
[96] See *supra*, Chap. 2, pt. 2.

of such a right, in principle both intra-brand and inter-brand competition can be restricted or even prohibited. It is submitted that the case law of the Court concerning the applicability of the principle of free movement of goods or services to intellectual property rights is of prime importance in this respect because it determines the framework for the establishment of a competitive market structure in the internal market.

The rules on the free movement of goods apply in principle to the circulation of all goods, whether protected by intellectual property rights or not. The free movement of goods protected by intellectual property rights is a precondition to safeguarding intra-brand competition in the internal market, whereas the free movement of both protected and unprotected goods may be necessary to safeguard inter-brand competition. It is, of course, true that inter-brand and intra-brand competition would not necessarily take place if Article 36 E.C. could not be invoked with respect to intellectual property rights. Conversely, when Article 36 E.C. is invoked in relation to intellectual property rights it has of necessity a repercussion on both intra-brand and inter-brand competition and may therefore affect the competitive market structure. As such, it seems to be important that national intellectual property law invoked to derogate from the principle of free movement of goods should be justified and proportional under the first sentence of Article 36 and not be contrary to the second sentence of Article 36 E.C.[97]

In other words, it is the scrutiny of intellectual property law under Article 36 E.C. that should determine the legal framework against which the rules on competition need to be applied. The reason for this is that, at least in principle, the purpose of the rules on competition does not seem to be to create a competitive market structure, for instance by rendering inter-brand competition obligatory.[98] The aim of the latter is rather to sustain the competitive market structure through curtailing anti-competitive behaviour, for instance by imposing limitations on the way in which an intellectual property owner makes undue use of his exclusive right in a given market. It is therefore submitted that the case law of the Court concerning the application of the rules on competition to intellectual property rights complements its case law on free movement of goods, but can by no means replace it.[99]

(c) Convergence of Articles 30–36 and 85–86

Keeping the different objective of the different Treaty rules in mind, it is all the more surprising that, in respect of intellectual property rights, the basis for the Court's case law on both Articles 30–36 E.C. (and by analogy Articles 59 *et seq.* E.C.) and Articles 85–86 E.C. was laid down in early competition law cases.[1] In this context, the effect of Article 36 E.C. on the rules on competition was explained in terms of the so-called existence/exercise dichotomy. The peculiarity lies in the fact that this distinction was later transposed to the case law on the free movement of goods and services, apparently without taking

3.32

---

[97] See *supra*, at pt. 2(2).
[98] But see *infra*, Chap. 5, pt. 4(3), concerning the "affirmative action" in the *Magill* cases.
[99] See also *supra*, at pt. 2(4)(b).
[1] See *infra*, at pt. (2).

the peculiarities of those rules, or of intellectual property rights, into account. In order to try to understand on what basis the Court delineates between what constitutes a normal use as opposed to a misuse or an abuse of the system of intellectual property protection, it is therefore necessary to retrace the early case law.

(2) The distinction between existence and exercise of intellectual property rights

(a) The origin

(i) *Consten Grundig*: issues

3.33   The Court first clarified the effect of Article 36 E.C. on the competition rules in the *Consten Grundig v. Commission* case of 1966.[2] The question arose as to whether the application of competition rules could be circumvented by reliance on national intellectual property rights.

The Commission maintained that a clause in a distribution contract whereby one party (Consten) is given the right to register the trade mark "GINT" in a given Member State, whereas that trade mark is internationally registered in the name of the other party (Grundig), amounts to creating an absolute territorial protection which is prohibited by Article 85 E.C. It therefore inserted in its contested decision an injunction to restrain the use of the trade mark to block parallel imports. Consten and Grundig to the contrary argued that the Commission had infringed Articles 36 and 222 E.C. by holding that the trade mark could not be used to prohibit parallel imports because the absolute territorial protection was the effect of the exclusive right granted by national intellectual property law and not of restrictive clauses to that effect in their agreement.

The Court settled this issue by ruling that although the exclusive right in the trade mark was conferred by national law, it was the agreement that enabled Consten to register the trade mark in the first place. The agreement could therefore be held to infringe Article 85(1) E.C. More difficult was the question of whether the Commission could impose the obligation upon the parties to refrain from using their trade mark, which was conferred by national law, to block parallel imports. In this respect, the Court pointed out that the prohibition under Article 85 E.C. would be meaningless if Consten could still use its exclusive right under national trade mark law to obtain absolute territorial protection.

(ii) The Court on the relationship between Articles 36 and 85

3.34   The Court for the first time expressly clarified the relationship between the intellectual property rights exception of Article 36 E.C. and Article 85 E.C. It held that Articles 36 and 222 E.C. "do not exclude any influence whatever of Community law on the exercise of national industrial property rights" and

---

[2] Joined Cases 56 and 58/64, *Etablissements Consten SARL and Grundig-Verkaufs-GmbH v. Commission*, Judgment of July 13, 1966: [1966] E.C.R. 299; [1966] C.M.L.R. 418.

that "Article 36 EEC [. . .] cannot limit the field of application of Article 85".[3] This did not imply that the very existence of national intellectual property rights could be disregarded under the competition rules. The Court namely further ruled that:

> "the injunction [. . .] to refrain from using the rights under national trade mark law in order to set an obstacle in the way of parallel imports does not affect the *grant* of those rights but only limits their *exercise* to the extent necessary to give effect to the prohibition under Article 85(1)."[4]

As such, it was only the "improper use" of trade mark law to "frustrate" the rules on competition that was struck down under Community law.[5]

(iii) *Parke Davis*: issues

The Court reiterated this distinction between the "existence" of intellectual property rights which is subject to national legislation, and the "exercise" of those rights which can be limited by virtue of the Community rules on competition in the *Parke Davis* case of 1968.[6] The Court was asked in a preliminary ruling whether the patent holder's reliance on his national patent right to claim that the courts should prevent any circulation, sale, hire, delivery, storage or use of the same product imported from another Member State where no exclusive right was granted to manufacture and sell that product was compatible with the Articles 85(1), 86, 36 and 222 E.C. The secondary question was whether the price difference between the products concerned would lead to a different answer. The Commission summarised the questions as the extent to which Articles 85 and 86 E.C. may limit the rights of a patent holder obtained by virtue of the law of one of the Member States.[7]

3.35

Having remarked that in the absence of the unification of patent law, the variations between the different legislative systems concerning patents may potentially create obstacles to the free movement of the patented products and to competition within the Common Market, the Court merely proceeded with the interpretation of the competition rules in the light of the distinction made in the *Consten Grundig* case. The possible application of the rules on the free movement of goods was thus totally disregarded. The Court emphasised that

---

[3] Concerning the applicability of Article 222 EEC, Advocate General Roemer held that "its object is solely to guarantee in a general manner the freedom of the Member States to organise their own systems of property but not to provide a guarantee that the Community institutions may not in any way intervene in subjective rights of property. The concept of property being extremely wide in the national legal systems, any other argument would result finally in the paralysis of the powers of the Community", Opinion of April 27, 1966, [1966] E.C.R. 352 at 366. It seems that Article 222 E.C. is concerned with safeguarding national property systems, such as privatisation or nationalisation of industry; not intellectual property. The Court expressly ruled that: " . . . the provisions of the Treaty, and in particular Article 222 . . ., cannot be interpreted as reserving to the national legislature, in relation to industrial and commercial property, the power to adopt measures which would adversely affect the principle of free movement of goods within the Common Market as provided for and regulated by the Treaty." See Case C–30/90, *Commission v. United Kingdom*, Judgment of February 18, 1992: [1992] E.C.R. I-829: [1992] 2 C.M.L.R. 709, at para. 18.

[4] Joined Cases 56 and 58/64: [1966] E.C.R. 299 at 345; [1966] C.M.L.R. 418 (emphasis added).

[5] *id.*, *op. cit.*, p. 346.

[6] Case 24/67, *Parke, Davis & Co v. Probel, Reese, Beintema-Interpharm and Centrafarm*, Judgment of February 29, 1968: [1968] E.C.R. 55; [1968] C.M.L.R. 47.

[7] Case 24/67: [1968] E.C.R. 55 at 62.

a patent, taken by itself, is merely the expression of a legal status granted by a state to products meeting certain criteria, and as such does not infringe the E.C. Treaty provisions. Looking at the wording of Article 85(1) E.C., it is clear that unilateral action by a patentee cannot fall under the prohibitions thereof.[8] The difficult question was whether reliance on this exclusive right in court could constitute an abuse of a dominant position within the meaning of Article 86 E.C.

(iv) The Advocate General on patent enforcement and Article 86

3.36 Advocate General Roemer, in his opinion on the case, expressed the view that the possibility of resorting to defensive measures to reinforce the legal patent right, when a patented product has been put into circulation without the consent of the patent holder in countries where the product is not patentable, is part of the essence of the right and has to remain unchanged.[9] He stated:

> "a patent law emptied of its substance and devaluated to this point could hold up technical progress."

He pointed out that if the patent protection is not sufficient, the likely alternative for the inventor would be to resort to secrecy and to diminish the grant of licences. Whether or not the use of a patent infringes Article 86 E.C. depends on commercial realities, such as the possibility of fixing prices and terms, the existence of several licences maintaining competition, the commercial value of a patent, and the presence of substitutable products on the market. Thus, in the view of Advocate General Roemer, it has to be established that there was an "abuse" in the exercise of patent rights as opposed to their proper use in accordance with their nature which can never be prohibited under Article 86 E.C.[10] He held that the difference in price has to be evaluated according to the same commercial criteria. An excessively high price structure might be a factual indication that a dominant position on the market is being abused, but of itself is not proof.[11] An analysis of the different costs involved would therefore be indispensable.

(v) The rule: a triple distinction

3.37 The Court followed the opinion of Advocate General Roemer without, however, pursuing the analysis of the objectives of patent protection. The Court ruled as follows:

> "1. The *existence* of the rights granted by a Member State to the holder of a patent is not affected by the prohibitions contained in Articles 85(1) and 86 of the Treaty;"

> "2. The *exercise* of such rights cannot of itself fall either under Article 85(1), in the absence of any agreement, decision or concerted practice

---

[8] See *infra*, Chap. 5, pt. 2(2).
[9] Case 24/67, Opinion by Advocate General Roemer, delivered on February 7, 1968: [1968] E.C.R. 55 at 77.
[10] *id.*, at pp. 78–79.
[11] *id.*, at pp. 79–80.

prohibited by this provision, or under Article 86, in the absence of any abuse of a dominant position;"

"3. A higher sale price for the patented product as compared with that of the unpatented product coming from another Member State does not necessarily constitute an abuse."[12]

In other words, the Court introduced a triple distinction as the guiding principle to strike the balance between national intellectual property rights and the Community rules on competition. First, the "existence" of intellectual property rights is not affected by the rules on competition. Secondly, the "normal exercise" of those rights is not affected by the rules on competition either. Thirdly, the "abusive exercise" of those rights is prohibited by the rules on competition. The main problem is, of course, to determine what the difference is between these three concepts, and how to distinguish between them in practice.

(b) The concept

In *Consten Grundig*, as in the *Parke Davis* case, the Court assumed that the intellectual property right concerned was granted and used in conformity with the first sentence of Article 36 E.C. so that its existence should be taken for granted and not be affected by Community law. This is different from the approach taken by Advocate General Roemer in both cases. The Advocate General considered whether or not the way in which the given right was used lived up to the function of intellectual property rights under national law in order to conclude whether the right was abused and could be limited under Community law. Although the conclusions of the Court and the Advocate General were basically the same, it is submitted that the different reasoning followed in reaching their conclusions is not without importance.

3.38

(i) In relation to the function of intellectual property rights

Even though the rules on the free movement of goods were not invoked in the *Consten Grundig* case, Advocate General Roemer considered whether the Commission's injunction under Article 85(1) E.C. interfered with rights which need protection. In other words, with rights that can be justified under Article 36 E.C. and hence should be left untouched. He came to the conclusion that the GINT trade mark did not fulfil the function of a trade mark which he held to be to guarantee the origin of the product to the consumer.[13] Under the given circumstances, the GINT trade mark was used neither as an indication of origin relating to either the manufacturer or the dealer, nor as an indication of sales networks. His conclusion was that:

3.39

"if it thus appears that in effect the sole aim of the GINT trade mark consists in circumventing legal provisions on cartels [...], the Commission may certainly take this situation into account without being guilty of unwarranted interference in trade mark law."[14]

---

[12] Case 24/67: [1968] E.C.R. 55 at 73–74. (Emphasis added.)
[13] On the function of trade marks, see *supra*, Chap. 2, pt. 3(4).
[14] Joined Cases 56 and 58/64: [1966] E.C.R. 299 at 366.

In the *Parke Davis* case, Advocate General Roemer again considered the specific function of the intellectual property right invoked. He held that the essence of patent law is to grant:

> "(a) legal monopoly to exploit an invention, which is intended to guarantee the chance of a reasonable return for the inventor."[15]

As seen above, he maintained that to prohibit the patent holder from using his exclusive right to block the importation of goods put on the market of another Member State without his consent would empty the patent of its substance. In other words, the patent would no longer be able to fulfil the main function for which it was granted.

(ii) Disregarding the function of intellectual property rights

3.40 If one disregards the preliminary analysis made in the light of the function of the right invoked, it would seem that Advocate General Roemer, and also the Court in its judgments, came to two contradictory conclusions. In the *Consten Grundig* case he allowed the national trade mark to be emptied of its substance in the sense that it could no longer be used to prohibit importations, whereas in the *Parke Davis* case he expressly stated that the patent should not be emptied of its substance through prohibiting the use of the exclusive right to block importations, and yet in both cases it was held by both the Court and the Advocate General that the existence of the exclusive right was left untouched whereas it was only the abusive exercise of the right that was limited by Community law. In the *Consten Grundig* case, it is clear that to a large extent the national trade mark only continued to exist in theory, because in practice it was stripped of most of its legal effect.

(iii) A theoretical concept

3.41 This illustrates that drawing a distinction between the existence and the exercise of intellectual property rights without taking into account additional criteria, such as the function of intellectual property rights, to determine to what extent the Community rules on competition may or should limit the exclusive right is a purely theoretical one. It creates uncertainty as to where the Court draws the line between the "existence" and the "exercise" of intellectual property rights, not in the least because the existence of a right is in essence constituted by the various ways in which it can be exercised,[16] and it definitely creates uncertainty as to when the exercise of such an exclusive right will be considered as a "normal use" and when it will amount to an "abuse".

(iv) Rationale in terms of competition rules

3.42 The formal distinction between, on the one hand, the existence and, on the other hand, the exercise of intellectual property rights can nevertheless easily

---

[15] Case 24/67: [1968] E.C.R. 55 at 78. Compare with the function of patents as described *supra*, Chap. 2, pt. 3(2).

[16] See V. Korah, "Dividing the Common Market through national industrial property rights" (1972) 35 Mod.L.Rev. 634 at 636; P. Blok, "Articles 30–36 of the EEC Treaty and intellectual property rights: a Danish view" [1982] I.I.C. 729 at 731; R. Joliet, "Patented articles and the free movement of goods within the EEC" [1975] *Current Legal Problems* 15, at 23, although the latter maintains that the distinction makes sense under Articles 85–86, but not under Articles 30–36.

be explained in so far as the application of the rules of competition are concerned. As mentioned above, the objective of the competition rules is to curtail
the anti-competitive behaviour of economic actors, and not to bring national
laws into conformity with E.C. Treaty objectives.[17] As such, those rules are
specifically concerned with the exercise of rights, or the use of market power,
and are not meant to affect the legal status conferred by national law. This
basic principle was most recently confirmed, if not elaborated upon, by the
Court in the *Ohra* case.[18]

(v) Transposition to free movement of goods

The distinction between the "existence" of intellectual property rights which   **3.43**
is determined by national law and the "exercise" which is subject to scrutiny
under Community law, has also been used in the context of the Articles 30–36
E.C.[19] The application of this distinction is, however, less obvious under the
rules on the free movement of goods than under the rules on competition. The
Court has consistently held that Articles 30–36 E.C. apply in the first place to
national measures. It is therefore submitted that it is the existence and
enforcement of provisions of national intellectual property laws which are not
justified and not proportional that should not be upheld by the rules on the
free movement of goods, rather than the exercise of the exclusive right by the
intellectual property owner.[20]

(c) Plea for a functionality test
(i) The function of intellectual property rights as criterion

Through referring merely to the distinction between "existence", "normal   **3.44**
exercise" and "abusive exercise" of intellectual property rights as the guiding
principle in the early intellectual property cases, it is not only the relationship
between Community law and national law that has been determined in a
rather vague way. It also implies that the limitations imposed on intellectual
property rights by the Community rules on competition are based on precarious grounds. It seems to leave it up to the Court to determine whether, and
when, national intellectual property rights should be set aside for the purpose
of accelerating the integration of the internal market.[21] It is submitted that this
uncertainty could be remedied through introducing the criterion of "the use of
the exclusive right in conformity with the function for which it was granted".
This would then be the determining factor between, on the one hand, the normal exercise of an intellectual property right which should be left untouched

---

[17] See *supra*, at pt. 2(4)(b).
[18] Case C–245/91, *Ohra*, Judgment of November 17, 1993: [1993] E.C.R. I-5851.
[19] See *infra*, Chap. 4.
[20] See also E. White, "In search of the limits to Article 30 of the EEC Treaty" [1989] C.M.L.Rev.
235 at 266 where he writes: "This approach is in conflict with the principle that Article 30
applies to state measures"; G. Marenco, K. Banks, "Intellectual property and the Community
rules on free movement of goods: discrimination unearthed" (1990) 15 E.L.Rev. 224, at 226.
[21] See also G. Friden, "Recent developments in EEC intellectual property law: the distinction
between existence and exercise revisited" (1989) 26 C.M.L.Rev. 193. At p. 193, he writes:
"This potential lack of clarity which gives the possibility to the court to use the distinction as an
instrument of judicial policy should not conceal the fact that the distinction can be given an
exploitable theoretical construction" (emphasis added).

and, on the other hand, the abusive exercise of that exclusive right which could be curtailed under the Community rules on competition. To avoid situations arising, as in the *Consten Grundig* case, whereby the existence of the trade mark was formally upheld but practically emptied of its substance, it would seem to be even more consistent to examine the existence of an intellectual property right granted by national law in the light of conformity with Community law, rather than to obtain the same result through the back door act of striking down its exercise under the competition rules. The appropriate way of challenging the very existence of an intellectual property right would be to examine intellectual property measures under Article 36 E.C., as is done for the other objectives mentioned in that Article.

(ii) Justification under Article 36

3.45   The rules on free movement of goods are directed to the Member States so that the concept of "measures having equivalent effect to quantitative restrictions" applies to all measures emanating from the state or a public authority.[22] As such, both the provisions of national intellectual property law and the individual decisions whereby intellectual property rights are granted, for instance by a national patent office, could in principle be subject to scrutiny under Articles 30–36 E.C.[23] As repeatedly stated before, Article 36 E.C. does not reserve an exclusive competence to Member States but merely allows for certain measures under certain conditions to derogate from the principle of free movement of goods. This would imply that the justification test and proportionality test inherent in the first sentence, as well as the exception embodied in the second sentence of Article 36 E.C., would have to be effectively applied to such legislation or decision.[24] It would seem to be logical that in order to be upheld, the exclusive right would have to be granted in conformity with the function of the intellectual property law concerned, whereas the latter should be drafted in such a way as not to exceed the function of the intellectual property rights concerned.

---

[22] See A. Dauses, "*Mesures d'effet équivalent à des restrictions quantitatives à la lumière de la jurisprudence de la Cour de Justice des Communautés européennes*" [1992] R.T.D.E. 607 at 611. On this concept applied to intellectual property rights, see *infra*, Chap. 7, pt. 3.

[23] Joliet argues that it is national law which is the measure having an equivalent effect, rather than judicial decisions enforcing those rights. However, he does not consider decisions whereby public authorities grant the right. See R. Joliet, "Patented articles and the free movement of goods within the EEC" [1975] *Current Legal Problems* 15, at 25–27. Barents, to the contrary, maintains that the Court's *Bouchereau* judgment (Case 30/77, [1977] E.C.R. 1999; [1977] 2 C.M.L.R. 800) means court decisions can also constitute measures having an equivalent effect. See R. Barents, "New developments in measures having equivalent effect" [1981] C.M.L.Rev. 271 at 275. This latter view has been confirmed by the Court in Case 58/80, *Dansk Supermarked*: [1981] E.C.R. 194; [1981] 3 C.M.L.R. 590.

[24] Marenco and Banks rightly point out that "what one can say in the context of the rules on the free movement is that they do not prejudice an intellectual property right in its general conception, but can only affect a particular feature of the law – which is not the same distinction as between existence and exercise": see G. Marenco, K. Banks, "Intellectual property and the Community rules on free movement: discrimination unearthed" (1990) 15 E.L.Rev. 224 at 226–227.

(iii) Example: denominations of origin

In the *Delhaize* case, the Court adopted this approach with regard to denomi-   **3.46**
nations of origin.[25] The Court in particular held that national measures which
are contrary to Article 34 E.C. can be justified for reasons of industrial and
commercial property in the sense of Article 36 E.C. only if they are necessary
to ensure that the denomination of origin fulfils its specific function.[26] The
Court furthermore gave a Community definition of the specific function of
denominations of origin. It held that denominations of origin have the specific
function of safeguarding that the product concerned comes from a well-
defined geographical area and presents certain specific features.[27]

The main difference between denominations of origin and other intellectual property rights lies in the fact that the former do not confer exclusive
rights based on the principle of territoriality to individuals which the latter do.
Although the Court apparently seems to attach great importance to this distinction it is, nonetheless, submitted that there is no obvious reason why a
similar approach to Article 36 E.C. could not also be applied to other intellectual property rights.

(iv) Essence of a functionality test

Introducing what could be called a "functionality test" as a basis for the tra-   **3.47**
ditional distinction between the existence and the exercise, whether normal or
abusive, of intellectual property rights would have the merit of rendering the
impact of Community law on intellectual property rights more transparent
and coherent. The existence of intellectual property rights would not be affected by Community law if the exclusive right were granted in conformity with
the function of the intellectual property right concerned, and its exercise
would not be struck down under the competition rules if the exclusive right
were subsequently used in conformity to the function for which it was
granted. On the other hand, abusively granted and/or abusively used intellectual property rights could be struck down under, respectively, the rules on the
free movement of goods or the rules on competition. It is obvious in this
respect that to safeguard the uniform interpretation of Community law, the
concept of the "essential function" of a particular intellectual property right
should not be established in each case with reference to the national law concerned, but rather should be given a Community definition.[28]

---

[25] Case C–47/90, *Etablissement Delhaize Frères et Compagnie Le Lion SA v. Promalvin SA et AGE Bodegas Unidas SA*, Judgment of June 9, 1992: [1992] E.C.R. I-3669.

[26] On the analysis of the Court under Article 34 E.C. in this case, see *infra*, Chap. 7, pt. 3(2).

[27] Case C–47/90: [1992] E.C.R. I-3669, at paras. 16–17.

[28] Mertens de Wilmar points out that the establishment of Community definitions of a particular concept is the first rule to be observed by the Court when interpreting Community law, see J. Mertens de Wilmar, "*Réflexions sur les methodes d'interpretation de la Cour de Justice des Communautés Européennes*" [1986] C.D.E. 5, at 12. Specifically in relation to Article 36 EEC, see J. Mertens de Wilmar, "*De Communautaire rechtspraak over het vrij verkeer van goederen*" [1984] R.W. 1 at 13. On the different functions of different types of intellectual property rights, see *supra*, Chap. 2, pt. 3.

(v) Approach taken by the Court

3.48   The Court has merely transposed the existence/exercise dichotomy which, as seen above, can only be explained with reference to the specific nature of the competition rules, to its case law on the free movement of goods. As will be seen in the next chapter, in some cases the Court has thereby invoked a functionality criterion in particular concerning trade marks and performance rights. This criterion is not, however, coherently and consistently applied by the Court in all intellectual property cases. It may therefore be inferred that a functional criterion does not necessarily underlie the distinction between the existence and the exercise of intellectual property rights. Although the Court has, in an important number of judgments, gradually elaborated upon these concepts, it is still not always clear where the existence of the right, and thus the undisturbed national right, ends and where its exercise, and thus the possibility of imposing limitations under Community law, begins. It is even less obvious whether the exercise of an intellectual property right will be held to be abusive or not, as is illustrated by the examination of the case law of the Court given in the following chapters.

4. "Misuse" of Intellectual Property Rights under the Rules on the Free Movement of Goods

1. The Community Exhaustion Principle

(1) The origin

One of the most significant cases dealt with by the European Court of Justice **4.01** in the field of intellectual property rights was the *Deutsche Grammophon* case of 1971.[1] The Hanseatisches Oberlandesgericht Hamburg made a reference for a preliminary ruling concerning the application of Community rules on competition to rights akin to copyright. However, the Court in its answer interpreted the rules on the free movement of goods and introduced the principle of Community exhaustion.

(a) Deutsche Grammophon Gesellschaft: facts

The essential facts of the case were as follows. The Deutsche Grammophon **4.02** Gesellschaft Company (DGG) distributed gramophone records directly or through subsidiaries in several E.C. Member States. In Germany, the records were sold directly through retail and wholesale booksellers. The controlled retail selling price was DM 19. In other countries, the records were distributed under exclusive licensing agreements with subsidiaries, such as Polydor of Paris. Metro SB of Hamburg refused to sign a written agreement to observe the retail selling price. Instead, it purchased Polydor records through a third undertaking, Rosner & Co. of Hamburg, and sold them on the German market at a lower price than the one set by DGG. This led DGG to bring an action before the national courts, claiming that Metro had infringed its right of exclusive distribution in the Federal Republic.

In the first question, the Oberlandesgericht Hamburg asked the Court to rule whether the exclusive right to distribute intellectual property protected articles, conferred by national law, may be invoked to prevent the marketing in a national territory of products which were distributed by such a manufacturer, or with his consent, in the territory of another Member State without infringing Community provisions, in particular Articles 5, para. 2 and 85(1) E.C. In other words, the question was whether the use of intellectual property

---

[1] Case 78/70, *Deutsche Grammophon Gesellschaft mbH v. Metro-SB-Großmärkte GmbH*, Judgment of June 8, 1971: [1971] E.C.R. 487; [1971] C.M.L.R. 631.

rights so as to prevent intra-brand competition in the given case constituted a "normal" use compatible with the rules on competition, or an "abusive" use of the exclusive right which should be struck down. The second question was whether the exclusive distribution rights infringed Article 86 E.C. if the controlled retail price was higher than the price of the original product reimported from another Member State, and if the principal performers were bound by exclusive contracts to the manufacturer of the sound recordings.[2]

(b) Existence/exercise dichotomy transposed to Article 36

4.03　Contrary to the approach taken in the *Sirena* case,[3] the first question was dealt with by the Court mainly in the light of Articles 30 to 36 E.C. The Court thereby made the assumption that Article 36 E.C., although only expressly referring to industrial and commercial property, also applies to a right related to copyright. However, instead of analysing under Article 36 E.C. whether or not the national legislation conferring the exclusive right was justified and proportional, as a precondition to its possible invocation and predominance over the free movement of goods, the Court transposed the distinction made in the context of the application of the rules on competition in the *Parke Davis* case.[4] It held that if the "exercise" of the exclusive right was not contrary to Articles 85 and 86 E.C., one still had to look at whether this *exercise* was not contrary to other provisions of the E.C. Treaty.[5] This means that the Court implicitly considered the "existence" of the right to be unaffected by *all* Community rules, and not only by the rules on competition, and merely looked at the impact of the "exercise" of the exclusive right by the intellectual property owner on the free movement of goods. This legacy of the early intellectual property competition cases was also to determine the evolution of subsequent case law.

(c) Principle of territoriality as "exercise"

4.04　Advocate General Roemer had taken a similar approach, referring to the prior case law concerning the application of the rules on competition to conclude that the existence of intellectual property rights should be left intact.[6] He looked at whether there was an improper exercise of the right that should be prohibited by Community law in the given case. He pointed out that the problem arose because the goods had been marketed with the intellectual property owner's consent in another Member State so that on the basis of the principle of territoriality the exclusive right could possibly be invoked to prohibit the

---

[2] On this question, see *infra*, Chap. 5, pt. 2(3)(d).

[3] Case 40/70, *Sirena v. Eda*, Judgment of February 18, 1971: [1971] E.C.R. 69; [1971] C.M.L.R. 260. The relevant preliminary question in this case was the following: "Must the said Articles 85 and 86 be interpreted as preventing the proprietor of a trade mark lawfully registered in one Member State from exercising the absolute right derived from the trade mark to prohibit third parties from importing from other Countries of the Community products bearing the same trade mark, lawfully attached to them in their place of origin?"

[4] See *supra*, Chap. 3, pt. 4(2)(a).

[5] Case 78/70: [1971] E.C.R. 487; [1971] C.M.L.R. 631, at para. 7.

[6] Case 78/70, opinion of Advocate General Roemer delivered on April 28, 1971: [1971] E.C.R. 503; [1971] C.M.L.R. 631.

importation of those goods. This was different from the situation arising with regard to marketing with consent within German territory, because in the latter event the principle of exhaustion of rights as laid down in German law applied.[7] He reflected on the question of whether the principle of territoriality, which is inherent in intellectual property law, forms part of the existence of intellectual property rights so that it should be unconditionally upheld or whether, to the contrary, it is part of the exercise of the exclusive right so that it could be curtailed by Community law. The Advocate General tended in favour of the latter view.[8] He held that in any event the decisive factor was that the objective of the intellectual property right was attained through the first marketing of the goods because this offered the possibility of obtaining a monopolistic reward. It was pointed out that "it would undoubtedly go beyond the objective of that right if the holder was permitted to control further marketing...".[9]

(d) Principle of exhaustion to safeguard the internal market objective

The Court thus introduced the principle of Community exhaustion of intellec-   **4.05**
tual property rights upon first marketing with consent to curtail the effect of the principle of territoriality.[10] The principle of exhaustion implies that if the intellectual property owner consented to putting the intellectual property protected product on the market in one Member State, he may no longer invoke his intellectual property right in another Member State to prohibit the parallel importation of that product. The Court explained that allowing citizens of Member States to partition the Common Market through invoking national provisions would be contrary to the essential purpose of the E.C. Treaty which is to unite the national markets into one single market.[11] That the application of the principle of exhaustion to curtail intellectual property rights is stringently linked to the Treaty objective of creating one internal

---

[7] According to Marenco, the Community principle of exhaustion exactly aims at eliminating the discrimination inherent in the national exhaustion principle. See G. Marenco, "*Pour une interpretation traditionelle de la notion de mesure d'effet equivalent à une restriction quantitative*" [1984] C.D.E. 291, at 344. However, if the aim of the Court were only to eliminate discrimination, then the application of the principle of Community exhaustion would be dependent on whether or not the national law invoked contains the principle of national exhaustion, and hence would apply differently according to the country of importation and the intellectual property right invoked. Even Marenco has to admit that discrimination is not the decisive element in the analysis of the Court concerning measures having equivalent effect (see p. 346). See also *infra*, Chap. 7, pt. 3(4)(a)(ii).

[8] Case 78/70: [1971] E.C.R. 487, at 508 where he writes: "...there is in fact much to be said for the view that the principle of territoriality, which is so uncertain in outline, does not form part of the existence of the right."

[9] *id.*: [1971] E.C.R. 487 at 508.

[10] This is different from the *Sirena* case, where the Court came to a similar conclusion through the application of the rules on competition. See Case 40/70: [1971] E.C.R. 69; [1971] C.M.L.R. 260, at para. 11, where the Court held: "Article 85, [...], is applicable to the extent to which trade mark rights are invoked so as to prevent imports of products which originate in different Member States, which bear the same trade mark by virtue of the fact that the proprietors have acquired it, or the right to use it, whether by agreements between themselves or by agreements with third parties."

[11] Case 78/70: [1971] E.C.R. 487; [1971] C.M.L.R. 631, at para. 12.

market was all the more evident in the *Polydor v. Harlequin* case.[12] This case presented striking resemblances to the *DGG* case, only it concerned parallel importation from a third country instead of another Member State. The Court held that the principle of exhaustion could not be transposed to an international context merely on the basis of provisions similar to Articles 30 and 36 E.C. in a free trade agreement with a third country. Rather, it stipulated that regard needed to be had to the content, objective and formulation of the agreement concerned which was different from that of the E.C. Treaty.

(e) Introduction of the "specific subject-matter" concept

4.06 Concurrent with the introduction of the principle of exhaustion, the Court in the *DGG* case also gave a restrictive interpretation of the scope of Article 36 E.C. specifically in relation to intellectual property rights. It stated that:

> "...Article 36 only admits derogations from [the free movement of goods] to the extent to which they are justified for the purpose of safeguarding rights *which constitute the specific subject-matter of such property.*"[13]

However, contrary to Advocate General Roemer, the Court did not explain what, in its view, constitutes the specific subject-matter or the objective of intellectual property rights. This concept, which thus distinguishes between what constitutes a normal use, as opposed to a misuse, of intellectual property protection under the rules on the free movement of goods, was only gradually elaborated upon in subsequent case law.[14]

(2) The concept

(a) Proportionality principle applied to the "exercise" of intellectual property rights

4.07 According to Gormley, the introduction of the concept of "specific subject-matter" to delineate the scope of application of Article 36 E.C. in so far as intellectual property rights are concerned is the "prime example" of the appli-

---

[12] Case 270/80, *Polydor v. Harlequin*, Judgment of February 9, 1982: [1982] E.C.R. 329; [1982] 1 C.M.L.R. 677. However, the principle of "regional" exhaustion has now been formally written into the EEA-Agreement so that it will apply also to the EFTA countries concerned. This is logical as the objective is to extend the internal market objective to those countries. Some controversy has nevertheless arisen as to whether or not it should only apply to goods originating in the EEA, considering that the EEA does not establish a customs union; compare M. Abbey, "Exhaustion of IP rights under the EEA agreement does not apply to third country goods" (1992) 13 E.C.L.R. 231; F. Prändl, "Exhaustion of IP rights in the EEA applies to third-country goods placed on the EEA market" [1993] E.C.L.R. 43. See also J. Brown, and G. Robert, "The European Economic Area: how important is it?" (1992) 14 E.I.P.R. 379.

[13] *id.*, at para. 11 (emphasis added).

[14] On the subsequent case law elaborating upon the concept "specific subject-matter", see *infra*, pt. 2.

cation of the proportionality principle.[15] This would probably have been true had the proportionality test been applied to determine whether or not the national measure conferring the exclusive right fell within the scope of the first sentence of Article 36 E.C., rather than merely to curtail the use made of that right by the intellectual property owner. Transposing the distinction between the "existence" of the right, which is left untouched, as opposed to the "exercise", which is curtailed by Community law, to the context of free movement of goods implies that the Court assumed that intellectual property law *per se* falls within the ambit of the first sentence of Article 36 E.C. But at the same time it is obvious, to use Gormley's words, that:

> "it is the national right (to, for example, oppose the importation of products on the ground of infringement of a patent) which is the measure having equivalent effect to a quantitative restriction, even though it is the private parties who seek to invoke that right."[16]

As such, it is submitted that in the absence of harmonisation the correct approach should have been to review the intellectual property law for its compatibility with Article 36 E.C.[17]

(b) Alternative: proportionality principle applied to the "existence" of intellectual property rights

The Court could have come to the same conclusion, namely exhaustion of rights, through applying the justification and proportionality tests under the first sentence of Article 36 E.C. to the "existence" of intellectual property rights. This would have implied that the Court looked at whether or not the national measure was justified by objective circumstances corresponding to the need of the intellectual property right concerned.[18] The Court would thus have had to take the function of the intellectual property right concerned into account and determine whether or not the right to oppose the importation of protected goods marketed with the right-owner's consent, under a system of parallel protection, was granted in accordance with that function. Secondly, the Court would have had to establish whether granting that right was

4.08

---

[15] L. Gormley, *Prohibiting restrictions on trade within the EEC* (1985, T.M.C. Asser Instituut, North-Holland), p. 126. He writes: "The proportionality principle has been developed most significantly in relation to industrial and commercial property, in which context the Court has chosen to express the concepts of necessity and action least onerous to intra-Community trade by limiting the permissible derogations under this heading to those necessary to give effect to the 'specific object' of the right relied upon." See also at pp. 184–186.

[16] L. Gormley, *op. cit.*, p. 262. After convincingly arguing that Articles 30–36 E.C. apply to state measures and not to the behaviour of private parties (see especially pp. 260–261), he then proceeds to try and fit in the case-law of the Court on intellectual property rights by stating that "the view that Articles 30–36 do not bind private parties as such does not mean that they have no effect on private parties".

[17] Similarly, see E. White, "In search of the limits to Article 30 of the EEC Treaty" (1989) 26 C.M.L.Rev. 235 at 269. He writes: "national provisions which grant rights (to take action against third parties) must be subject to Article 30 in the same way as other national measures." See also M. Quinn and M. MacGowan, "Could Article 30 impose obligations on individuals?" (1987) 12 E.L.Rev. 163 at 173. They write: ". . . it is suggested that the fundamental problem is the rights conferred on private parties by the national law concerned, without which he would be powerless to prevent imports."

[18] On the feasibility of a functionality test, see *supra*, Chap. 3, pt. 4(2)(c).

necessary to safeguard the achievement of the function of the intellectual property right or whether, to the contrary, the particular right granted under national law was disproportionate in relation to its objective.[19] The practical conclusion under such an approach would most likely have been similar to the conclusion reached by the Court in the *DGG* case. The reward and incentive functions of copyright could be said to have been duly safeguarded under the system of parallel protection in the Member State of exportation, so that no further restrictions on the free movement of goods were necessary in the Member State of importation on the basis of the need to protect intellectual property rights. In other words, it could also have been concluded that the national intellectual property law could not be invoked to prevent the importation of goods which had been put on the Community market with the consent of the intellectual property owner. It is submitted, however, that the latter approach, focusing on the fulfilment of the functions of intellectual property rights, might have prevented the Court from gradually deviating from the original meaning of "consent" in so far as the application of the principle of exhaustion is concerned.[20] As will be illustrated below, the approach taken by the Court, which focuses on the exercise of intellectual property rights by the right-owner, has led to the application of this principle even in the absence of parallel protection.

(c) Difference between the two approaches

4.09 A fundamental difference between the two approaches lies in the fact that with the above-mentioned alternative approach it would have been clarified from the start that national intellectual property rules and practices are not *per se* exempt from the application of Community law and may be subject to scrutiny of their content. This is now firmly established by the *Phil Collins* case.[21] It would also have been more transparent than the creation of an additional distinction concerning the exercise of intellectual property rights, namely the juxtaposition of "normal use" and "misuse", under the rules on the free movement of goods, to the "normal use" and "abuse" under the competition rules. Under the approach adopted by the Court it seems that the exercise of intellectual property rights considered to be "normal" under the rules on free movement of goods can still be considered as "abusive" under the competition rules. This is despite the fact that it may well be the national intellectual property right itself which has an effect equivalent to a quantitative restriction and is the cause of the obstruction of trade, rather than the exercise made of his exclusive right by the intellectual property owner.[22]

---

[19] See *infra*, pt. 2(1)(a), where it is illustrated that in the *Sterling Drug* case, the Court initially took this approach to the exhaustion principle as applied to patents.

[20] See *infra*, Chap. 6, pt. 5.

[21] It should be recalled that in this case the Court held that the general principle of non-discrimination (Article 6 E.C.) applies to intellectual property law, see *supra*, Chap. 2, pt. 4(1)(c)(iv).

[22] The Court has expressly acknowledged this in certain cases. See for instance Case C–9/93, *Ideal-Standard*, Judgment of June 22, 1994: [1994] E.C.R. I-2789, at para. 33. Case 16/74, *Centrafarm v. Winthrop*, Judgment of October 31, 1974: [1974] E.C.R. 1183; [1974] 2 C.M.L.R. 480, at paras. 7–11. See also *infra*, pt. 2(1)(c)(ii).

(d) Importance of Article 36 and Article 177 procedure

The question therefore arises of whether the reluctance of the Court to effec-   **4.10**
tively apply Article 36 E.C. to national intellectual property law is perhaps
determined by the nature of this provision and/or by the fact that most questions concerning intellectual property rights were raised in preliminary proceedings based on Article 177 E.C. With respect to Article 177 E.C., the Court
has clarified that the following division of functions applies:

> "Since the purpose of the Court's jurisdiction under Article 177 of the
> Treaty is to ensure the uniform interpretation of Community law in all
> the Member States, the Court confines itself to inferring from their word-
> ing and spirit the meaning of Community rules at issue. It is then for the
> national court alone to apply the provisions of Community law so inter-
> preted, taking into account the circumstances of fact and law in the case
> which has come before them."[23]

It should be pointed out that the Court under Article 177 procedures has,
nonetheless, not refrained from analysing whether the national law invoked
to derogate from the principle of free movement of goods under Article 36
E.C. was prima facie justified and proportional in so far as denominations of
origin, or the other objectives mentioned in Article 36 E.C. were concerned.[24]
This may be illustrated by the following examples.

(i) Examples of justification test

In the *Campus Oil* case, the Court expressly held that: **4.11**

> " . . . to come within the ambit of Article 36, the rules in question must be
> justified by objective circumstances corresponding to the needs of public
> security."[25]

After weighing the arguments advanced in favour of the contested measures, the Court held that the application to petroleum products of measures
having equivalent effect to quantitative restrictions was justified because of
these products' exceptional function as an energy source and their fundamental importance for the very existence of a state. Similarly, in the *De Peijper*
case, the Court maintained that:

---

[23] Case C–231/89, *K. Gmurzynska-Bscher v. Oberfinanz-direktion Köln*, Judgment of
November 8, 1990: [1990] E.C.R. I-4003, at para. 21. Concerning "interpretation of
Community law", see Case 61/79, *Denkavit Italiana*, Judgment of March 27, 1980: [1980]
E.C.R. 1205; [1981] 3 C.M.L.R. 694. On the co-operation procedure between the Court of
Justice and the national courts, see Case 244/80, *Foglia v. Novello*, Judgment of December 16,
1981: [1981] E.C.R. 3045; [1982] 1 C.M.L.R. 585; and Case C–83/91, *Meilicke*, Judgment of
July 16, 1992: [1992] E.C.R. I-4871.

[24] On the *Delhaize* case, see *supra*, Chap. 3, pt. 4(2)(c)(iii). Besides intellectual property
protection, the only other "*per se* exception" under Article 36 E.C. seems to be the public
security objective as applied to dual use goods. See Case C–367/89, *Minister of Finance of the
Grand-Duchy of Luxembourg v. Aimé Richardt*, Judgment of October 4, 1991: [1991] E.C.R.
I-4621, as discussed in I. Govaere, P. Eeckhout, "On dual use goods and dualist case law: the
Aimé Richardt judgment on export controls" (1992) 29 C.M.L.Rev. 941 at 949–952.

[25] Case 72/83, *Campus Oil Ltd v. Minister for Industry and Energy*, Judgment of July 10, 1984:
[1984] E.C.R. 2727; [1984] 3 C.M.L.R. 544, at para. 36.

> "it emerges from Article 36 that national rules or practices which do re-
> strict imports of pharmaceutical products or are capable of doing so are
> only compatible with the Treaty to the extent to which they are necessary
> for the effective protection of health and life of humans."[26]

In other words, in each particular case the specific national measure
invoked has to be scrutinised for its justification in the light of the relevant
objective mentioned in Article 36 E.C.[27]

(ii) Examples of proportionality test

4.12 Similarly, the Court under Article 177 procedures also proceeds with the
application of the proportionality test to the national measures invoked. This
essentially means that although the measures might at first sight be justifiable
under Article 36 E.C., they will not come within the scope of that Article if
other measures could be enforced which are less restrictive of intra-Community trade. For instance, in the *De Peijper* case, the Court held that:

> "Article 36 cannot be relied on to justify rules or practices which, even
> though they are beneficial, contain restrictions which are explained pri-
> marily by a concern to lighten the administration's burden or to reduce
> public expenditure, unless, in the absence of the said rules or practices,
> this burden or expenditure would exceed the limits of what can reason-
> ably be required."[28]

Also, in the *Campus Oil* case, the Court proceeded to look at whether the
specific measure adopted was proportional and gave indications to the
national court to apply the proportionality test to the given facts.[29]

(iii) No apparent problem of competence

4.13 The reason why the Court refrained from looking at whether the existence of
the intellectual property right was in conformity with Article 36 E.C. in the
Deutsche Grammophon case cannot easily be explained by the division of
competence under Article 36 E.C. That is to say, the Court did not use a similar existence/exercise dichotomy for the other objectives mentioned in Article
36 E.C. Neither can the reluctance of the Court to examine the national intellectual property law concerned be explained by the division of competence

---

[26] Case 104/75, *De Peijper*, Judgment of May 20, 1976: [1976] E.C.R. 613; [1976] 2 C.M.L.R. 271, at para. 16.

[27] A similar justification test applies to the so-called mandatory requirements ensuing from the *Cassis de Dijon* judgment (Case 120/78, *Rewe*, Judgment of February 20, 1979: [1979] E.C.R. 649; [1979] 3 C.M.L.R. 494), such as the rules on unfair competition and consumer protection. See, for instance, Case C–315/92, *Clinique*, Judgment of February 2, 1994: [1994] E.C.R. I-317, at paras. 20–22.

[28] *id.*, at para. 18. At para. 17, the Court in general held that "national rules or practices do not fall within the exception specified in Article 36 if the health and life of humans can as effectively be protected by measures which do not restrict intra-Community trade so much".

[29] Case 72/83: [1984] E.C.R. 2727; [1984] 3 C.M.L.R. 544, at paras. 44 *et seq*. The proportionality test is also applied to mandatory requirements. See for instance Case C–238/89, *Pall Corp. v. Dalhausen*, Judgment of December 13, 1990: [1990] E.C.R. I-4827, where the application of national rules on unfair competition to prohibit the use of the trade mark registration symbol ®, in case the trade mark is not registered in the Member State concerned although it is in another Member States, was held to be contrary to Article 30 E.C.

between the national and the Community Court under the preliminary procedure of Article 177 E.C. As illustrated above, under this procedure the Court has looked at whether national measures based on other objectives mentioned in Article 36 E.C. were prima facie justified and proportional.[30]

(e) Merits and shortcomings

Although the *Deutsche Grammophon* judgment did not go as far as it could have done, its importance cannot be denied. For the first time, the Court based its judgment almost entirely on the free movement of goods although this could have been circumvented by applying the rules on competition as had been done in the *Sirena* case. Furthermore, the introduction of the doctrine of Community exhaustion put an important limitation on the exercise of intellectual property rights in order to safeguard the principle of free movement of goods and intra-brand competition of intellectual property protected products. The judgment also fell short in at least two respects. First, it created the assumption that intellectual property law is not subject to scrutiny under Community rules. In Chapter 6 below it will be seen that, already before the ruling in the *Phil Collins* judgment, this was not always necessarily true. Secondly, it introduced a rather vague concept, namely the "specific subject-matter" of intellectual property rights, to constitute the delineating factor between "normal use" and "misuse" of intellectual property rights under the rules on the free movement of goods. In the next section, attention will be given to how the Court has had to elaborate upon this crucial concept with regard to the different intellectual property rights concerned in its subsequent case law.

2. THE CONCEPT OF "SPECIFIC SUBJECT-MATTER"

(1) Patents

(a) Parallel protection

(i) *Centrafarm v. Sterling Drug*: facts

The Court for the first time gave an indication of the concept of "specific sub-   **4.15**
ject-matter" of a patent right in the *Centrafarm v. Sterling Drug* case.[31] As in the *Deutsche Grammophon* case, the preliminary question was posed as to whether the owner of parallel intellectual property rights, *in casu* patents, could invoke his exclusive right under national law to prohibit the parallel

---

[30] There are numerous cases and articles confirming this. As Verloren van Themaat pointed out, the case law subsequent to the *Cassis de Dijon* judgment confirms that the fact that a national regulation is based on objectives such as one of those mentioned in Article 36 E.C., does not suffice to exclude the ensuing restrictions on importation from the basic prohibition on measures having equivalent effect as laid down in the *Dassonville* judgment: see P. Verloren van Themaat, *"La libre circulation des marchandises après l'arrêt 'Cassis De Dijon'"* [1982] C.D.E. 123 at 128.
[31] Case 15/74, *Centrafarm BV and Adriaan De Peijper v. Sterling Drug Inc.*, Judgment of October 31, 1974: [1974] E.C.R. 1147; [1974] 2 C.M.L.R. 480.

importation of protected goods, namely medicinal preparations sold under the trade mark "Negram", without infringing the E.C. Treaty. An additional problem in this case arose from the fact that the price was artificially held low in the Member State of exportation, the United Kingdom, due to certain government measures.

(ii) Effect of principle of exhaustion

4.16 The introduction of the doctrine of exhaustion of intellectual property rights in order to prevent the prohibition of parallel imports under national law means, in practical terms, that the right-owner can no longer benefit from the particular characteristics of a national market. Setting the prices according to the demand-supply ratio of the different territorial markets would lead to the unlimited importation of goods distributed on the market with the lowest price to the markets where originally higher prices were fixed. The intellectual property owner is therefore likely to safeguard revenue from his work by setting higher prices on the first sale, and/or by charging higher licence royalties, to make up for the potential losses due to parallel importations,[32] or to prevent parallel importation from being at all beneficial. However, this possibility was severely limited in the *Sterling Drug* case because of government interference with the prices in the United Kingdom market.

(iii) Definition of specific subject-matter

4.17 The Court confirmed its ruling in the *Deutsche Grammophon* case, namely that Article 36 E.C. only admits derogations from Articles 30–34 E.C. to safeguard rights which constitute the specific subject-matter of intellectual property. But the Court went further and stipulated that:

> "In relation to patents, the specific subject-matter of the industrial property is the guarantee that the patentee, *to reward the creative effort* of the inventor, has the exclusive right to use an invention with a view to manufacturing industrial products and *putting them into circulation for the first time*, either directly or by the grant of licences to third parties, as well as the right to oppose infringements."[33]

In the view of the Court, once the product has been put on the market in the Member State of exportation by the patentee, or with his consent, the industrial property right in the Member State of importation is held to be exhausted and may no longer be invoked to prevent parallel importation.

(iv) The reward theory

4.18 It was generally thought that the reference to the "reward for the creative effort" was the decisive factor in the definition of the subject-matter of patents. This led to the introduction of the so-called "reward theory". The idea was that if the inventor had been able to obtain a reward, then the specific subject-matter of his patent was fulfilled and he could no longer invoke his

---

[32] V. Korah, "The limitations of copyright and patent by the rules for the free movement of goods in the European Common market" [1982] *Case Western Reserve Journal of International Law* 7 at 18.

[33] Case 15/74: [1974] E.C.R. 1147; [1974] 2 C.M.L.R. 480, at para. 9, (emphasis added).

exclusive right to oppose parallel importations.[34] It should be noted in this respect that in spite of the lack of a thorough analysis of the justification for issuing patent legislation,[35] the Court held that the subject-matter of national patents confers a positive right upon the patentee, namely the right to market his products. However, the holder of, for instance, an improvement patent may be unable to exploit his patent without infringing the original patentee's rights. National intellectual property rights are, in the first place, prohibitive rights. This means that they do not, as such, confer a positive right, but rather they confer the right to prohibit certain acts and to exclude certain products from the market. With respect, it would therefore have been more correct for the Court to state that an industrial property right is basically the right to prevent others from manufacturing and selling the protected product, and to have elaborated upon the reasons for this exclusive right.[36]

(v) Government interference with level of reward

Instead, the Court rejected the patentee's justification based on the argument that governmental measures in the Member State of exportation caused important price differences which distorted normal intra-brand competition when the products were eventually imported. In the Court's reasoning, Member States cannot justify the maintenance, or introduction, of measures infringing the free movement of goods. Neither can the latter be relied upon by individuals to reduce the effect of factors in other Member States that are likely to distort competition within the Common Market. It is the task of the Community authorities to eliminate such obstacles through harmonisation of national measures.[37] Although, in theory, this approach is fully in accordance with the purpose of the E.C. Treaty it disregards the practical problems arising from the evolution from separate national markets to one Common Market. Economic actors may be forced to comply with Community rules, whereas Member States sometimes refrain from bringing their laws into conformity with Community objectives, or do this only gradually. This implies that as long as no harmonisation is achieved, individuals and firms find themselves in between the economic reality of separate national markets and the ideal of a single market, as outlined in the E.C. Treaty and pursued by the Court. In the *Sterling Drug* case, the practical impact of this approach was that Centrafarm could not freely determine its reward in the Member State of exportation, whereas it could not prevent intra-brand competition in the Member State of importation from occurring, so that the effect of the United Kingdom Government measures was partially extended to that market.

4.19

(b) *Absence of parallel protection*

(i) *Merck v. Stephar:* facts

The burden posed upon the economic actors to consider the Community market as an integrated market, despite divergent national law, is further

4.20

---

[34] See for instance T. Schaper, "*Het 'specifiek voorwerp' van de industriële en commerciele eigendom in de EEG-rechtspraak*" [1977] R.M.T. 556, at 561 *et seq.*

[35] On the function of patents, see *supra*, Chap. 2, pt. 3(2).

[36] See also V. Korah, *op. cit.* (1982), p. 19.

[37] Case 15/74: [1974] E.C.R. 1147; [1974] 2 C.M.L.R. 480, at paras. 22–25.

illustrated by the *Merck v. Stephar* judgment.[38] Merck is an American firm, holding patents for a drug known as "Moduretic" and for its manufacturing process in most E.C. Member States. At the time the product was first marketed in 1962, Italian patent law did not include pharmaceuticals, or their manufacturing processes, within the scope of the legal protection offered. Nonetheless, Merck put its product on sale in the Italian market. When, eventually, patents became possible for drugs in Italy, Merck was refused patent protection owing to the lack of novelty of the product. Stephar imported Moduretic from Italy into the Netherlands and resold it there at a price lower than Merck. The latter brought a legal action before the national court for infringement of its patent right. These facts led to a similar preliminary question as in the *Deutsche Grammophon* and *Sterling Drug* cases, namely, the compatibility of invoking this exclusive right to prohibit parallel importations with the rules on the free movement of goods. However, the major difference was that in this case the parallel importation took place in the absence of parallel patent protection in the Member State of exportation.

(ii) Effect of principle of exhaustion

4.21 Applying the doctrine of exhaustion in the absence of parallel protection implies that the patent holder would most likely not be able to obtain a return for R&D investment through raising the price of his product upon first marketing. This is due to the fact that on the Italian market the product can be freely copied so that Merck has to sell its product there at competitive prices. Furthermore, subjecting the Dutch patented product to intra-brand competition from the competitively priced Italian products would obviously entail either the Dutch product being driven out of the market or its price having to be set so as to be competitive with the price of the imported Italian product.[39] This is manifestly contrary to the reward and incentive functions inherent in patent law.

(iii) Clarification of specific subject-matter
— "Right to first marketing"

4.22 In line with its earlier judgments, whereby the Court merely analysed the behaviour of the intellectual property owner rather than the legal context against which this took place,[40] the Court held that the patentee is free to decide how to make use of his right of first marketing the product in his best interest, taking account of the various circumstances involved. According to the Court, this includes:

[38] Case 187/80, *Merck & Co Inc. v. Stephar BV*, Judgment of July 14, 1981: [1981] E.C.R. 2063; [1981] 3 C.M.L.R. 463.
[39] See M. Waelbroeck, "Competition, integration and economic efficiency in the EEC from the point of view of the private firm" in *The Art of Governance* (Michigan Law Review Association ed. 1987) (Nomos), pp. 301–308. He argues that the Court's approach is to be rejected because it enforces the rules on the free movement of goods for the sake of enforcing those rules, thereby disregarding its negative impact on free competition, which is also a Community objective, and economic efficiency. However, he seems to suggest that intellectual property rights should be left untouched to the extent that no harmonisation has been achieved, rather than smoothing out the differences through analysing intellectual property law under Article 36 E.C.
[40] See especially also Joined Cases 55 and 57/80, *Musik-Vertrieb*, Judgment of January 20, 1981: [1981] E.C.R. 147; [1981] 2 C.M.L.R. 44, as explained below.

"the possibility of marketing in a Member State where the law does not provide patent protection for the product in question. *If he decides to do so he must then accept the consequences of his choice as regards the free movement of the product within the Common Market.*"[41]

— "Reward for creative effort"

On the previous argument of the Court in the *Sterling Drug* case that the specific subject-matter of patents is to reward the patentee through the exclusive right to use the invention with a view to manufacturing industrial products and putting them into circulation for the first time, the Court followed Advocate General Reischl's opinion that a patent merely provides the proprietor with the *possibility* of obtaining a reward for his creative effort.[42] However, the Court failed to consider whether Merck was in fact provided with the possibility of obtaining such a reward.[43] The Court merely held:

4.23

> "That right of first placing the product on the market enables the inventor, by allowing him a monopoly in exploiting his product, to obtain the reward for his creative effort *without, however, guaranteeing that he will obtain such a reward in all circumstances.*"[44]

From the wording of the judgment, it seems that the hypothetical case in which the patentee could have obtained patent protection in the Member State of exportation yet refrained from applying for it, should be regarded in the same way as when no protection was possible.

(c) Specific subject-matter versus function

(i) Different concepts

It is clear from this judgment that the essence or the function of the patent, which basically is the grant of a temporary exclusive right on a new product or process to reward the creative effort of the inventor and to stimulate further investment in research and development,[45] is not tantamount to the specific subject-matter of the patent. The latter is reduced to the right to put the goods

4.24

---

[41] Case 187/80: [1981] E.C.R. 2063; [1981] 3 C.M.L.R. 463, at para. 11 (emphasis added).

[42] Case 187/80, Opinion of Advocate General Reisch, delivered on June 3, 1981: [1981] E.C.R. 2084 at 2090, where he writes: "However, where [the reward] is one of the objectives of a patent right it is not, in my view, inherent in that right but must be seen as being separate from it, for it is open to any proprietor of a patent to put his invention on the market without seeking the recompense described above. Furthermore, it should not be forgotten that the return on research investment is merely a *possibility*, the realisation of which depends on numerous market factors such as the presence of substitute products, commercial exploitability and similar conditions" (emphasis added).

[43] See *infra*, Chap. 6, pt. 2(5)(d)(iii).

[44] Case 187/80: [1981] E.C.R. 2063; [1981] 3 C.M.L.R. 463, at para. 10, (emphasis added).

[45] See *supra*, Chap. 2, pt. 3(2). Similarly, see Advocate General Trabucchi who expressly held in the *Sterling Drug* case that the essence of trade marks, which is to guarantee the origin of the product to the consumers, is different from the essence of patents. He wrote: "the real essence of the protection conferred on the patent owner is the exclusive right to manufacture and market the patented product, given to compensate him as the inventor of a process and to bring him a financial reward for his efforts and for the commercial risks he runs, and it is recognised on a purely temporary basis". See Case 15/74, opinion delivered on September 18, 1974: [1974] E.C.R. 1169 at 1172.

into circulation for the first time either by the intellectual property owner himself or with his consent.[46]

(ii) Initial convergence

4.25 From the reasoning used in the *Sterling Drug* case, it could be assumed that the Court implicitly considered that there was an indispensable relationship between the function and the subject-matter of the patent. Although in the final ruling the Court held that the *exercise* of the right by the patent holder was incompatible with the rules on the free movement of goods in the E.C., in the reasoning for the judgment it held that:

> "An obstacle to the free movement of goods *may* arise out of the *existence*, within a national legislation concerning industrial and commercial property, of provisions laying down that a patentee's right is not exhausted when the product protected by the patent is marketed in another Member State, with the result that the patentee can prevent importation of the product into his own Member State when it has been marketed in another Member State."[47]

Furthermore, the Court held that this obstacle to the free movement of goods *may* be justified on the ground of industrial property protection in a case where it concerns parallel importation in absence of parallel protection of goods that have been marketed without the patent holder's consent.[48] This double use of the conditional tense thus seemed to imply that reliance on Article 36 E.C. would only be upheld in a case where a national rule conferring the right to oppose importations did not exceed what was needed to fulfil the function, or the objective, of the industrial property right concerned. This is reinforced by the fact that the Court continued to state that such an obstacle to the free movement of goods cannot be justified if the goods had been marketed with the patent holder's consent, in particular in the case of parallel patents, because:

> "if a patentee could prevent the import of protected products marketed by him or with his consent in another Member State, he would be able to partition off national markets and thereby restrict trade between Member States, *in a situation where no such restriction was necessary to guarantee the essence of the exclusive rights flowing from the parallel patents.*"[49]

---

[46] Advocate General Reischl was of a different opinion in the *Merck* case. He held that "the essence of a patent right lies primarily in the fact that the inventor is guaranteed an *exclusive right* to manufacture and market the product in question", whereas he held concerning the reward for the creative effort that "whilst it is one of the objectives of a patent right it is not, in my view, inherent in that right but must be seen as being separate from it". See Case 187/80: [1981] E.C.R. 2063 at 2090. Beier's main critique of the use of the criterion "specific subject-matter" as a demarcation is precisely that it does not cover the essence of the right, see F.-K. Beier, "Industrial property and the free movement of goods in the internal market" [1990] I.I.C. 131 at 148.

[47] Case 15/74: [1974] E.C.R. 1147; [1974] 2 C.M.L.R. 480, at para. 10, (emphasis added).

[48] *id.*, at para. 11.

[49] *id.*, at paras. 11–12 (emphasis added).

(iii) Point of divergence: the consent theory

However, the Court clarified in the subsequent *Merck* case that the function of a patent is to be totally disregarded.[50] The only criterion withheld to determine whether or not the exercise of the exclusive right exceeds the specific subject-matter of the patent is whether or not the substance of the patent right, which "lies essentially in according the inventor an exclusive right of first placing the product on the market",[51] has been safeguarded. As such, the so-called "consent theory" seemed to have replaced the "reward theory".   **4.26**

(2) Copyright and akin rights

(a) Distribution rights

(i) Article 36 applied to copyright

The first time the Court expressly clarified the reason why copyright protection falls within the ambit of Article 36 E.C., which only mentions "industrial and commercial property", was in the *Musik-Vertrieb and K-Tel* cases of 1981.[52] The question arose of whether a management company entrusted with the exploitation of copyright could invoke provisions of national copyright law to claim the payment of additional royalties upon importation of records that had been marketed in other Member States for lower royalties, due to government interference, with the consent of the owner of the musical works concerned, without infringing the Treaty rules. The Court stated: **4.27**

> "It is true that copyright comprises moral rights of the kind indicated by the French Government. However, it also comprises other rights, notably the right to exploit commercially the marketing of the protected work, particularly in the form of licences granted in return for payment of royalties. It is this economic aspect of copyright which is the subject of the question submitted by the national court and, in this regard, *in the application of Article 36 of the Treaty there is no reason to make a distinction between copyright and other industrial and commercial rights.*"[53]

This uniform approach to copyright and industrial and commercial property rights seems to be entirely justified in so far as the applicability of Article 36 E.C. is concerned, for the commercial implications of intellectual property

---

[50] See also F.-K. Beier, "Industrial property and the free movement of goods in the internal European market" [1990] I.I.C. 131. At p. 148, he argues that the "specific subject-matter" is not a suitable criterion for demarcation and should be replaced by the distinction between legitimate and improper use. He points out that it has become clear that the "specific subject-matter" does not mean the "essential function" or the "very essence" of the right.

[51] Case 187/80: [1981] E.C.R. 2063; [1981] 3 C.M.L.R. 463, at para. 9.

[52] Joined Cases 55 and 57/80, *Musik-Vertrieb GmbH and K-Tel International v. GEMA*, Judgment of January 20, 1981: [1981] E.C.R. 147; [1981] 2 C.M.L.R. 44. The Court had already implicitly recognised this in the *Deutsche Grammophon Gesellschaft* case of 1971, see *supra*, pt. 1(1); and explicitly in the *Coditel I* case, see *infra*, pt. (b).

[53] *id.*, at para. 12. On the question of whether or not the moral right of the copyright holder comes within the scope of the E.C. Treaty, see L. Ubertazzi, "Copyright and the free movement of goods" [1985] I.I.C. 46 at 72–74. In general he gives a positive answer to that question, but excludes the application of the principle of exhaustion to moral rights.

protection is not very different from that of, for instance, patents.[54] The fact that copyright also embodies a moral right does not render its economic impact insignificant within the Common Market. It seems to be less coherent, however, to extend the uniformity in approach beyond that point.[55] Each industrial, commercial and intellectual property right has a specific function to fulfil so that the justification for maintaining such a right may thus vary from one right to another.[56]

(ii) Straightforward application of consent theory

4.28   The Court did not, however, give a definition of the specific subject-matter of copyright in the *Musik-Vertrieb* case. The Court, applying the consent theory, went on to note that the author is free to choose the place where he puts his work into circulation according to his best interests:

> "which involve not only the level of remuneration provided in the Member State in question but other factors such as, for example, the opportunities for distributing his work and the marketing facilities which are further enhanced by virtue of the free movement of goods within the Community."[57]

As such, differences in the rates of remuneration existing in the various Member States cannot justify the reliance on national intellectual property rights to claim additional fees on the importation of the works. Similarly as in the *Sterling Drug* case, but contrary to the opinion of Advocate General Warner, the Court held that the fact that the lower royalties in the Member State of exportation are due to restrictions imposed by national law is not relevant.[58]

(iii) Specific subject-matter versus function

4.29   The best example of the fact that the Court takes an overall uniform approach to the application of Article 36 E.C. to intellectual property rights is probably the *Dansk Supermarked* case.[59] The question was posed of whether national provisions concerning both copyright and trade marks could be invoked to prohibit the parallel importation of goods, *in casu* second-rate goods, that had been marketed with the consent of the intellectual property owner in

---

[54] See also B. Harris, "Community law and intellectual property: recent cases in the Court of Justice" [1982] C.M.L.Rev. 61 at 63, where he writes that "had the expression 'intellectual property' been more favourable at the time the EEC Treaty was drafted, it might well have been used instead of 'industrial and commercial property'". Furthermore, he points to the "fine dividing-line" between copyright and other intellectual property rights, for instance concerning computer software, to conclude that "a separation between copyright and other intellectual property rights could be rather arbitrary".

[55] See also A. Dietz, "The harmonisation of copyright in the European Community" [1985] I.I.C. 379 at 390, where he writes: "... copyright cannot be viewed merely as one of many intellectual property rights, paying no attention to values."

[56] See *supra*, Chap. 2.

[57] Joined Cases 55 and 57/80: [1981] E.C.R. 147; [1981] 2 C.M.L.R. 44, at para. 25.

[58] See *supra*, pt. (1)(a)(v), and the contrary opinion of Advocate General Warner, delivered on November 11, 1980: [1981] E.C.R. 167 at 178–180.

[59] Case 58/80, *Dansk Supermarked v. Imerco*, Judgment of January 22, 1981: [1981] E.C.R. 181; [1981] 3 C.M.L.R. 590.

another Member State. The Court reiterated its point of view that Article 36 E.C. only admits derogations to Articles 30-34 E.C. to the extent that these are justified for the purpose of safeguarding rights which constitute the specific subject-matter of intellectual property. However, the Court ruled in a general way that:

> "The exclusive right guaranteed by the legislation on industrial and commercial property is exhausted when a product has been lawfully distributed on the market of another Member State by the actual proprietor of the right or with his consent."[60]

The Court did not distinguish between possible different justifications for enforcing the exclusive right in the copyright or in the trade mark. It also disregarded the fact that copyright gives protection against unauthorised reproduction of the protected work, whereas a trade mark gives protection against the unauthorised use of the trade mark but does not affect the possibility of marketing the product as such. It seems from this case that, according to the Court, the specific subject-matter of copyright is not related to the objective for which the exclusive right is granted nor to the characteristics which make each intellectual property right specific. Rather, in aiming to safeguard the internal market objective, the concept "specific subject-matter" is reduced to the one common denominator attributed to all intellectual property rights, namely the right to put the product on the market for the first time, at least in so far as distribution rights are concerned.

(b) Performance rights

(i) Main difference from distribution rights

Under the rules on the free movement of goods the Court had to rule on literary and artistic works where placing them at the disposal of the public was inseparable from the material form of the work. It was with the first intellectual property cases brought to its attention under the rules on services that the specific issue of performance rights was raised. The question was posed in the *Coditel* cases of whether an assignee of performing rights in a film could prohibit the exhibition of that film by means of cable diffusion when it was broadcast in another Member State with the consent of the original owner of the right.[61] The Court acknowledged that the peculiarity of these cases resided in the fact that performances of literary and artistic works, such as films, may be repeated infinitely so that the assignee of a performance right may have a legitimate interest in charging fees upon each public performance of the work.[62]

4.30

---

[60] *id.*, at para. 11.
[61] Case 62/79, *Coditel v. Ciné Vog Films (Coditel I)*, Judgment of March 18, 1980: [1980] E.C.R. 881; [1981] 2 C.M.L.R. 362. Case 262/81, *Coditel v. Ciné Vog Films (Coditel II)*, Judgment of October 6, 1982: [1982] E.C.R. 3381; [1983] 1 C.M.L.R. 49. On these cases, see for instance R. Joliet, P. Desaux, "Copyright in the case-law of the Court of Justice of the European Communities" in *Copyright in free and competitive markets* (W. Cornish ed. 1986) (ESC), pp. 21–40.
[62] Case 62/79: [1980] E.C.R. 881; [1981] 2 C.M.L.R. 362, at para. 12. Case 262/81: [1982] E.C.R. 3381; [1983] 1 C.M.L.R. 49, at para. 11.

(ii) Essential function versus specific subject-matter

4.31 Although in the *Coditel* cases the Court applied Article 36 E.C. by analogy and, in so doing, transposed the existence/exercise dichotomy to the rules on services,[63] it should be emphasised that the approach taken with regard to the exercise of intellectual property rights for performance rights differs from that for distribution rights. As seen above, for distribution rights, the principle of exhaustion applies upon the first marketing of the protected work with the consent of the intellectual property owner because the specific subject-matter of copyright is then held to be fulfilled. Considering that performances may be infinitely repeated, and are not inseparably linked to the material form of the work, the same rule will not necessarily apply to performance rights. Rather than the straightforward application of the specific subject-matter test, which would have entailed the exhaustion of the right in this specific case, the Court came to a contrary conclusion to the *Coditel* cases on the basis that:

> " ... the right of a copyright owner and his assigns to require fees for any showing of a film is *part of the essential function of copyright* in this type of literary and artistic work."[64]

In other words, in so far as performance rights are concerned it is the need to safeguard the essential function, rather than the specific subject-matter, that will determine whether the exercise of the intellectual property right should be upheld or struck down under Community law.

(c) Distinguishing between distribution and performance rights

4.32 In practice, distribution and performance rights may of course relate to one and the same literary and artistic work so that the question arises of which approach should prevail. This specific problem was submitted to the Court in the *Tournier* case concerning sound recordings.[65] The national court asked, *inter alia*, whether Articles 30 and 59 E.C. prohibit the application of national law which considers the public performance of a musical work to constitute an infringement of copyright, regardless of the fact that royalties for the reproduction of the work had been paid to the author in another Member State. In other words, the Court was asked whether an additional royalty could be imposed in the Member State of importation where the public performance was to take place, having regard to the prior judgments in the *Musik-Vertrieb* and *Coditel* cases. Rather than let one approach prevail over the other, the Court sought to reconcile its prior case law in the following manner:

> "It is true that the present case raises the specific question of the distinction between the conditions applicable to those two situations, in so far

[63] See *supra*, Chap. 3, pt. 2(3).
[64] Case 62/79: [1980] E.C.R. 881; [1981] 2 C.M.L.R. 362, at para. 14. See also Case 262/81: [1982] E.C.R. 3381; [1983] 1 C.M.L.R. 49, at para. 12.
[65] Case 395/87, *Ministère Public v. Tournier*, Judgment of July 13, 1989: [1989] E.C.R. 2521; [1991] 4 C.M.L.R. 248.

as sound-recordings are products covered by the provisions on the free movement of goods contained in Article 30 *et seq.* of the Treaty but are also capable of being used for public performance of the musical work in question. In such circumstances, the requirements relating to the free movement of goods and the freedom to provide services and those deriving from the observance of copyright must be reconciled in such a way that the copyright owners, or the societies empowered to act as their agents, may invoke their exclusive rights in order to require the payment of royalties for music played in public by means of a sound-recording, even though the marketing of that recording cannot give rise to the charging of any royalty in the country where the music is played in public."[66]

The Court thus reiterated the distinction between distribution and performance rights. Furthermore, it expressly clarified that whereas the charging of additional royalties may be prohibited in relation to distribution, it may nevertheless be upheld with regard to public performance of one and the same protected work.

(3) Trade marks

(a) Specific subject-matter and confusingly similar trade marks

As is apparent from the *Dansk Supermarked* case mentioned above, the Court **4.33** applies the same definition of "specific subject-matter" in so far as trade marks are concerned. It is held to be the right to the first marketing of the product bearing the trade mark by the trade mark proprietor or with his consent.[67] However, considering that the function of trade marks is to guarantee the origin of the product to the consumer so that it offers protection not only against the use of the same, but also confusingly similar, trade marks the Court has had to elaborate upon the scope of the specific subject-matter concept.[68] The Court thus acknowledged in *Terrapin v. Terranova* that a trade mark owner can also invoke his exclusive right to prohibit the importation of goods that have been lawfully marketed by a third party in another Member State under a confusingly similar trade mark, without infringing the rules on the free movement of goods.[69] It should be noted in this respect that in *Renault v. Audi* the Court ruled that the criteria for deciding whether or not there is a risk of confusion is a matter for national trade mark law to determine, at least in the absence of harmonisation, and is subject to the prohibition of arbitrary discrimination or disguised restrictions on intra-Community trade as laid

[66] Case 395/87: [1989] E.C.R. 2521; [1991] 4 C.M.L.R. 248, at para. 13.
[67] See *supra*, pt. (2)(a)(iii). See for instance also Case 16/74, *Centrafarm BV and Adriaan De Peijper v. Winthrop BV*, Judgment of October 31, 1974: [1974] E.C.R. 1183; [1974] 2 C.M.L.R. 480.
[68] Marenco points out that one of the problems with the definition of the specific subject-matter criterion is that it "has to be modified with every new case in order to fit the particular problem under consideration and to justify the solution to be given to it". See G. Marenco, and K. Banks, "Intellectual property and the Community rules on free movement: discrimination unearthed" (1990) 15 E.L.Rev. 224 at 230.
[69] Case 119/75, *Terrapin v. Terranova*, Judgment of June 22, 1976: [1976] E.C.R. 1039; [1976] 2 C.M.L.R. 482.

down in the second sentence of Article 36 E.C.[70] Two specific problems lay at the basis of a further elaboration of the concept of "specific subject-matter of trade marks". As is seen in the two sections below, it concerns the issue of repackaging of marked products by third parties on the one hand, and the issue of independent trade marks with a common origin on the other.

(b) Repackaging by third parties

(i) Hoffman-La Roche v. Centrafarm: issue

4.34 In the *Hoffman-La Roche* case, the preliminary question was posed of whether a trade mark owner could invoke his exclusive right to prohibit the importation of goods that had been put on the market of another Member State with his consent.[71] The peculiarity of the case was that the goods had been repackaged and the trade mark reaffixed to the new packet by a third party without the consent of the proprietor of the trade mark. Merely applying the exhaustion principle on the basis of a straightforward application of the consent theory, namely with as sole reference the first marketing of the goods and thereby paying no attention to the objectives of trade mark protection, would obviously have disregarded the function of the trade mark. The Court in *Terrapin v. Terranova* had held the latter to be to guarantee the origin of the product to the consumers.[72]

(ii) Link between essential function and specific subject-matter

4.35 In his approach to the *Hoffman-La Roche* case, Advocate General Capotorti took as a premise that:

> "it must be established whether there is a necessary connexion between the *essential function* of the mark and the right which German law appears to attribute to the plaintiff...."[73]

As such, he held that the national court had to look at whether the right to prohibit the repackaging of the product could be justified in this specific case by the need to avoid confusion as to the origin of the product.[74] The Court

---

[70] Case C–317/91, *Deutsche Renault AG V. Audi AG*, Judgment of November 30, 1993: [1993] E.C.R. I-6227, at paras. 29–39, concerning the use of the designations "Quadra" and "Quattra" for cars. Compare, however, to Case 16/83, *Prantl*, Judgment of March 13, 1984: [1984] E.C.R. 1299; [1985] 2 C.M.L.R. 238, especially also at paras. 34–38, where the Court seemingly applied the principle of mutual recognition also in the context of Article 36 E.C.

[71] Case 102/77, *Hoffman-La Roche v. Centrafarm*, Judgment of May 23, 1978: [1978] E.C.R. 1139; [1978] 3 C.M.L.R. 217. In an earlier case between the same parties, the same question was already posed by the national court, but the judgment of the European Court of Justice dealt mainly with the interpretation of Article 177 E.C.: see Case 107/76, *Hoffman-La Roche v. Centrafarm*, Judgment of April 24, 1977: [1977] E.C.R. 957; [1977] 2 C.M.L.R. 334.

[72] Case 119/75: [1976] E.C.R. 1039; [1976] 2 C.M.L.R. 482, at para. 6. On the function of trade marks, see *supra*, Chap. 2, pt. 3(4).

[73] Case 102/77, Advocate General Capotorti, opinion delivered on March 14, 1978: [1978] E.C.R. 1168 at 1173 (emphasis added).

[74] *id.*, at p. 1177. The Advocate General wrote: "I consider that it would be in breach of Article 36 of the Treaty to recognise the right of the proprietor of a mark to object in general to any alteration whatever in the packaging in order to ensure that the identity of the product is not misrepresented, without the need to establish whether in a given case there is an actual danger of this nature, having regard to the conditions under which the repackaging is carried out."

took a slightly different approach. Rather than look at the justification of the national legislation concerned, the Court rephrased the concept of specific subject-matter of trade marks. It was thereby expressly stated that this concept should be applied with regard to the specific function of trade marks.

(iii) Elaboration of specific subject-matter

The Court clarified and elaborated upon the specific subject-matter concept in relation to trade marks in the following manner: **4.36**

> "In relation to trade marks, the *specific subject-matter* is in particular to guarantee to the proprietor of the trade mark that he has the exclusive right to use that trade mark for the purpose of putting a product into circulation for the first time and therefore to protect him against competitors wishing to take advantage of the status and reputation of the trade mark by selling products illegally bearing that trade mark.
>
> In order to answer the question whether that exclusive right involves the right to prevent the trade mark being affixed by a third person after the product has been repackaged, *regard must be had to the essential function* of the trade mark, which is to guarantee the identity of the origin of the trade marked product to the consumer or ultimate user, by enabling him without any possibility of confusion to distinguish that product from products which have another origin.
>
> This *guarantee of origin* means that the consumer or ultimate user can be certain that a trade marked product which is sold to him has not been subject at a previous stage of marketing to interference by a third person, without authorisation of the proprietor of the trade mark, such as to affect the original condition of the product.
>
> The right attributed to the proprietor of preventing any use of the trade mark which is likely to impair the guarantee of origin so understood is therefore part of the specific subject-matter of the trade marked right."[75]

(iv) Justification in terms of essential function

One could maintain that, for the first time, the Court really looked at whether a specific feature of a specific type of intellectual property law, and thus the "existence" of a national provision, was justified under the first sentence of Article 36 E.C., although formally the distinction between the existence and the exercise of the right was upheld. This seems to be confirmed by the statement of the Court, at paragraph 8, that: **4.37**

> "It is accordingly justified under the first sentence of Article 36 to recognise that the proprietor of a trade-mark is entitled to prevent an importer of a trade-marked product, following repackaging of that product, from affixing the trade-mark to the new packaging without the authorisation of the proprietor."

The Court did not merely put the fact that it concerned the prohibition of parallel importation of protected goods in the balance against the rules on the

---

[75] Case 102/77: [1978] E.C.R. 1168; [1978] 3 C.M.L.R. 217 at para. 7 (emphasis added).

free movement of goods, but additionally looked at the justification invoked for granting the right to prohibit parallel importations. The Court also gave a general definition of the function of a trade mark, which, although commonly accepted in all Member States, seems to be a Community concept which cannot be subject to, or altered by, national law.

(v) "Misuse" in terms of essential function

4.38   However, the Court also pointed out that the "exercise" of the intellectual property right may nevertheless be prohibited under the second sentence of Article 36 E.C.:

> "if it is established that the *use* of the trade mark right by the proprietor, having regard to the marketing system he has adopted, will contribute to the artificial partitioning of the markets between Member States."[76]

It was specified that this will be the case if, in addition to the adverse effect on intra-Community trade, it is established that the repackaging cannot adversely affect the original condition of the product, the proprietor of the mark received prior notice of the marketing of the repackaged product, and it is stated on the new packaging by whom the product has been repackaged. These criteria were subsequently applied in the *Pfizer* case.[77] Here it was held that the trade mark proprietor could not rely on Article 36 E.C. to prohibit the importation by a third person of goods that had been marketed with his consent. In this particular case the third person had replaced the external wrapping by a transparent wrapping so that the internal packaging, which was left intact, and the trade mark were visible. It was further indicated on the external wrapping that the product was manufactured by the subsidiary of the trade mark proprietor and repackaged by the importer.

(vi) Clarification of "guarantee of origin" and misuse

4.39   The Court also confirmed this "new approach" to trade marks in *Centrafarm v. American Home Products*.[78] The question was raised of whether a trade mark owner, who put his product on the market in different Member States under different trade marks, could invoke his exclusive right to prohibit the importation of products which had been marketed with his consent in another Member State but to which a third party had affixed the trade mark of the Member State of importation instead of the trade mark of the Member State of exportation. The Court reiterated the link already established between the specific subject-matter and the function of trade marks in the *Hoffman-La Roche* case, but specified that the guarantee of origin, which is the essential function of a trade mark, implies that:

---

[76] *id.*, at para. 10 (emphasis added).
[77] Case 1/81, *Pfizer v. Eurim-Pharm GmbH*, Judgment of December 3, 1981: [1981] E.C.R. 2913; [1982] 1 C.M.L.R. 406.
[78] Case 3/78, *Centrafarm BV v. American Home Products Corporation*, Judgment of October 10, 1978: [1978] E.C.R. 1823; [1979] 1 C.M.L.R. 326.

"... only the proprietor may confer an identity upon the product by affixing the mark."[79]

Hence the right to prohibit the parallel importation in the given case was held to be justified under the first sentence of Article 36 E.C. However, the Court again emphasised that the exercise of this right might, nonetheless, be contrary to the second sentence of Article 36 E.C. if it were to be established by the national court that:

"the proprietor of different marks has followed the practice of using such marks for the purpose of artificially partitioning the markets."[80]

(c) Trade marks with a common origin

(i) HAG II: issue

The Court further specified the relationship between the function and the specific subject-matter of trade marks in the *HAG II* case.[81] As in *HAG I*,[82] the preliminary question was posed of whether a trade mark owner could invoke his exclusive right to prohibit the importation of similar products bearing the same mark where the trade mark had originally belonged to the same owner in the Member States concerned but had subsequently been divided due to government interference in the form of expropriation of enemy property. But taking into account the development of its case law in relation to intellectual property rights subsequent to the *HAG I* case, the Court in *HAG II* expressly reversed its ruling in the *HAG I*.[83]

4.40

(ii) The theory of common origin refuted

Advocate General Jacobs convincingly argued that the theory of common origin, as elaborated in *HAG I* and meaning that the proprietor of a trade mark cannot invoke his exclusive right to prohibit the importation of goods bearing an identical trade mark with the same origin, rested on a misinterpretation of the function of trade marks. He pointed out that the guarantee of origin refers to the commercial, rather than to the historical, origin of the marked goods.[84] As such, the basic function of a trade mark is to give the guarantee to the consumers that the product has been produced under the responsibility of one

4.41

---

[79] Case 3/78: [1978] E.C.R. 1823; [1979] 1 C.M.L.R. 326, at para. 13. See also F.-K. Beier, "The doctrine of exhaustion in EEC trade mark law – scope and limits" [1979] I.I.C. 20, where on the basis of a comparative study of the legislation of the Member States, he comes to the conclusion that the exclusive right of affixation belongs to the indispensable substance of trade mark protection.

[80] Case 3/78: [1978] E.C.R. 1823; [1979] 1 C.M.L.R. 326, at paras. 21–23. See also Joined Cases 266–267/87, *Royal Pharmaceutical Society of Great Britain*, Judgment of May 18, 1989: [1989] E.C.R. 1295; [1989] 2 C.M.L.R. 751, at para. 20.

[81] Case C–10/89, *SA CNL-Sucal NV v. Hag GF AG*, Judgment of October 17, 1990: [1990] E.C.R. I-3752; [1990] 3 C.M.L.R. 571.

[82] Case 192/73, *Van Zuylen Frères v. Hag AG*, Judgment of July 3, 1974: [1974] E.C.R. 731; [1974] 2 C.M.L.R. 127.

[83] Case C–10/89: [1990] E.C.R. I-3752; [1990] 3 C.M.L.R. 571, at para. 10.

[84] Case C–10/89: [1990] E.C.R. I-3752; [1990] 3 C.M.L.R. 571, Opinion of Advocate General Jacobs delivered on March 13, 1990, pt. 24 where he writes: "The consumer is not, I think, interested in the genealogy of trade marks; he is interested in knowing who made the goods that he purchases."

and the same person so that an expectation as to the quality of the goods, in other words goodwill, can be created. Negating the right to use the exclusive right to prohibit the importation of goods bearing the same trade mark but which are not produced by the trade mark proprietor, as was the result of *HAG I*, obviously effectively negates the very distinctive function of the trade mark and potentially destroys goodwill.[85] Or, as Advocate General Jacobs succinctly put it:

> "...it is difficult not to conclude that the essential function of the mark is compromised, its specific subject-matter is affected and – most seriously of all – its very existence is jeopardised. But none of those consequences ensued from the fragmentation of the HAG mark in 1944; they ensued from the Court's judgment in *HAG I*."[86]

(iii) Essential function as crucial criterion

4.42   The Court to a large extent followed up Advocate General Jacob's opinion through expressly acknowledging that:

> "For the trade mark to be able to fulfil (its) role, it must offer a guarantee that all goods bearing it have been produced under the control of a single undertaking which is accountable for their quality."[87]

It was thus held that the decisive factor was the absence of consent on behalf of the trade mark proprietor to put a similar product bearing a similar trade mark on the market by another independent undertaking. The Court stated that in spite of the common origin of the trade mark:

> "In such circumstances, *the essential function of the trade mark would be jeopardised* if the proprietor of the trade mark could not exercise the right conferred on him by national legislation to oppose the importation of similar goods bearing a designation liable to be confused with his own trade mark, because, in such a situation, consumers would no longer be able to identify for certain the origin of the marked goods and the proprietor of the trade mark could be held responsible for the poor quality of goods for which he was in no way accountable."[88]

Hence, it seems that the concept "essential function" is of a crucial importance in order to interpret the specific subject-matter of trade marks.[89] The practical result is that both the independent HAG trade mark holders in both

---

[85] The disregard of the function of the right was the main criticism of *HAG I*, as well as of other cases. See for, instance, A.-M. Constant, *"L'épuisement du droit à la marque: problématique et conséquences"* [1992] Ing.-Cons. 1 at 10; F. Gotzen, *"La libre circulation des produits couverts par un droit de propriété intellectuelle dans la jurisprudence de la Cour de Justice"* [1985] R.T.D.C. 467, especially at 472. However, the latter seems to suggest that instead of giving a real Community definition of the function of each specific intellectual property right, the Court should, in each case, refer back to national law. This would obviously lead to very different results in comparable cases and therefore be unacceptable.

[86] Opinion to Case C–10/89: [1990] E.C.R. I-3752; [1990] 3 C.M.L.R. 571, pt. 24.

[87] Case C–10/89: [1990] E.C.R. I-3752; [1990] 3 C.M.L.R. 571, at para. 13.

[88] Case C–10/89: [1990] E.C.R. I-3752; [1990] 3 C.M.L.R. 571, at para. 16 (emphasis added).

[89] Similarly, see W. Rothnie, "HAG II: putting the common origin doctrine to sleep" [1991] E.I.P.R. 24, at 28. He furthermore points out that "there is room for doubt about when "consent" will be crucial and when the essential function will prevail".

Member States concerned can, since the *HAG II* judgment, prohibit the importation under the same trade mark of each others goods.

(iv) Voluntary assignments: *Ideal-Standard*

Not surprisingly, the question has arisen in the subsequent *Ideal-Standard* case[90] of whether this reasoning can be transposed to the context of trade marks that have been subject to voluntary assignments or whether, to the contrary, it only applies in cases of government intervention as the Court seemed to suggest in *HAG II*.[91] It obviously would have been fundamentally inconsistent to make a distinction between these two cases.[92] The cause of the division of the trade mark does not affect the analysis of the essential function of the trade mark, whereas it is difficult to maintain that whether or not the function of the trade mark should be taken into account should depend on the historical background of the trade mark.[93] The Court fully acknowledged this in the *Ideal-Standard* case. It expressly held that the considerations elaborated upon in *Hag II*, in particular in terms of the need to safeguard the essential function of trade marks, apply:

> "...whether the splitting of the trade mark originally held by the same owner is due to an act of public authority or a contractual assignment."[94]

(v) The meaning of "consent"

The Court rejected the argument that the trade mark proprietor implicitly consented to marketing products bearing the trade mark through assigning it to third parties so that he should therefore accept the consequences of his choice in so far as the free movement of goods is concerned. The Court quite rightly emphasised the difference between licences and assignments, the ownership and possibility of control being retained with regard to the first but not with the latter. In the words of the Court:

> "In case of a licence, the licensee can control the quality of the licensee's products by including in the contract clauses requiring the licensee to comply with his instructions and giving him the possibility of verifying such compliance.[95] The origin which the trade mark is intended to guarantee is the same; it is not defined by reference to the manufacturer but by reference to the point of control of manufacture...

4.43

4.44

---

[90] Case C–9/93, *Ideal-Standard*, Judgment of June 22, 1994: [1994] E.C.R. I-2789.

[91] Case C–10/89: [1990] E.C.R. I-3752; [1990] 3 C.M.L.R. 571, at para. 19. After *HAG II* many articles already raised this issue. See, for instance, the following article by the Juge-Rapporteur in the *Ideal-Standard* case: R. Joliet, "*Droit de marques et libre circulation des marchandises: l'abandon de l'arrêt HAG I*" [1991] R.T.D.E. 169–185.

[92] See for instance G. Kunze, "Waiting for Sirena II – Trade mark assignment in the case law of the European Court of Justice" [1991] I.I.C. 327; I. Govaere, "*HAG II of de ommekeer in de rechtspraak van het Europese Hof van Justitie inzake merken met een gemeenschappelijke oorsprong*" [1992] R.W. 105.

[93] See also C. Shelley, "Abolition of the doctrine of common origin: some reflections on *HAG II* and its implications" [1991] *European Business Law Review* 87 at 90.

[94] Case C–9/93: [1994] E.C.R. I-2789, at para. 46.

[95] On the compatibility with Article 85 E.C. of intellectual property licensing agreements containing provisions with regard to type-approval and quality controls, see *infra*, Chap. 5, pt. 3(3)(d).

It should furthermore be stressed that the decisive factor is the possibility of control over the quality of goods, not the actual exercise of that control . . . .

Articles 30 and 36 thus debar the application of national laws which allow recourse to trade mark rights in order to prevent the free movement of a product bearing a trade mark whose use is under unitary control.

(The situation where unitary control of the trade mark has been severed following assignment for one or several Member States only) must be clearly distinguished from the case where the imported products come from a licensee or a subsidiary to which ownership of the trade mark has been assigned in the exporting State: a contract of assignment by itself, that is in the absence of any economic link, does not give the assignor any means of controlling the quality of products which are marketed by the assignee and to which the latter has affixed the trade mark."[96]

This distinction led the Court to clarify the meaning of the concept "consent" which entails exhaustion in the following manner:

"The consent implicit in any assignment is not the consent required for the application of the doctrine of exhaustion of rights. For that, the owner of the right in the importing State must, directly or indirectly, be able to determine the products to which the trade mark may be affixed in the exporting State and control their quality. That power is lost if, by assignment, control over the trade mark is surrendered to a third party having no economic link with the assignor."[97]

The potential practical effect of this ruling cannot be ignored. It was pointed out that upholding the right to exercise the exclusive rights inherent in the trade mark in the case of voluntary assignment of trade marks may, perhaps, tempt more than one manufacturer to resurrect national barriers through selling their right to the trade mark in another Member State. But, as the Court indicated, one should be aware of the possible application of Article 85 E.C. in this respect.[98]

(4) Industrial designs

(a) Basic concept

4.45 In so far as industrial designs are concerned, the Court has refrained from following a similar approach to that for trade marks. As for patents and for distribution rights related to copyright, the Court does not seem to take the specific function of the intellectual property right concerned into account but rather it makes a straightforward application of the principle of exhaustion on the basis of the consent theory. It is specifically with regard to industrial designs that the shortcomings of the specific subject-matter concept have been exposed.

---

[96] Case C–9/93: [1994] E.C.R. I-2789, at paras. 37–41.
[97] Case C–9/93: [1994] E.C.R. I-2789, at para. 43.
[98] See *infra*, Chap. 5, pt. 2(2).

(b) Shortcomings of specific subject-matter approach exposed

(i) *Keurkoop v. Nancy Kean*: issues

The Court was for the first time asked to pass a judgment concerning the pro-   **4.46**
tection of designs in the light of Article 36 E.C. in *Keurkoop v. Nancy Kean
Gifts*.[99] The first question raised the issue of whether the Uniform Benelux Act
on Designs and Models could be applied without infringing Article 36 E.C.
The effect of that Benelux Act is to grant exclusive rights in a design to the first
person to file it with the competent authorities, thereby applying the principle
of relative novelty.[1] It provides that only the person claiming to be the author
of the design, the employer, or the person commissioning the design, can challenge the right of the person who filed the design and defeat an application for
an injunction lodged by that person. The second question raised was whether
the application for an injunction in a Member State could be defeated if it
concerned products that the defendant had lawfully obtained in a Member
State where the applicant's design rights were not infringed through the marketing of the product. These questions arose out of an injunction by Nancy
Kean Gifts BV before the Dutch courts against Keurkoop BV for breach of its
exclusive design rights on a handbag. Keurkoop imported similar products
into the Netherlands. It obtained these products of Taiwanese origin through
a German company which marketed the handbags freely in Germany. Keurkoop objected that Nancy Kean Gifts was not the author of the design it had
filed nor had it filed it with the author's consent.

(ii) Conditions and procedures not subject to scrutiny

In its answer to the first question, the Court for the first time interpreted   **4.47**
Article 36 E.C. in relation to designs. It held:

> "By way of a preliminary observation it should be stated that, as the
> Court has already held as regards patent rights, trade marks and copy-
> right, *the protection of designs comes under the protection of industrial
> and commercial property within the meaning of Article 36* inasmuch as
> its aim is to define exclusive rights which are characteristic of that
> property."[2]

Nevertheless, the Court did not examine whether the exclusive right
granted on the basis of the principles of first to file and relative novelty was in
conformity with the function of industrial designs and models.[3] It merely held
that so far as the issue of whether this principle is compatible with Article 36
E.C. is concerned:

> "... the Court can only state that in the present state of Community law
> and in the absence of Community standardisation or harmonisation of

---

[99] Case 144/81, *Keurkoop BV v. Nancy Kean Gifts BV*, Judgment of September 14, 1982: [1982]
E.C.R. 2853; [1983] 2 C.M.L.R. 47.
[1] On the compatibility of the principle of relative novelty with E.C. law, see *infra*, Chap. 6, pt.
3(2).
[2] Case 144/81: [1982] E.C.R. 2853; [1983] 2 C.M.L.R. 47, at para. 14 (emphasis added).
[3] On the function of industrial designs, see *supra*, Chap. 2, pt. 3(5).

laws the determination of the conditions and procedures under which protection of designs is granted is a matter for national rules...."[4]

In other words, the Court regarded the conditions and procedures for obtaining design protection laid down in national law as coming under the "existence" of industrial and commercial property which is not to be affected by Community provisions.[5] It should again be recalled, however, that the Court subsequently held in the *Phil Collins* case that national intellectual property law is subject to the general principle of non-discrimination as laid down in Article 6 E.C.[6]

(iii) Conditions to "normal use"

4.48   In line with the existence/exercise dichotomy, the Court in its answer to the second question held that the exercise of the exclusive right can nonetheless be subject to Community principles. Without giving an express definition of the specific subject-matter of a design,[7] the Court held that the proprietor of a right to a design may prevent the importation of similar products from another Member State, provided that the following three conditions are all met:

> "...*that* the products in question have not been put into circulation in the other Member State by, or with the consent of, the proprietor of a right or a person legally or economically dependent on him, *that* as between the natural or legal persons in question there is no kind of agreement or concerted practice in restraint of competition *and finally that* the respective rights of the proprietors of the right to the design in the various Member States were created independently of one another."[8]

This last condition, which does not refer to a specific Treaty provision, was obviously inspired by Advocate General Reischl's opinion. He reflected upon the impact of the disparities that exist in national design law and was apparently concerned about the fact that the theory of common origin, as elaborated with respect to trade marks, might also be applied to industrial designs.

(iv) Impact of the theory of common origin

4.49   Advocate General Reischl pointed to the hypothetical situation in which different persons independently obtain a right to the same design in different Member States in accordance with national provisions. He argued that if these designs were traced back to the same creative work, and considered as

---

[4] Case 144/81: [1982] E.C.R. 2853; [1983] 2 C.M.L.R. 47, at para. 18.

[5] Marenco points out that this is precisely where the subject-matter approach falls short, because "the risk of having to assess the wisdom of the national legislator came into the open with *Keurkoop v. Nancy Kean*, the case which constituted the moment of truth for this test and from which it has never fully recovered". See G. Marenco, and K. Banks, "Intellectual property and the Community rules on free movement: discrimination unearthed" (1990) 15 E.L.Rev. 224, at 232.

[6] See *supra*, Chap. 2, pt. 4(1)(c)(iv).

[7] Advocate General Reischl, in his opinion to the case, proposed to take the same overall approach as concerns patents and copyright and thus to define, although not exhaustively, the subject-matter of designs as the right of the proprietor to market the product of a given industrial design for the first time, see Case 144/81: [1982] E.C.R. 2853, Opinion of Advocate General Reischl delivered on June 8, 1982, at p. 2880.

[8] Case 144/81: [1982] E.C.R. 2853; [1983] 2 C.M.L.R. 47, at para. 29 (emphasis added).

having an identical origin, and if the rule of common origin as the Court had elaborated in the *HAG I* case were to be transposed to the context of designs, then national law which merely required the filing of the design to benefit from protection would be deprived of its substance.[9] As such, it seems that neither the Advocate General nor the Court were concerned with safeguarding the essential function of a design when implicitly rejecting the theory of common origin, as had been the case for the refutation of the theory of common origin in relation to trade marks in the subsequent *HAG II* case.[10] The aim was rather merely to leave the "existence" of national design law intact.

It should be emphasised, however, that this endeavour to exclude the transposition of the theory of common origin to industrial designs found its expression in the introduction of the formal condition that the designs should have been created independently of one another. With the express departure from the theory of common origin concerning trade marks in the subsequent *HAG II* and *Ideal-Standard* cases, questions currently arise concerning the impact of voluntary assignments of industrial designs. Apparently this issue cannot simply be settled by analogy to the *Ideal-Standard* case without at least partly overruling the *Keurkoop* case. In instances of voluntary assignments of design rights it is obvious that the design rights are not created independently of one another. However, attaching importance to this fact amounts to reintroducing the theory of common origin, whereas the reasoning followed in the *Keurkoop* case aimed at rendering the latter inapplicable in so far as industrial designs were concerned. It therefore remains to be seen whether or not the Court would reiterate the condition that design rights have to be created independently of one another if it were to be asked to give a ruling in a case concerning voluntary assignments of industrial designs.

(c) Specific subject-matter and reversed consent theory

The Court for the first time gave an express definition of the specific subject-matter of industrial designs in the so-called spare parts cases of 1988. For instance in the *Volvo* case, it was held that: **4.50**

> "... the right of the proprietor of a protected design to prevent third parties from manufacturing and selling or importing, without its consent, products incorporating the design constitutes the very subject-matter of his exclusive right."[11]

Not only did the Court in this case refrain from taking the function of industrial designs into account, it also omitted the usual reference to the need to provide for the possibility of obtaining a reward in its definition of the specific subject-matter. The peculiarity nevertheless lies in the fact that although the formulation of this definition was, to a large extent, dictated by the facts of the case, the Court seemed to fully acknowledge that intellectual property rights are essentially prohibitive rights. Namely, they are exclusive rights that give

[9] Case 144/81: [1982] E.C.R. 2853 at 2883.
[10] See *supra*, pt. (3)(c).
[11] Case 238/87, *Volvo v. Veng*, Judgment of October 5, 1988: [1988] E.C.R. 6211; [1989] 4 C.M.L.R. 122, at para. 8.

the intellectual property owner the right to oppose certain acts by third parties. This view of intellectual property rights logically entails the application by the Court of what could be called a reversed consent theory, whereby the emphasis is put on the right to prohibit certain acts done not with, but rather without, the consent of the intellectual property owner.[12]

3. Traditional Approach to Establishing "Misuse" of Intellectual Property Rights

4.51   Under the rules on the free movement of goods and, by analogy, services, the Court has adopted a three-tier approach to determine whether or not intellectual property rights may be curtailed by Community law. Although these principles generally apply to all types of intellectual property rights without distinction,[13] trade marks and performance rights should be singled out because in some cases, at least, the Court has recognised their specific characteristics and taken their essential functions into account.

The first basic principle is the existence/exercise dichotomy which is derived from the application of the competition rules to anti-competitive behaviour of intellectual property owners. In essence, this means that the national intellectual property law, as such, will not be subject to scrutiny under Article 36. It is mainly the way in which the intellectual property owner makes use of his exclusive right that may be held to be incompatible with the principle of free movement of goods and services.[14]

Secondly, to delineate between normal use and misuse of intellectual property rights under the rules on the free movement of goods and services, the Court has introduced the concept of the "specific subject-matter" of intellectual property rights. For patents, copyright and industrial designs, the Community definition of the specific subject-matter is held to be merely the right to put the protected goods on the market for the first time by the intellectual property owner or with his consent. Whether or not the essential function of the intellectual property right concerned is thereby fulfilled seems to be irrelevant, or at least is ignored.[15] Instead of refining what was known as the reward theory, through determining what the real function of the exclusive right concerned is in a particular case, the development of the case law of the Court has given rise to the much simpler, but also less adequate, consent theory.[16]

This is different for trade marks and performance rights. With regard to these intellectual property rights, the Court has held that the concept of "specific subject-matter" is to be understood in the light of the essential function of the specific intellectual property right concerned. Furthermore, the Court has elaborated a Community definition of what constitutes this essential func-

---

[12] For a more detailed analysis, see *infra*, Chap. 7, pt. 4.

[13] Except for denominations of origin, to which a proper functionality test is applied, see *supra*, Chap. 3, pt. 4(2)(c)(iii).

[14] But see also *infra*, Chap. 6.

[15] See also F. Gotzen, "*La libre circulation des produits couverts par un droit de propriété intellectuelle dans la jurisprudence de la Cour de Justice*" [1985] R.T.D.C. 467 at 475.

[16] For an evaluation of the consent theory, see *infra*, Chap. 6, pt. 2(5).

tion, so that the latter is not subject to national laws or interpretation. It should be pointed out that in so far as trade marks are concerned, the consent of the proprietor of a trade mark to putting the protected goods on the market also plays an important role in defining the specific subject-matter. However, this is no longer considered to be the only viable criterion but is withheld only if the function of the trade mark is thereby duly safeguarded.

The third basic principle under the rules on the free movement of goods is the exhaustion of intellectual property rights. This essentially means that the intellectual property right concerned can no longer be invoked to prohibit the importation and sale of infringing goods, once the specific subject-matter of the exclusive right as described above is held to be fulfilled. In general this will be so when the intellectual property owner had consented to the protected product being put on the Community market. This basic principle, which has clearly been elaborated to safeguard the internal market objective to the full, does not apply as such to performance rights.

This three-tier approach to delineate between the normal use and abuse of **4.52** intellectual property rights under the rules on the free movement of goods and services is now firmly established, if not generally accepted. It will be illustrated in Chapter 6 that this approach has led to fundamental inconsistencies in the Court's case law, in particular when considering the inherent functions of the various exclusive rights and the impact on intellectual property owners. Further, in more recent cases this approach, based on the existence/exercise dichotomy, has proved to be inadequate in coming to terms with several important distortions posed to intra-Community trade by certain specific features of intellectual property law. It is not surprising, therefore, that a tendency to depart from the traditional approach is to be discerned in the latest case law on the free movement of goods so that this three-tier approach to intellectual property rights no longer applies unconditionally.[17]

---

[17] See *infra*, Chap. 6.

5. "Abuse" of Intellectual Property Rights under the Competition Rules

1. The Concepts "Misuse" and "Abuse"

It is apparent from the preceding chapter that the European Court of Justice is reluctant to tackle the existence of intellectual property rights under the rules on the free movement of goods. In the *Consten Grundig* and *Parke Davis* cases, the Court already made it clear that, at least theoretically, the existence of intellectual property rights should also be left untouched by the rules on competition.[1] It is only the "exercise" of an intellectual property right that can be curtailed if it constitutes an "abuse", rather than a "normal use", of the exclusive right. The question thus arises of how to distinguish between the "normal use" and "abuse" of intellectual property rights under the rules on competition. The criterion of "specific subject-matter" as used by the Court to delineate between "normal use" and "misuse" of intellectual property rights under Article 36 E.C. cannot be unconditionally applied in the context of the competition rules.[2] The extent to which the intellectual property owner can exercise his exclusive right to put the product on the market and to prohibit a third party making and marketing the protected product, or in other words the extent to which he may exercise the rights covered by the specific subject-matter of intellectual property rights, is precisely what is subject to scrutiny under the rules on competition.[3] This implies that the "abuse" of intellectual property rights under the rules on competition is not tantamount to the "misuse" of intellectual property rights under the rules on the free movement of goods. If these were not so, then as soon as the potentially anti-competitive behaviour of an intellectual property owner is "cleared" under Article 36 E.C., it would also automatically be "cleared" under Articles 85–86 E.C. It was submitted above that the application of a test based on the criterion of

5.01

---

[1] See *supra*, Chap. 3, pt. 4(2), and especially pt. 4(2)(b), where it is submitted that those two judgments are irreconcilable if one disregards the function of the intellectual property right concerned, because in the *Consten Grundig* case the trade mark is in fact virtually emptied of its substance.

[2] On the specific subject-matter concept, see *supra*, Chap. 4, pt. 4(2).

[3] For a contrary view, see A. Reindl, "The Magic of Magill: TV guides as a limit of copyright law?" [1993] I.I.C. 60. He argues that the Court has shifted from the exercise/existence test to the specific subject-matter test, rather than considering them to be complementary tests, and concludes that the rights coming within the "specific subject-matter" of intellectual property rights may not be limited by Community law in general. Though he admits in n. 31 that the Court in some recent Article 36 cases still referred to the existence/exercise dichotomy.

safeguarding the function of intellectual property rights would lead to an overall coherent and transparent Community approach to intellectual property rights.[4] However, the latter is currently not consistently used by the Court.[5]

The first section of this chapter deals with the Court's rulings about the basic principles underlying the relationship between the Community rules on competition and national intellectual property rights. The second section briefly analyses the Commission's approach to intellectual property licensing agreements under Article 85 E.C. and the appraisal made thereof by the Court. The Commission's approach to intellectual property rights under Article 86 E.C., as well as the consideration of this by the Community courts, in particular in the *Hilti* and *Magill* cases, is examined in the third section. The final section highlights the incidence of Articles 85 and 86 E.C. as clarified in the *Tetra Pak* case.[6]

2. Basic Principles Introduced by the Court

(1) The basic rule

5.02   From the early cases one learns that the general rule is that the rules on competition are fully applicable to intellectual property rights.[7] But the exception to the rule is probably more important, namely, the "essence" or the "normal use" of intellectual property rights cannot be curtailed in order to safeguard competition in the market.[8] The problem is that the Court has not given a definition of the "essence" of intellectual property rights, but has taken a case by case approach. From the *Parke Davis* case it is clear that an intellectual property right taken by itself will not infringe Articles 85 or 86 E.C.[9] As soon as a licence is given or a concerted practice is established the question arises of whether, and when, Article 85 E.C. will apply. Similarly, in order for Article 86 E.C. to apply an anti-competitive element additional to the "normal" use of the intellectual property right will be needed. Rather than give clear indications as to when this requirement will be fulfilled the Court has, in its case law, only gradually elaborated upon the concept of "abuse" of intellectual property rights in the context of the competition rules.

---

[4] See *supra*, Chap. 3, pt. 4(2)(c).

[5] But see *infra*, the *Magill* cases, at pt. 4(3), where it is submitted that both the Commission and the Court of First Instance for the first time introduced the concept of the "essential function" of an intellectual property right in cases concerning intellectual property rights other than trade marks or performance rights.

[6] For a general introduction to E.C. competition law and practice, and a detailed analysis of the procedural rules, it is suggested the reader consults the following books: V. Korah, *An introductory guide to E.C. competition law and practice* (5th ed., 1994, Sweet & Maxwell); C.S. Kerse, *EEC antitrust procedure* (3rd ed., 1994, Sweet & Maxwell).

[7] See Joined Cases 56 and 58/64, *Consten and Grundig v. Commission*: [1966] E.C.R. 299; [1966] C.M.L.R. 418, see *supra*, Chap. 3, pt. 4(2)(a).

[8] See Case 24/67, *Parke Davis v. Probel et al.*: [1968] E.C.R. 55; [1968] C.M.L.R. 47, see *supra*, Chap. 3, pt. 4(2)(v).

[9] *id.*, Case 24/67: [1968] E.C.R. 55; [1968] C.M.L.R. 47.

(2) Article 85 E.C. and intellectual property rights

Article 85 E.C. reads as follows: 5.03

> "1. The following shall be prohibited as incompatible with the common market: all agreements between undertakings, decisions by associations of undertakings and concerted practices which may affect trade between Member States and which have as their object or effect the prevention, restriction or distortion of competition within the common market, and in particular those which:
>
> (a) directly or indirectly fix purchase or selling prices or any other trading conditions;
>
> (b) limit or control production, markets, technical development, or investment;
>
> (c) share markets or sources of supply;
>
> (d) apply dissimilar conditions to equivalent transactions with other trading partners, thereby placing them at a competitive disadvantage;
>
> (e) make the conclusion of contracts subject to acceptance by the other parties of supplementary obligations which, by their very nature or according to commercial usage, have no connection with the subject of the contracts.
>
> 2. Any agreements or decisions prohibited pursuant to this Article shall be automatically void.
>
> 3. The provisions of paragraph 1 may, however, be declared inapplicable in the case of (any such agreement, decision or concerted practice) which contributes to improving the production or distribution of goods or to promoting technical or economic progress, while allowing consumers a fair share of the resulting benefit, and which does not:
>
> (a) impose on the undertakings concerned restrictions which are not indispensable to the attainment of these objectives;
>
> (b) afford such undertakings the possibility of eliminating competition in respect of a substantial part of the products in question."

(a) Enforcement of intellectual property rights

The relationship between Article 85 E.C. and intellectual property rights is, at   5.04
first sight, rather simple. The Court has consistently held that Article 85(1) E.C. does not apply to the mere unilateral enforcement of an intellectual property right, which, being a legal right granted by national law and not an agreement or a concerted practice, does not fulfil the requirements of that provision.[10] It is therefore submitted that the Court was not quite accurate in ruling in the *HAG I* case that Article 85(1) E.C. did not apply to the facts because no legal, financial, technical or economic link existed between the two independent proprietors of a trade mark with a common origin.[11] Article

---

[10] See for instance, concerning patents: Case 24/67, *Parke Davis*: [1968] E.C.R. 55; [1968] C.M.L.R. 47; concerning copyrights and akin rights: Case 78/70, *Deutsche Grammophon Gesellschaft*: [1971] E.C.R. 487; [1971] C.M.L.R. 631, at para. 5; concerning designs: Case 144/81, *Keurkoop*: [1982] E.C.R 2853; [1983] 2 C.M.L.R. 47, at para. 27; concerning trade marks: Case 51/75, *EMI Records*: [1976] E.C.R. 811; [1976] 2 C.M.L.R. 235, at para. 26.
[11] Case 192/73, *HAG I*: [1974] E.C.R. 731; [1974] 2 C.M.L.R. 127, at paras. 4–5.

85(1) E.C. did not apply simply because there was no agreement or concerted practice between the two intellectual property owners in the sense of Article 85(1) E.C. that lay at the basis of the division of the mark.[12]

(b) Undertakings belonging to a same concern

5.05 The Court specified in the *Centrafarm v. Sterling Drug* case that Article 85(1) E.C. does not apply either to agreements or to concerted practices relating to intellectual property rights between undertakings that belong to a same concern, as a parent company and a subsidiary, if the following conditions are fulfilled. Namely, they form an economic unit, the subsidiary cannot determine freely its market behaviour, and the agreement merely concerns the internal allocation of tasks.[13] It was confirmed subsequently by the Court that, as a general rule, Article 85(1) E.C. does not apply to such agreements.[14]

(c) Agreements of minor importance

5.06 The Court also clarified that for agreements to come under the scope of Article 85(1) E.C. they must have an "appreciable" effect on intra-Community trade. In the *Völk v. Vervaecke* case of 1969, it was held that whether or not agreements are of minor importance must be established by reference to the actual circumstances of the agreement. The Court thus introduced the so-called *de minimis* rule by stating:

> "Consequently an agreement falls outside the prohibition in Article 85 when it has only an insignificant effect on the markets, taking into account the weak position which the persons concerned have on the market of the product in question."[15]

The Commission subsequently issued a Notice on Agreements of Minor Importance in which it quantified the concept of "appreciable effect on intra-Community trade". In the Commission's view, an agreement does not fall within Article 85(1) E.C. if:

> "– the goods or services which are the subject of the agreement [...] together with the participating undertaking's goods or services which are considered by users to be equivalent in view of their characteristics, price and intended use, do not represent more than 5% of the total market for such goods or services [...] in the area of the common market affected by the agreement and
> – the aggregate annual turnover of the participating undertakings does not exceed 300 million ECU"

or

---

[12] See also J. Johannes, and G. Wright, "In defense of Café Hag" (1976) 1 E.L.Rev. 230 at 236, where they criticise the Court's reasoning without, however, contesting the conclusion.
[13] Case 15/74, *Centrafarm v. Sterling Drug*: [1974] E.C.R. 1147; [1974] 2 C.M.L.R. 480, at para. 41.
[14] See for instance Case 30/87, *Corinne Bodson v. Pompes funèbres des régions libérées SA*, Judgment of May 4, 1988: [1988] E.C.R. 2479; [1989] 4 C.M.L.R. 984, at para. 19.
[15] Case 5/69, *Völk v. Vervaecke*, Judgment of July 9, 1969: [1969] E.C.R. 295; [1969] C.M.L.R. 273, at para. 5/7.

"...if the abovementioned market share or turnover is exceeded by not more than one tenth during two successive financial years."[16]

It should be pointed out that this notice is in no way binding upon the Court; it merely indicates the approach the Commission will take. Furthermore, the notice expressly stipulates that it will not apply where competition is restricted by the cumulative effects of parallel networks of similar agreements established by several manufacturers or dealers.[17] This means that it does not always suffice to consider the effect of the agreement on its own for, as the Court has consistently held, if similar agreements do exist this may be "a factor in the economic and legal context within which the contract must be judged".[18] In the *Delimitis* case, the Court thus clarified that if the agreement is part of a supplier's network of exclusive purchasing agreements having a cumulative effect on competition, then it may nevertheless come under Article 85(1) E.C. if it "makes a significant contribution to the sealing-off effect brought about by the totality of those agreements in their economic and legal context", having regard to the position of the contracting parties in the relevant market and the duration of the agreement.[19]

(d) All other restrictive practices

The difficulty thus arises when those three hypotheses do not apply to the facts, for in all other cases the application of Article 85 E.C. to the exercise of intellectual property rights cannot simply be discarded. Neither can it be taken for granted. The Court has, in several cases, held that the exercise of intellectual property rights will be contrary to Article 85(1) E.C.: **5.07**

"...each time it manifests itself as the subject, the means or the result of an agreement (or a concerted practice) which, by preventing imports from other Member States of products lawfully distributed there, has as its effect the partitioning of the market."[20]

or

"...where they serve to give effect to an agreement, decision or concerted practice which may have as its object or effect the prevention, restriction or distortion of competition in the common market."[21]

As such, the exercise of an intellectual property right may fall within the scope of Article 85(1) E.C. if it is the subject, the means or the consequence of a restrictive practice which, furthermore, has an appreciable effect on

---

[16] [1986] O.J. C231/2, at pts. 7 and 8. (For the latest amendment raising the turnover threshold from 200 to 300 million ECUs, see [1994] O.J. C368/20.)

[17] *id.*, pt. 16.

[18] Case 23/67, *Brasserie de Haecht v. Wilkin*, Judgment of December 12, 1967: [1967] E.C.R. 407; [1968] C.M.L.R. 26.

[19] Case C–234/89, *Delimitis v. Henninger Bräu*, Judgment of February 28, 1991: [1991] E.C.R. I-935; [1992] 5 C.M.L.R. 210, at para. 27. On the implications of this case, see for instance M. Levitt, "Delimitis and De Minimis" [1994] E.C.L.R. 283.

[20] Case 78/70, *Deutsche Grammophon Gesellschaft*: [1971] E.C.R. 487; [1971] C.M.L.R. 631, at para. 6.

[21] Case 262/81, *Coditel II*: [1982] E.C.R. 3361; [1982] 1 C.M.L.R. 49, at para. 14.

intra-Community trade. This means that both the effect of the agreement, or the concerted practice, and the intention of the parties may be taken into account. It also implies that not only intellectual property licensing agreements,[22] but also concerted practices[23] and agreements whereby the intellectual property right is assigned to a third party or created or confirmed in its own right, might be prohibited by Article 85(1) E.C. The Court already clarified in the *Consten Grundig* case that the fact that the national exclusive intellectual property right may originate in legal or factual circumstances other than the agreement or the concerted practice such as, for instance, the registration of a trade mark in conformity with national procedures, does not preclude the application of Article 85(1) E.C.[24] The Court reiterated this principle in relation to trade mark delimitation contracts in the *BAT* case, where it held that:

> "... agreements known as 'delimitation agreements' are lawful and useful if they serve to delimit, in the mutual interest of the parties, the spheres within which their respective trade marks may be used, and are intended to avoid confusion or conflict between them. That is not to say, however, that such agreements are excluded from the application of Article 85 of the Treaty if they also have the aim of dividing up the market or restricting competition in other ways."[25]

In the *Ideal-Standard* case of 1994, the Court settled the controversy with regard to the applicability in principle of Article 85(1) E.C. to trade mark assignments by unequivocally stating:

> "..., where undertakings independently of each other make trade mark assignments following a market-sharing agreement, the prohibition of anti-competitive agreements under Article 85 applies and assignments which give effect to that agreement are consequently void. However, [...], that rule and the accompanying sanction cannot be applied mechanically to every assignment. Before a trade mark assignment can be treated as giving effect to an agreement prohibited under Article 85, it is

---

[22] See *infra*, pt. 3.

[23] See for instance Joined Cases 110 and 241–242/88, *Lucazeau v. SACEM*, Judgment of July 13, 1989: [1989] E.C.R. 2811; [1991] 4 C.M.L.R. 248, at paras. 17–20.

[24] See Joined Cases 56 and 58/64, *Consten Grundig v. Commission*: [1966] E.C.R. 299; [1966] C.M.L.R. 418. (See also *supra*, Chap. 3, pt. 4(2)(a) and Case 40/70, *Sirena v. Eda*: [1971] E.C.R. 79; [1971] C.M.L.R. 260, at para. 11.)

[25] Case 35/83, *BAT v. Commission*, Judgment of January 30, 1985: [1985] E.C.R. 363; [1985] 2 C.M.L.R. 470, at para. 33. For an analysis of trade mark delimitation agreements in E.C. law, see for instance B. Smulders, P. Glazener, "*Delimiteringsovereenkomsten en de bepalingen van het EEG-verdrag inzake het vrij verkeer van goederen en de mededinging*" [1991] B.I.E. 103.

necessary to analyse the context, the commitments underlying the assignment, the intention of the parties and the considerations for the assignment."[26]

The problem is, however, to establish when those conditions will be held to be fulfilled in practice.

(i) Examples given by the Court

As mentioned above, in the *Consten Grundig* case of 1966 the Court held an **5.08** agreement whereby one party was given the right to register a trade mark in a particular Member State, whereas the trade mark was internationally registered in the name of the other party, to be incompatible with Article 85(1) E.C.[27] In subsequent cases the Court did not offer clear criteria for the national courts to determine when an agreement transferring rights, or concerted practices between independent intellectual property owners, would be contrary to Article 85(1) E.C. but merely gave other examples of when this could be so.

For instance, in the *Sirena* case, the Court held that the combination of different assignments of national trade marks concerning the same product might be contrary to Article 85(1) E.C. if the result is that barriers are resurrected between the Member States.[28] In *EMI Records v. CBS* it was held that an agreement concerning trade marks between traders inside and outside the Community, whereby the Common Market as a whole would be isolated, could be contrary to Article 85(1) E.C. This was held to be the case in particular if the trader outside had subsidiaries inside the Community which could have used the trade mark within the Community in the absence of the agreement.[29] In the *Lucazeau* case concerning copyright, it was held that although reciprocal representation contracts between copyright collecting societies are not, as such, contrary to Article 85(1) E.C., it might be otherwise if those contracts entailed exclusivity by virtue of the fact that those collecting societies undertook not to grant access to their musical repertoires to anyone established outside their territory.[30] However, the conferment of exclusivity is not the decisive factor which will "trigger" Article 85(1) E.C. In the *Coditel II* case the Court held that an agreement conferring an exclusive right to exhibit a film for a specific period in the territory of a Member State is not, as such, contrary to Article 85 E.C. It added, however, that the manner in which the exclusivity conferred by the contract is exercised should not be "subject to a situation in the economic or legal sphere the object or effect of which is to prevent or

---

[26] Case C–9/93: [1994] E.C.R. I-2789, at para. 59. On this controversy in legal doctrine, and in favour of the solution as subsequently adopted by the Court in *Ideal-Standard*, see I. Govaere, *"HAG II of de ommekeer in de rechtspraak van het Europese Hof van Justitie inzake merken met een gemeenschappelijke oorsprong"* [1992] R.W. 105 at 110–112. In the same sense, see H. Johannes, *"La propriété industrielle et le droit d'auteur dans le droit des Communautés Européennes"* [1973] R.T.D.E. 537 at 578, where he points out that the theory which holds that Article 85 does not apply to trade mark assignments, because this kind of agreement does not contain an element of duration, does not explain where it finds the requirement for such an additional element since it is not mentioned in Article 85 E.C.

[27] See *supra*, Chap. 3, pt. 4(2)(a).

[28] Case 40/70, *Sirena v. Eda*: [1971] E.C.R. 69; [1971] C.M.L.R. 260, at para. 10.

[29] Case 51/75, *EMI Records v. CBS (U.K.) Ltd.*: [1976] E.C.R. 811; [1976] 2 C.M.L.R. 235, at para. 28–29.

[30] Joined Cases 110 and 241–242/88: [1989] E.C.R. 2881; [1991] 4 C.M.L.R. 248, at para. 14.

restrict the distribution of films or to distort competition within the cinematographic market, regard being had to the specific characteristics of that market".[31] Also, in the *Keurkoop* case concerning industrial designs, the Court
held that Article 85(1) E.C. can apply to a situation whereby "persons simultaneously or successively file the same design in various Member State in order
to divide up the markets within the Community among themselves".[32]

(ii) Restrictive practices before the E.C. Treaty entered into force

5.09 Restrictive practices such as licensing agreements or assignments of intellectual property rights which took effect before the E.C. Treaty came into force
or before a state adhered to the E.C. are not, as such, immune from the application of the E.C. rules on competition. The Court has held in this respect that
for Article 85(1) E.C. to apply it is "both necessary and sufficient that they
continue to produce their effects after that date".[33] However, the Court specified in the *EMI Records v. CBS* case that Article 85 E.C. will not apply if the
effects of a trade mark assignment do not exceed those that constitute the
normal exercise of the right.[34] The underlying rationale is clarified by Advocate General Warner in his opinion on the case. He pointed out that the agreement itself was not contrary to the E.C. Treaty in the *EMI Records* case
because it was concluded before the entry into force of the E.C. Treaty. He
therefore concluded that the exercise of intellectual property rights originating in an agreement that was not prohibited could not themselves be prohibited.[35] This case was often invoked to support the view that trade mark
assignments, as such, did not come under Article 85(1) E.C.[36] However, this
view has now been formally rejected by the Court in the above-mentioned
Ideal-Standard case.

(3) Article 86 E.C. and intellectual property rights

5.10 Article 86 E.C. reads as follows:

> "Any abuse by one or more undertakings of a dominant position within
> the common market or in a substantial part of it shall be prohibited as
> incompatible with the common market in so far as it may affect trade
> between Member States.
>
>   Such abuse may, in particular, consist in:
> (a) directly or indirectly imposing unfair purchase or selling prices or
> other unfair trading conditions;
> (b) limiting production, markets or technical development to the preju-
> dice of consumers;

---

[31] Case 262/81, *Coditel II*: [1982] E.C.R. 3361; [1982] 1 C.M.L.R. 49, at para. 20.
[32] Case 144/81, *Keurkoop v. Nancy Kean Gifts*: [1982] E.C.R 2853; [1983] 2 C.M.L.R. 47, at para. 28. See also *supra*, Chap. 4, pt. 2(4)(b)(iii).
[33] Case 40/70, *Sirena*: [1971] E.C.R 69; [1971] C.M.L.R. 260, at para. 12.
[34] Case 51/75, *EMI Records v. CBS*: [1976] E.C.R 811; [1976] 2 C.M.L.R. 235, at para. 32.
[35] Case 51/75: [1976] E.C.R. 811; [1976] 2 C.M.L.R. 235, opinion delivered on March 31, 1976: [1976] E.C.R. 852.
[36] See for instance P.-J. Slot, "The application of Articles 3(F), 5 and 85 to 94 EEC" (1987) 12 E.L.Rev. 179 at 188, where he illustrates the statement: "the exemptions to Article 30 extend to agreements under Article 85" by a reference to the *EMI* case.

(c) applying dissimilar conditions to equivalent transactions with other trading parties, thereby placing them at a disadvantaged position;
(d) making the conclusion of contracts subject to acceptance by the other parties of supplementary obligations which, by their nature or according to commercial usage, have no connection with the subject of such contracts."

(a) Enforcement of intellectual property rights

The relationship between intellectual property rights and Article 86 E.C. is somewhat different. Contrary to Article 85 E.C., no agreement or concerted practice is required for Article 86 E.C. to apply.[37] This implies that the mere unilateral enforcement of the exclusive right by an intellectual property owner may, in principle, suffice to render this provision applicable. The conditions for the application of Article 86 E.C., as stipulated in the E.C. Treaty, are threefold. There has to be a dominant position in the Community market or a substantial part thereof, which is abused by undertakings, and whereby intra-Community trade is affected. The Court has consistently held that the exercise of intellectual property rights does not come within the scope of this provision if those three elements are not present.[38] Considering the special competitive position intellectual property rights confer on the right-owner, the fundamental question is to determine when those conditions will be held to be fulfilled.   **5.11**

(b) Dominant position

Intellectual property rights are exclusive rights which means that the right-owner can prohibit the marketing of infringing goods, regardless of whether or not they are imported from another Member State. As such, they create a privileged position on the market for the intellectual property owner because they confer market power. The Court has held that the use of the exclusive right to prohibit importations of infringing goods, which is allowed by Article 36 E.C., does not automatically imply that the intellectual property owner has a dominant position in the market.[39] Concurrent with the exclusive right, intellectual property rights usually also confer the right to distribute the protected product. The Court has also held that the mere exercise of this right, which is also lawful under Article 36 E.C., does not in itself constitute a dominant position.[40]   **5.12**

In other words, the existence and the normal exercise of intellectual property rights under Article 36 E.C. is not necessarily tantamount to conferring a dominant position in the sense of Article 86 E.C. Rather, the Court has clarified that one has to look at whether the intellectual property owner can impede the maintenance of effective competition in a substantial part of the

---

[37] On the incidence of Articles 85 and 86 E.C., see *infra*, pt. 5.
[38] See for instance Case 24/67, *Parke Davis*: [1968] E.C.R. 55; [1968] C.M.L.R. 47. Case 78/70, *Deutsche Grammophon*: [1971] E.C.R. 487; [1971] C.M.L.R. 631.
[39] Concerning the right to prohibit the marketing and importation of infringing products, see for instance Case 40/70, *Sirena*: [1971] E.C.R 69; [1971] C.M.L.R. 260, at para. 16.
[40] Concerning the exercise of the right by way of distribution, see Case 78/70, *Deutsche Grammophon*: [1971] E.C.R. 487; [1971] C.M.L.R. 631, at para. 16.

relevant market.[41] This means that regard should be had to the existence, or possible entry, of competing products into the market that could be substituted for the protected products.[42]

(c) Abuse of a dominant position

5.13   It does not suffice to prove that an intellectual property owner occupies a dominant position in the relevant market for Article 86 E.C. to apply to the exercise of intellectual property rights. A further requirement is that the dominant position is also abused. In the *Hoffman-La Roche* case the Court held that:

> "... to the extent to which the exercise of a trade mark right is lawful in accordance with the provisions of Article 36 of the Treaty, such exercise is not contrary to Article 86 of the Treaty *on the sole ground* that it is the act of an undertaking occupying a dominant position on the market if the trade mark right has not been used as an instrument for the abuse of such a position."[43]

The Court seems to imply that if the existence of a dominant position is established one has first to ascertain whether or not the contested exercise of the intellectual property right is lawful under Article 36 E.C. If it is not, then its exercise cannot become lawful under the rules on competition. But this rule does not apply vice versa.[44] If the exercise is covered by the specific subject-matter of the intellectual property right under Article 36 E.C., it will not be automatically lawful under the rules on competition. An additional element, however, will be needed to hold that the intellectual property right has been abused under Article 86 E.C.[45] This reasoning was reiterated in the *Basset v. SACEM* case. The Court held that the mere use of the intellectual property right to charge a supplementary mechanical reproduction fee, which had been upheld under Article 36 E.C., "does not *in itself* constitute abusive conduct for the purpose of Article 86 of the Treaty", before giving examples of conduct that nevertheless could be held to be abusive.[46] The question thus arises as to what additional element is needed for the exercise of intellectual property rights by an undertaking in a dominant position to be qualified as abusive.

[41] See for instance, Case 78/70, *Deutsche Grammophon*: [1971] E.C.R. 487; [1971] C.M.L.R. 631, at para. 17. Case 51/75, *EMI v. CBS*: [1976] E.C.R. 811; [1976] 2 C.M.L.R. 235, at para. 36. For an analysis of the relevant market concept in relation to intellectual property protected products, see *infra*, Chap. 8, pt. 3.

[42] See for instance Case 40/70, *Sirena*: [1971] E.C.R 69, [1971] C.M.L.R. 260, at para. 16.

[43] Case 102/77, *Hoffman-La-Roche*: [1978] E.C.R. 1139; [1978] 3 C.M.L.R. 217, at para. 16, (emphasis added).

[44] It is submitted that Reindl neglected the *Hoffman-La Roche* judgment through merely applying an *a contrario* reasoning without paying attention to the Court's further qualification, see A. Reindl, *op. cit.*, p. 64 *et seq.*

[45] For an analysis of the concept of "abuse" of a dominant position by an intellectual property owner, see *infra*, Chap. 8, pt. 4.

[46] Case 402/85, *Basset v. SACEM*: [1987] E.C.R. 1747; [1987] 3 C.M.L.R. 173, at para. 18, (emphasis added). This was also implicitly held in Case 51/75, *EMI Records*: [1976] E.C.R. 811; [1976] 2 C.M.L.R. 235, at para. 37, where the Court held that the exercise of the right to prohibit importation of infringing goods does not constitute an abuse of a dominant position.

(d) Examples of abusive conduct given by the Court

The Court has not offered clear and precise criteria to distinguish between the normal and the abusive exercise of intellectual property rights. In response to the facts of the cases brought before it, which mostly concerned copyright collecting societies, the Court has merely given examples of practices that, provided they may affect trade between Member States,[47] could be held to be contrary to Article 86 E.C. For instance, the Court has consistently rejected the argument that higher prices are proof of an abuse. The Court has, nonetheless, added that higher prices may be indicative of an abuse if they cannot be justified by objective criteria.[48] Similarly, the Court has held in the above-mentioned *Basset v. SACEM* case that imposing unfair conditions could be contrary to Article 86 E.C.[49] In *BRT II*, the Court held that the imposition on its members, by an undertaking entrusted with the exploitation of copyright, of obligations which are not indispensable for the attainment of its objective constitutes unfair conditions contrary to Article 86 E.C.[50] The concept of "unfair conditions" was further elaborated upon in the *Tournier* and *Lucazeau v. SACEM* cases in relation to third parties. It was held to include the non-objectively justifiable imposition of higher rates of royalties compared to other Member States.[51] In the *Volvo* case concerning industrial designs, analysed in detail below,[52] the Court held that an arbitrary refusal to deliver spare parts to independent repairers, the fixing of prices for spare parts at an unfair level, or a decision to no longer produce spare parts for a particular model even though many cars of that model remain in circulation, may be contrary to Article 86 E.C.

The absence of clear guidelines given by the Court means that the application of Article 86 E.C. to intellectual property rights has to take place on a case by case basis and may give rise to controversy. As in the case of Article 85 E.C., the Commission's approach to Article 86 E.C., and the consideration of this by the Community Courts namely in the *Hilti* and *Magill* cases,[53] provides somewhat more clarity without necessarily providing more legal certainty.

5.14

---

[47] On the concept of "affecting intra-Community trade" in relation to intellectual property rights, see *infra*, Chap. 8, pt. 5.
[48] Case 78/70, *Deutsche Grammophon*: [1971] E.C.R. 487; [1971] C.M.L.R. 631, at para. 19. Case 40/70, *Sirena*: [1971] E.C.R 69; [1971] C.M.L.R. 260, at para. 17.
[49] Case 402/85, *Basset v. SACEM*: [1987] E.C.R. 1747; [1987] 3 C.M.L.R. 173, at para. 19.
[50] Case 127/73, *BRT v. SABAM and NV Fonior*, Judgment of March 27, 1974: [1974] E.C.R. 313; [1974] 2 C.M.L.R. 238, at para. 15.
[51] See Case 395/87, *Ministère Public v. Jean-Louis Tournier*, Judgment of July 13, 1989: [1989] E.C.R. 2521; [1991] 4 C.M.L.R. 248, at para. 46; Joined Cases 110 and 241–242/88: [1989] E.C.R. 2881; [1991] 4 C.M.L.R. 248, at para. 33. It should be pointed out, however, that the Commission has in the past rejected complaints in this respect. See Case T–114/92, *BEMIM v. Commission* and Case T–5/93, *Tremblay, Lucazeau and Kestenberg v. Commission*, both Judgments of January 24, 1995: [1995] E.C.R. II-147. In both cases the Court of First Instance partly annulled the contested decisions of the Commission. It did so in so far as the latter rejected the applicants' allegations that the market had been partitioned as a result of an alleged agreement between SACEM and the copyright management societies in other Member States. This was based on the lack of sufficient statement of reason as required by Article 190 E.C.
[52] Case 238/87, see *infra*, Chap. 8, pt. 4(4).
[53] See *infra*, pt. 4.

3. Commission's Approach to Intellectual Property Licensing Agreements

(1) The "essence of intellectual property rights" criterion under Article 85

5.15 It was shown above that the "existence" or the "essence" of intellectual property rights is not affected by the rules on competition.[54] This implies that only those provisions in intellectual property licensing agreements that are not thought to belong to the "essence" of intellectual property rights are caught by the prohibitions of Article 85(1) E.C. and may entail nullification by a national court under Article 85(2) E.C. In cases where such an agreement is notified to it, the Commission will, in principle, give a negative clearance if it considers that it merely concerns the "essence" of intellectual property rights. If it does not, it will need to establish whether all the conditions are fulfilled to grant an individual exemption under Article 85(3) E.C.[55] It should, however, be pointed out that concerning patent and know-how licensing agreements notification to the Commission will often not be necessary. The Commission has issued so-called block exemptions, or group exemptions, in relation to these kind of agreements which indicate which provisions are held to be exempted or prohibited under Article 85 E.C.,[56] by virtue of the competence conferred on it by Regulation 19/65.

5.16 The uneasiness of Community institutions faced with the application of Community law to intellectual property rights is best illustrated by the "U-turn" the Commission made in its approach to intellectual property licensing agreements, in particular concerning patents, under Article 85(1) E.C.[57] The understanding of what constitutes the "essence" of a patent which is unaffected by the rules on competition has significantly varied with time. Initially, the Commission was of the opinion that Article 85(1) E.C. did not apply to exclusive patent licences, whereas later on it seemed to assume that exclusive patent licences necessarily came within the scope of Article 85(1) and always needed exemption under Article 85(3) E.C. This was again departed from in the block exemption regulation for patent licences in which the Commission adopted an in-between approach. The evolving of the Com-

---

[54] See *supra*, pt. 2(1).

[55] See also H. Johannes, "*La propriété industrielle et le droit d'auteur dans le droit des Communautés Européennes*" [1973] R.T.D.E. 557 at 558.

[56] Group exemption for patent licences, Regulation 2349/84 of July 23, 1984: [1984] O.J. L219/85 (Corrigendum [1985] O.J. L113/34). For an analysis, see V. Korah, *Patent licensing and the EEC competition rules: Regulation 2349/84* (1985, ESC). Group exemption for know how licences, Regulation 556/89 of November 30, 1988: [1989] O.J. L61/1. For an analysis, see V. Korah, *Know how licensing agreements and the EEC competition rules: Regulation 556/89* (1989, ESC). Both Regulations were subsequently modified by Regulation 151/93 of December 23, 1992: [1993] O.J. L21/8, which extended their scope to include certain patent licensing agreements with joint ventures and certain reciprocal agreements (see Article 3). Furthermore, awaiting the formal adoption and coming into force of the group exemption for technology transfer licensing agreements which was to replace both the patent and know how group exemptions (see *infra*, pt. (4)), the duration of the patent licensing group exemption was extended in duration until June 30, 1995 (see [1994] O.J. C313/6). On the procedural aspects of Article 85, see the book by Kerse, *op. cit.*.

[57] On the Commission's approach to trade mark licensing agreements see, for instance, the *Moosehead/Whitbread* decision: [1990] O.J. L100/32; [1991] 4 C.M.L.R. 391.

mission's approach to patent licences will be briefly illustrated with reference to the Court's judgments that lay at the basis of this change.

(2) The Commission's "U-turn" on patent licences

(a) The "Christmas Message"

On December 24, 1962, the Commission issued a Communication on the future attitude it would take towards patent licenses.[58] This was the so-called "Christmas Message". Several clauses in patent licensing agreements were considered not to be contrary to Article 85(1) E.C. amongst which were limitations as to use, time, quantity, exploitation method, space or person. The general idea was that practices covered by the scope of the patent could not be contrary to competition rules because:

> "they entail only the partial maintenance of the right of prohibition contained in the patentee's exclusive right in relation to the licensee, who in other respects is authorised to exploit the invention."[59]

5.17

In other words, the premise was that the exclusive right inherent in the patent gives the patentee the right to prohibit certain actions by third parties. Writing restrictions and prohibitions into a licensing agreement is merely the expression of the exclusive right of the patentee, but the advantage is that the patentee allows third parties to participate in his privileged position. This means that in the Commission's view, the patentee could impose all kinds of restrictions and that, for instance, undertakings on behalf of the licensor not to authorise third parties to exploit the invention and/or not to exploit it himself were, in principle, allowed.[60,61]

(b) Departing from the "Christmas Message"

The Commission had already modified its view somewhat in its decisions of the early 1970s. It is significant that the Commission no longer only looked at the relationship between the licensor and the licensee, but also took the position of third parties into account. This is evident in the first formal decisions taken by the Commission concerning patent licences notified to it. In the *Burroughs* decisions of December 1971,[62] the Commission stated that exclus-

5.18

[58] Communication on Patent Licensing Agreements: [1962] O.J. C139/2922.
[59] *id.*, IV.
[60] Similarly, see the distinction made between restrictions coming "within" the scope of patent law and those falling outside the scope, G. Schrans, *Octrooien en octrooilicenties in het Europees mededingingsrecht* (1966, Story-Scientia), pp. 536 *et seq.*
[61] However, the Commission stated by way of precaution that other competent authorities, in particular the courts, might have a different interpretation (pt. III). As such, the impact of the "Christmas Message" was in legal terms purely informative. Although the Commission's communications do not have legal effect, they do create legitimate expectations and are often regarded as constituting "soft-law". See I. Govaere, and F. Helin, "Implementing the Internal Market: problems and perspectives" in *The 1992 Challenge at National Level* (Schwarze, Govaere, Hélin, Van den Bossche eds. 1990) (Nomos Verlagsgesellschaft), pp. 681–703 at pp. 696–703.
[62] The *Burroughs-Delplanque* decision of December 22, 1971: [1972] O.J. L13/50; [1972] C.M.L.R. D67. The *Burroughs-Geha* decision of December 22, 1971: [1972] O.J. L13/53; [1972] C.M.L.R. D72.

ive licences *may* be caught by the prohibition of Article 85(1) E.C. as they prevent the licensor contracting with other applicants for a licence and as such may restrict competition.[63] The *Davidson-Rubber* decision of June 1972 is even more significant because here the Commission did consider the exclusive patent and know-how licensing agreements to be contrary to Article 85(1) E.C.[64] Although the sale of contract articles could freely be made between Member States, the Commission found that the exclusivity, combined with the limited number of competing processes, had as a consequence considerably altered the position of third parties and therefore noticeably restricted competition.[65]

5.19   These early decisions were already an important move away from the "Christmas Message". It cannot go unnoticed that between the 1962 notice and these decisions, the Court had ruled in the *Consten Grundig* case that Article 85(1) E.C. applies to vertical as well as to horizontal agreements.[66] Concerning the applicability of Article 85(1) E.C. to sole distributorship contracts, the Court clarified that:

> "Competition may be distorted within the meaning of Article 85(1) not only by agreements which limit it as between the parties, but also by agreements which prevent or restrict the competition which might take place between one of them and third parties. For this purpose, *it is irrelevant whether the parties to the agreement are or are not on a footing of equality as regards their position and function in the economy.*"[67]

In its First Report on Competition Policy of 1972, the Commission expressed the view that:

---

[63] Though this was not held to be the case for the agreements concerned due to the low market share of the licensees and their freedom to sell the licensed products in the whole of the common market. See also B. Cawthra, "Exclusive, sole and non-exclusive rights in patent licensing agreements" [1977] I.I.C. 430 at 434.

[64] The *Davidson-Rubber* decision of June 9, 1972: [1972] O.J. L143/31; [1972] C.M.L.R. D52. Contrary to the *Burroughs* decisions, the licensees held a considerable market share in the protected articles.

[65] Cawthra points out that the flaw in the Commission's decision is that it failed to state that it was the combination of exclusivity with the export prohibition that affected trade between Member States, see *op. cit.*, p. 436. The Commission pursued its analysis under Article 85(3) E.C. and granted an individual exemption. For a more detailed analysis, see B. Cawthra, *Patent licensing in Europe*, (2nd ed., 1986, Butterworth's), pp. 29–30. The same day, the Commission issued a negative clearance in the *Raymond-Nagoya* decision: [1972] O.J. L143/39; [1972] C.M.L.R. D45. The matter concerned a patent and utility model agreement between a French partnership and a Japanese company. The exclusive character of the agreement was considered not to be prohibited by Article 85(1) E.C., for it only eliminated potential competitors in the Far East and did not affect the competitive situation within the Common Market. The export prohibition, imposed on the Japanese undertaking, was also thought not to be contrary to Article 85(1) E.C. owing to the improbability that the licensee would export to the Community. Once again, however, the Commission implied that such a restriction, when affecting competition within the Common Market, might come under Article 85(1) E.C.

[66] Joined Cases 56 and 58/64, *Consten and Grundig v. Commission*, Judgment of July 13, 1966: [1966] E.C.R. 229; [1966] C.M.L.R. 418. On this case, see also *supra*, Chap. 3, pt. 4(2)(a).

[67] *id.*, at para. 339 (emphasis added).

"... where the owner of a patent undertakes to restrict the exercise of his exclusive rights to a single enterprise in the assigned area, thus conferring upon that single enterprise the sole right to exploit the invention and to prevent other enterprises from exploiting it, he loses the freedom to enter into agreements with other applicants for licences. The exclusive character of such a licence may amount to a restriction of competition and thus fall within the category of prohibited agreements in so far as it has an appreciable effect on market conditions."[68]

As such, it was now firmly accepted that Article 85 E.C. could, in principle, apply to patent licences. The question nonetheless remained unanswered of when Article 85(1) E.C. would also effectively be held to apply to patent licensing agreements. The Commission expressed its uncertainty about the proper application of Article 85 E.C. to patent licensing agreements, and thus about what constitutes the "essence" of a patent, in its Fourth Report on Competition Policy of 1975.[69] In the latter it was held that:

"The assessment of patent licensing agreements under the Treaty *calls upon a consideration of interests and issues which go beyond the field of competition policy*..."

"On a legal plane, the Commission faces the *problems of definition* exposed by the Court of Justice in its distinction between the *existence* of nationally protected industrial property rights, which is not to be affected by Community law, and the *exercise* of these rights, which can be subject to the Treaty rules."[70]

From its further comments concerning several common types of patent licensing provisions, it seemed that in future the Commission would regard all export restrictions as needing an exemption under Article 85(3) E.C. and thus as not belonging to the "essence" of the patent. Field-of-use restrictions would only be prohibited by Article 85(1) E.C. where they cause the elimination of competition between licensees or between the parties. Restrictions concerning the duration of the agreement were, in principle, allowed if this did not exceed the life of a single licensed patent. Non-competition clauses were thought to fall under Article 85(1) with little possibility of exemption under Article 85(3) E.C. Also quantitative output restrictions were, in the Commission's view, contrary to Article 85(1) E.C.

Three months after the publication of this report, the Commission held in   **5.20**
the *Kabelmetal-Luchaire* decision that exclusive licences are caught by Article 85(1) E.C. because the obligation not to grant licences to other parties does not belong to the "essence" of the patent.[71] As Frank pointed out, the Commission did not specify what it understood by the concept "essence" of a

---

[68] Annex to the Fifth General Report on the Activities of the Communities, April 1972, pt. 78.
[69] Annex to the Seventh General Report on the Activities of the Communities, April 1975.
[70] *id.*, at pts. 19 and 20 (emphasis added).
[71] The *Kabelmetal-Luchaire* decision of July 18, 1975: [1975] O.J. L222/34; [1975] 2 C.M.L.R. D40. The Commission did, however, grant an exemption for an exclusive licence to use a patented process. But in order to benefit from the individual exemption under Article 85(3) E.C., a ban on export to other Member States, an obligation to transfer to Kabelmetal the ownership of jointly developed improvements, and a non-challenge clause were deleted from the original agreement at the Commission's request.

patent in the *Kabelmetal* decision. The subsequent decisions were therefore important in that they exemplified the meaning of the latter in the Commission's view.[72] For instance, in its provisional *Bronbemaling-Heidemaatschappij* decision of July 1975, the Commission expressly stated that:

> "...an undertaking by a patent holder to restrict his own freedom to grant licences is *not the essence of his right* as a patent holder, even where the licensees have gone through the trouble and expense of improving the invention."[73]

(c) "Per se" prohibition

5.21   In its Fifth Report on Competition Policy, the Commission tried to correct the general impression created by its previous report, and its subsequent decisions, that it regarded some clauses in patent licensing agreements as "*per se*" infringements.[74] It confirmed that the matter of the applicability of Article 85(1) E.C. requires consideration of the economic power of the parties, the nature of the market or business in which they are engaged, their share of the market, the number of competitors and the significance of the licensed invention or know-how.[75] The Commission further stated that an exclusive manufacturing and sales licence of limited duration qualifies for an exemption under Article 85(3) E.C. if it provides the licensee with an incentive to penetrate either a geographic or a product market not yet worked by the licensor.[76]

But the Commission's practice proved to be different. Ever since the *Davidson Rubber* decision of 1972,[77] the Commission had consistently held that exclusive patent licences infringe Article 85(1) E.C. and need exemption under Article 85(3) E.C.[78] Similarly, in its *Maize Seed* decision of 1978,[79] the Commission held that Article 85(1) E.C. was infringed by clauses in an exclusive licensing agreement concerning plant breeders' rights obliging the licensor

---

[72] See G. Frank, "Intellectual property rights in the European Economic Community and the Treaty of Rome – conflict or harmony" [1977] *Journal of the Patent Office Society* 274 at 296–297.

[73] The *Bronbemaling-Heidemaatschappij* decision of July 25, 1975: [1975] O.J. L249/27; [1975] 2 C.M.L.R. D67 (emphasis added). The Commission refused to grant an exemption for the patent licensing agreement containing a clause making the granting of future licences dependent on the consent of the majority of the existing licensees. An exemption was also refused in the *AOIP-Beyrard* decision of December 2, 1975: [1976] O.J. L6/8; [1976] 1 C.M.L.R. D14. Here the Commission noted that although, in principle, an exemption can be granted in a case where the patent licensing agreement contains a provision whereby the licensor gives the licensee the exclusive right to manufacture certain products within a specified part of the territory of the Common Market, other clauses such as a no-challenge and a non-competition clause prevented the applicability of Article 85(3) E.C. in this particular case.

[74] Annex to the Eighth General Report on the Activities of the Communities, April 1976. This "*per se*" approach to exclusivity in the early decisions had been strongly criticised. See for instance B. Cawthra, *op. cit.*, p. 436; G. Albrechtskirchinger, "The impact of the Luxembourg Conference for the establishment of a Community patent on the law of license agreements" [1976] I.I.C. 447 at 458–459.

[75] *id.*, pt. 10.

[76] *id.*, pt. 65.

[77] See *supra*, pt. (b).

[78] See also R. Ludding, "Groepsvrijstelling octrooilicenties" [1985] S.E.W. 332 at 335.

[79] The *Nungesser* decision of September 21, 1978: [1978] O.J. L286/23; [1978] 3 C.M.L.R. 434.

to refrain from authorising other undertakings to produce or use plant varieties protected through a breeder's right in the licensed territory, and to refrain from producing or using such varieties himself. The Commission pointed out that such clauses eliminate the licensor as a competitor and deprive him of the ability to issue licences to other undertakings within the contract territory. Other provisions found to infringe Article 85(1) E.C. concerned the obligation on the parties to prevent third parties from exporting the product to the contract territory.[80] The Commission stated that such obligations restrain the breeder from exploiting his right freely and results in market sharing through preventing imports into, and exports from, the licensed territory by third parties. It did not grant an exemption under Article 85(3) E.C. for the reason that no new market was being penetrated or a new product launched. This was also the tenor of the draft block exemption regulation for patent licensing published in 1979.[81] However, the final version of this block exemption was somewhat modified on this point in order to comply with the distinction made by the Court in the *Maize Seed* case between "open" and other exclusive licences.[82]

(3) The Court's appraisal of the Commission's approach

(a) Exclusive intellectual property licences

In June 1982 the Court passed an important judgment in the *Nungesser v. Commission* case. Although the latter concerned plant breeders' rights the Court by implication considered the Commission's approach in the late 1970s to patent licensing agreements in general.[83] Nungesser contested the above-mentioned Commission's *Maize Seed* decision of 1978 and objected to the Commission's approach that every exclusive licence is by its very nature to be regarded as an agreement prohibited by Article 85(1) E.C.[84] In particular, Nungesser criticised the Commission's disregard of the fact that for newly-developed seeds exclusive licences constitute the sole means of promoting competition between the new product and comparable products on the market. The Court distinguished between the arguments that had led the Commission to conclude that the agreement was incompatible with Article 85(1) of the Treaty. It held:

5.22

---

[80] It should be noted that since the *Valley Printing Co. – BBC* case of 1976 ([1976] 2 E.C. Bull. 26), it is clear that the Commission looks upon export bans in copyright licences in the same way as it does for patent licences. Due to the Commission's investigation into a complaint by a third party, namely a sub-licensor of the BBC which was prevented from selling its products in the Netherlands, the BBC agreed to refrain from impeding exports of these copyright products in the future. As such, the proceedings were terminated without a formal decision. Nevertheless, this investigation into possible infringements of the rules on competition proves that the Commission is likely to follow the same line for copyright licences as it does for patent licensing agreements.

[81] [1979] O.J. C58/12. In the draft regulation, the Commission drew a distinction between exclusivity with respect to manufacture and use, which was unconditionally exempted, and exclusivity with respect to sale which could only be exempted under certain conditions.

[82] See *infra*, pt. (3)(a).

[83] Case 258/78, *Nungesser KG and Kurt Eisele v. Commission (Maize Seed)*, Judgment of June 8, 1982: [1982] E.C.R. 2015; [1983] 1 C.M.L.R. 278.

[84] See *supra*, pt. (2)(c).

"It should be observed that those two sets of considerations relate to two legal situations which are not necessarily identical. The first case concerns a so-called *open exclusive licence or assignment* and the exclusivity of the licence relates solely to the contractual relationship between the owner of the right and the licensee, whereby the owner merely undertakes not to grant other licences in respect of the same territory and not to compete himself with the licensee on that territory. On the other hand, the second case involves an *exclusive licence or assignment with absolute territorial protection*, under which the parties to the contract propose, as regards the products and the territory in question, to eliminate all competition from third parties, such as parallel importers or licensees for other territories."[85]

(i) "Open" exclusive licences

5.23   The Court took into account the argument that the total prohibition of exclusive licences would be detrimental to the dissemination of knowledge and new techniques in the Community. Especially the German Government had emphasised in its intervention that the protection of breeders' rights constitutes a means of encouraging agricultural innovation. It pointed out that allowing exclusive licences for a limited period of time, first, provides an additional incentive to such innovative efforts and, secondly, without it undertakings in other Member States might not take the risk of cultivating and marketing the product in competition with comparable existing products. The specific nature of the products concerned, and the function of breeders' rights, led the Court to conclude that:

"... the grant of an open exclusive licence, [...], is not *in itself* incompatible with Article 85(1) of the Treaty."[86]

As such, the Court rejected the theoretical "*per se*" approach taken by the Commission.[87] Instead, it seemed to acknowledge that economic realities should be weighed against legal considerations in order not to jeopardise competition and innovation in the long run. One can also deduce from the Court's reasoning that safeguarding the function of intellectual property rights may be an important factor in determining what constitutes the "essence" of the intellectual property right,[88] which is to be left unaffected by Article 85(1) E.C.

---

[85] Case 258/78: [1982] E.C.R. 2015; [1983] 1 C.M.L.R. 278, at para. 53 (emphasis added).

[86] Case 258/78: [1982] E.C.R. 2015; [1983] 1 C.M.L.R. 278, at para. 58 (emphasis added). The Court reiterated this approach to licensing agreements concerning plant breeders rights in Case 27/87, *Louis Erauw-Jacquery SàRL v. La Hesbignonne*, Judgment of April 19, 1988: [1988] E.C.R. 1919; [1988] 4 C.M.L.R. 576. However, in this case the Court held that the inclusion of a clause imposing minimum prices might, depending on the economic and legal context of the agreement, be contrary to Article 85(1) E.C.

[87] It is not surprising, therefore, that this case is taken as the example to illustrate the pragmatic approach of the Court, see U. Everling, "The Court of Justice as a decision making authority" in *The art of governance* (Michigan Law Review Association ed. 1987) (Nomos Verlagsgesellschaft) 156 at 168.

[88] Compare to the function of patents, see *supra*, Chap. 2, pt. 3(2).

(ii) "Non-open" exclusive licences and exhaustion

However, in the line of the earlier *Consten Grundig* judgment, the Court held   **5.24**
that a non-open exclusive agreement, enabling parallel imports to be controlled and artificial boundaries to be resurrected between national markets,
is prohibited by Article 85(1) E.C. It contested the view taken by the Government of the United Kingdom that a contract between two parties cannot have
this effect owing to the previously established case law concerning the free
movement of goods introducing the principle of exhaustion[89] and, therefore,
should not come under Article 85(1) E.C. The Court emphasised that the
Commission's powers to ensure the observance of the rules on competition is
in no way restricted by the existence of other Treaty provisions upon which
other persons can rely to escape the implications of an agreement between two
parties. On the whole, the Court held that the absolute territorial restriction
was not indispensable for the improvement of production or promotion of
technical progress. It supported the Commission's opinion that this was a sufficient reason not to grant an exemption under Article 85(3) E.C.

(iii) Impact on block exemption for patent licences

Subsequent to the *Maize Seed* judgment of the Court, the Commission issued   **5.25**
Regulation 2349/84 on the application of Article 85(3) of the Treaty to certain categories of patent licensing agreements.[90] The impact of the *Maize Seed*
case is obvious in Recital 11, which reads:

> "Exclusive licensing agreements, *i.e.* agreements in which the licensor
> undertakes not to exploit the 'licensed invention', [. . .], in the licensed
> territory himself and not to grant further licences there, *are not in them-*
> *selves incompatible with Article 85(1)* where they are concerned with the
> introduction and protection of a new technology in the licensed territory,
> by reason of scale of the research which has been undertaken and the risk
> that is involved in manufacturing and marketing a product which is
> unfamiliar to users in the licensed territory at the time the agreement is
> made. This may also be the case where the agreements are concerned
> with the introduction and protection of a new process for manufacturing
> a product which is already known . . . ."[91]

Such provisions could thus, in principle, have been included in the white-list
of Article 2. Article 2 essentially lists provisions which are thought to constitute the "essence" of patents, which in principle do not come under the prohibition of Article 85(1) E.C. but for which an exemption is granted "just in
case". Article 1, on the other hand, lists those provisions which are thought to
come within the scope of Article 85(1) E.C., but which are exempted because
they generally contribute to the improvement of the production of goods and
promote technical progress. The recital goes on to state that such "open

---

[89] On this case law, see *supra*, Chap. 4.
[90] See *supra*, pt. (1). For a detailed commentary, see V. Korah, *Patent licensing and EEC*
competition rules, Regulation 2394/84 (1985, ESC). See also J. Venit, "EEC patent licensing
revisited: The Commission's patent licence regulation" [1985] *Antitrust Bull.* 457; R. Ludding,
"*Groepsvrijstelling octrooilicenties*" [1985] S.E.W. 332.
[91] (Emphasis added.) This clearly concerns only the so-called "open exclusive licences".

exclusive licensing" provisions are nevertheless included in Article 1 because there are also cases in which they do come within the ambit of Article 85(1) and thus need exemption.[92] As such, contrary to the draft block exemption in which the Commission adopted a *"per se"* prohibition approach,[93] the final regulation radically departed from this and takes a lenient approach to open exclusive licences in general, which is also the approach adopted in the group exemption for technology licensing agreements.[94] Of course, due regard should still be had to the provisions blacklisted in Article 3 E.C.[95]

(b) Determination of material scope of patent

5.26   On February 25, 1986 the Court passed another very important judgment in the *Windsurfing* case.[96] Windsurfing International Inc. (WSI) had challenged the Commission's decision of 1983 whereby its non-exclusive patent licensing agreements were found to infringe the rules on competition and a fine of 50,000 ECUs was imposed.[97] Since the Commission had established its decision along the criteria laid down in the block exemption for patent licensing agreements this judgment indirectly gave an appraisal of Regulation 2349/89. The Commission had objected in particular to clauses extending the licensor's control beyond the material scope of the patent which led to it being impossible for third parties to enter the market.[98] It also objected to obligations imposed on the licensees which prevented them from acting independently as well as from competing with the licensor.

The preliminary issue was whether, and to what extent, the Commission is competent to rule on the material scope of a patent granted in a Member State. Legal proceedings to determine the precise scope of the German patent granted, namely, did the patent only cover the rig or also the board of a sailboard, were still pending before national courts at the time of the Com-

---

[92] See the first four clauses mentioned in Article 1.

[93] See *supra*, pt. (2)(c).

[94] see *infra*, pt. (4).

[95] Article 3 lists those provisions which are prima facie considered to be not exempt under Article 85(3) E.C. due to their detrimental effect on competition and market behaviour. Patent licensing agreements containing blacklisted clauses cannot benefit from the opposition procedure but can, in principle, still be notified in order to obtain an individual exemption. Though the group exemption provides the guidelines and criteria on which the Commission will most likely base its decision, as is illustrated by the first decision concerning a patent licensing agreements after the coming into force of the block exemption, namely the *Velcro-Aplix* decision of July 12, 1985: [1985] O.J. L233/22; [1989] 4 C.M.L.R. 157. The infringements listed are mainly blacklisted provisions; no individual exemption was granted under Article 85(3) E.C. In this case the Commission made no findings as to the validity of the agreements prior to the expiry of the basic patents and did not impose any fines, presumably due to the early notification of the agreement, namely on January 30, 1963.

[96] Case 193/83, *Windsurfing International Inc. v. Commission*, Judgment of February 25, 1986: [1986] E.C.R. 611; [1986] 3 C.M.L.R. 489. See especially J. Venit, "In the wake of Windsurfing: Patent licensing in the Common Market" [1987] I.I.C. 1.

[97] The *Windsurfing* decision of July 11, 1983: [1983] O.J. L229/1; [1984] 1 C.M.L.R. 1.

[98] In American law, similar provisions would probably be prohibited on the basis of the "patent misuse doctrine" which found its origin in the *Morton Salt Co v. GS Suppiger Co* case concerning restraints of competition in the market of unpatented products on the basis of a patent licence, see (1942) 314 U.S. 488. See J. Wallace, "Proper use of the patent misuse doctrine – an antitrust defense to patent infringement actions in need of rational reform" [1976] *Patent Law Review* 357.

mission's decision. The Court held that although the Commission is not competent to determine the material scope of a patent, it must be able to exercise its powers in accordance with Regulation 17 to determine whether or not the competition rules have been infringed. Where the scope of the patent is relevant to do so, it should not refrain from acting only because the scope of patent protection is the subject of national legal proceedings. As such, the crucial issue is whether or not the Commission has made a *reasonable assessment* of the scope of the patent. The Court found that in this particular case the Commission was justified in assuming that the German patent covered only the rig and not the board of the sailboard owing to the wording of the patent and the outcome of previous test cases.

(c) Calculation of royalties

In the above-mentioned *Windsurfing* case, the Court generally upheld the Commission's decision except with respect to the provision on the calculation of royalties on the net selling price of a complete sailboard. Contrary to the Commission's view, the Court held that using the selling price of both protected (rigs) and unprotected products (board) as the basis of calculation of the royalties was not aimed at restricting competition in the sale of separate rigs. The Court pointed to the fact that the licensees acknowledged that it would have been equitable to accept a higher rate of royalty if the licensor's remuneration were calculated on the price of the rig alone. As such, the Court seemingly undermined the absolute character of Article 3(4) of Regulation 2349/84.[99] Nevertheless, it did not totally empty this provision of its substance for it went on to note that royalties on the net selling price of a complete sailboard may restrict competition with regard to the sale of boards alone, since they are not covered by the patent.[1] In the *Ottung v. Klee* case the Court further held that the contractual obligation to pay royalties for an indeterminate period, and therefore also after the expiry of the patent, is not contrary to Article 85(1) E.C. unless the licensee is not given the opportunity to terminate the agreement with reasonable notice or if his freedom of action after termination is restricted.[2]

5.27

(d) Type-approval and quality controls

In the *Windsurfing* case the Court impliedly agreed with Article 2(9) of Regulation 2349/84[3] by sustaining the Commission's objection to the obligation to submit new board types, on which the protected rigs were to be used, to the licensor's prior approval. The Court reiterated the Commission's justification

5.28

---

[99] Article 3(4) of Regulation 2349/89 blacklists: "The licensee is charged royalties on products which are not entirely or partially patented or manufactured by means of a patented process."

[1] Case 193/83: [1986] E.C.R. 611; [1986] 3 C.M.L.R. 489, at paras. 65–67.

[2] Case 320/87, *Kai Ottung v. Klee & Weilbach A/S and Thomas Schmidt A/S*, Judgment of May 12, 1989: [1989] E.C.R. 1177; [1990] 4 C.M.L.R. 915, at para. 13.

[3] Article 2.1(9) of Regulation 2349/89 stipulates that the following is not incompatible with Article 85(1): "An obligation on the licensee to observe specifications concerning the minimum quality of the licensed product, *provided that such specifications are necessary for a technically satisfactory exploitation of the licensed invention*, and to allow the licensor to carry out related checks" (emphasis added).

in terms of the specific subject-matter of intellectual property rights, and held that:

> "*It is necessary to determine whether quality controls on the sailboards are covered by the specific subject-matter of the patent.* As the Commission rightly points out, such controls do not come within the specific subject-matter of the patent unless they relate to a product covered by the patent since their sole justification is that they ensure 'that the technical instructions as described in the patent and used by the licensee may be carried into effect'. In this case, however, it has been established that it may reasonably be considered that the German patent does not cover the board."[4]

The use of the concept of "specific subject-matter" in this context is, to say the least, confusing because the Court applies the criterion of the material scope of the patent to hold that quality controls may not be enforced on unprotected products. The Court has consistently held in the context of the rules on the free movement of goods that the specific subject-matter of patents is the right to first place the protected product on the market either by the patent holder himself or with his consent.[5] One could perhaps argue that the concept of "consent" does not cover poor quality goods put on the market by a licensee in disregard of quality requirements contractually imposed by the licensor. It is doubtful, however, if the Court would accept this reasoning with regard to patents for it expressly rejected it with regard to trade marks. In the *Ideal-Standard* case the Court unequivocally held:

> "... a national law allowing the licensor to oppose importation of the licensee's products on grounds of poor quality would be precluded as contrary to Articles 30 and 36: if the licensor tolerates the manufacture of poor quality products, despite having contractual means of preventing it, he must bear the responsibility. Similarly if the manufacture of products is decentralised within a group of companies and the subsidiaries in each of the Member States manufacture products whose quality is geared to the particularities of each national market, a national law which enabled one subsidiary of the group to oppose marketing in the territory of that State of products manufactured by an affiliated company on grounds of those quality differences would also be precluded. Articles 30 and 36 require the group to bear the consequences of its choice."[6]

It should be emphasised, however, that in the *Windsurfing* case the question of quality controls arose in the context of the application of the competition rules and not the rules on the free movement of goods. This distinction is important because, as the Court acknowledged in the *Ideal-Standard* case, even though the licensor may not invoke intellectual property rights to prohibit the free movement of poor quality goods:

> "... the licensor can control the quality of the licensee's products by including in the contract clauses requiring the licensee to comply with his

---

[4] Case 193/83: [1986] E.C.R. 611; [1986] 3 C.M.L.R. 489, at para. 45 (emphasis added).
[5] See *supra*, Chap. 4, pt. 2(1).
[6] Case C–9/93: [1994] E.C.R. I-2789, at para. 38. See also *supra*, Chap. 4, pt. 2(3)(v).

instructions and giving him the possibility of verifying such compliance."[7]

In this respect the Court introduced an important qualification in the *Windsurfing* case. It held that even if the board was covered by the patent, then quality and safety criteria would still need to be agreed upon in advance on the basis of objectively verifiable criteria in order to be compatible with the rules on competition.[8] This condition was not fulfilled in the case in question.

(e) Sales tie-in

In the *Vaessen-Moris* decision of 1979 the Commission found that a patent   5.29
licensing agreement was prohibited by Article 85(1) E.C. due to a non-challenge and a tie-in clause.[9] It held that a tie-in clause constitutes an unlawful extension by contractual means of the monopoly given by the patent.[10] The tie-in clause in the *Windsurfing* case, whereby rigs could only be sold in conjunction with boards approved by the licensor, was confirmed to be contrary to Article 85(1) E.C. by the Court.[11] The Court recalled that only the rig is held to be patented, not the board, and refused to accept that this particular tie-in clause was indispensable to the exploitation of the patent. Conversely, this would seem to imply that if the tie-in was indispensable to the satisfactory exploitation of the patent, then Article 85(1) E.C. might not have been held to be infringed. The latter reasoning also finds expression in Articles 2.1(1) and 3(9) of Regulation 2349/89. It cannot go unnoticed, however, that the *Windsurfing* case concerned an obligation on the licensee *to sell* unprotected products together with a patented product whereas the block exemption merely deals with the *purchasing* of goods from the licensor.[12]

(f) Non-competition clause

The Court held in the *Ottung v. Klee* case that clauses whereby the licensee is   5.30
prohibited from manufacturing and marketing the goods after the expiry of the agreement, as well as of the patent, is contrary to Article 85(1) E.C. on the

---

[7] Case C–9/93: [1994] E.C.R. I-2789, at para. 37.
[8] It is interesting to note that the Court did not uphold the argument based on the protection against slavish imitation because this would substitute WSI's discretion for the decision of the national courts which have sole competence in such matters. For the same reasons, the Court rejected WSI's justification of the need to maintain territorial restrictions on the manufacturing place of the licensed product, combined with the right to terminate the agreement immediately in case of infringement, which was said to be needed to carry out quality controls. See Case 193/83: [1986] E.C.R. 611; [1986] 3 C.M.L.R. 489, at paras. 82–88.
[9] The *Vaessen-Moris* decision of January 10, 1979: [1979] O.J. L19/32; [1979] 1 C.M.L.R. 511.
[10] *id.*, p. 35, pt. 15. No individual exemption was granted because the four conditions enumerated in Article 85(3) E.C. were not considered to be fulfilled.
[11] Case 193/83: [1986] E.C.R. 611; [1986] 3 C.M.L.R. 489, at paras. 54–59.
[12] Article 2.1(1) of Regulation 2349/89 reads: "an obligation on the licensee *to procure* goods or services from the licensor, [...], in so far as such products or services are necessary for a technically satisfactory exploitation of the licensed invention" (emphasis added). Article 3(9) reads: "the licensee is induced at the time the agreement is entered into to accept further licences which he does not want or to agree to use patents, products or services which he does not want, unless such patents, products or services are necessary for a technically satisfactory exploitation of the licensed invention."

condition that intra-Community trade is affected.[13] The *Windsurfing* judgment shows that the insertion of provisions by which competition by the
licensee is not prohibited, but is rendered more difficult, may also be "caught"
by Article 85 E.C.[14] Both the obligation on the licensees to affix to the boards
notices stating that the product was licensed by WSI, and the no-challenge
clause with respect to WSI's trade marks, were held to be incompatible with
the rules on competition. The Court agreed with the Commission that these
conditions unduly restricted the licensees' competitiveness *vis-à-vis* the
licensor.

(g) No-challenge clause

5.31   Besides the no-challenge clause in relation to WSI's trade marks, the Court
also held the no-challenge clause with regard to the patent to be incompatible
with Article 85 E.C. in the *Windsurfing* case. The Court stated:

> "it is in the public interest to eliminate any obstacle to economic activity
> which may arise where a patent was granted in error."[15]

It should be pointed out that the Court apparently changed its view on the
matter. It clarified in the subsequent *Bayer v. Süllhöfer* case that a no-challenge clause will not always come under the prohibition of Article 85(1) E.C.,
thereby disregarding the public interest element.[16] In the latter case the Court
held that:

> "A no-challenge clause in a patent licensing agreement *may, depending
> on the legal and economic context*, restrict competition within the mean-
> ing of Article 85(1) of the EEC Treaty. Such a clause does not, however,
> restrict competition when the agreement in which it is contained granted
> a free licence and the licensee does not, therefore, suffer the competitive
> disadvantage involved in the payment of royalties *or* when the licence
> was granted subject to payment of royalties but relates to a technically
> outdated process which the undertaking accepting the no-challenge
> clause did not use."[17]

It was rightly pointed out by Friden that the Court in the *Bayer* case disregarded the effect of an erroneously granted patent on the competitive
situation of third parties who can be denied access to the technology.[18] It is

[13] Case 320/87: [1989] E.C.R. 1177; [1990] 4 C.M.L.R. 915, at para. 13. Non-competition clauses were blacklisted in Article 3(3) of Regulation 2349/89.
[14] Case 193/83: [1986] E.C.R. 611; [1986] 3 C.M.L.R. 489, at paras. 68–81.
[15] Case 193/83: [1986] E.C.R. 611; [1986] 3 C.M.L.R. 489, at para. 92.
[16] Case 65/86, *Bayer AG and Maschinenfabrik Hennecke GmbH v. Heinz Süllhöfer*, Judgment of September 27, 1988: [1988] E.C.R. 5249; [1990] 4 C.M.L.R. 182. See also S. Singleton, "Intellectual property disputes: settlement agreements and ancillary licences under E.C. and U.K. competition law" [1993] E.I.P.R. 48 at 49.
[17] Case 65/86: [1988] E.C.R. 5249; [1990] 4 C.M.L.R. 182, at para. 21 (emphasis added).
[18] See G. Friden, "Recent developments in EEC intellectual property law: the distinction between existence and exercise revisited" (1989) 26 C.M.L.Rev. 193 at 213. He further points out that in a royalty-free licence, other restrictions might be imposed on the licensee "which are likely to be significant to compensate the licensor for the absence of royalties".

obviously not the function of patent protection to create entry barriers for products that do not live up to the requirements for patent protection. It is therefore submitted that a patent should always be free to be challenged upon its validity. Furthermore, a contradictory result of this judgment was that an agreement in which a no-challenge clause was inserted could not benefit from either the block exemption or the opposition procedure, since it was a black-listed clause in Regulation 2349/84, whereas the same agreement could be held to be compatible with Article 85(1) E.C. when notified in order to obtain an individual exemption.[19]

(4) Block exemption for technology transfer agreements

The Commission is currently elaborating a new block exemption, namely the block exemption for technology transfer agreements. It is to replace the two existing block exemptions for patent licences and know-how licensing agreements. This single regulation will therefore apply to both "pure" patent and "pure" know-how licences, as well as to "mixed" patent and know-how licensing agreements. However, the draft exemption received a lot of criticism and will most likely be thoroughly re-examined.[20] Only the most controversial features of it will therefore be highlighted here.   **5.32**

In so far as exclusive licences are concerned, the Commission reiterated in the draft exemption for technology transfer agreements the distinction already made between open and non-open exclusive licences in the previous block exemptions subsequent to the *Maize Seed* case.[21] An innovatory feature, however, is that a limit to market share was set above which territorial restrictions would not be exempted in block but for which an individual exemption should be applied for.[22] The adoption of the latter approach was strongly criticised in legal writings.[23] The exclusion from the block exemption of parties operating in a oligopolistic market, presumably due to the *Tetra Pak* case,[24] gave rise to further criticism. It was, *inter alia*, pointed out that legal certainty would be jeopardised not in the least because the calculation of market share is dependent on the definition given to the relevant product and geographical markets. Furthermore, the market share test does not seem to be limited to the time at which the licence is granted but apparently may be applied throughout the duration of the licensing agreement. A constant monitoring of market shares would therefore seem to be required.

The blacklist of prohibited provisions was also considerably shortened in the draft technology transfer block exemption in comparison to the patent   **5.33**

---

[19] Although this, of course, also depends on the other clauses inserted in the agreement, as well as on the "legal and economic context" which, according to the Court, has to be taken into account to determine whether or not the no-challenge clause is contrary to Article 85(1) E.C.

[20] For the draft exemption, see [1994] O.J. C178/3 (Corrigendum [1994] O.J. C187/16).

[21] See Recital 9 of the preamble of the draft block exemption for technology transfer licences. In relation to the patent licensing block exemption, see *supra*, pt. (3)(a)(iii).

[22] See Articles 1.5 and 1.6 of the draft block exemption.

[23] See for instance R. Whaite, "The draft technology transfer block exemption" [1994] E.I.P.R. 259; V. Korah, "The preliminary draft of a new E.C. group exemption for technology licensing" [1994] E.I.P.R. 263; N. De Souza, "The Commission's draft group exemption on technology transfer" [1994] E.C.L.R. 338.

[24] See *infra*, pt. 5.

and know-how licensing block exemptions.[25] Non-competition clauses were still blacklisted, but mention was, for instance, no longer made of no-challenge clauses or tie-ins of the licensee. As the Commission indicated the fact that the latter, and other anti-competitive provisions, were no longer expressly mentioned did not imply that they could not be found to be contrary to Article 85 E.C.[26] It therefore seemed to be necessary to pay due attention to the prior decisions of the Commission and the case law of the Court in this respect.[27] The shortening of the blacklist thus entailed further legal uncertainty as to which provisions in agreements would nevertheless be held to be incompatible with Community law even though they were not, as such, prohibited by the block exemption.

Furthermore, contrary to the block exemptions it is intended to replace, the draft block exemption for technology transfer licences no longer mentioned the possibility of recourse to the so-called opposition procedure. The latter means that agreements which contain provisions that are neither expressly exempted nor expressly prohibited by the group exemption can be notified to the Commission and will be held to be exempted if the Commission does not oppose to the agreement within six months. The fact that the Commission did not reiterate the opposition procedure in the draft was strongly criticised, in particular in view of the fact that the Commission concurrently considerably shortened the blacklist and introduced the market share test. In other words, whereas the draft block exemption, on the one hand, created legal uncertainty about its application, on the other hand, it did away with the simplified procedure designed precisely to remedy this kind of situation.

It was pointed out in legal writings that the uncertainty about whether or not an agreement would benefit from the block exemption would necessarily entail recourse to notification for individual exemption for most agreements concerned. This would place a heavy burden both on industry and on the Commission. A block exemption is, however, aimed at reducing the need for individual exemptions by providing clear guidelines to industry on the application of Article 85 E.C. to certain categories of agreements by the Commission.[28] In other words, it was spelled out that the draft did not live up to the very objective for which block exemptions are issued. It remains to be seen to what extent the Commission will take this strong and rather fundamental criticism voiced on the draft block exemption into account, and how it will remedy these major shortcomings in the final block exemption for technology transfer licensing agreements. The latter is due to be adopted soon.

---

[25] The blacklist is to be found in Article 3 of the draft regulation. The blacklist contains those clauses which are held to be contrary to Article 85(1) E.C. and cannot be exempted owing to their detrimental impact on competition. In one sense, the blacklist can be called the most important provision in a block exemption for it considerably limits the scope and effect thereof as a whole.

[26] See Article 4 draft block exemption.

[27] See *supra*, at pts. (2) and (3).

[28] See, for instance, Regulation 4087/88 concerning the application of Article 85(3) of the Treaty to certain categories of franchising agreements of November 30, 1988: [1988] O.J. L359/46. On this regulation see, for instance, V. Korah, *Franchising and the EEC competition rules: Regulation 4087/88* (1990, European Competition Law Monographies); L. Van Allen, "*De EEG-groepsvrijstelling voor franchise-overeenkomsten*" [1990] S.E.W. 3.

4. COMMISSION'S APPROACH TO CERTAIN ABUSIVE INTELLECTUAL PROPERTY PRACTICES UNDER ARTICLE 86

(1) Contested issues

Not only did the Commission issue some contested decisions concerning the applicability of Article 85 E.C. to intellectual property licensing agreements, this was also the case in so far as the applicability of Article 86 E.C. to the unilateral enforcement of exclusive rights by intellectual property owners is concerned. With respect to the latter, it is particularly significant that legal actions were initiated before the Court of First Instance (CFI) against both the *Hilti* decision and what has become known as the *Magill* decision of the Commission. The ruling of the CFI in both cases was subsequently challenged on appeal before the European Court of Justice.[29]

5.34

The *Hilti* case, in essence, raised the issue of to what extent the holder of a patent can eliminate competition in the related market for unprotected accessories, whereas the *Magill* cases concerned the question of to what extent a copyright holder can invoke his exclusive right to prevent the creation of a derivative market in a new product. The *Volvo* and *Renault* cases, which were preliminary procedures and which are extensively analysed in Chapters 7 to 9, posed a complementary question, namely, to what extent may the owner of an industrial design invoke his exclusive right to eliminate competition in the after-sales market of replacement parts.[30] The most difficult issue in all three cases proved to be to establish what constitutes the additional element to the normal exercise of intellectual property rights which may trigger Article 86 E.C. The *Hilti* and *Magill* cases, which are analysed below, have in common that they illustrate the approach adopted to this issue by the Commission, the CFI and the European Court of Justice, respectively.

(2) Tie-in of unprotected products

(a) The Commission's Hilti decision

(i) Issue

The *Hilti* decision concerned the alleged abuse of a dominant position by Hilti, a proprietor of patents on nail guns and compatible cartridge strips, in the related market in nails to be used in those nail guns and cartridge strips.[31] Two independent companies which specialised in the manufacture and marketing of nails, namely Eurofix and Bauco, had lodged a complaint with the Commission against the commercial practice of Hilti. The latter mainly consisted of tying the sale of nails to the sale of cartridge strips in order to exclude competitors from the market for nails compatible with Hilti products.

5.35

---

[29] See *infra*, at pts. (2) and (3).
[30] See *infra*, Chaps. 7 and 8; and especially Chap. 8 for the analysis under the rules on competition.
[31] The *Eurofix-Bauco v. Hilti* decision of December 22, 1987: [1988] O.J. L65/19; [1989] 4 C.M.L.R. 677.

(ii) Dominant position and relevant market concept

5.36   Hilti maintained that the above-mentioned practice was not contrary to Article 86 E.C. because it did not occupy a dominant position in the relevant product market.[32] In its view the latter was the market for nail guns, cartridge strips and nails which form one integral system, and for fastening systems for the construction industry in general. The Commission, however, held the relevant product markets as being the separate markets for Hilti nail guns, Hilti-compatible cartridge strips and Hilti-compatible nails on the basis that although those products are interrelated they have different sets of supply and demand conditions.[33] The Commission pointed out that Hilti could prevent competition in the market for cartridge strips on the basis of its patent, whereas no such "institutional barrier" to competition existed in the market for Hilti-compatible nails.

Considering that the relevant product markets were held to be the markets in Hilti-compatible products and that Hilti had a patent on the cartridges, on the basis of which it could legitimately exclude competition, the Commission had no difficulty in concluding that Hilti held a dominant position in the market for Hilti-compatible cartridge strips. It was derived from its important market share in nail guns, and the patent protection on the cartridges, that Hilti had a strong economic position which enabled it to prevent effective competition being maintained in the market for Hilti-compatible nails. The Commission justified this finding by referring to Hilti's ability to act independently of either competitors or consumers.

(iii) Abuse of dominant position, effect on trade and safety concerns

5.37   Hilti abused its dominant position, according to the Commission, in both the markets for Hilti compatible cartridge strips and nails by preventing, or limiting, the entry of independent producers into those markets.[34] Although the cartridges were patented in the United Kingdom they were subject to licences of right, which in essence means that anyone applying for a licence may obtain one.[35] Hilti demanded unreasonably high royalties which, in practice, amounted to a refusal to license and stated that the license of right did not affect its copyright in the cartridge strips. In the Commission's view this constituted an abuse since Hilti was deliberately frustrating the objective of legitimately available licences of right with the sole aim of preventing competition in the market for cartridge strips in which it held a dominant position.

The practices held by the Commission as constituting an abuse of a dominant position by Hilti can be summarised as follows:

---

[32] For the concept of "relevant market", see *infra*, Chap. 8, pt. 3(1).

[33] The Commission held: "they are separate markets, because from the supply side nails and cartridge strips are produced with totally different technologies and often by different firms. On the demand side it is true that a user needs an equal complement of nails and cartridges, but they are not necessarily purchased together in identical quantities...", see pt. 55. The relevant geographical market was considered to be the whole of the E.C.

[34] On the concept of "abuse" of a dominant position, see *infra*, Chap. 8, pt. 4(2).

[35] See also *infra*, Chap. 6, pt. 3(1)(b), concerning the application of the rules on the free movement of goods to licences of right.

— Tying sales of nails to the sale of cartridges and discriminating against cartridge-only orders, for instance through reducing discounts;[36]

— Inducing independent distributors not to fulfil certain export orders with the aim of preventing independent nail makers from obtaining supplies of cartridge strips;

— Refusal to fill complete orders for cartridges from long-standing customers who might resell them;

— Refusal to honour guarantees if non-Hilti nails were used, which was not objectively justified by reason of quality of the nails used;

— Offering special discriminatory prices to its competitors' customers whilst maintaining higher prices for its own customers;

— Operating unilaterally and secretly a policy of differential discounts for supported and unsupported plant-hire companies and dealers in the United Kingdom.

It is obvious that the attempts to block exports had a potential effect on intra-Community trade. The Commission further held that the attempts to exclude independent nail makers was bound to affect the competitive market structure. It also pointed out that the trade flow would potentially develop along different lines in the absence of Hilti's abusive behaviour.[37]

Hilti objected that its behaviour was justified in view of its concern about **5.38** the reliability and safety of its products. This argument was rejected on the basis that Hilti's commercial behaviour was not the least restrictive action necessary to attain this objective. The Commission in essence held that a company may not resort to abusive behaviour which is contrary to Article 86 E.C. because there are other legitimate and more efficient ways of safeguarding safety.

(b) The Court of First Instance's appraisal

(i) Issues raised

Hilti challenged this decision of the Commission before the CFI.[38] Hilti par- **5.39** ticularly called into question the finding of a dominant position, although it recognised that if it had been in a dominant position some aspects of its contested behaviour could have been considered abusive. Hilti further argued

---

[36] For an economic analysis of tie-ins and the Commission's *Hilti* decision in general, see D. Price, "Abuse of a dominant position – the tale of nails, milk cartons, and TV guides" [1990] E.C.L.R. 80. At p. 87 she points out that although economists from the Chicago school would reject the Commission's conclusion that the tying policy creates barriers to entry in the market for *Hilti*-compatible nails because a second monopoly profit cannot be derived from the market for the tied product, Article 86 E.C. is not limited to the pursuit of purely economic goals but is also applied to protect competitors *per se*. On the E.C. competition policy objectives, see also *infra*, Chap. 9, pt. 2.

[37] On the concept "effect on intra-Community trade", see *infra*, Chap. 8, pt. 5.

[38] Case T–30/89, *Hilti AG v. Commission*, Judgment of December 12, 1991: [1991] E.C.R. II-1439; [1992] 4 C.M.L.R. 16.

that its commercial behaviour was not capable of affecting intra-Community trade.[39]

(ii) Relevant market and dominant position

5.40   The main argument advanced by Hilti to contest the finding of a dominant position was that the Commission had not correctly defined the relevant product market. It reiterated the point of view that nail guns, cartridges and nails are not three distinct markets, but rather constitute one indivisible whole that belongs to the market for all fastening systems which are substitutable in any PAF (powder-actuated fastening) application. The CFI rejected that argument and upheld the Commission's view that there are three distinct markets in nail guns, Hilti-compatible cartridges and nails. The Court held that the Commission's findings of the absence of a cross-price-elasticity, and the limited interchangeability of the products, were sufficiently convincing and had not been invalidated by the plaintiff's arguments.

Moreover, the CFI pointed out that the existence of independent producers making only Hilti-compatible nails is evidence of the fact that there is a specific market for those nails. It should, however, be pointed out that the independent manufacturers could not also manufacture the Hilti-compatible cartridges without infringing the patent, otherwise they might have done so. The CFI proceeded to state that accepting Hilti's point of view would entail that the use of competing nails in Hilti nail guns would be excluded, whereas:

> "... in the absence of general and binding standards or rules, any independent producer is quite free, as far as Community competition law is concerned, to manufacture consumables intended for use in equipment manufactured by others, *unless in doing so it infringes a patent or some other industrial or intellectual property right.*"[40]

In this case, the important factor was that Hilti did not have a patent on the nails, but only on the cartridges, so that it could not legitimately exclude others from the market for Hilti-compatible nails.[41] Through refusing to accept that the relevant market is constituted by both patented and unprotected products, the CFI impliedly reiterated the view that a tie in is prohibited

---

[39] *Hilti* also raised some procedural issues which will not be dealt with here. On this point, see S. Farr, "Abuse of a dominant position – the *Hilti* case" [1992] E.C.L.R. 174 at 175 and 177.

[40] Case T–30/89: [1991] E.C.R. II-1439; [1992] 4 C.M.L.R. 16, at para. 68 (emphasis added).

[41] Compare with the case law of the Court concerning exclusive rights granted by the state to private undertakings in the public interest (Art. 90), and especially the *Telemarketing* case in which it was held that "an abuse within the meaning of Article 86 is committed where, without any objective necessity, an undertaking holding a dominant position on a particular market reserves to itself or to an undertaking belonging to the same group an ancillary activity which might be carried out by another undertaking as part of its activities on a neighbouring but separate market, with the possibility of eliminating all competition from such undertaking", Case 311/84, *CBEM v. CLT and IPB*, Judgment of October 3, 1985: [1985] E.C.R. 3261; [1986] 2 C.M.L.R. 558, at para. 27. On the application of the competition rules to exclusive rights granted in the public interest, see C. Ehlermann, "Managing monopolies: the role of the state in controlling market dominance in the European Community" [1993] E.C.L.R. 61.

under Community competition law so that the exclusive effect of a patent which may be compatible with Article 86 E.C. cannot be extended beyond the material scope of the patent.[42]

Having confirmed the Commission's definition of the relevant market,[43] the CFI proceeded to uphold the finding that Hilti had a dominant position in the market for Hilti-compatible nails. The CFI pointed out that Hilti had a market share of between 70 per cent and 80 per cent of the market which is indicative of the existence of a dominant position. It also agreed with the Commission's contention that the existence of a patent on cartridge strips, and the invoking of copyright protection in the United Kingdom strengthened Hilti's position in the market for Hilti-compatible consumables in general.[44]

(iii) Abuse of dominant position, effect on trade and safety concerns

Hilti had admitted that some of its behaviour could constitute an abuse if it were held to be in a dominant position. Nevertheless, it objected to the Commission's conclusion that it had sought to frustrate the legitimately available licences of right as well as to the alleged discriminatory policy against the business of competitors and their customers. The CFI pointed out that under the system of licences of right, Hilti had demanded royalties about six times higher than the level that the competent authority finally set. This behaviour, which needlessly delayed the proceedings, was held to "undeniably" constitute an abuse.[45] The CFI was as brief about the discriminatory policy pursued by Hilti, stating that the Commission had proved the existence of this behaviour sufficiently in order to conclude that this was "not a legitimate mode of competition on the part of an undertaking in a dominant position".[46]   **5.41**

The CFI also rejected the alleged objective justification for Hilti's behaviour in terms of the need to safeguard the safety of its products. It pointed out that: **5.42**

> "... it is clearly not the task of an undertaking in a dominant position to take steps on its own initiative to eliminate products which, *rightly or wrongly*, it regards as dangerous or at least as inferior in quality to its own products. It must further be held in this connection that the effectiveness of the Community rules on competition would be jeopardised if the interpretation by an undertaking of the laws of the various Member States regarding product liability were to take precedence over those rules."[47]

As such, there was no need to examine whether the competing goods were in fact of lesser quality or reliability, because this could in any event not justify the abusive behaviour.[48]

---

[42] On the determination of the material scope of a patent and on tie-in clauses under Article 85 E.C., see *supra*, pt. 3(3)(b) and (c).

[43] The CFI equally upheld the Commission's qualification of the relevant geographical market as constituting the whole of the E.C.

[44] Case T–30/89: [1991] E.C.R. II-1439; [1992] 4 C.M.L.R. 16, at para. 93.

[45] Case T–30/89: [1991] E.C.R. II-1439; [1992] 4 C.M.L.R. 16, at para. 99.

[46] Case T–30/89: [1991] E.C.R. II-1439; [1992] 4 C.M.L.R. 16, at para. 100.

[47] Case T–30/89: [1991] E.C.R. II-1439; [1992] 4 C.M.L.R. 16, at paras. 118–119 (emphasis added).

[48] On the safety justification in relation to intellectual property rights, see *infra*, Chap. 7, pt. 6(2).

5.43   The CFI equally held the abusive behaviour to have an effect on intra-Community trade. It stated that the commercial interests of the independent manufacturers were not only harmed in the United Kingdom, but that simultaneously their ability to export to other Member States was prejudiced by the abusive behaviour of Hilti which was aimed at limiting their entry into the market. The export possibilities were held to be real and potentially lucrative considering the differences in price in the different Member States. On the basis of all those reasons the CFI dismissed Hilti's application for annulment of the Commission's decision.

(c) The European Court of Justice's judgment on appeal

(i) Issues at stake

5.44   The CFI thus fully concurred with the Commission's decision that Hilti had abused its dominant position in the market for Hilti-compatible nails. A *de facto* extension of the exclusivity inherent in patent protection to unprotected by-products was held to be incompatible with Article 86 E.C. This conclusion could only be reached by defining the relevant product market as the market in the Hilti-compatible by-product concerned. It is not surprising, therefore, that Hilti in its appeal before the European Court of Justice challenged "the grounds on which the Court of First Instance arrived at a definition of the market which enabled it to find that the position held by Hilti was a dominant one, and also certain reasoning in the judgment relating to the discharging of the burden of proof by the Commission".[49]

(ii) Nature of judicial review in appeal

5.45   It should be pointed out that, as the *Hilti* case illustrates, an appeal to the European Court of Justice concerning judgments from the CFI is not tantamount to yet another full trial, a kind of second chance in case no satisfaction was obtained before the CFI. In his opinion to the case, Advocate General Jacobs recalled that the rationale of the establishment of a Court of First Instance, by a Council Decision of 1988, was not simply to insert an intermediary court between the Commission and the European Court of Justice, at least in competition cases, but rather for it "to take over a substantial part of its jurisdiction".[50] Concerning the nature of judicial review in appeal, the Court unequivocally held:

> "It should be pointed out, before considering Hilti's pleas, that the Court of Justice has consistently held that pursuant to Article 168A of the EEC Treaty and Article 51 of the Statute of the Court of Justice of the EEC an appeal may rely only on grounds relating to the infringement of rules of law, to the exclusion of any appraisal of the facts . . . ."[51]

[49] Case C–53/92 P, *Hilti AG v. Commission,* Judgment of March 2, 1994 (Appeal): [1994] E.C.R. I-667; (1994) 1 C.M.L.R. 590, at para. 7.

[50] Case C–53/92 P: [1994] E.C.R. I-667; (1994) 1 C.M.L.R. 590, Opinion delivered on November 10, 1993, at paras. 10–11. Council Decision 88/591 of June 24, 1988 establishing a Court of First Instance: [1988] O.J. L319/1.

[51] Case C–53/92 P: [1994] E.C.R. I-667; [1994] 1 C.M.L.R. 590, at para. 10. The Court thereby in particularly refers to the following judgments concerning E.C. officials: Case C–283/90 P, *Vidrànyi v. Commission,* Judgment of October 1, 1991: [1991] E.C.R. I-4339, at para. 12; Case C–346/90 P, Judgment of April 8, 1992: [1992] E.C.R. I-2691, at para. 7.

On appeal, the Court will thus only examine whether or not a rule of law was infringed by the CFI, without re-examining the appraisal made by the CFI of the facts of the case. Nevertheless, as Advocate General Jacobs pointed out, if it were to be established that the CFI did not take relevant facts of the case into consideration, this might also constitute an infringement of a rule of law and be grounds for annulling the judgment. He argued:

> "It is clear that a failure to take relevant factors into consideration in reaching a conclusion of law is in itself an error of law which might render the judgment liable to be annulled. It is to be noted that, in such a case, this Court is not reviewing the findings of fact made by the Court of First Instance, but rather examining whether sufficient findings have been made to support the legal conclusions drawn."[52]

(iii) No infringement of a rule of law

The issue at stake in the *Hilti* case was therefore whether or not the CFI had infringed a rule of law either through wrongly interpreting and applying E.C. law, or through reaching legal conclusions which were not substantiated by sufficient findings. The Court rejected Hilti's main plea that the CFI failed to apply the correct test for defining the relevant product market by pointing out that, from its judgment, it appeared the CFI had duly considered the question of the substitutability of the products in question.[53] It also systematically rejected the six other pleas made by Hilti, mainly arguing that the CFI had failed to take all the evidence put before it by Hilti into consideration, had made an incorrect or insufficient appraisal of the facts, or had taken a wrong approach to the burden of proof. Having regard to the limited nature of judicial review in appeal, the Court pointed out that these claims related to findings of facts, whereas on the whole the considerations given by the CFI in its judgment were held to be sufficient to support the conclusions reached. In other words, Hilti's appeal was dismissed and the judgment of the CFI fully upheld.

5.46

(3) The extension of intellectual property exclusivity to a derivative market

(a) The Commission's Magill decision

(i) Issues

The Commission's *Magill* decision of 1988 was far more controversial than the *Hilti* decision, because it touched on the central nerve of the delicate question of where to draw the boundaries to the exclusive rights of intellectual property owners in view of the need to safeguard competition in the Common Market.[54] The key issue was whether, and to what extent, an owner of copy-

5.47

---

[52] Case C–53/92 P: [1994] E.C.R. I-667; [1994] 1 C.M.L.R. 590, Opinion, at para. 28.
[53] Case C–53/92 P: [1994] E.C.R. I-667; [1994] 1 C.M.L.R. 590, at para. 11–14. For the Court's response to *Hilti's* allegation that the CFI had wrongfully applied the criteria laid down by the Court in the prior *Hugin* case, see *infra*, Chap. 8, pt. 3(b)(iii).
[54] The *Magill TV Guide/ITP, BBC and RTE* decision of December 21, 1988: [1989] O.J. L78/43; [1989] 4 C.M.L.R. 749.

right in advance listings of forthcoming television and radio programmes can rely on his exclusive right to exclude potential competitors from the derivative market of weekly TV guides without infringing Article 86 E.C. The essential facts were the following. Magill TV Guide Ltd, the publisher of a weekly TV guide, had lodged a complaint with the Commission against the Independent Television Publications Ltd (ITP), the British Broadcasting Corporation (BBC) and Radio Telefis Eireann Authority (RTE), all three being providers of public broadcasting services. Magill wanted to bring a comprehensive weekly TV guide onto the market in Ireland and Northern Ireland, comprising the programmes offered by ITP, BBC and RTE. ITP, BBC and RTE each marketed a weekly TV guide, but only comprising their own programmes, so that a consumer who wanted to have complete advance information had to buy several TV guides. ITP, BBC and RTE, who held copyright in their respective advance listings of forthcoming programmes, gave licences free of charge to newspapers on the express terms that they might only reproduce daily listings. Upon the marketing of a comprehensive weekly TV guide by Magill, ITP, BBC and RTE obtained a Court injunction to stop the infringement of their copyright. According to Magill, their behaviour which led to its exclusion from the market in weekly TV guides was incompatible with the Community rules on competition. The Commission agreed with Magill and held that the practices and policies of the three television broadcasters constituted an abuse of a dominant position in the sense of Article 86 E.C.

(ii) Relevant market and dominant position

5.48   The relevant product market was held to be the market in the advance weekly listings of each of the broadcasters. The Commission pointed out that their listings were complementary, rather than interchangeable, since they covered different programmes and were each constituent elements of a comprehensive guide. Weekly listings were also only interchangeable to a limited extent with daily listings because the latter did not allow the television viewer to plan ahead. Finally, the different TV guide markets were considered to be separate from the markets for broadcasting services, although they are derived from, and ancillary to, the latter. The relevant geographical market was held to be Ireland and Northern Ireland. Comprehensive weekly TV guides would be marketed in both those areas so that cross-border trading would occur if they were allowed to be marketed.

The Commission pointed out that the broadcasters had both a factual and a legal monopoly on the production and first publication of their weekly listings. The factual monopoly is due to the fact that the weekly listings are a by-product of the broadcasting schedule. These listings obviously cannot be produced by third parties themselves but have to be obtained from the broadcasting organisation so that third parties, such as Magill, are in a position of economic dependence *vis-à-vis* broadcasters such as ITP, BBC and RTE. The legal monopoly results from the claims to copyright protection on the listings in order to exclude competition by third parties.[55] On this basis, the Commission held that ITP, BBC and RTE each occupied a dominant position in the market for their respective weekly listings.

(iii) Copyright enforcement and abuse of a dominant position

The most delicate issue was the finding as to whether or not there had also been an abuse of this dominant position, because this implied the appraisal of whether or not BBC, ITP and RTE had made a normal use of their copyright under the Community rules on competition. The Commission relied heavily on the example given in point (b) of Article 86 E.C. of an abusive practice by an undertaking in a dominant position, namely limiting production or markets to the prejudice of consumers. It was held that ITP, BBC and RTE prevented the substantial potential consumer demand for a comprehensive weekly TV guide to be met in order to protect their individual TV guides against competition. In particular, the Commission held the licensing terms which prevented the publication of the listings, other than on a daily and sometimes two-daily basis, to be unduly restrictive of competition to the prejudice of consumers. The justification of the broadcasters' policies in terms of the need to ensure a comprehensive high-quality coverage of all their programmes was rejected as being disproportionate and inconsistent, because no obligations to this end were imposed by virtue of the licences given so far. BBC, ITP and RTE were therefore held to have abused their dominant position within the meaning of Article 86 E.C.

The Commission also, rather plainly, rejected the argument based on the copyright protection on the advance listings in the following terms:

> "The argument put forward by the parties in relation to copyright do not affect this conclusion. On the contrary the Commission considers that the practices and policies of ITP, BBC and RTE in the present case in fact *use copyright as an instrument of abuse in a manner which falls outside the specific subject-matter of that intellectual property right.*"[56]

The Commission added that a further element of abuse lay in the fact that ITP, BBC and RTE, who held a dominant position in the market for their own listings, prevented competition from third parties in the derivative market for comprehensive weekly TV guides. In the *Decca* decision of the same day, the Commission had equally rejected a justification given for the abuse of a dominant position based on alleged copyright. It pointed out that there was no need to ascertain whether those copyrights really existed because the objective was to allocate markets and:

5.49

5.50

---

[55] See also D. Price, *op. cit.*, p. 85, where she points out that: "intellectual property rights are classic examples of barriers to entry and are recognised as such both by the Commission and the Chigaco school of economists." "In *Magill*, copyright in the advance weekly listings constituted an important barrier to entry."

[56] At pt. 23, p. 50 (emphasis added).

"the Community system of competition does not allow an improper use of rights under national copyright laws which frustrates Community competition rules."[57]

As such, the Commission created the impression that once it had established that a dominant position had been abused, then the protection of copyright could not be relied on to justify the behaviour of the dominant undertaking which was held to be incompatible with Article 86 E.C. In the *Magill* decision, the Commission apparently went a step further and stated that the only possible remedy was the supply of the advance listings to each other and to third parties on request, and on a non-discriminatory basis, as well as to permit the reproduction of those listings. The Commission pointed out that this could be done by means of licences on condition that the royalties are reasonable. As such, the Commission not only held that a copyright owner could not invoke his copyright to stop an infringement of his right. It further put the obligation on the copyright owner to let third parties use his protected work upon request.[58] It is obvious that this approach is difficult to reconcile with the traditional approach held by the Court, and that it apparently calls the whole existence/exercise dichotomy into question.[59] It is not surprising, therefore, that this decision by the Commission with its implicit call for "affirmative action" on behalf of a copyright owner proved to be highly controversial and was challenged by BBC, RTE and ITP separately before the CFI.

(b) The Court of First Instance's appraisal

(i) **Issues raised**

5.51 The judgments by the Court of First Instance in what became known as the *Magill* cases were as controversial as the Commission's *Magill* decision itself since they basically confirmed the latter.[60] The three undertakings concerned by the Commission's decision, namely the BBC, ITP and RTE, each appealed to the CFI to have the decision declared void. The CFI dealt with the cases separately even though the contents of the rulings are largely similar and the judgments were passed on the same day. The applicants contested the finding that they occupied a dominant position in the market since they disagreed with the definition of the relevant product market as being the market in the

---

[57] The *Decca Navigator System* decision of December 21, 1988: [1989] O.J. L43/27; [1990] 4 C.M.L.R. 627, at pt. 104. In this particular case, the claim for copyright protection had been rejected by most national courts.
[58] This is what Subiotto has called the *affirmative action* obligation, see R. Subiotto, "The right to deal with whom one pleases under EEC competition law: a small contribution to a necessary debate" [1992] E.C.L.R. 234 at 236.
[59] See also T. Vinje, "*Magill*: its impact on the information technology industry" [1992] E.I.P.R. 397 at 398. See *supra*, Chap. 3, pt. 4(2).
[60] The following are generally referred to as the *Magill* cases: Case T–69/89, *Radio Telefis Eireann v. Commission*: [1991] E.C.R. II-485; [1991] 4 C.M.L.R. 586. Case T–70/89, *The British Broadcasting Corporation and BBC Enterprises Limited v. Commission*: [1991] E.C.R. II-535; [1991] 4 C.M.L.R. 669. Case T–76/89, *Independent Television Publications Limited v. Commission*: [1991] E.C.R. II-575; [1991] 4 C.M.L.R. 745; all judgments of July 10, 1991.

advance weekly listings of their own programmes. Rather, ITP maintained that the relevant market was the market for TV guides in general,[61] the BBC that it was the market for broadcasting services or in the alternative the market for television programme information generally,[62] and RTE thought the appropriate market comprised all advance programme information supplied on a weekly or daily basis.[63] Secondly, they invoked the established case law concerning the "existence/exercise" dichotomy to support the argument that their behaviour could not be considered abusive because it constituted merely the legitimate exercise of their copyright. They pointed out that the Court had consistently held that for Article 86 E.C. to apply, an additional factor is needed besides the legitimate exercise of intellectual property rights.

(ii) Relevant product market and dominant position

The CFI rejected the alternative methods of defining the relevant product market as put forward by the plaintiffs. The BBC's first proposal was not upheld on the basis that publishing is a totally different economic activity from broadcasting. Equally, all the other definitions were put aside because, as the Commission had established and as was confirmed by the success of the weekly guides during the brief time-span they were available on the market, there was a specific, constant and regular potential demand for advance weekly listings. The CFI agreed with the Commission that daily listings are only to a limited extent a substitute, because only comprehensive weekly listings allow the television viewer to plan his leisure activities ahead.

5.52

The relevant product market was thus confirmed to be the market in the advance weekly listings of each of the plaintiffs. The CFI proceeded to state that as a consequence of their copyright on their listings, the BBC, ITP and RTE each held a dominant position in the relevant market. The BBC and ITP objected to this finding by pointing out that the Court has consistently held that the mere exercise of an intellectual property right does not suffice to establish that the owner has a dominant position in the market. Although this statement is correct, it should be added that the Court has never stated that intellectual property protection is an obstacle to establishing a dominant position. Rather, the Court has clarified that one needs to look at whether the intellectual property owner can impede the maintenance of effective competition in a substantial part of the relevant market so that intellectual property protection is neither an indication of, nor an obstacle to, the finding of a dominant position.[64] The CFI confirmed the validity of the test applied by the Commission, namely the reference to the economic dependence of third parties such as Magill and the possibility of preventing the emergence of effective competition in the market, a test which had already been upheld by the Court in the *Michelin* case.[65] As such, it should be emphasised that the Commission

---

[61] Case T–76/89: [1991] E.C.R. II-575; [1991] 4 C.M.L.R. 745, at para. 15.
[62] Case T–70/89: [1991] E.C.R. II-535; [1991] 4 C.M.L.R. 669, at paras. 16–17.
[63] Case T–69/89: [1991] E.C.R. II-485; [1991] 4 C.M.L.R. 586, at para. 30. *RTE* also preliminary invoked infringement of essential procedural requirements, but this was not upheld by the CFI.
[64] On this issue, see *supra*, pt. 2(3).
[65] Case 322/81, *Michelin v. Commission*, Judgment of November 9, 1983: [1983] E.C.R. 3461; [1985] 1 C.M.L.R. 282, at para. 30. On this issue, see also *infra*, Chap. 8, pt. 3.

and the CFI did not state that the plaintiffs were in a dominant position *because* of their copyright, but rather as a *consequence* of their copyright.[66]

5.53   RTE's argument seems therefore more appropriate, albeit somewhat exaggerated. RTE had argued that accepting the Commission's criterion to establish the relevant product market would entail that:

> "every undertaking – with the exception of 'producers of undifferentiated goods' – would hold a dominant position, within the meaning of Article 86, on the market for its own products".[67]

This is, of course, only true to the extent that no interchangeable products are present in, or may enter, the market and is not necessarily linked to the existence of intellectual property protection. It is, for instance, unlikely that the Commission would consider one particular reading book to be the relevant product because third parties can freely draw inspiration from the ideas expressed therein, which are not protected by copyright, on condition that they do not infringe the copyright of the author which covers the form of expression. Third parties could thus bring a competing and interchangeable product on to the market. This is a very different situation compared to the one at issue, namely listings of television programmes for which the relevant data is inseparable from its form. With respect to the latter there can be no interchangeable product on the market if effective competition is excluded as a consequence of the exercise of copyright. But even if RTE's argument had been accepted, and if it had been retained that the relevant market did not merely constitute the market in their own programmes but rather in all advance weekly listings, then one could still argue that the BBC, RTE and ITP abused a position of collective dominance. Smith points out that there was *in casu* perhaps no tacit agreement between the broadcasters in the sense of Article 85 E.C., but that for Article 86 E.C. to apply it suffices that there is "a parallel behaviour between parties whose aggregate market position is such that it would, if held by one undertaking, amount to dominance", with, as result, that the competitive conditions differ from the normal ones.[68] He maintains that in this particular case, parallel behaviour was unlikely to occur normally because alternatives existed to the applications for court injunctions made individually by the broadcasters against Magill. He therefore concludes that there is a "prima facie case for considering the parallel behaviour to be the result of abusive conduct."[69] However, the CFI did not reflect on this possibility since, as stated above, it upheld the Commission's definition of the relevant product market and consequently the finding that the broadcasters occupied a dominant position in that market. The most difficult issue the CFI had to address was whether or not this dominant position had also been abused.

---

[66] See also T. Vinje, "*Magill*: its impact on the information technology industry" [1992] E.I.P.R. 397 at 400 where he observes that the Commission and the Court apply traditional economic criteria in testing for dominance and concludes: "it would be far-fetched to assert that *Magill* equates dominance with simple ownership of copyright."

[67] Case T–69/89: [1991] E.C.R. II-485; [1991] 4 C.M.L.R. 586, at para. 32.

[68] J. Smith, "Television guides: the European Court doesn't know 'there's so much in it'" [1992] E.C.L.R. 135 at 137.

[69] J. Smith, *op. cit.*, p. 138. In his view, there is no doubt that the case concerned abusive behaviour of an oligopoly. He therefore regrets that the CFI ignored this.

(iii) Abuse of a dominant position

The applicants raised the argument that they had merely sought to protect the
specific subject-matter of their copyright, behaviour which the Court has consistently held not to constitute an abuse under Article 86 E.C. in the absence of
an additional element. In particular, they maintained that the prohibition on
Magill or other third parties to publish the weekly listings is:

5.54

> "the direct result of the exclusive right to use the protected creation with
> a view to the manufacture and first sale of commercial products, which
> constitutes the substance of the right."[70]

The Commission and the CFI each took a different approach to counter this
argument. The practical result was nonetheless the same in that the plaintiffs
could not successfully invoke their national copyright to justify their behaviour under the Community rules on competition. The Commission came to
this conclusion by challenging the very existence of the intellectual property
right under Community law. The CFI's reasoning aimed at proving that there
was an additional element present which constituted an abusive exercise of
the intellectual property right.

According to the Commission, one has first to ascertain the legitimacy of
copyright in programme listings before reflecting upon the scope of the specific subject-matter of the right. To do so, regard must be had to:

5.55

> "... *inter alia*, the nature of the property protected from the technologi-
> cal, cultural or innovative point of view, together with the purpose and
> justification in domestic law of the copyright in listings."[71]

In other words, it has to be ascertained whether the "essential function" of
copyright is fulfilled.[72] With regard to programme listings, the Commission
observed that they are merely factual information which is not secret, innovative or related to research so that the conferment of copyright protection "can
only be explained by the desire to "reserve a monopoly" to its owner".[73] The
Commission takes this reasoning a step further and maintains that the refusal
to authorise third parties to publish the information is arbitrary because it
cannot be justified in terms of safeguarding the essential function of copyright, *i.e.* for requirements of secrecy, research and development, or other
objectively verifiable considerations and hence constitutes an abuse.[74]
According to the Commission, the discriminatory licensing policy is, to the
contrary, clearly aimed at preventing the emergence of competing products on
the derivative market for comprehensive weekly guides.

---

[70] See for instance Case T–69/89: [1991] E.C.R. II-485; [1991] 4 C.M.L.R. 586, at para. 38.

[71] Case T–69/89: [1991] E.C.R. II-485; [1991] 4 C.M.L.R. 586, at para. 45.

[72] On the function of copyright, see *supra*, Chap. 2, pt. 3(3).

[73] Case T–69/89: [1991] E.C.R. II-485; [1991] 4 C.M.L.R. 586, at para. 46. The Commission
points to the opinion of Advocate General Mischo in Case 35/87, *Thetford v. Fiamma*,
concerning the principle of relative novelty under the rules on the free movement of goods. He
held that the "normal" exercise of intellectual property rights might be contrary to Community
law because there might be a protectionist intention underlying the grant of the intellectual
property right. On this issue, see *infra*, Chap. 6, pt. 3(2).

[74] This analysis has been strongly criticised on the basis that it bears on the existence of the right,
whereas the Commission should have taken the existence/exercise dichotomy as a premise. See
for instance P. Glazener, "*Verplichte licenties in het Gemeenschapsrecht*" [1992] I.E.R. 10 at
14.

5.56   The CFI did not follow the Commission in its analysis of the grounds for national copyright protection for programme listings under Community law. Rather, it sought to reconcile the conclusion drawn by the Commission with the principles so far established by the Court. Contrary to the Commission, it took the existence/exercise dichotomy as a given fact, recalling that in the absence of harmonisation the procedures and conditions for granting copyright protection are a matter for national law to determine. The CFI also reiterated the established case law that the exclusive right to reproduce a protected work is covered by the specific subject-matter of copyright and does not, in itself, infringe Article 86 E.C. But here it added the following important qualification:

> "However, while it is plain that the exercise of the exclusive right to reproduce a protected work is not in itself an abuse, that does not apply when, *in the light of the details of each individual case*, it is apparent that right is exercised in such ways and circumstances as in fact to pursue an aim manifestly contrary to the objectives of Article 86. In that event, *copyright is no longer exercised in a manner which corresponds to its essential function*, within the meaning of Article 36 of the Treaty, *which is to protect the moral rights in the work and to ensure a reward for the creative effort, while respecting the aims of, in particular, Article 86.* [...] In that case, the primacy of Community law, particularly as regards the principles as fundamental as those of the free movement of goods and freedom of competition, prevails over any use of a rule of national intellectual property law in a manner contrary to those principles."[75]

5.57   The CFI rather unconvincingly stated that this analysis is "borne out" by the Court's decisions in the *Volvo* and *Renault* cases and in particular by the Court's submission that the arbitrary refusal by the owner of industrial designs to supply spare parts to third parties might constitute an abuse under Article 86 E.C.[76] The CFI equated this with the refusal to authorise third parties to publish the weekly programme listings. However, it has been pointed out by Subiotto that the Court in the spare parts cases merely referred to the supply of protected products and did not impose the obligation to share intellectual property rights.[77] Or in other words, the CFI used a sophism by equating refusal to supply with refusal to license. Whereas the Court failed to look at the anti-competitive effect of the court injunctions upholding exclusive rights and preventing third parties from using the intellectual property rights

---

[75] Case T–69/89: [1991] E.C.R. II-485; [1991] 4 C.M.L.R. 586, at para. 71 (emphasis added).

[76] For an analysis of these cases and the difference in approach as compared to the *Magill* cases, see *infra*, Chap. 8, pt. 4.

[77] R. Subiotto, "The right to deal with whom one pleases under EEC competition law: a small contribution to a necessary debate" [1992] E.C.L.R. 234 at 241. He writes: "...it seems that one must distinguish between the licensing of intellectual property rights, over which the Court in *Volvo* and *Renault* recognises that the owner has absolute discretion, on the one hand, and the obligations which may be imposed on the owner with respect to the physical products resulting from its use of the protected rights, on the other hand. It is clear that what someone does with a product has nothing to do with the exercise of intellectual property rights, including where the manufacture of the product has necessitated the use of intellectual property rights." Also Flynn remarks that the CFI's analogy would amount to interpreting the *Volvo* judgment as requiring third parties to manufacture the panels, see J. Flynn, "Intellectual property and antitrust: E.C. attitudes" [1992] E.I.P.R. 49 at 53.

in the spare parts cases, this was precisely what the CFI was concerned with in the *Magill* cases. The CFI held:

> "Conduct of that type – characterised by preventing the production and marketing of a new product, for which there is potential consumer demand, on the ancillary market of television magazines and thereby excluding all competition from that market solely in order to secure the applicant's monopoly – *clearly goes beyond what is necessary to fulfil the essential function of the copyright as permitted in Community law.*"[78]

As such, it has been said that rather than confirming existing case law, the ruling of the CFI in the *Magill* cases is revolutionary because it is the first time that a refusal to licence has been held to be incompatible with the rules on competition by a Community court.[79] But this is merely the consequence of applying a test which aims at restraining the use of intellectual property rights beyond what is needed to safeguard the essential function of the right. It is therefore submitted that it is the introduction of this test that is revolutionary and to be welcomed.[80] It should be recalled that the functionality test is not novel in itself because apart from fully applying to denominations of origin,[81] it has already partly been applied with regard to trade marks and performance rights. However, this was previously done mainly with the aim of specifying the specific subject-matter of trade marks rather than to limit its scope.[82] The CFI gave the beginning of a Community definition of the concept of "essential function of a copyright" by referring to the protection of the moral rights in the work and the need to ensure a reward for the creative effort while respecting the aims of Article 86 E.C. The Commission gave a different, though complementary, appraisal of the essential function of copyright. The latter referred to the nature of the property protected from the technological, cultural or innovative point of view.[83] Both definitions imply a case-by-case analysis of whether or not the function is fulfilled in the given circumstances but they are, at least formally, situated at a different level. The Commission's definition is clearly directed at challenging the validity of the copyright in question, and thus the national measure granting the copyright. The CFI's definition is prima facie directed at the behaviour of private parties.

(c) *The European Court of Justice's judgment on appeal*

(i) Issues at stake

The main problem was that it is difficult to reconcile the practical result of the CFI's final ruling with its premise, namely the formal existence/exercise

5.58

---

[78] Case T–69/89: [1991] E.C.R. II-485; [1991] 4 C.M.L.R. 586, at para. 73 (emphasis added).
[79] See I. Forrester, "Software licensing in the light of current E.C. competition law considerations" [1992] E.C.L.R. 5 at 16. According to this author, the *Magill* decisions are complementary to, rather than conflicting with, the spare parts cases.
[80] This is in line with the proposed functionality test, see *supra*, Chap. 3, pt. 4(2)(c).
[81] See the *Delhaize* case (Case C–47/90), *supra*, Chap. 3, pt. 4(2)(c)(iii).
[82] See *supra*, Chap. 4, pt. 2(2)(b) and 2(3).
[83] It is likely that the Commission used this broad definition which embodies concepts of industrial property law, such as the protection of innovation, in order to include functional or utilitarian copyrights which are not always necessarily original or creative in the artistic sense of the word.

dichotomy. Through curtailing the straightforward exercise of copyright on the grounds that this is abusive and contrary to Article 86 E.C., the CFI came extremely close to negating the very existence of the intellectual property right. It is not surprising, therefore, that this was one of the main arguments raised on appeal before the European Court of Justice by RTE and ITP against the judgment of the CFI.[84] They pointed out that:

> "... one of the essential rights of the owner of a copyright, without which that right would be deprived of its substance, is the exclusive right of reproduction. That right, which has not been placed in question by the Treaty rules, entitles its holder to be rewarded by the exclusive sale of the products incorporating the protected work and to prevent competition by a third party in respect of those products."[85]

It is precisely the disregard in practice by the CFI of the existence/exercise dichotomy, as previously elaborated upon by the Court, that led Advocate General Gulmann to conclude in his opinion to the case that the Court should put the judgment of the CFI aside and itself give a final judgment on the matter.[86] On the basis of a comprehensive analysis of the case law of the Court relating to the specific subject-matter concept, the latter held that the CFI's conclusion establishing an abuse under Article 86 E.C. was not justified.[87] He was therefore inclined to accept the argument raised by RTE and ITP that Article 86 E.C. was applied not because the exercise made of their intellectual property right was considered to be inherently abusive, but rather because the programme listings concerned were not regarded as meriting copyright protection. He pointed out the following in this respect:

> "As indicated at the outset it may reasonably be claimed that the effort involved in drawing up listings *is not so deserving of protection* as to justify acceptance that the author may prevent the emergence of comprehensive weekly television guides. The preparation of the programme listings does not require any incentive since the listings do not consist of anything more than the setting out on paper of certain information which must in any event be produced and compiled for the purpose of television broadcasting service. If that factor is taken into consideration I see no difficulty in holding that the refusal to grant licences in these cases are indications of an improper exercise of copyright. The question is, however, whether the Court of Justice is able to attach significance to the nature of the work protected by copyright."[88]

He, not surprisingly, answered the latter question in the negative on the basis of the application of the existence/exercise dichotomy. It should be

---

[84] On the arguments raised, see also T. Skinner, "The oral hearing of the *Magill* case" [1994] E.C.L.R. 103.

[85] Joined Cases C–241/91 P & C–242/91 P, *Radio Telefis Eirann (RTE) and Independent Television Publications Ltd (ITP) (Magill appeal)*: [1995] E.C.R. I-743; [1995] 4 C.M.L.R. 718 at para. 34.

[86] Joined Cases C–241/91P & C–242/91P, *Radio Telefis Eirann (RTE) and Independent Television Publications Ltd (ITP) (Magill appeal)*, Opinion of June 1, 1994.

[87] In favour of Advocate General Gulmann's opinion, see for instance M. Van Kerckhove, "The Advocate General delivers his opinion on *Magill*" [1994] E.C.L.R. 276. For a qualified approach, see S. Haines, "Copyright takes the dominant position" [1994] E.I.P.R. 401.

[88] Joined Cases C–241/91P & C–242/91P, *op. cit.*, at para. 123.

pointed out that he thereby disregarded the fact that the Court had already set this distinction aside in some recent cases concerning Article 36 E.C. The latter are analysed in Chapter 6 below. It could thus be expected that with the current evolution in the case law concerning the free movement of goods whereby the existence/exercise dichotomy is more and more put under strain, and sometimes even put aside in favour of what could be called a "functionality test", a similar approach could be adopted in competition law cases. It is submitted that this would call for a coherent approach with clear indications of when Community rules would prevail. Legal certainty would most likely be obtained if the functionality test as used by the CFI were to be further elaborated upon by the Court.

Even if the question posed by the Advocate General becomes less relevant in view of the case law of the Court prior to the *Magill* appeal judgment, it remains important to know whether, and to what extent, the CFI was bound by the existence/exercise dichotomy. As Reindl points out, the CFI might have been restrained by a problem of jurisdiction. The fact that the CFI could only adjudicate on the compatibility of private parties conduct with Community rules on competition might have been the reason why it did not pursue the Commission's view on the validity, and thus the "existence", of national copyright.[89] In view of the conclusion drawn it would have been more logical, and would have provided more legal certainty, had the CFI held that the broadcasters' exercise of their copyright was not justified because the copyright itself was not granted in accordance with its essential function, and hence did not benefit from a special status under Community law. However, the CFI most likely lacked the competence to scrutinise the existence of intellectual property rights for their compatibility with E.C. law. The judgment by the Court in appeal therefore became all the more important. The Commission submitted that even if the Court quashed the judgment by the CFI on a particular point, it should nevertheless confirm the operative parts of the judgment, which are sound, whilst substituting its own reasoning for that of the CFI.[90] However, there was no need to do so because the Court fully upheld the judgments of the CFI and dismissed the appeals.

(ii) Abuse of a dominant position

The Court first of all reiterated that whereas the mere ownership of an intellectual property right does not confer a dominant position, it is no obstacle to this finding.[91] It upheld the judgment of the CFI in this respect on the grounds that RTE and ITP had a *de facto* monopoly over the information used in the programme listings so that they could prevent effective competition in the market in weekly television magazines.

With respect to the question of whether or not the exercise of intellectual property rights may amount to an abuse under Article 86 E.C., the Court gave the following clarification:

> "With regard to the issue of abuse, the arguments of the appellants and IPO wrongly presuppose that where the conduct of an undertaking in a

---

[89] See A. Reindl, *op. cit.*, n. 32.
[90] Joined Cases C–241/91P and C–242/91P, *op. cit.*, para. 19.
[91] See also *supra*, pt. (3)(b).

dominant position consists of the exercise of a right classified by national law as 'copyright', such conduct can never be reviewed in relation to Article 86 of the Treaty.

Admittedly, in the absence of Community standardisation or harmonisation of laws, determination of the conditions and procedures for granting protection of an intellectual property right is a matter for national rules. Further, the exclusive right of reproduction forms part of the author's rights, so that refusal to grant a licence, even if it is the act of an undertaking holding a dominant position, cannot in itself constitute abuse of a dominant position (judgment in Case 238/87, *Volvo*, paragraphs 7 and 8).

However, it is also clear from that judgment (paragraph 9) that the exercise of an exclusive right by the proprietor may, *in exceptional circumstances*, involve abusive conduct."[92]

The exceptional circumstances triggering Article 86 E.C. in this particular case were held to be the following: reliance on copyright to prevent the appearance of a new product for which there was a potential consumer demand, and the reservation to themselves of the secondary market of weekly television guides by excluding all competition on the market. According to the Court, the CFI had therefore not erred in law in concluding that Article 86 E.C. applied.[93] The Court also dismissed, as unfounded, the pleas as to the alleged misapplication of the concept of an effect on intra-Community trade by the CFI, and the failure by the latter to take the Berne Convention into account.[94]

In other words, the Court fully upheld the approach taken by the CFI which consisted in formally acknowledging the existence/exercise dichotomy whilst practically emptying the intellectual property right of its substance. The appeal judgment will therefore most likely be as controversial as the judgment of the CFI, if not more so. It was, for instance, clearly illustrated in legal writings that the CFI's *Magill* judgment was not "borne out" of the *Volvo* ruling of the Court but is, to the contrary, difficult to reconcile with it.[95] The Court in appeal expressly stated that there is a link between the two judgments, but failed to subsequently indicate the precise nature of the link. In Chapter 8 it is illustrated that there are indeed important similarities between the two cases. This finding makes it all the more difficult to understand on what basis the Court apparently comes to contradictory conclusions. It is important to point out in this respect, particularly in view of the criticism expressed subsequent to the judgment of the CFI, that the Court did not explain why Article 86 E.C. may apply to the refusal to license intellectual property rights, and not just to the refusal to sell protected products as seemed to follow from paragraphs 8 and 9 of the *Volvo* case.

5.62   It is furthermore to be regretted that the Court did not pursue, or even reiterate, the reasoning of the CFI in terms of the function of copyright. The

[92] Joined Cases C–241/91P & C–242/91P, *op. cit.*, paras. 48–50 (emphasis added).
[93] On the nature of the Court's review in appeal, see *supra*, the *Hilti* case, pt. 4(2)(c)(ii).
[94] On the application of the Berne Convention in E.C. law, see *supra*, Chap. 2, pt. 4(1)(c).
[95] See the CFI's *Magill* judgment *supra*, pt. (b)(iii), and the *Volvo* judgment *infra*, Chap. 8, pt. 4.

Court apparently endorsed the reasoning of the CFI merely in so far as the anti-competitive effects of the behaviour of the intellectual property owner are concerned, such as the prevention of the appearance of a new product on the market for which there is potential consumer demand. Contrary to the CFI, the Court failed to point out that such behaviour was abusive *because* it could not be justified in terms of the function of copyright. The latter put the emphasis on the fact that basic information on programme scheduling, on which copyright was enforced, is the indispensable raw material for compiling a weekly television guide.[96] The lack of analysis in terms of the function of intellectual property rights might open the door to unwarranted and unjustifiable interference of E.C. law with respect to other intellectual property rights such as patents. For example, would it suffice that third parties claim that they need to use protected inventions or technology to create a new product for the enforcement of a nationally granted patent to be held to be incompatible with Article 86 E.C.? Although this is obviously highly objectionable, from the point of view of safeguarding the very essence of intellectual property protection, the reasoning adopted by the Court in *Magill* would seem to imply a positive answer. It is therefore submitted that if the function of intellectual property rights is not upheld as a viable criterion then it will be all the more difficult to draw the line between abuse and use of intellectual property rights under Article 86 E.C. because intellectual property rights are, at least in the short run, inherently anti-competitive. It was generally expected that the Court would seize the opportunity to unequivocally clarify the relationship between intellectual property rights and Article 86 E.C. in *Magill*. However, guidance from the Court seems to be highly necessary, especially after the *Magill* appeal judgment, considering the potentially far-reaching implications it entails for all kinds of intellectual property rights.

(iii) Affirmative action obligation

The potential implications of the *Magill* judgment are all the more far-reaching since the Court expressly ruled that the Commission was entitled to impose compulsory licences under Article 3 of Regulation 17.[97] The Court settled the controversy, arisen in this respect subsequent to the *Volvo* case,[98] by pointing out the following: **5.63**

> "It is appropriate to observe that Article 3 of Regulation 17 is to be applied according to the nature of the infringement found and may include an order to do certain acts or things which, unlawfully, have not been done as well as an order to bring an end to certain acts, practices or situations which are contrary to the Treaty . . . ."[99]

In other words, the Court agreed with the CFI that the Commission may impose an "affirmative action" obligation on intellectual property owners if

---

[96] Joined Cases C–241/91P and C–242/91P, *op. cit.*, para. 53 and 56.

[97] On this particular issue, see also G. Van der Wal, "Article 86 E.C.: The limits of compulsory licensing" [1994] E.C.L.R. 230.

[98] On the controversy arisen in this respect in particular after the *Volvo* judgment and on the potential implications of compulsory licences, see *infra*, Chap. 9, pt. 5(1)(b).

[99] Joined Cases C–241/91P & C–242/91P, *op. cit.*, para. 90.

this is the only way to bring an infringement of Article 86 E.C. to an end.[1] In particular, the Court held:

> "In the present case, after finding that the refusal to provide undertakings such as Magill with the basic information contained in television programme listings was an abuse of a dominant position, the Commission was entitled under Article 3, in order to ensure that its decision was effective, to require the appellants to provide that information. As the Court of First Instance rightly found, the imposition of that obligation – with the possibility of making the authorisation of publication dependent on certain conditions, including payment of royalties - was the only way of bringing the infringement to an end."[2]

The fact that the obligation to license may be made conditional upon the payment of royalties does not alter the fact that, in essence, intellectual property owners may thus be obliged to share their protected intellectual property with third parties.

5.64   The approach adopted in the *Magill* case seems difficult to reconcile with the ruling in the *Volvo* case. In both judgments the existence/exercise dichotomy was formally upheld. However, the Court expressly acknowledged in the *Volvo* case that:

> "... an obligation imposed upon the proprietor of a protected design to grant third parties, even in return for a reasonable royalty, a licence for the supply of products incorporating the design would lead to the proprietor thereof being deprived of the substance of his exclusive right ...."[3]

It was precisely this concern not to deprive the intellectual property owner of the substance of his exclusive right that led the Court in the latter case to plainly state that a refusal to license cannot in itself constitute an abuse of a dominant position. In the view of the Court there was apparently no need to examine the potential anti-competitive effects this refusal could entail. It is significant in this respect that the Court particularly refrained from examining the exceptional circumstances of the case which consisted of a tie-in of car owners in the spare parts market through the enforcement of design protection on components of complex products.[4] In the *Magill* case the Court came to the contrary conclusion, and thus allowed for the intellectual property right to be emptied of its substance through the imposition of compulsory licences. The Court thereby pointed to the allegedly exceptional circumstances of the case, namely the fact that copyright was enforced to prevent the appearance of a new product in a derivative market and to reserve a monopoly in a secondary market. As Advocate General Gulmann pointed out, the latter approach is obviously irreconcilable with its premise, the existence/exercise dichotomy.

---

[1] On the affirmative action obligation imposed by the Commission in the *Magill* decisions, see *supra*, pt. (a)(iii).

[2] Joined Cases C–241/91P & C–242/91P, *op. cit.*, para. 91.

[3] Case 238/87, *Volvo v. Veng*: [1988] E.C.R. 6211; [1989] 4 C.M.L.R. 122, at para. 8. See *infra*, Chap. 8, in particular pt. 4(3)(c) and pt. 4(4)(a).

[4] For a detailed analysis of *Volvo* in comparison to *Magill*, see *infra*, esp. at Chap. 8.

(iv) Evaluation

The Court's judgment in appeal does not manage to fully dissipate the impression, which was apparently also shared by Advocate General Gulmann,[5] that Article 86 E.C. was applied in the *Magill* cases not so much because the exercise of intellectual property rights was held to be abusive, but rather because the programme listings concerned were not regarded as meriting copyright protection. This impression is reinforced by the fact that even though the Court formally upheld the existence/exercise dichotomy, it did not refrain from emptying the copyright concerned of its substance. Contrary to the CFI, the Court thereby apparently did not consider the need to fulfil the function of intellectual property rights as the decisive criterion in order to distinguish between the normal exercise, and the abuse, of intellectual property rights under Article 86 E.C. It rather seems that the so-called exceptional circumstances of the case and, in particular, the anti-competitive effects of the enforcement of intellectual property rights will be the decisive criteria to trigger the application of Article 86 E.C. in the future. The problem is how to define the concept of "exceptional circumstances", other than on an arbitrary basis, having regard to the fact that this was not considered in the *Volvo* case to which the Court refers.   5.65

In adopting this rather untransparent approach in the long-awaited *Magill* judgment, it is submitted that the Court not only potentially exposed itself to criticism in legal writings but, furthermore, set a dangerous precedent for the future. It should be emphasised that intellectual property rights are inherently anti-competitive, at least in the short run, whereas the reference to the "exceptional" circumstances of the case does not offer much legal certainty for intellectual property owners that their exclusive rights will not be unduly impinged upon. In other words, the Court seems to have set the door wide open to unpredictable and unwarranted interference by E.C. law not only in relation to copyright but in the field of intellectual property protection as a whole.   5.66

It should be pointed out in this respect that the exceptionally anti-competitive circumstances referred to by the Court in the *Magill* case clearly result from granting copyright on facts, rather than from an abusive exercise of his exclusive right by the intellectual property owner. It might therefore have sufficed to simply point out, having regard to the copyright idea/expression dichotomy, that copyright is not intended to reserve a monopoly on ideas but only grants the right to prohibit the unauthorised reproduction of the form in which these ideas are expressed.[6] It could thus be said that copyright exceeds its essential function, and cannot be upheld as a justification for anti-competitive behaviour under the competition rules, if having regard to the specific circumstances of the case, and in particular considering the fact that no alternative ways of expression are possible without infringing the copyright, it

---

[5] See *supra*, pt. (i).
[6] See *supra*, Chap. 2, pt. 3(3).

confers a monopoly on mere facts or ideas.[7] The anti-competitive behaviour which triggers Article 86 E.C. would then consists of invoking copyright on the form of expression in order to enforce a monopoly on a product, and thus prevent competition from occurring. The latter approach would avoid the rather delicate appraisal of the "creative effort" or "originality" of a work in competition cases, as well as the need to refer to the derivative market. There are, furthermore, grounds to believe that works involving creativity or originality, in the sense that they are not dictated solely by the function of the work, would not confer a monopoly on a product but would allow for alternative ways of expressing the same idea.

5.67   It is of course true that the functionality test, whether applied as set out above or as defined by the Commission and the CFI, would, in the first place, affect functional and utilitarian products whilst leaving literary and artistic works to a large extent untouched. Subiotto objects to this by pointing out that it is precisely that kind of copyright that stimulates research and development and hence should be left untouched.[8] It should be emphasised, however, that applying the functionality test merely avoids the abuse of the system of intellectual property rights. It is not tantamount to rendering the concept of functional or utilitarian copyright meaningless as such. It is undeniable that research and development in general would be hampered if one undertaking could prevent the use of information which is indispensable for further innovation by others.[9] It is not surprising, therefore, that the *Magill* judgments are of major importance to the information technology industry for which safeguarding inter-operability through curtailing abuses of intellectual property rights is essential to the continuing development and innovation of the market.[10] Although the final outcome of the *Magill* cases is to be welcomed for this reason, the major drawback lies in the fact that the rather vague indications given by the Court on appeal give grounds to fear that competition policy objectives may in the future well outweigh the legitimate claims for protection of intellectual property owners.

---

[7] It was maintained above that it is for the same reason, namely the monopoly position as a consequence of the copyright, that the relevant product market is determined as being the market in the own protected products. It had been pointed out that although the CFI referred to the essential function of copyright it failed to subsequently indicate why Article 86 had been breached. See J. Feenstra, and S. Krawczyk, "*De Magill-arresten: de uitoefening van het auteursrecht en misbruik van machtspositie*" [1992] *Informatierecht* 43 at 45. Unfortunately, the appeal judgment of the Court does not offer more guidance in this respect.

[8] R. Subiotto, *op. cit.*, p. 240.

[9] It is probably in this sense that the controversial statement to the press by Sir Leon Brittan, namely that "*Magill* shows that enterprises cannot unreasonably sit on their intellectual property rights in order to stifle enterprise and prevent the emergence of new forms of competition", should be understood.

[10] See especially T. Vinje, "*Magill*: its impact on the information technology industry" [1992] E.I.P.R. 397. For the appendices, see [1993] E.I.P.R. 71. See also I. Forrester, "Software licensing in the light of current E.C. competition law considerations" [1992] E.C.L.R. 5.

5. The incidence of Articles 85 and 86 E.C.

(1) Issue at stake

From the foregoing sections it is apparent that the approach adopted differs **5.68**
according to whether Article 85 or Article 86 E.C. is concerned. Under Article
85 E.C. intellectual property rights are not, as such, curtailed by virtue of the
use of the market power they confer, whereas this is exactly what is at stake
under Article 86 E.C. It is not surprising, therefore, that the question of the
incidence of Articles 85 and 86 E.C. has for the first time arisen with regard to
intellectual property rights, namely patents.

(2) Background to the *Tetra Pak* judgment

(a) The ruling

In the *Tetra Pak I* case, the Court of First Instance upheld the Commission's **5.69**
view that the granting of an exemption under Article 85(3) E.C. does not preclude the application of Article 86 E.C.[11] Tetra Pak objected to the Commission's finding that it had infringed Article 86 E.C. by taking over a
company which held a patent licence concerning competing technology,
exempted under Regulation 2349/84.[12]

(b) The essential facts

In the *Tetra Pak I* decision, the Commission held that Tetra Pak was in a **5.70**
dominant, almost monopolistic (91 per cent), position in the market for the
supply of machines for sterilising and filling cartons in aseptic conditions, and
the cartons to be used with those machines.[13] On the basis of its acquisition of
Liquipak, Tetra Pak took over Liquipak's exclusive patent licensing agreement with BTG. This agreement did not contain provisions contrary to Regulation 2349/84 and hence was thought to benefit from the block exemption
for as long as the Commission had not expressly withdrawn the exemption.

(c) Commission's findings under Article 85

The Commission objected to the exclusive nature of the licensing agreement **5.71**
because of Tetra Pak's already dominant position in the market. It maintained
that in the given circumstances exclusivity could not be justified under Article
85(3) E.C. by the need to protect research and development or the improvement of production and distribution. The benefit of the block exemption was,
nonetheless, not withdrawn because the agreement was altered to take into
account the Commission's objections and became non-exclusive in nature.

[11] Case T–51/89, *Tetra Pak Rausing SA v. Commission*, Judgment of July 10, 1990: [1990]
E.C.R. II-309; [1991] 4 C.M.L.R. 334.
[12] On Regulation 2349/84, see *supra*, pt. 3.
[13] Commission decision of July 26, 1988, *Tetra Pak I (BTG-licence)*: [1988] O.J. L272/27; [1990]
4 C.M.L.R. 47. Case T–51/89 is an appeal against this decision.

(d) Commission's findings under Article 86

5.72 The Commission nevertheless held that Tetra Pak had abused a dominant position, in the sense of Article 86 E.C., by obtaining the exclusive patent licence from BTG through acquiring Liquipak, for as long as the exclusivity lasted. According to the Commission, the latter not only had the effect of strengthening the dominant position which Tetra Pak already occupied in the market, but further frustrated the attempts of potential competitors to enter the market.[14]

(3) Legal appraisal

(a) Complementary provisions pursuing the same objective

5.73 Tetra Pak initiated proceedings before the CFI in order to have the Commission's decision declared void. It thereby based its claim exclusively on legal issues. Tetra Pak's main argument was that Article 86 E.C. cannot be applied if an exemption has been granted under Article 85 E.C. because both articles pursue the same objective. It maintained that any other interpretation would seriously jeopardise legal certainty as well as the uniform application of Community law. According to Tetra Pak, the mere fact that an undertaking which holds a dominant position in the market becomes party to an agreement exempted under Article 85(3) E.C. does not constitute an abuse in the absence of other elements extrinsic to the agreement and attributable to that undertaking. If the abuse relates to the agreement, then Article 86 E.C. could only be applied once the exemption had been withdrawn. The Commission pointed out that this would imply that an exemption is granted equally under Article 86 E.C. considering that the withdrawal of an exemption does not have retroactive effect.

The CFI recalled that although Articles 85 and 86 are complementary provisions pursuing the same objective they are, nevertheless, two distinct legal instruments that address different situations. The CFI partly agreed with Tetra Pak, stating that:

> "... the mere fact that an undertaking in a dominant position acquires an exclusive licence does not *per se* constitute abuse within the meaning of Article 86 EEC."[15]

(b) Additional element to establish "abuse" under Article 86

5.74 However, the CFI rejected the argument that an element external to the agreement was needed to constitute an abuse. It proceeded to state, in line with the

---

[14] In the *Tetra Pak I* decision, no fine was imposed considering the relative novelty of the infringement. However, the Commission has issued its *Tetra Pak II* decision on July 24, 1992: [1992] O.J. L72/1; [1992] 4 C.M.L.R. 551, in which a global appreciation of the infringement of Article 86 E.C. by Tetra Pak was given, and a fine imposed of 75 million ECUs. This fine was recently upheld by the CFI in Case T–83/91, *Tetra Pak II*, Judgment of October 6, 1994: [1994] E.C.R. II-755. The latter is currently being challenged on an appeal before the Court of Justice (Case C–333/94 P).

[15] Case T–51/89: [1990] E.C.R. II-309; [1991] 4 C.M.L.R. 334, at para. 23 (emphasis added).

Commission's approach, that the additional element for the finding of the abuse could be constituted by the factual background against which the acquisition of the exclusive licence took place:

> "For the purpose of applying Article 86, the circumstances surrounding the acquisition, and in particular its effects on the structure of competition in the relevant market, must be taken into account."[16]

It was held that in this specific case, the decisive factor for establishing the abuse was Tetra Pak's position in the market and particularly the fact that only the right to use BTG's patented process was capable of providing a third undertaking with the means to compete effectively with Tetra Pak. The acquisition of Liquipak, and the exclusive licence with BTG, thus had the effect of preventing competition from occurring.

(c) No Article 85(3) exemption under Article 86

The CFI further pointed out that linking the application of Article 86 E.C. to **5.75** the non-retroactive withdrawal of the exemption granted under Article 85(3) E.C. would be tantamount to granting an exemption under Article 86 E.C. Yet the E.C. Treaty does not foresee possible exemptions to Article 86 E.C. whereas secondary legislation cannot derogate from Treaty provisions.[17] The CFI plainly rejected the argument based on the legal certainty which was supposedly conferred by the exemption under Article 85(3) E.C., by stating that:

> "...an undertaking cannot rely on the alleged unpredictability of the application of Article 86 EEC in order to escape the prohibition there laid down."[18]

Equally, the argument that the uniform interpretation of Community law is at stake was refuted on the basis that national courts are acting as Community courts when applying Article 86 E.C., a system which is safeguarded by the preliminary questions procedure. Thus, Article 86 E.C. remains fully applicable regardless of what the outcome of the analysis under Article 85 E.C. is.

(d) Individual and group exemptions

Having convincingly explained the legal relationship between Articles 85 and **5.76** 86 E.C., the CFI then proceeded to draw an artificial, and it is submitted unnecessary, distinction between individual and group exemptions.[19] The premise is that individual exemptions are granted on a case-by-case basis whereby the factual circumstances, including the possibility of restricting competition in the market, should be taken into account, whereas the block exemption only refers to the provisions embodied in the agreement. When applying Article 86 E.C. to an agreement that has been individually exempted, the Commission must rely on the same findings unless the legal or factual

[16] Case T–51/89: [1990] E.C.R. II-309; [1991] 4 C.M.L.R. 334, at para. 23.
[17] Case T–51/89: [1990] E.C.R. II-309; [1991] 4 C.M.L.R. 334, at para. 25.
[18] Case T–51/89: [1990] E.C.R. II-309; [1991] 4 C.M.L.R. 334, at para. 37.
[19] Case T–51/89: [1990] E.C.R. II-309; [1991] 4 C.M.L.R. 334, at para. 28–29.

context has changed.[20] It is different when applying Article 86 E.C. to an agreement that fulfils the criteria of a group exemption because here no positive assessment has been made under Article 85(3) E.C. The CFI thus seems to imply that an individual exemption will offer greater protection and legal security, in so far as the application of Article 86 E.C. is concerned, than the invoking of a block exemption. The latter gave rise to certain contrary critiques. According to James, the fact that the CFI held that earlier relevant analysis has to be taken into account by the Commission "satisfies legitimate concerns as to legal certainty".[21] Daltrop and Ferry, to the contrary, point out that this implies that undertakings will now "face the dilemma of deciding whether to provide such greater immunity through notification but having to submit to Commission scrutiny".[22] It is apparent that this factual distinction is difficult to reconcile with the legal analysis about the difference in purpose and structure of Articles 85 and 86 E.C. It furthermore raises the question in which of the two categories the implied exemption on the basis of the opposition procedure, foreseen in most block exemption regulations, needs to be classified.[23]

(e) Main implications

5.77 The main importance of this judgment therefore consists in the fact that it was for the first time clearly stated that Article 86 E.C. is an instrument to safeguard competition in its own right, without being subject to the outcome of scrutiny under Article 85 E.C. A dominant undertaking acquiring exclusive intellectual property licences will therefore have to examine carefully whether or not in so doing it infringes not only Article 85 E.C. but also Article 86 E.C.

6. ESTABLISHING "ABUSE" OF INTELLECTUAL PROPERTY RIGHTS

5.78 The first obvious conclusion to be drawn from the case law is that the existence/exercise dichotomy is merely a formal distinction which raises more questions than it gives answers to. Upholding the formal immunity of national intellectual property rights prejudices legal certainty for economic actors with regard to the application of both the rules on the free movement of goods and the rules on competition. It is the latter that eventually have to account for incompatibilities between national intellectual property rights and Treaty rules.

The distinction between "normal use" and "misuse" of intellectual property rights under the rules on the free movement of goods is drawn with refer-

---

[20] Though it should be pointed out that the factual situation will always change in case of acquisitions or take-overs.
[21] H. James, "*Tetra Pak*: Exemption and abuse of dominant position" [1990] E.C.L.R. 267 at 269.
[22] J. Daltrop, J. Ferry, "The relationship between Articles 85 and 86: *Tetra Pak* (T–51/89)" [1991] E.I.P.R. 31 at 33.
[23] Although it should be recalled that the opposition procedure was no longer written into the draft block exemption for technology licensing agreements, contrary to the block exemptions for patent and know how licences it is intended to replace, see *supra*, pt. 3(4).

ence to the specific subject-matter of the intellectual property rights concerned. Except for trade marks and performance rights, this concept has not been defined so as to take the specifics and the essential function of intellectual property rights into account. In order to safeguard the internal market objective, regard is merely had as to whether or not the intellectual property owner consented to the first marketing of the protected product after which the principle of exhaustion is quasi-automatically applied. The legal or factual context against which the intellectual property rights are exercised, or the need to safeguard the inherent functions of the exclusive right, is thereby largely neglected.

The distinction between "normal" and "abusive" exercise of intellectual property rights under the competition rules is even more problematic. The application of Article 85 E.C. to agreements relating to intellectual property rights has been subject to major shifts in policy due to the changing perception of what constitutes the "essence" or the "existence" of the intellectual property right concerned. The latter, in turn, affects the definition of "normal" exercise which is not contrary to Article 85(1) E.C. Analysis under Article 85(3) E.C. gives rise to further legal uncertainty as it is not always clear when the enhancement of research and development and technological innovation will prevail over the temporary restraint of competition in the market. Or in other words, the question remains largely unanswered on what basis, and to what extent, the function of the intellectual property right is taken into account.

Nevertheless, Article 85 E.C. does not in principle affect the principle of exclusivity inherent in the intellectual property right concerned, but merely curtails anti-competitive agreements or concerted practices with third parties. Clarification that an analysis under Article 85 E.C. does not prejudice the application of Article 86 E.C. is therefore of major importance. Article 86 E.C. is concerned with the abusive exercise of the exclusivity, and thus market power, conferred by intellectual property rights on an undertaking holding a dominant position in the market.

The basic rule with respect to Article 86 E.C. is that an element additional to the normal use is needed to establish an abuse of intellectual property rights. This is not an effective bar, however, preventing the very "existence" or "essence" of the intellectual property right being affected by the rules on competition. There are no clear criteria provided by the Court to establish what this additional element will be considered to be in any particular case so that in this respect legal uncertainty prevails. The latter is most clearly illustrated by the outcome of the *Magill* cases. Whereas the Court formally upheld the existence/exercise dichotomy, it in fact emptied the copyright of its substance and allowed compulsory licences to be imposed. Instead of pursuing the analysis of the additional element in terms of the function of intellectual property rights as introduced by the CFI, the Court referred to the exceptionally anti-competitive circumstances of the case. The latter were, however, clearly the direct consequence of granting copyright protection on mere facts instead of on an original form of expression. The impression is therefore created that, like the CFI and the Commission, the Court considered that the programme listings did not merit copyright protection, rather than that the exercise made of his exclusive right by the intellectual property owner was abusive. In other words, it seems that the normal use of intellectual property rights considered to be abusively granted may well be equated with an abuse of intellectual property rights in so far as the application of Article 86 E.C. is concerned.

5.79   In the next chapter, it will be further illustrated that the existence/exercise dichotomy can lead but a formal existence. A closer analysis reveals the fundamental incompatibilities inherent in that principle. The Court seems to have accepted the shortcomings of this distinction, at least under Articles 30–36 E.C., and has in some recent cases opened the door to a new approach towards intellectual property rights in general. It is to be regretted that the Court did not seize the opportunity in the *Magill* case to openly acknowledge the more than evident shortcomings of this distinction also under Article 86 E.C. and thus failed to offer clear guidelines on the approach to be followed in the future. Until such time, one should be aware that in view of the reasoning used by the Court in *Magill,* it is not impossible that intellectual property owners may be held to have abused their intellectual property rights, and infringed the Treaty rules, merely because they enforce their exclusive rights.

6. Disparities in National Intellectual Property Law and Free Movement of Goods

1. Predominance of Free Movement of Goods Over Intellectual Property Rights Revisited

From the preceding chapter, it is apparent that the approach so far adopted by   **6.01** the European Court of Justice is inadequate to deal with the various problems arising in a Community context from the enforcement of national intellectual property rights. Merely curtailing the exercise of those rights on the basis of either the rules on the free movement of goods and services or the rules on competition often leads to a situation of legal uncertainty for intellectual property owners. Although the approach adopted under the rules on the free movement of goods and services seems to be more or less established, it still seems to be uncertain when an exercise of intellectual property rights will be held to be "abusive" under the rules on competition, and especially under Article 86 E.C. The main cause for this uncertainty is the reluctance of the Court to strike down intellectual property rights that are abusively granted by national legislation and, *a fortiori*, to give guidance concerning the criteria to be applied to establish which features of intellectual property law may be held to be incompatible with Community law. As such, it is logical for the intellectual property owner to expect that he will be able to exercise the nationally granted exclusive right without infringing Community law. In several cases, however, the Community courts have virtually emptied the exclusive right of its substance through curtailing the exercise of the exclusive right under the competition rules to such an extent that it challenges the very existence of the right.[1] It is therefore submitted that it would be more coherent and more transparent for the courts to scrutinise the very existence of the intellectual property right for its compatibility with Article 36 E.C. before looking at whether the intellectual property owner has abusively exercised his exclusive right.[2]

The European Court of Justice has in several recent cases opened the door to challenging the very existence of intellectual property rights under Article

---

[1] It might suffice to recall the *Consten Grundig* and *Magill* cases, see *supra*, respectively Chap. 3, pt. 4(2)(b), and Chap. 5, pt. 4(3).

[2] Similarly, see E. White, "In search of the limits to Article 30 of the EEC Treaty" (1989) 26 C.M.L.Rev. 235 at 167–270. See also *supra*, Chap. 3, pt. 4(2)(c), where it is submitted that this should be done through the application of the functionality test, as is done with regard to denominations of origin.

36 E.C. Before looking into those cases, a classification will be made of the majority of the cases, namely those that have so far been decided through the application of the consent theory. In all the cases to which the consent theory has been applied, it can be submitted that the Court considered the major problem to be the principle of territoriality inherent to intellectual property rights.[3] All other aspects of intellectual property rights which are potentially detrimental to the functioning of the Common Market were thereby neglected.

2. CASES DECIDED THROUGH THE APPLICATION OF THE CONSENT THEORY

(1) Parallel intellectual property protection

(a) "Comparable" intellectual property protection

6.02   The early cases brought before the Court all concerned problems of parallel importation against the background of comparable parallel intellectual property rights.[4] The term "comparable" parallel intellectual property protection points to the conditions for obtaining the intellectual property protection and not to distortions subsequently created by other government measures such as price fixing for medicinal preparations or limits imposed on the intellectual property owner's remuneration. The Court has consistently held that the latter are not relevant to the outcome of the case.[5] With the exception of performance rights and trade marked goods that have been repackaged or to which the trade mark has been reaffixed[6] the Court has, since the *Deutsche Grammophon* case, consistently held that the fact that the goods have been put on the market in the Member State of exportation with the intellectual property owner's consent implies that the principle of exhaustion should apply.[7] This means that in those circumstances the principle of free movement of goods prevails over the intellectual property right concerned.

---

[3] See *supra*, Chap. 4, pt. 1(1).

[4] See, for instance, Case 78/70, *Deutsche Grammophon Gesellschaft v. Metro*, Judgment of June 8, 1971: [1971] E.C.R. 487; [1971] C.M.L.R. 631. Case 15/74, *Centrafarm v. Sterling Drug*, Judgment of October 31, 1974: [1974] E.C.R. 1147; [1974] 2 C.M.L.R. 480. Case 16/74, *Centrafarm v. Winthrop*, Judgment of October 31, 1974: [1974] E.C.R. 1183; [1974] 2 C.M.L.R. 480. Case 58/80, *Dansk Supermarked v. Imerco*, Judgment of January 22, 1981; [1981] E.C.R. 181; [1981] 3 C.M.L.R. 590. For more details of those cases, see *supra*, Chap. 4.

[5] Concerning distortions created due to price fixing by the government see, for instance, Case 15/74, *Centrafarm v. Sterling Drug*, Judgment of October 31, 1974: [1974] E.C.R. 1147; [1974] 2 C.M.L.R. 480. Concerning distortions due to government interference with the level of royalties for copyright, see Joined Cases 55 and 57/80, *Musik-Vertrieb and K-Tel International v. GEMA*, Judgment of January 20, 1981: [1981] E.C.R. 147; [1981] 2 C.M.L.R. 44. For an analysis of the impact of the Court's decisions, see *supra*, Chap. 4, respectively pts. 2(1)(a) and 2(2)(a).

[6] See *supra*, Chap. 4, respectively pts. 2(2)(b) and 2(3)(b).

[7] On the exhaustion principle and on Case 78/70, *Deutsche Grammophon*: [1971] E.C.R. 487; [1971] C.M.L.R. 631. See *supra*, Chap. 4, pt. 1.

(b) Parallel intellectual property protection yet substantially different conditions

The application of the principle of exhaustion based on the consent theory is **6.03** the general rule in cases of parallel protection. The Court has, in subsequent cases, been confronted with the question of whether this rule also applies in case where there is parallel intellectual property protection in the Member States concerned but the conditions under which intellectual property protection is granted differ substantially from one Member State to another. It will be seen below that the principle of exhaustion will not necessarily apply to those cases.[8]

(2) Absence of parallel intellectual property protection

(a) No intellectual property rights in Member State of exportation

The Court clarified in *Merck v. Stephar* that the application of the exhaustion **6.04** principle is not linked to the existence of parallel intellectual property protection, but rather to the consent of the intellectual property owner to market the protected goods for the first time.[9] This case concerned a situation in which intellectual property protection was not provided for in the Member State of exportation. The Court held that the intellectual property owner can choose whether or not to bring his product on to that market but, if he decides to do so, he must then accept the consequences of his choice. Thus the free movement of goods prevails here over the national intellectual property right.

It has already been shown that the application of the exhaustion principle in the absence of parallel intellectual property protection implies that the exclusive right in the Member State of importation is potentially emptied of its substance.[10] Although the effect of the ruling is, apparently, only to create intra-brand competition one can submit that, indirectly, inter-brand competition is also introduced as a consequence of the Court's judgment. As such, the impact of this judgment extends far beyond the elimination of the prejudicial effect of the principle of territoriality inherent in intellectual property rights. This ruling is to be severely criticised from the point of view of the function of intellectual property rights. In the light of the Court's rulings it seems that the same finding would be made where the possibility of obtaining parallel intellectual property protection existed but the intellectual property

---

[8] See *infra*, pt. 3(3). Case 158/86, *Warner Brothers v. Christiansen*: [1988] E.C.R. 2605; [1990] 3 C.M.L.R. 684.

[9] Case 187/80, *Merck v. Stephar*, Judgment of July 14, 1981: [1981] E.C.R. 2063; [1981] 3 C.M.L.R. 463. See *supra*, Chap. 4, pt. 2(1)(b).

[10] See *supra*, Chap. 4, pt. 2(1)(b)(ii), where it is shown that this implies that the effect of the potential inter-brand competition in the Member State of exportation is transposed to the Member State of importation.

owner refrained from applying for intellectual property protection in the Member State of exportation.[11]

(b) Model 1: Consent theory

6.05 This finding makes it possible to draw a first simplified model of the application of the consent theory as shown below. The model, as the Court's approach, is based on the assumption that the balance between national intellectual property law and the free movement of goods can be found merely by looking at the behaviour of the intellectual property owner without taking into account special provisions in national law. A second basic assumption is that the goods will only be imported from Member State B into Member State A if the product's selling price is lower there, although in all cases export from A to B is theoretically feasible.

SCHEME 1: CONSENT THEORY

	A = MS of importation		B = MS of exportation
1.	IPR reward = X	(_____	IPR, and consent reward – or = X
2.	IPR reward = X	(_____	no IPR, yet consent reward – X (*)
3.	IPR reward = X	(____/____	no IPR, no consent reward 0

MS = Member State
IPR = intellectual property right

(*) The reward is considered to be less than the monopoly-reward X in this case, because inter-brand competition cannot be prohibited due to the lack of intellectual property protection. Whether or not inter-brand competition will effectively occur depends on the type of the product and on the situation in the market.

(3) Differing durations of intellectual property protection

(a) Expiry of intellectual property rights in Member State of exportation

6.06 The Court held in *EMI v. Patricia Im – und Export*,[12] that when parallel intellectual property protection ceased to exist due to the expiry of the duration of the intellectual property protection offered in the Member State of exportation, the intellectual property owner in the Member State of importation

---

[11] It is clear from the *Merck* case that the Court does not make a distinction between a patentee voluntarily placing himself in a position of not having parallel protection, through not applying for it, and this occurring involuntarily because no parallel protection is available. Frank advanced the view that exhaustion should only occur in the first situation because the cause in the second situation is the disparity between national patent systems. See G. Frank, "Intellectual property rights in the European Economic Community and the Treaty of Rome – conflict or harmony" [1977] *Journal of the Patent Office Society* 274 at 292.

[12] Case 341/87, *EMI Electrola v. Patricia Im – und Export and others*, Judgment of January 24, 1989: [1989] E.C.R. 79; [1989] 2 C.M.L.R. 413.

can still invoke his exclusive right to prevent the importation of goods that have been lawfully marketed without his consent. Applying an *a contrario* reasoning, this implies that if the goods had been marketed with his consent even after the expiry of the protection in the Member State of exportation, he would not be able to prevent the importation because his intellectual property right would be held to be exhausted. Referring to Scheme 1 above, this means a shift upon the expiry of the intellectual property right from the application of hypothesis 1 to hypotheses 2 and 3 if the goods are marketed, respectively, with and without the intellectual property owner's consent. This implies that whether or not parallel intellectual property protection existed previously is not taken into account when applying the principle of exhaustion of intellectual property rights.

(b) Underlying rationale

Advocate General Darmon pointed out that any other interpretation would lead to the harmonisation of the duration of intellectual property rights on the basis of the shortest period of protection offered in a Member State of the Community.[13] He further argued that "there is no reason to distinguish between the situation in which the product *cannot* be protected and the situation in which it can *no longer* be protected", because otherwise this would entail the paradoxical consequence that the expiry of intellectual property protection is more serious for the intellectual property owner than the total absence of intellectual property protection.[14] This interpretation will therefore most probably apply not only to the circumstances of the case in which the maximum duration of national intellectual property protection came to an end, but also to the situation when the intellectual property protection expired due to the choice, or the negligence, of an intellectual property owner who fails to extend the period of intellectual property protection where this is still possible.

6.07

(4) Compulsory licences

(a) Parallel intellectual property rights worked under compulsory licences

Compulsory and akin licences are probably the clearest example of the fact that intellectual property rights are also, if not as much, in the interest of states providing such protective laws as in the interest of the intellectual property owner. In essence, obligatory licences are licences granted by a national authority to a third person usually, though not necessarily, without the consent of the intellectual property owner, for reasons of public interest and mainly because of the failure to exploit the right sufficiently by the intellectual property owner himself.[15] The first case brought to the attention of the Court of Justice in this respect, the *Pharmon v. Hoechst* case, concerned the

6.08

---

[13] Case 341/87, Opinion of Advocate General Darmon delivered on November 29, 1988: [1989] E.C.R. 86 at 91.

[14] *id.*, at p. 90.

[15] See also *infra*, pt. 3(1).

importation of a patented product into a Member State, where the patent holder worked his patent, from another Member State where his parallel patent was worked by a third person on the basis of a compulsory licence.[16] At issue was whether the patent holder could prevent the importation on the basis of his exclusive right in the Member State of importation, or whether this intellectual property right was exhausted due to the fact that the patent was worked under a compulsory licence in the Member State of exportation. Secondly, the preliminary question was posed of whether the fact that the patent holder received a reward under the compulsory licence influenced the outcome of the case.

(b) Compulsory licence does not imply consent

6.09   In line with the *Merck* judgment, one could argue that the intellectual property right is indeed exhausted because the patent holder should have known the law in force in the Member State of exportation as well as the risk of not working his patent so that he has to accept the consequences of his choice as regards the free movement of the product within the Common Market.[17] However, the Court did not pursue this line of reasoning. To the contrary, it held that the principle of exhaustion does not apply to the parallel importation of goods that have been manufactured by a third party under a compulsory licence as the patent holder cannot be said to have consented to putting those goods on the market.[18] It should be noted that this is different from the solution proposed by Advocate General Mancini who suggested that it should be left to the national court to determine whether or not the patentee had expressly, or impliedly, indicated his consent.[19] The Court categorically stated:

> "It is necessary to point out that where, as in this instance, the competent authorities of a Member State grant a third party a compulsory licence which the patentee would normally have the right to prevent, *the patentee cannot be deemed to have consented to the operation of that third party.* Such a measure deprives the patent proprietor of his right to determine freely the conditions under which he markets his products."
>
> "... the substance of a patent lies essentially in according the inventor an exclusive right of first placing the product on the market so as to allow him to obtain a reward for his creative effort. *It is therefore necessary to allow the patent proprietor to prevent the importation and marketing of*

---

[16] Case 19/84, *Pharmon v. Hoechst*, Judgment of July 9, 1985: [1985] E.C.R. 2281; [1985] 3 C.M.L.R. 775.

[17] This view was advanced by Pharmon.

[18] According to Guy, the Court has clarified that voluntary and compulsory licences have "nothing in common", see D. Guy, "*Pharmon v. Hoechst*: compulsory licences clarified" [1986] E.I.P.R. 252 at 252.

[19] Case 19/84, Opinion of Advocate General Mancini delivered on April 23, 1985: [1985] E.C.R. 2282 at 2289–2290. He gives examples of when, under compulsory licences, the interests of the state and the patent holder may coincide and concludes that one cannot categorically state that the proprietor never consents to having his intellectual property right exploited by a third party under a compulsory licence.

products manufactured under a compulsory licence in order to protect the substance of his exclusive rights under his patent."[20, 21]

The practical effect of this judgment concerning parallel patents is that the patent holder might benefit from having his product exploited under compulsory licences in the Member State of exportation in order to protect a more profitable market in the Member State of importation, rather than marketing the products himself in both markets or giving voluntary licences.[22] This is especially so since the Court ruled that it was irrelevant to know whether or not the patent holder was given a fair return under the system of compulsory licences.[23]

(c) Model 2: parallel intellectual property protection

Scheme 2 below shows that under the normal system of parallel patents (1), **6.10** the patent holder does obtain a reward in both markets possibly even the same reward as under compulsory licences (2). However, his overall reward will be less than under the system of compulsory licences as he cannot prevent price competition from occurring between his own goods.

SCHEME 2: PARALLEL PROTECTION*

	$A = MS$ of importation		$B = MS$ of exportation
1.	worked patent reward = X	(_ _ _ _ _ _ _	worked patent reward – or = X
2.	worked patent reward = X	(_ _ _/_ _ _	compulsory licence reward – or = X

* For the basic assumptions, see *supra*, Scheme 1.

---

[20] Case 19/84: [1985] E.C.R. 2281; [1985] 3 C.M.L.R. 775, respectively at paras. 25 and 26 (emphasis added).

[21] White correctly points out that it is significant that the Court omitted to specify, as it had done in previous cases, that the subject or specific subject-matter of patents is putting the goods into circulation for the first time, either directly or *by the grant of licences to third parties.* He writes: "... one notices that the omission of any reference to exploitation through the granting of licences [...] allows the conclusion the Court wishes to arrive at to follow more easily": see E. White, "Case 19/84, *Pharmon BV v. Hoechst AG*" (1986) 23 C.M.L.Rev. 719 at 722.

[22] This consequence is clearly demonstrated and severely criticised by P. Demaret, "Industrial property rights, compulsory licences and the free movement of goods under Community law" [1987] I.I.C. 161. See also the criticism by E. White, "Case 19/84, *Pharmon v. Hoechst AG*" (1986) 23 C.M.L.Rev. 719.

[23] Gormley points out that the Court was more concerned with the protectionist effect than with the actual reward. He writes: "It might be thought that the argument that, if royalties are paid the patentee has been assured of his reward, would have carried some weight with the Court. However, it seems that the Court has accepted that to give extra-territorial effect to patent licences would encourage freeloading by the industry of certain Member States on the back of the inventiveness of others", see L. Gormley, "Recent cases on Articles 30–36 EEC: compulsory patent licensing" (1985) 10 E.L.Rev. 431 at 449.

(5) Evaluation of the consent theory

(a) The rule: consent entails exhaustion

6.11   Although the consent theory at first sight seems to be a coherent and workable model, a closer look shows that a rigid application of this theory entails paradoxical consequences, especially in terms of the function of the various intellectual property rights, which are difficult to explain. As concerns trade marks and performance rights, the Court modified its approach to take the function of the exclusive right into account so that the mere marketing of the goods with the intellectual property owner's consent does not automatically entail the exhaustion of the right.[24] But as concerns the other types of intellectual property, the Court has consistently applied the consent test without taking the objectives of the exclusive right concerned into account. This implies that as soon as it is established that the intellectual property owner consented to putting the product on the market in the Member State of exportation his exclusive right is held to be exhausted and he can no longer invoke parallel intellectual property rights to oppose the importation of those goods into other Member States.

(b) Relation between consent and parallel rights

(i) Paradoxical consequences of consent theory

6.12   The paradoxical consequences the consent theory entail are most clearly illustrated by the comparison of the practical effects of the *Merck* and the *Pharmon* cases.[25] In both cases, the patent holder had a patent in the Member State of importation (A), but in the Member State of exportation (B) the situation and behaviour of the intellectual property owner in each case was diametrically opposed. In the *Merck* case, the patent holder marketed his product even though it could not benefit from patent protection, whereas the *Pharmon* ruling applies to a situation whereby the patent holder obtained a parallel patent but refrained from marketing its product.[26] This means that in the *Merck* case inter-brand competition was essentially enhanced in B. The *Pharmon* ruling applies to the contrary situation, namely where the exclusive right was not only invoked to prohibit inter-brand competition but furthermore the patented product was not at all brought onto the market in B by the patent holder, so that a compulsory licence could be given to a third party to remedy this situation.

---

[24] See *supra*, Chap. 4, respectively pts. 2(2)(b) and 2(3)(b).

[25] Compulsory licences can be granted for various reasons in the public interest. In the *Pharmon* case, the compulsory licence was granted on the basis of section 41(2) of the U.K. 1949 Patent Act which was aimed at ensuring low prices for food and medicine, etc. whilst guaranteeing a fair return for the inventor. However, since the Court did not distinguish between the different forms of compulsory licences in *Pharmon*, the hypothesis to this example is the extreme case whereby the patent holder obtains a patent but refrains from exploiting his patent at all.

[26] In this hypothesis, the patent holder does not at all live up to the demands of the Member State concerned. On fulfilling the needs of the market through importation of goods from other Member States, and the case law of the Court on compulsory licences, see *infra*, pt. 3(1).

(ii) Model 3: Comparison between *Merck* and *Pharmon*

The straightforward application of the consent theory by the Court gives the   **6.13**
following result, as set out in Scheme 3 below:

SCHEME 3: MERCK AND PHARMON*

A = MS of importation		B = MS of exportation
1. worked patent		no IPR, consent
reward = X	(_____	reward – X (*)
2. worked patent		IPR, no consent
reward = X	(____/____	reward – or = X

(*) For the basic assumptions, see *supra* Scheme 1

In the *Merck* case (1), the patent holder is penalised for his competitive effort in B because his intellectual property right is thought to be exhausted in A so that his products in market A are, through the intra-brand competition the exhaustion of rights entails, indirectly confronted by the inter-brand competition in B. Following the *Pharmon* ruling (2), the patent holder is rewarded for his anti-competitive behaviour in B because he can protect his market in A from competition by goods which have been manufactured under a compulsory licence and for which he may, furthermore, receive a reward in B.

(iii) Parallel intellectual property protection not a relevant criterion

Both the *Merck* and the *Pharmon* cases prove that it is not the existence of   **6.14**
parallel patents but merely the marketing of the protected goods with the consent of the intellectual property owner that is the decisive factor used by the Court in applying the principle of exhaustion. In the first case there was no parallel intellectual property protection but the principle of exhaustion was applied. In the latter case, even though there was parallel protection the principle of exhaustion was not applied.

(c) The original meaning of "consent" departed from

Both Joliet and Marenco have quite rightly pointed out that the Court has   **6.15**
deviated from the original meaning of "consent", which was the consent by the intellectual property owner to the exercise of his exclusive right by a licensee.[27] Understood in this sense, the principle of exhaustion upon marketing with consent prevented the possibility of obtaining a benefit twice on a single unit of production by invoking the territorial character of intellectual property rights in the context of the internal market. The inconsistency in the case law of the Court results from having applied the consent theory to the mere marketing of the product instead of to the use of the exclusive right with

---

[27] See R. Joliet, "Patented articles and the free movement of goods within the EEC" [1975] *Current Legal Problems* 15 at p. 37. He argues in terms of safeguarding the function of the right. See also G. Marenco and K. Banks, "Intellectual property and the Community rules on free movement: discrimination unearthed" (1990) 15 E.L.Rev. 224 at 247–248.

the result that the principle of exhaustion was also applied even in the absence of parallel intellectual property protection. As was mentioned before this gradual, but decisive, deviation from the original meaning of "consent" might not have happened had the Court applied from the start the proportionality test under Article 36 E.C. to the national law concerned rather than to the exercise of the intellectual property right by the right-owner.[28]

(d) Relation between consent criterion and reward function

(i) Further paradoxical consequence of consent theory

6.16 It was maintained above that a paradox of the Court's case law on intellectual property rights is that the holder of a parallel patent is better off having his parallel patent worked under a compulsory licence rather than working the patent himself in the Member State of exportation. In the latter case the principle of exhaustion applies so that his products are subject to intra-brand competition in the Member State of importation.[29] Demaret points out that this paradox is further enhanced when comparing the *Pharmon* case with the *Musik-Vertrieb* case. In the latter, the Court held that an intellectual property right is exhausted even though the parallel intellectual property right is subject to government interference in so far as the possibility of obtaining a reward is concerned.[30] In *Pharmon*, the intellectual property right was not held to be exhausted even though the patent holder did obtain a reward under the parallel patent. Demaret therefore argues for the abandonment of the consent test altogether.[31]

(ii) Alternative: "economic substance of intellectual property rights" as criterion

6.17 Instead of the consent theory, Demaret therefore proposes a test focusing on "the economic substance of the exclusive rights". This would entail the application of the principle of exhaustion only if two cumulative conditions are fulfilled. First, the same invention must be protected by a parallel exclusive right. Secondly, there should be no restrictions in the country of export which prevent the proprietor of the intellectual property right setting the level of royalties he thinks appropriate.[32] Such an approach would indeed have led to more acceptable and coherent judgments concerning the exhaustion of intellectual property rights. But it would still imply that the Court only curtails the exercise of intellectual property rights whereas the existence would, in prin-

---

[28] See *supra*, Chap. 4, pt. 1(2)(b).

[29] See *supra*, pt. 2(4).

[30] See *supra*, Chap. 4, pt. 2(2)(a).

[31] He points out that the consent test is only a valid and useful criterion as it is applied to trade marks, because it is "consistent with the protection of the basic legal function of trade marks, that is the indication of origin", whereas the way in which it is applied to patents and copyright cases is "rather questionable", see P. Demaret, *op. cit.*, pp. 176–177.

[32] See P. Demaret, *Patents, territorial restrictions and EEC law* (1978, VCH Verlagsgesellschaft), pp. 59–76. Marenco also is of the opinion that the principle of exhaustion should not apply in case the disparities in the national law are the cause of the divergence in commercialisation, see G. Marenco, *"Pour une interpretation traditionelle de la notion de mesure d'effet équivalent"* [1984] C.D.E. 291 at 345. He finds it in particular difficult to justify the *Musik-Vertrieb* and *Merck* judgments.

ciple, be left intact. It also seems to disregard the fact that the Court has consistently held that Article 36 E.C. cannot be invoked to justify measures that are economic in nature,[33] unless the objective of an economic nature is ancillary to another objective mentioned in Article 36 E.C.[34]

(iii) Refinement: "function of intellectual property rights" as criterion

— Rationale

Rather than emphasise the importance of safeguarding the economic sub-   **6.18**
stance of an intellectual property right, it would seem to be more appropriate to advance the criterion of safeguarding the essential function of the intellectual property right concerned.[35] It has been submitted above that this should be done through looking at whether the intellectual property right was, in the first place, granted in accordance to its function and subsequently used by the intellectual property owner in accordance with its function.[36] The function of patents can be described as to grant a temporarily exclusive right to the patentee on his protected product or process in order to provide the possibility of obtaining a reward, to give an incentive to stimulate research and development, and to let society benefit from the invention rather than having it kept secret.[37] As such the aim is, in the first place, to shield the intellectual property owner from inter-brand competition in order to give him an incentive to commercially exploit his invention and to give him the possibility of obtaining a reasonable return and reward for his investment. Although this criterion has a lot in common with the "economic substance of intellectual property rights" criterion it is, nevertheless, broader in at least two ways. First, it implies an analysis of the conditions under which national intellectual property rights are granted. Secondly, besides the economic interests of the intellectual property owner, it takes the public interest into account.

---

[33] See for instance, Case 7/61, *Commission v. Italy*, Judgment of December 19, 1961: [1961] E.C.R. 633; [1962] C.M.L.R. 39.

[34] Case 72/83, *Campus Oil v. Ministry for Industry and Energy*, Judgment of July 10, 1984: [1984] E.C.R. 2727; [1984] 3 C.M.L.R. 544, at para. 36. Barents points out that what is seemingly prohibited is "the use of Article 36 as a pure instrument of economic policy", see R. Barents, "New developments in measures having equivalent effect" (1981) 18 C.M.L.Rev. 271 at 278–279. Demaret himself invokes the argument that Article 36 E.C. only applies to non-economic measures to conclude that the domestic manufacturing clause under the system of compulsory licences is incompatible with Article 30 and unjustifiable under Article 36 E.C. On this issue, see *infra*, pt. 3(1)(a).

[35] Joliet had already pointed this out in 1975. He wrote that the application of the principle of exhaustion to parallel imports under parallel patents is "compatible with the policy justification behind the patent system, *i.e.* with the patent function. True, the patentee would be able to obtain certain additional income if the flexibility of demand in the two national markets for which he holds parallel patents were to differ, making a price discrimination possible and if he was in a position to keep those markets separated. But the loss of this additional income does not appear to jeopardise the fundamental function of the patent: thanks to his patent, he will have had at any rate the chance to obtain monopoly profits in the exporting country". He furthermore argued that if a functionality test – in the sense of the monopoly-profit-incentive thesis – were applied, then restrictions on imports would be justified in case there is a price control scheme in the exporting country or a local working condition in the country of importation. See R. Joliet, "Patented articles and the free movement of goods within the EEC" [1975] *Current Legal Problems* 5 at 33–34.

[36] See *supra*, Chap. 3, pt. 4(2)(c).

[37] On the characteristics and the function of the different intellectual property rights, see *supra*, Chap. 2.

— Examples: *Merck* and *Pharmon*

6.19   This may be illustrated by reference to the *Merck* and *Pharmon* cases. The Court was obviously right, in the *Merck* case, to hold that a patent merely confers the *possibility* of obtaining a reward without ensuring that this will always be obtained. However, with respect, the Court was wrong in introducing the exhaustion principle with reference to goods that, although they were marketed with the intellectual property owner's consent, had been exposed to inter-brand competition because in practice this comes down to eliminating the very "possibility" of obtaining a reward.[38] Similarly, in the *Pharmon* case, the Court disregarded the fact that a patent is also granted in the public interest, namely to let the public benefit from the invention. Instead, it merely referred to the subject-matter of the right which it held to be to bring the product on to the market for the first time and to oppose infringements. The situation in which the patent holder refrains from bringing the patented product on to the market can hardly be said to be in accordance with the function of the right, but more likely constitutes an abuse of the exclusive right.[39] This logically implies that he should be less, and not more, protected than a patent holder who makes normal use of his right. It is submitted that it is the lack of analysis in the light of the function of a patent that has led to the current situation whereby a holder of parallel patents who uses his exclusive right in accordance with its function is put in a disadvantaged position compared to the intellectual property owner who potentially abuses his exclusive right.[40] This situation is the consequence of the straightforward application of the consent theory. It is submitted that a refinement of the reward theory as correctly put forward, but wrongly applied, in the *Merck* case, so as to reflect the various functions of intellectual property rights, could only have led to more acceptable and consistent results.

3. CASES WHERE THE VERY EXISTENCE OF THE INTELLECTUAL PROPERTY RIGHT WAS CHALLENGED

6.20   Up till now one can discern three sets of cases in which the Court has, sometimes radically, departed from its traditional approach based on the existence/exercise dichotomy. The first set of cases concerns new questions raised with regard to obligatory licences. In the second, the Court has taken a new approach concerning the principle of relative novelty. In the third, the Court has given a remarkable judgment concerning rental and lending rights inherent in national copyright law.

---

[38] Similarly, see N. Koch, "Article 30 and the exercise of industrial property rights to block imports" [1986] *Fordham Corp. L. Inst.* 605 at 620; G. Marenco and K. Banks, *op. cit.*, p. 248.

[39] It is significant in this respect that the Commission did not object to the patentee's obligation, under national patent laws, to work the patent and satisfy the domestic demand for the patented product, and did not challenge the system of obligatory licences, as such, in Cases C–235/89 and C–30/90, *Commission v. Italy* and *Commission v. United Kingdom* respectively, see *infra*, pt. 3(1).

[40] See *supra*, Scheme 2.

(1) Obligatory licences

The Court elaborated further on the question of the compatibility of national **6.21** systems of obligatory licences with the rules on the free movement of goods in four cases subsequent to the *Pharmon* judgment.[41] Two of those cases were initiated by the Commission against Member States on the basis of Article 169 E.C. The other two were preliminary rulings. Nevertheless, they all have in common that the Court has challenged the very existence of certain provisions of national patent law rather than hold on to the traditional existence/exercise dichotomy.[42] The first set of cases analysed below concerned provisions in national patent law which allowed the competent authority to grant compulsory licences for lack of sufficient exploitation of the patent in the national territory. The second set of cases concerned the discriminatory treatment of importers under the system of licences of right. It should be pointed out, however, that this does not reflect the chronological order in which the cases were actually dealt with by the Court.

(a) Local manufacturing clause

(i) Legal issue

The Commission had undertaken to challenge certain provisions of Italian **6.22** and British legislation concerning compulsory licences on their compatibility with Articles 30–36 E.C. It initiated proceedings before the Court on the basis of Article 169 E.C. in order to establish whether the national provisions of the Member States concerned, whereby compulsory licences are granted for lack of sufficient exploitation of the patent in the national territory, were in conformity with the objectives of the Treaty.[43] It should be emphasised that it was not the system of obligatory licences as such that was put into question, but only well-specified features of it. The Commission in particular objected to the fact that in order to establish whether or not the patent has been sufficiently worked or exploited, and thus conclude whether or not a compulsory licence should be granted, reference was only made to manufacturing in the national territory by the patent holder himself or by his licensees. The national provisions concerned expressly provided that the importation of the goods did not constitute "working" the patent.[44] According to the Commission, this disregarded the fact that the patent holder might meet the needs of the national market through the importation of the product from another

---

[41] See *supra*, pt. 2(4). The term "obligatory licences" is used here to mean all licences which are imposed by the competent authorities rather than being granted voluntarily by the intellectual property owner, and thus covers both compulsory licences and licences of right.

[42] On these cases, see also N. MacFarlane, C. Wardle, J. Wilkinson, "The tension between intellectual property rights and certain provisions of E.C. law" [1994] E.I.P.R. 525.

[43] Case C–235/89, *Commission v. Italy*, Judgment of February 18, 1992: [1992] E.C.R. I-777; [1992] 2 C.M.L.R. 709. Case C–30/90, *Commission v. the United Kingdom*. Judgment of February 18, 1992: [1992] E.C.R. I-829; [1992] 2 C.M.L.R. 709.

[44] The national provisions concerned are section 48(3) and section 50 of the U.K. 1977 Patents Act and, for Italy, sections 52–54 of the modified R.D. No. 1127 of June 29, 1939 as well as section 14 of the modified R.D. No. 974 of August 12, 1975. These provisions have in common that they provide for compulsory licences if, after three years from the grant of the exclusive right, the right-owner has failed to work the patent in the national territory. It is expressly stipulated that importation of goods will not be considered as "working" the patent.

Member State where he had a parallel patent. The consequence of this was that the patent holder was encouraged to locate his production in the United Kingdom, and/or in Italy, so that the sale of imported products would be reduced. This, the Commission held, was contrary to Article 30 E.C. and could not be justified by the need to protect industrial and commercial property.[45]

(ii) Private rights versus public interest

6.23   The governments concerned did not deny that the result of the contested measure was to give an incentive to the patent holder to manufacture his product in the national territory. To the contrary, they claimed that this was the envisaged counterpart, in the public interest, to the granting of monopoly rights to individuals. The Italian Government pointed out that under the system of compulsory licences, although the patent holder would lose his exclusive right in the market he could still import goods from other countries which would then be in competition with the goods manufactured in Italy by a third party under the compulsory licence.[46] The United Kingdom Government argued that in the light of the lack of harmonisation of patent legislation:

> "... [the] abolition of the local working rules would mean, for example, that where a patent can be obtained for a product of a particular kind in State X but not in State Y, an undertaking manufacturing a product in State Y could obtain a monopoly for the product in State X although it is not manufactured there whereas an undertaking in State X would have no possibility of obtaining a monopoly for a product of the same kind in State Y. State Y would therefore become a patent haven, encouraging investment there by copyists to serve export opportunities."[47]

(iii) Article 36: intellectual property rights as private rights

6.24   Having established that the contested provisions were in fact discriminating against imported goods coming from other Member States, and thus were contrary to Article 30 E.C., the Court briefly analysed whether they could be justified on the basis of Article 36 E.C. However, with respect, the approach taken to Article 36 E.C. was based on a wrong premise. The Commission had advanced the view that Article 36 E.C. could not be invoked to justify national measures that limit, instead of protect, intellectual property rights. Advocate General Van Gerven agreed with this and held that:

> "I am unable to see how national rules which, under certain circumstances, *deprive* the patent proprietor of a major part of the protection afforded him by the patent, could be justified on grounds of industrial and commercial property."[48]

The Court expressed the same opinion. In its findings under Article 30 E.C., the Court pointed out that since it had already ruled that a mere publicity

---

[45] Case C–30/90 and Case C–235/89, Reports of the Hearing.
[46] Case C–235/89, Report of the Hearing.
[47] Case C–30/90, Report of the Hearing.
[48] Case C–235/89 and Case C–30/90: [1992] E.C.R. I-777; [1992] 2 C.M.L.R. 709; and [1992] E.C.R. I-829; [1992] 2 C.M.L.R. 709, Opinion of Advocate General Van Gerven, delivered on December 13, 1991, at pt. 12.

campaign organised by the authorities of a Member State to promote domestic products constituted a measure having an equivalent effect[49] this, *a fortiori*, also applied to the given case. It indicated the approach it would take under Article 36 E.C. by stating that:

> "Those provisions cannot be justified by the derogating provisions of Article 36 of the Treaty since the object of the contested rules is not to ensure the protection of industrial and commercial property but, on the contrary, to limit the rights conferred by such property."[50]

(iv) Specific subject-matter approach

The Court reiterated the principle that derogations on the basis of Article 36   **6.25** E.C. can only be invoked in so far as they are justified to safeguard the specific subject-matter of a patent, which is the right to the first marketing of the protected goods. The threat posed to the patent holder by having his exclusive right adversely affected if he does not exploit the patent in the Member State concerned, induces the proprietor to manufacture his product in that Member State. The Court went on to state that:

> "Although the penalty for lack of insufficiency of exploitation of a patent may be regarded as the necessary counterpart to the territorial exclusivity conferred by the patent, there is *no reason relating to the specific subject-matter* of the patent to justify the discrimination inherent in the contested provisions between exploiting the patent in the form of production on the national territory and exploiting it by importation from the territory of other Member States."[51]

The governments concerned had argued that the justification for the discrimination is to be found in the national legislator's concern to encourage domestic production. They held that it was a legitimate concern under the system of intellectual property to see that a person that had been granted a national patent, and hence may prevent national manufacture by others, himself manufactures locally. As such, they maintained that the obligation to manufacture locally is inherent in the patent right itself. The Court pointed out, however, that this justification could not be upheld because it comes down to frustrating the objectives of the Community as laid down in Articles 2 and 3 E.C.[52]

(v) Protectionism versus single market objective

— Justification in terms of specific subject-matter
It is indeed difficult to reconcile the protectionist goal of the domestic manu-   **6.26** facturing clause, which impinges upon the interests of other Member States,

---

[49] Case 249/81, *Commission v. Ireland*, Judgment of November 24, 1982: [1982] E.C.R. 4005; [1983] 2 C.M.L.R. 104.
[50] Case C–30/90: [1992] E.C.R. I-829; [1992] 2 C.M.L.R. 709, at para. 14. Case C–235/89: [1992] E.C.R. I-777; [1992] 2 C.M.L.R. 709, at para. 10.
[51] Case C–30/90: [1992] E.C.R. I-829; [1992] 2 C.M.L.R. 709, at para. 28. Case C–235/89: [1992] E.C.R. I-777; (1992) 2 C.M.L.R. 709, at para. 24, (emphasis added).
[52] Case C–30/90: [1992] E.C.R. I-829; [1992] 2 C.M.L.R. 709, at para. 30. Case C–235/89: [1992] E.C.R. I-777; [1992] 2 C.M.L.R. 709, at para. 26

with the aim to establish one single integrated European market. But, with respect, the Court's reasoning in coming to this conclusion is rather blurred. The justification test in terms of the specific subject-matter of patents is derived from the case law which curtails the "exercise" of the intellectual property right whilst leaving the existence of the right untouched. However, the Court was precisely asked whether provisions of national law which regulate the existence of an intellectual property right (which logically implies the conditions under which the right is both granted and maintained in force) are compatible with the E.C. Treaty. The justification in terms of the specific subject-matter implies that the Court was of the opinion that national measures have to be justified in relation to the exclusive right of the patent holder, which is taken for granted, rather than having to justify the reason for the existence of this exclusive right under Article 36 E.C., and subsequently to justify the reasons for reducing the scope of protection offered. This approach was probably largely inspired by the, with respect, erroneous view of the Commission and the Advocate General which stated that Article 36 E.C. cannot be invoked to justify measures that impinge upon the rights of the intellectual property owner.

— Justification in terms of function of intellectual property rights

6.27   It seems, to the contrary, more coherent to state that Article 36 E.C. can, in principle, be invoked to justify *all* national measures governing the conditions under which an intellectual property right is granted and kept in force, but that the justification has to show that the measure concerned is needed to safeguard the essential function of that right. In this sense, Demaret pointed out that domestic manufacturing provisions:

> "... are motivated by considerations foreign to the essential purpose of a modern patent system, which is to stimulate invention and innovation, not to induce the uneconomic location of industrial activity."[53]

Having regard to Articles 2 and 3 of the E.C. Treaty, one can indeed argue that although intellectual property rights are still national prerogatives granted on the basis of the principle of territoriality, their function and effect have to be considered in the context of the internal market rather than in a national context. This is reinforced by the fact that Article 36 E.C. can only be invoked with regard to non-economic measures so that the justification for the domestic manufacturing provisions, in the sense that the function of a patent is to stimulate innovation and invention and subsequently the national economic development, would in itself seem to be unacceptable under Com-

---

[53] P. Demaret, "Industrial property rights, compulsory licences and the free movement of goods under Community law" [1987] I.I.C. 161 at 181. He made these comments long before these cases were decided. Burst and Kovar pointed out the same with regard to the *Allen v. Hanburys* case, see J-J. Burst and R. Kovar, "*Les licences imposées et le droit communautaire*" [1990] C.D.E. 249 at 271.

munity law.[54] It is to be regretted that the Court has failed to address this issue and, in so doing, has also failed to give a Community definition of the function of patent rights.

(vi) Discrimination criterion

Throughout both judgments the Court put the emphasis on the discrimi- **6.28** nation against imports embodied in the national provisions, and ruled that the governments concerned had "failed to fulfil [their] obligations under Article 30 of the Treaty". It is significant that the Court did not add that, and indicate why, the contested provisions could not come under the exception of Article 36 E.C.[55]

— Discriminatory measures under Article 36

It should be pointed out in this respect that it is not so much the fact that the **6.29** national provisions discriminate against importations from other Member States, but rather that this discrimination cannot be justified to safeguard the function of intellectual property rights that should be the decisive factor to establish whether or not Article 36 can be successfully invoked. The Court has consistently held that measures that discriminate against imports may, never-theless, be justified under Article 36 EC[56] subject to the second sentence of Article 36 E.C. which stipulates that those measures should not constitute an arbitrary discrimination or a disguised restriction to intra-Community trade. This is the difference with mandatory requirements ensuing from the *Cassis de Dijon* judgment,[57] such as consumer protection and rules on unfair compe-tition, in relation to which measures necessarily have to be indistinctly appli-cable in order to be upheld.[58]

— Prohibition of arbitrary discrimination

It seems that the distinguishing factor between "accepted" and "arbitrary" **6.30** discrimination under the second sentence of Article 36 E.C. is to be found in whether or not such discrimination can be justified in terms of being indis-pensable to safeguard the objectives mentioned in the first sentence of Article

---

[54] On the non-invokeability of Article 36 E.C. for economic reasons, see *supra* pt. 2(5)(d)(ii). See also P. Demaret, *op. cit.*, p. 181. Compare to Case C–17/92, *Fedicine*, Judgment of May 4, 1993; [1993] E.C.R. I-2239, especially at para. 22; in the latter case relating to services, the Court expressly held that national measures, reserving licences to dub foreign films in a national language to distributors undertaking also to distribute national films, clearly envisages a purely economic objective and thus does not constitute a public policy reason under Article 56 E.C.

[55] Compare, for instance, to Case 104/75, *De Peijper*, Judgment of May 20, 1976: [1976] E.C.R. 613; [1976] 2 C.M.L.R. 271.

[56] See, for instance, also P. Verloren van Themaat, "*La libre circulation des marchandises après l'arrêt 'Cassis de Dijon'*" [1982] C.D.E. 123 at 131.

[57] Case 120/78, *Rewe*, Judgment of February 20, 1979: [1979] E.C.R. 649; [1979] 3 C.M.L.R. 494.

[58] The Court once again reiterated this distinction in Joined Cases C 1 and 176/90, *Aragonesa*, Judgment of July 25, 1991: [1991] E.C.R. I-4151, where it stated at para. 13: "...Article 36 also applies where the contested measure restricts only imports, whereas according to the Court's case-law the question of imperative requirements for the purpose of the interpretation of Article 30 cannot arise unless the measure in question applies without distinction to both national and imported products...".

36 E.C.[59] This would imply that, if discriminatory measures are in principle justifiable under the first sentence of Article 36 E.C., they should not be applied at random but according to objectively justifiable criteria so that they are not diverted from their real purpose.[60] It is clear that in the cases concerned the discriminatory measures could not be justified under the first sentence of Article 36 E.C. because they were not needed to safeguard the function of the patent. Thus there was no need to invoke the second sentence of Article 36 E.C.

(vii) Evaluation

6.31 Although the result in these specific cases is the same when applying the "functionality test" or the "specific subject-matter test", it is to be regretted that the Court has not seized this opportunity to come to terms with the inclusion of intellectual property rights in Article 36 E.C. These judgments do have the merit that the Court has held certain contestable provisions of national patent law to be incompatible with the rules on the free movement of goods. However, it came to this conclusion not through looking at the reasons for the existence of certain provisions in national patent law but through assuming that the exercise of an exclusive right, once granted, should not be unduly restricted by those national provisions.

(b) Licences of right

6.32 The Court has so far been confronted with what could be called a triptych of patent cases concerning obligatory licences under the rules on the free movement of goods. As seen above, in the *Pharmon* case the Court held that the importation of goods that have been marketed under a compulsory licence can be prohibited on the basis of a parallel patent.[61] From the *Commission v. Italy* and *Commission v. United Kingdom* cases it is clear that the granting of a compulsory licence is incompatible with the E.C. Treaty if the patent holder was willing, and able, to satisfy the needs of the market concerned by importing his product from other Member States.[62] Finally, the Court has had to rule on the compatibility with Community law of national provisions determining to which third parties, and on what conditions, licences of right can be granted.[63]

---

[59] Similarly, see R. Barents, "New developments in measures having equivalent effect" (1981) 18 C.M.L.Rev. 271 at 281–282.

[60] This would seem to be the function of the proviso laid down in the second sentence of Article 36 E.C. as defined by the Court in the *Henn and Darby* case, see *supra*, Chap. 3, pt. 2(2)(b). Similarly, see L. Gormley, *Prohibiting restrictions on trade within the EEC* (1985, North-Holland), pp. 210–218. At p. 217, he writes: "... it is submitted that the proper function of the second sentence of Article 36 is to act as an overriding requirement to ensure that apparently justified measures are not applied in such a manner as to partition the Community artificially. Indeed, it has been suggested that it acts as something as an 'emergency brake' in Community law." See also P. Verloren van Themaat, "The contribution to the establishment of the internal market by the case-law of the Court of Justice of the European Communities" in *1992: one European market?* (Bieber et al. eds. 1988) (Nomos Verlagsgesellschaft), pp. 109–126 at p. 116.

[61] See *supra*, pt. 2(4).

[62] See *supra*, pt. 3(1).

[63] On the compatibility with Article 86 E.C. of charging "unreasonably" high royalties under licences of right, see the *Hilti* case, *supra*, Chap. 5, pt. 4(2).

(i) Legal issues

In the *Allen and Hanburys v. Generics* case, the issue was raised of whether a   **6.33**
patent holder could invoke national legislation concerning licences of right to
prevent a third party from importing the protected products from another
Member State where they were marketed without his consent.[64] Whereas
under the national law concerned any person was, in principle, entitled to a
licence of right, this did not necessarily apply to importers, as one of the terms
that could be imposed was a prohibition on importing the protected product.
In the *Generics v. Kline* case, the complementary preliminary question was
posed of whether national provisions that require the competent national
authority "to refuse a licence (of right) to import from another country when
the patentee works the patent by manufacture in the United Kingdom but to
grant a licence (of right) to import from a third country where the patentee
works the patent by importation of products manufactured in other Member
States of the EEC", are compatible with Articles 30 to 36 E.C.[65]

These two cases have certain features in common. Both cases concerned
licences of right which means, in essence, that any person is entitled to a
licence under the patent on such terms as may be settled by agreement or, in
default, by the competent national authority.[66] In both cases the patent had
been endorsed "licences of right" on the basis of transitional provisions governing the extension of the duration of patent protection from 16 to 20
years.[67] In both cases, rather than limiting itself to analysing the behaviour of
the patent holder, the Court looked into the reasons for the provisions of the
national legislation discriminating against importers. There are also, however, significant differences between the two cases. The most important one
being that the dispute in the first case concerned importation into the United
Kingdom of goods coming from other Member States, whereas in the second
case it concerned the importation of goods coming from third countries.[68]

(ii) Importation of products from other Member States

— Applicability of consent theory

The *Allen and Hanburys v. Generics* case could, in theory, have been decided   **6.34**
on the basis of the consent theory.[69] Allen and Hanburys, the patentee, argued
that the Court should apply the same reasoning as it had done in the *Pharmon*

---

[64] Case 434/85, *Allen and Hanburys Ltd v. Generics (UK) Ltd*, Judgment of March 3, 1988:
    [1988] E.C.R. 1245; [1988] 1 C.M.L.R. 701.
[65] Case C–191/90, *Generics (UK) Ltd and Harris Pharmaceuticals Ltd v. Smith Kline and French
    Laboratories Ltd*, Judgment of October 27, 1992: [1992] E.C.R. I-5335; [1993] 1 C.M.L.R.
    89.
[66] See section 46(3)(a) of the 1977 U.K. Patents Act.
[67] See Schedule 1 to the 1977 U.K. Patents Act.
[68] In the latter, the question was also posed of whether Portugal and Spain should be considered as
    third countries, or as Member States, considering that at the material time patents were still
    governed by the transitional provisions of their respective Acts of Accession. This question will
    not be dealt with here.
[69] See also G. Friden, "Recent developments in EEC intellectual property law: the distinction
    between existence and exercise revisited" (1989) 26 C.M.L.Rev. 193 at 202 where he writes:
    "These facts clearly seemed to require a traditional application of the Court's case-law on
    exhaustion and the conclusion that, as consent was absent for the manufacture or sale in Italy,
    the right was not exhausted and thus EEC law did not prevent the grant of an injunction."

case.[70] They stressed the importance of the fact that Generics imported the products without their consent from a Member State, Italy, where no patent protection existed for medicinal products at that time. The argument went that if they could have held a parallel patent in Italy they could have prevented Generics from copying their product and marketing it there in the first place, so that the latter could not have applied for a licence of right to import the unauthorised product into the United Kingdom. The Court did not, however, approach the facts from the angle of curtailing or upholding the exercise of the intellectual property right. Rather, it looked at the reasons inherent in United Kingdom law discriminating against imports, and thus examined whether these measures were justified under Article 36 E.C. It should be pointed out that this significant shift to a new approach, whereby the existence of the right is challenged on its compatibility with Community rules, was not openly stated as such.

— Introduction of a reward test

6.35 The Court reiterated its previous case law in which it had held that derogations under Article 36 E.C. are only admitted in so far as they are needed to safeguard the specific subject-matter of intellectual property, which is the right to first place the product on the market and to oppose infringements. But instead of going ahead with applying the consent test to see whether the intellectual property right should be held to be exhausted, the Court went on to state that the specific subject-matter of patents under licences of right was appreciably altered. The latter was described as being constituted merely by the right to get a fair return. The reason given for this was that the national law itself deprived the patentee of the right to oppose domestic infringements.[71] The consent test was thus held to be inapplicable and substituted by a reward test. In the words of the Court:

> "In those circumstances it must be considered that the power of national courts to prohibit the importation of the product in question may be justified under the provisions of Article 36 on the protection of industrial and commercial property *only if that prohibition is necessary in order to ensure that the proprietor of such a patent has, vis-à-vis importers, the same rights as he enjoys as against producers who manufacture the product in the national territory, that is to say the right to a fair return from his patent*."
>
> "That is therefore the test which must be applied in examining the merits of a number of arguments raised before the Court, both by Allen and Hanburys and by the United Kingdom, in order to justify an injunction prohibiting imports granted against an importer-infringer."[72]

In other words, it had to be proved that the discrimination against importers was necessary to safeguard a reward for the patentee in order for the national provisions and practices to come under the derogation of Article 36 E.C.

[70] See *supra*, pt. 2(4).
[71] Case 434/85: [1988] E.C.R. 1245; [1988] 1 C.M.L.R. 701, at paras. 9–13.
[72] Case 434/85: [1988] E.C.R. 1245; [1988] 1 C.M.L.R. 701, at paras. 14 and 15 (emphasis added).

— Arbitrary discrimination

The Court rejected the justifications forwarded by the United Kingdom 6.36
Government in support of its legislation which were based on the alleged lack
of adequate assets in the national territory belonging to importers and on the
difficulty of carrying out checks as to the origin and the quantity of imported
goods.[73] The Court pointed out that the same problems could arise with
regard to domestic manufacturers whereas no court injunction could be
obtained in that situation. Instead, the Court came to the conclusion that the
application of the national provisions amounted to an arbitrary discrimination in the sense of the second sentence of Article 36 E.C., since they were
not indistinctly applicable to domestic manufacture and imports and could
not be justified on the basis of the protection of industrial and commercial
property.[74]

(iii) Importation of products from third countries

— Clarification of scope of Articles 30–36

The Court also focused on the discriminatory factor in its findings under Arti- 6.37
cles 30–36 E.C. in the *Generics v. Kline* case. This may seem surprising, considering that it is well-established case law that the rules on the free movement
of goods only apply to intra-Community trade.[75] In so doing, the Court thus
impliedly clarified in *Generics v. Kline* that if Member States apply discriminatory criteria with respect to imports from third countries that would
adversely affect intra-Community trade, these measures will be held to be
contrary to Articles 30–36 E.C.[76] It should therefore be stressed that the decisive factor which will trigger the application of Articles 30–36 E.C. is the
adverse effect of the national measure, whether directly or indirectly, on intra-
Community trade rather than the fact that it effectively applies to, and regu-
lates, intra-Community trade. This does not imply, however, that the intellectual property owner also loses his right to oppose the direct importation of
infringing products coming from third countries. The Court only held the discriminatory feature of the contested legislation to be incompatible with Article 36 E.C., and not the right of the intellectual property owner to prohibit
importation from third countries as such.

— Differential treatment

In this particular case the contested practice was held to be discriminatory 6.38
because the patentee was discouraged from importing his product from other
Member States rather than manufacturing them domestically. The Court
briefly stated that this different treatment could not be justified in terms of the
specific subject-matter of a patent but, to the contrary, was clearly inspired by

---

[73] Case 434/85: [1988] E.C.R. 1245; [1988] 1 C.M.L.R. 701, at paras. 16–19.
[74] See also J. Turner, "*Allen and Hanbury's v. Generics*, acte claire – and wrong" [1988] E.I.P.R.
186.
[75] Concerning the non-applicability of the case law concerning intellectual property to trade with
third countries, see Case 51/75, *EMI Records Ltd v. CBC United Kingdom Ltd*, Judgment of
June 15, 1976: [1976] E.C.R. 811; [1976] 2 C.M.L.R. 235. Case 270/80, *Polydor v. Harlequin*,
Judgment of February 9, 1982: [1982] E.C.R. 329; [1982] 1 C.M.L.R. 677.
[76] Case C–191/90: [1992] E.C.R. I-5335; [1993] 1 C.M.L.R. 89, at paras. 17–18.

protectionist objectives which are contrary to the objectives of the Community as expressed in Articles 2 and 3 of the Treaty.[77]

— Departing from the reward test

6.39   It is significant that the Court did not reiterate the definition of the specific subject-matter of patents under licences of right in terms of constituting the right to get a fair return in the *Generics v. Kline* case. In the latter the usual definition of the specific subject-matter of patents was used whereas the Court endeavoured to rectify the conclusions drawn from the *Allen and Hanburys* case in the following, with respect, rather unconvincing manner:

> "The Court, (in the *Allen and Hanburys* case), did no more than take note of the United Kingdom legislation and did not establish a Community definition of a 'weak patent'."[78]

In the *Generics* case the Court thus refrained from using the above-mentioned reward test, namely, whether or not the contested provisions of the United Kingdom Patents Act were necessary to safeguard for the patentee a fair return under patents endorsed "licences of right". However, the Court did not give any indications concerning the underlying reason as to why the discrimination could not be justified in terms of the specific subject-matter of patents which it held to be the right to the first marketing of the patented product and to oppose infringements.

— Specific subject-matter under licences of right

6.40   The reason underlying this different approach in the *Generics v. Kline* case is partly, though not entirely convincingly, elucidated by Advocate General Van Gerven in his opinion to the case.[79] He points out that in principle the patentee, under the system of licences of right, cannot oppose the grant of a licence to a third party but only has the right to a fair return. However, the fact that his patent is endorsed "licences of right" does not imply that he totally loses his right to oppose importations coming from third countries. He retains his right to oppose importations from third countries on condition that he manufactures the product domestically. In other words, he only loses his right to oppose importations from third countries if he works his patent through importation of the patented product himself.[80] It could thus be said that the specific subject-matter of the patent is affected differently in cases of domestic production as opposed to importation from other Member States. As such, the argument goes that it cannot be maintained that the discriminatory measure is needed to safeguard the specific subject-matter of the patent, presum-

---

[77] Case C–191/90: [1992] E.C.R. I-5335; [1993] 1 C.M.L.R. 89, at paras. 22–25. Compare to the Court's approach to protectionist measures in Cases C–235/89 and C–30/90, see *supra*, pt. 3(1)(v).

[78] Case C–191/90: [1992] E.C.R. I-5335; [1993] 1 C.M.L.R. 89, at para. 37. The Court gave this explanation to counter the view of the Commission, the Spanish and United Kingdom Governments and Harris and Generics, who had argued that "patents endorsed licences of rights are 'weak' patents which are necessarily excluded from the scope of the derogating provisions of Articles 47 and 209 of the Act of Accession."

[79] Case C–191/90: [1992] E.C.R. I-5335; [1993] 1 C.M.L.R. 89, Opinion of Advocate General Van Gerven delivered on July 8, 1992.

[80] *id.*, pt. 9.

ably because it is precisely the discriminatory measure that causes the specific subject-matter to differ.

(iv) Evaluation

From these judgments it is clear that the Court will not hesitate to rule on the **6.41** compatibility of the provisions in national legislation imposing obligatory licences with the rules on the free movement of goods, and will declare them inapplicable, *per se*, where thought necessary to safeguard the objectives of the E.C. Treaty. As such, it is the very existence of those rights which is put in the balance against Community principles. The guiding principle seems to be that discriminatory treatment, whether directly or indirectly, of imports from other Member States under the system of licences of right is incompatible with the E.C. Treaty. Whether or not the goods concerned were marketed with the patentee's consent is therefore of no relevance.

The combination of the effect of these cases, with the ruling in the *Pharmon* **6.42** case, is to minimise the impact of obligatory licences on the free movement of goods through weakening the benefits a Member State can obtain by applying this system. This may be clarified by the following simplified scheme:

SCHEME 4 : OBLIGATORY LICENCES

Member State A		Member State B
obligatory licence	____/____)	parallel patent
Member State A		Member State C
obligatory licence	(_____	consent or not

The importation of products brought on to the market under compulsory licences in Member State A can be prevented on the basis of a parallel patent in Member State B. In contrast, products brought onto the market in Member State C, whether or not with the consent of the intellectual property owner, should have non-discriminatory access to the market of Member State A.

(2) The principle of relative novelty

(a) Legal issue

The Court also departed from the consent theory in the second case that was **6.43** put to it concerning the compatibility of the principle of relative novelty with the rules on the free movement of goods. The principle of relative novelty means, in essence, that industrial property protection is given for a reinvention. In both cases brought before the Court, this implied that the product had been "forgotten", *i.e.* not commercialised, during 50 years preceding the new application for protection and that during that period no other application had been filed within the national territory. As seen above, a common function of intellectual property protection is to give the inventor or artist the possibility of obtaining a reward for his inventive or creative effort, as well as to provide an incentive to invest time and money in research and development.[81] The principle of relative novelty raises questions about the concept of

---

[81] In general, see *supra*, Chap. 2, pt. 3(1).

"inventive or creative effort" for which protection is granted in the form of exclusive intellectual property rights.

The existence of national systems of obligatory licences shows that states also have an interest in having intellectual property rights worked in their territory.[82] Instead of introducing a system of obligatory licences, which reduces the scope of intellectual property protection offered in the public interest, Member States may be tempted to widen the scope of intellectual property protection they offer so as to attract industries and, subsequently, investment in the national economy. Take, for instance, an ordinary football. If under the legislation of a Member State an intellectual property right could be obtained on this common item, it would distort competition through reserving a legal monopoly for a manufacturer in a national market.[83] Could the use of that intellectual property right constitute an abuse of a dominant position or does this only occur once all competition from importers has been eliminated and, for instance, monopoly prices charged? Following the established case law it would be the latter since the normal use of intellectual property rights, including the possibility of being granted an injunction against imports if those goods were marketed without the consent of the right-owner, cannot of itself be contrary to the rules on competition.[84] This means that the problem comes down to the very "existence" of an intellectual property right when granted in spite of novelty. On two occasions the Court has had to rule on the compatibility of the principle of "relative novelty" with the concept of "industrial and commercial property rights" as written into Article 36 E.C. Although the underlying issue was largely similar in both cases, the approach adopted by the Court differed substantially in the second case.

(b) Case 1: Existence/exercise dichotomy

6.44 The first case, *Keurkoop v. Nancy Kean Gifts*, concerned design rights in a ladies' handbag.[85] The applicable Benelux law contained the principle of relative novelty combined with the principle of first-to-file whereby only the person claiming to be the author of the design or the person employing him or commissioning the design can object that the person filing the application is not the author. As mentioned before, the first preliminary question raised the issue of whether the application of a national law containing a provision whereby only a limited number of persons have the right to challenge the right of the person who filed the design is compatible with Article 36 E.C. The second preliminary question asked if the application for an injunction could be

---

[82] See *supra*, pt. 3(1), for the case law of the Court concerning the incompatibility of protectionist features of obligatory licences with Community law.

[83] See Case 35/87, *Thetford v. Fiamma*, Opinion of Advocate General Mischo delivered on April 28, 1988: [1988] E.C.R. 3594; [1988] 3 C.M.L.R. 549, pt. 21, where he writes: "If a Member State were in fact to grant a patent for such (a perfectly ordinary football) in everyday use, without doubt its motive would be to reserve a monopoly for a national manufacturer...." According to him, this would constitute a disguised restriction on trade in the sense of Article 36 E.C., second sentence.

[84] See *supra*, Chap. 5.

[85] Case 144/81, *Keurkoop BV v. Nancy Kean Gifts BV*, Judgment of September 14, 1982: [1982] E.C.R. 2853; [1983] 2 C.M.L.R. 47. See also *supra*, Chap. 4, pt. 4(b)(i).

defeated if the importer obtained the goods from another Member State where these rights were not infringed by the marketing of the goods.

In accordance with the distinction between the "existence" and the "exercise" of intellectual property rights, the Court applied the following reasoning in its answer to the first question:

> "On that issue the Court can only state that in the present state of Community law and in the absence of Community standardisation or a harmonisation of laws *the determination of the conditions and the procedures under which protection of designs is granted is a matter for national rules....*"[86]

In its answer to the second question, the Court reiterated that in order to come under the exception of Article 36 E.C., the prohibitions and restrictions on imports must be justified on grounds of the protection of industrial property and must not constitute a disguised restriction on trade. The Court held that such a disguised restriction on trade might come about through an "improper use" of those rights. For instance through maintaining, or creating, artificial barriers to the Common Market through agreements or concerted practices envisaged by Article 85 E.C. So it seemed that the Court was not willing to examine the impact of national provisions as such. The conditions and procedures constitute the existence of industrial property rights which are nationally determined and not curtailed by Community law. The exercise of those rights might be infringing Community law if the behaviour of the market participant leads to a disguised restriction on trade. Summarising the Court's approach in this way brings out the similarities between this case, mainly concerning Article 36 E.C., and the Court's ruling in the *Parke Davis* case concerning the rules on competition.[87]

(c) Case 2: Towards a justification test

The second case, *Thetford v. Fiamma*, concerned patents on portable toilets granted under the principle of relative novelty in the United Kingdom.[88] The first question, referred for a preliminary ruling, asked whether a patent granted under the principle of relative novelty constitutes industrial and commercial property entitled to protection under Article 36 of the Treaty. The second question raised the matter of whether, in case the answer to the first question was positive, the only relief justified under Article 36 E.C. would be an order for payment of a reasonable reward but not an injunction.   6.45

(i) No justification under first sentence Article 36

It is significant that the Court reformulated the first question in the following way: 6.46

---

[86] Case 144/81: [1982] E.C.R. 2853; [1983] 2 C.M.L.R. 47, at para. 18 (emphasis added).
[87] Case 24/67, *Parke Davis v. Probel e.a.*, Judgment of February 29, 1968: [1968] E.C.R. 55; [1968] C.M.L.R. 47. See *supra*, Chap. 3, pt. 4(2)(iii).
[88] Case 35/87, *Thetford Corporation a.o. v. Fiamma SpA a.o.*, Judgment of June 30, 1988: [1988] E.C.R. 3585; [1988] 3 C.M.L.R. 549.

"The [. . .] first question seeks to establish whether the derogation from Articles 30 to 34 of the EEC Treaty which is set out in the *first sentence of Article 36 necessarily applies to any patent granted pursuant to the legislation of a Member State* or whether, on the contrary, it does not apply to patents granted by virtue of the principle of relative novelty."[89]

Although the Court thus seemed to acknowledge the nature of the problem posed by the national court, it basically restated the first part of the *Keurkoop* judgment by ruling that the conditions and procedures of intellectual property protection are matters for national rules to determine. By thus implying that any patent granted under any national law of a Member State comes within Article 36 E.C., the Court once again failed to formulate a Community concept of a patent independently of national law.[90]

(ii) Justification under second sentence Article 36

6.47 The Court proceeded, nonetheless, to look at whether the application of the legislation concerned, *per se*, constituted an arbitrary discrimination or a disguised restriction on trade. The importance of this fact lies in that the Court did not merely proceed to state that the exercise of the intellectual property right, in particular circumstances, might be contrary to the second sentence of Article 36 E.C. as it had done in the *Keurkoop* case. Rather, it examined the scope of the legislation in general, and thus impliedly acknowledged that the existence of intellectual property rights may be curtailed by Community rules.[91]

— Rationale

6.48 This new approach to the principle of relative novelty, which goes along the same lines of the *Allen and Hanburys* ruling decided a couple of months earlier,[92] was probably inspired by the following reflection made by Advocate General Mischo in his opinion to the case:

"In fact, it could be that an injunction prohibiting the importation of a product, issued in view of the existence of a patent, may constitute such a (arbitrary) discrimination or such a (disguised) restriction (on trade) *simply because the patent was granted in circumstances indicative of a protectionist intention.*"[93]

— Scrutiny by the Court

6.49 The Court looked at whether the provisions of national law pointed to an arbitrary discrimination and, perhaps more significantly, looked at the justifi-

---

[89] Case 35/87: [1988] E.C.R. 3585; [1988] 3 C.M.L.R. 549, at para. 7 (emphasis added).

[90] See also R. Eccles, "Patentee's right to prevent importation – *Thetford Corporation v. Fiamma Spa*" [1982] E.I.P.R. 26 at 26.

[91] See also G. Friden, "Recent developments in EEC intellectual property law: the distinction between existence and exercise revisited" (1989) 26 C.M.L.Rev. 193 at 199 where he writes: "It follows that the Court's rulings to the effect that Treaty prohibitions do not affect the existence of intellectual property rights are no longer valid, to the extent that the Member State's freedom to create a right is now limited by the second sentence of Article 36, which previously only applied to the exercise of the right." However, it will be seen in Chap. 7 *infra* that this judgment is not as decisive a change as it promised to be, because the Court still uses the existence/exercise dichotomy in what seems to be an arbitrary manner.

[92] See *supra*, pt. 3(1)(b).

[93] Case 35/87: [1988] E.C.R. 3585; [1988] 3 C.M.L.R. 549, at pt. 19 (emphasis added).

cation of the law in order to establish whether its aim was to disguise restrictions on trade or not. The Court held that there was no discrimination because the rules applied without distinction according to the place where the invention was originally filed, in the United Kingdom or in another Member State, or according to the nationality of the applicant. It also ruled that in the given circumstances there was no disguised restriction on trade because the aim of the provision was merely to reward the rediscovery of an old and unused invention.[94]

— Geographical aspect disregarded

It is significant in this respect that the Court only dealt with the chronological aspect of the principle of relative novelty and not with its geographical aspect. Both the Commission and the Advocate General had pointed out that the use of an invention outside the United Kingdom in the 50 years preceding the application was not taken into account for establishing whether or not the invention had been "forgotten". A patent could therefore be granted on the basis of relative novelty in the United Kingdom for an invention that was freely used or duly published in another Member State.[95] This, they held, constitutes an arbitrary discrimination and is incompatible with Article 36 E.C.[96] The Court apparently followed the Advocate General's advice not to engage in this matter, in particular as the national court had not included this aspect in its preliminary question. This issue raised complex problems such as the applicability of Community rules to patents granted before the accession of the United Kingdom to the Community, legal certainty, legitimate expectations and vested rights.[97] The reluctance of the Court to rule on this matter might in addition find an explanation in that it concerned the 1949 United Kingdom Patents Act that has since been replaced, even though it would be found to infringe Article 36 E.C. if the law was still in force now.

6.50

(iii) Specific subject-matter approach

In its answer to the second question concerning the lawful exercise the intellectual property owner could make of his intellectual property right, the Court simply reiterated its established case law concerning the specific subject-matter of the right.[98] It held that the granting of an injunction, which is normally provided for in national law, is justified under Article 36 E.C. It thereby rejected the national court's suggestion that the payment

6.51

---

[94] Case 35/87: [1988] E.C.R. 3585; [1988] 3 C.M.L.R. 549, at paras. 17–18. Marenco gives the following definition of a disguised restriction on trade: "a protectionist measure in the form of a facially non discriminatory provision", G. Marenco and K. Banks, "Intellectual property and the Community rules on free movement: discrimination unearthed" (1990) 15 E.L.Rev. 224 at 235.

[95] Case 35/87: [1988] E.C.R. 3585; [1988] 3 C.M.L.R. 549. For the Commission's viewpoint, see Report of the Hearing, Answers to a question put by the Court; for the Advocate General's view, see at pt. 30.

[96] See also G. Friden, *op. cit.*, p. 201, where he points out that: "The obvious consequence of this logic is that an injunction could not be obtained on the basis of the Rule. The patent holder's rights would therefore diminish but it is unclear to what extent, if any, the patent would lose its validity. It would theoretically be possible to distinguish validity under U.K. law and effects within the Community but that would lead to a rather unpractical and uncertain situation."

[97] Case 35/87: [1988] E.C.R. 3585; [1988] 3 C.M.L.R. 549, at pt. 30.

[98] On the specific subject-matter of patents, see *supra*, Chap. 4, pt. 2(1).

of a reasonable reward might perhaps suffice with respect to intellectual property rights issued under the principle of relative novelty.

(iv) Evaluation

6.52 Although this case is very important, in that the Court puts the existence/exercise dichotomy aside in respect of the second sentence of Article 36 E.C., it is submitted that it falls short in not applying the justification and proportionality tests to the first sentence of Article 36 E.C. The Court does apply a discrimination test to see whether the existence of national rules can be upheld under the second sentence of Article 36 E.C., but only looks at the exercise by the right-owner under the first sentence of Article 36 E.C. There is, however, no coherent explanation for the difference in treatment under the first and second sentence of Article 36 E.C. to be found in the Treaty. Furthermore, it is submitted that the structure of Article 36 E.C. imposes an analysis as to the justification of the existence of the principle of relative novelty, under its first sentence, prior to the analysis of the compatibility of that principle with the proviso of the second sentence.[99]

(3) Renting and lending right

(a) Legal issue

6.53 The approach taken in the *Thetford v. Fiamma* case stands in contrast to the approach taken by the Court in the *Warner Brothers v. Christiansen* case, which was decided a month earlier.[1] The essential facts of the latter were as follows. Warner had parallel copyright protection in a video-film in both the United Kingdom and Denmark, but the scope of protection offered differed substantially. Under United Kingdom copyright law anyone buying the video can freely rent it out, whereas under Danish copyright law a specific authorisation by the author is needed to subsequently hire it out. Warner brought the video on to the market for sale in the United Kingdom. Christiansen bought the video marketed by Warner in the United Kingdom and imported it into Denmark where he hired out the video-cassette without Warner's authorisation. Warner invoked Danish copyright law to prohibit the hiring-out of the video without its consent. Christiansen objected that Warner's copyright was exhausted by putting the video on sale in the United Kingdom so that, in line with the *Musik-Vertrieb* case,[2] it should now accept the consequences of its choice as regards the free movement of goods in the Community.

---

[99] Mattera also considers the second sentence of Article 36 E.C. to be subordinate to an analysis under the first sentence. See A. Mattera, "*La libre circulation des oeuvres d'art à l'intérieur de la Communauté et la protection des trésors nationaux ayant une valeur artistique, historique ou archéologique*" [1993] *Revue du Marché Unique Européen* 9 at 17–18. He describes the second sentence of Article 36 E.C. as a supplementary intellectual precaution, a kind of "safety net" in order to ensure that the limits imposed on the application of that provision are watertight and prevent attempts to slip through the net of the first sentence. This also seemed to be acknowledged by the Court in the *Henn and Darby* case, see *supra*, Chap. 3, pt. 2(2)(b).

[1] Case 158/86, *Warner Brother Inc. and Metronome Video ApS v. Erik Viuff Christiansen*, Judgment of May 17, 1988: [1988] E.C.R. 2605; [1990] 3 C.M.L.R. 684.

[2] See *supra*, Chap. 4, pt. 2(2)(a).

(b) Applicability of consent theory

The Court's approach to this problem was totally different from Advocate **6.54** General Mancini's who had basically pursued Christiansen's argument.[3] Advocate General Mancini merely focused on the exercise of the intellectual property right and, invoking the case law whereby the consent theory was applied, came to the conclusion that Warner's intellectual property right was exhausted through the sale of its video-cassette in the United Kingdom. This implied that in his opinion any other solution would exceed the specific subject-matter of the right, defined by the Court as the right to the first marketing with the intellectual property owner's consent, and thus cannot benefit from the derogation under Article 36 E.C.[4] He referred to the *Musik-Vertrieb* case to conclude that the intellectual property owner may not rely on differences between national laws to resurrect barriers to intra-Community trade. The Court radically departed from this opinion. The approach taken by the Court consisted in looking at the justification invoked for the existence of the intellectual property right, rather than at the way in which it was exercised by Warner.

(c) Nature of measures having equivalent effect

The Court justified the difference in approach between the *Warner Brothers* **6.55** and the *Musik-Vertrieb* cases by pointing out that in the latter the law in force in the Member State of importation allowed the copyright holder to collect an additional fee upon importation of the goods. In the former case the contested right only applied once the goods had been imported.[5]

(i) Importance before *Keck* judgment

At the time of the judgment this distinction seemed to be rather artificial con- **6.56** sidering, in particular, that the Court had no problems with accepting the fact that the contested rules indirectly affected intra-Community trade and thus constituted measures having an equivalent effect to quantitative restrictions, in the sense of the *Dassonville* judgment,[6] which in principle come under Article 30 E.C. The Court held:

> "...it must be observed that the commercial distribution of video-cassettes takes the form not only of sales but also, and increasingly, that of hiring-out to individuals who posses video-tape recorders. The right to prohibit such hiring-out in a Member State *is therefore liable to influence trade in video-cassettes in that State and hence, indirectly, to affect intra-Community trade* in these products. Legislation of the kind which gave

---

[3] Case 158/86, Opinion of Advocate General Mancini delivered on January 26, 1988: [1988] E.C.R. 2618; [1990] 3 C.M.L.R. 684.

[4] Case 158/86: [1988] E.C.R. 2618; [1990] 3 C.M.L.R. 684, see especially pt. 8.

[5] Case 158/86: [1988] E.C.R. 2605; [1990] 3 C.M.L.R. 684, at para. 9.

[6] Case 8/74, *Procureur du Roi v. Dassonville*, Judgment of July 11, 1974: [1974] E.C.R. 837; [1974] 2 C.M.L.R. 436, at para. 5, where the Court gave the following definition: "all trading rules enacted by the Member States which are capable of hindering, directly or indirectly, actually or potentially, intra-Community trade are to be considered as measures having an effect equivalent to quantitative restrictions."

rise to the main proceedings must therefore, in the light of the established case-law, be regarded as a measure having an effect equivalent to a quantitative restriction on imports, which is prohibited by Article 30 of the Treaty."[7]

This was in conformity with the state of the case law on Article 30 E.C. at that time whereby the Court did not distinguish between whether the measures took effect at the border or whether they were internal measures.[8] It was also obvious from this judgment that the Court did not take the criterion of discrimination into account.[9]

(ii) Importance after *Keck* judgment

6.57   As is seen below,[10] the Court subsequent to the *Warner Brothers* case expressly qualified the definition of measures having equivalent effect in so far as specifically sales modalities are concerned in the very important *Keck* case.[11] Whether or not measures are enforced at the border thereby seems to have gained in importance in order to determine whether Article 30 E.C. applies at all to national measures, although apparently they do not necessarily have to be discriminatory.[12] As yet it is not totally clear whether the *Keck* ruling can merely be transposed to measures dealing with the hiring-out of products rather than imposing sales modalities. It therefore remains to be seen whether, in the future, similar measures will at all be held to come under Article 30 E.C.

(d) *Relation between Articles 30, 59 and 36*

(i) *Basset v. SACEM*

6.58   The Court had already made a similar distinction between charging additional royalties upon importation, as in *Musik-Vertrieb*, and charging a "supplementary mechanical reproduction fee" in addition to a performance royalty upon the public use of sound-recordings in the *Basset v. SACEM* judgment of 1987.[13] From the reasoning used it is not clear whether or not the

---

[7] Case 158/86: [1988] E.C.R. 2605; [1990] 3 C.M.L.R. 684, at para. 10 (emphasis added).

[8] See also E. White, "In search of the limits to Article 30 of the EEC Treaty" (1989) 26 C.M.L.Rev. 235 at 241.

[9] This is also admitted by Marenco, who argues in favour of the discrimination theory. See G. Marenco, and K. Banks, "Intellectual property and the Community rules on free movement: discrimination unearthed" (1990) 15 E.L.Rev. 224 at 241. On the discrimination-theory in general, see also L. Defalque, "*Le concept de discrimination en matière de libre circulation des marchandises*" [1987] C.D.E. 471; G. Marenco, "*Pour une interprétation traditionelle de la notion de mesure d'effet équivalent à une restriction quantitative*" [1984] C.D.E. 291. See also *infra*, Chap. 7, pt. 3(4).

[10] See *infra*, Chap. 7, pt. 3.

[11] Joined Cases C–267 and 268/91, *Keck and Mithouard*, Judgment of November 24, 1993: [1993] E.C.R. I-6097.

[12] Similarly, see L. Gormley, "Reasoning renounced? The remarkable judgment in *Keck & Mithouard*" [1994] *European Business Law Review* 63.

[13] Case 402/85, *G. Basset v. SACEM*, Judgment of April 9, 1987: [1987] E.C.R. 1747; [1987] 3 C.M.L.R. 173, at para. 12. On this case, see J. Shaw, "Performing rights and Community law" (1988) 13 E.L.Rev. 45. The Court passed another judgment, which concerned the same facts, the same questions, and the same defendant, merely with reference to this case, see Case C–270/86, *J. Cholay and Société "Bizon's Club" v. SACEM*, Judgment of December 12, 1990, [1990] E.C.R. I-4607.

Court considered the charging of the supplementary fee to be incompatible with Article 30 E.C.[14] In this case the Court looked mainly at whether the rule was discriminatory and, upon the finding that it was not, held:

> "It follows that, even if the charging of the fee in question were to be capable of having a restrictive effect on imports, *it does not constitute a measure having equivalent effect prohibited under Article 30 of the Treaty inasmuch as it must be regarded as a normal exploitation of copyright* and does not constitute a means of arbitrary discrimination or a disguised restriction on trade between Member States for the purpose of Article 36 of the Treaty."[15]

The reasoning used by the Court was, to say the least, confusing.[16] It follows from the E.C. Treaty and it is generally accepted that Article 36 E.C. is an exception to Article 30 E.C. As such, it is not because Article 36 E.C. applies that the rule itself is no longer qualified as a measure having an effect equivalent to a quantitative restriction. Article 36 E.C. can be invoked to maintain such a measure in force. If the measure is not regarded as having an effect equivalent to quantitative restrictions, then Article 30 E.C. simply does not apply so that it is obvious that no recourse should be had to Article 36 E.C. In the *SACEM* case the Court seemingly reversed the reasoning and first looked at the applicability of the second sentence of Article 36 E.C., apparently assuming that national copyright always comes within its first sentence, to conclude that since Article 36 E.C. applied there was no need to look at whether the measure was caught by Article 30 E.C. Another explanation may be that the Court impliedly reasoned in terms of the applicability of Article 36 by analogy to services, and therefore expressly stated that Article 30 E.C. did not apply to the case. This could be deduced from the fact that the Court held that the supplementary mechanical reproduction fee constitutes "part of the payment for an author's rights over the public performance of a recorded musical work" and is calculated not on the number of records bought or played but on the basis of a discotheque's turnover.[17] It should be recalled that in the earlier *Coditel* cases, and in the subsequent *Tournier* case, the Court held performance rights to be governed by the rules on services instead of Articles 30–36 E.C.[18]

(ii) *Warner Brothers*

Whatever the underlying reason, the least one can say is that the Court used a 6.59
highly confusing reasoning in *SACEM*. It is therefore to be welcomed that the Court rectified and clarified its approach in the *Warner Brothers* case by

---

[14] See also G. Marenco and K. Banks, *op. cit.*, p. 228.

[15] Case 402/85: [1987] E.C.R. 1747; [1987] 3 C.M.L.R. 173, at para. 16 (emphasis added).

[16] The Court used a similarly confusing reasoning in Case 40/82, *Commission v. United Kingdom (Newcastle disease)*, Judgment of July 15, 1982: [1982] E.C.R. 2793; [1982] 3 C.M.L.R. 497, at para. 31: "The national measures are therefore to be considered as measures having an effect equivalent to quantitative restrictions, prohibited by Article 30 of the Treaty unless it is established that they are justified under Article 36 on grounds of the protection of animal health." On this case, see L. Gormley, "Newcastle disease and the free movement of goods – I" [1983] *New Law Journal* 1037.

[17] Case 402/85: [1987] E.C.R. 1747; [1987] 3 C.M.L.R. 173, at para. 15.

[18] See *supra*, Chap. 4, pt. 2(2)(b) and (c).

expressly stating that the measure concerned came within the ambit of Article 30 E.C. before analysing whether Article 36 E.C. could be invoked. It has been argued by some authors that this does not exclude the fact that the rules on the free provision of services could also have applied to this case since it could be said to concern rights of performance.[19] There seems to be an importance difference, however, between the cases decided under the rules on services and the *Warner Brothers* case. In the latter, the royalties are not calculated on the basis of an estimated number of persons viewing the film but, to the contrary, merely reflects the number of times the material form of the work, namely the video cassette, is hired out. It would therefore seem to be premature, in the present state of the case law, to unequivocally state that the rules on services would be held to be applicable in such a case by the Court. It is significant in this respect that the Court expressly rejected the application of the rules on services in the *Cinéthèque* case. It held that in respect of cinematographic works transmitted to the public indirectly by means of recordings such as video cassettes, "... the transmission to the public merges with the putting of the works on the market".[20] As in *Warner Brothers*, the Court reached it findings solely with regard to Articles 30–36 E.C.

(e) Justification test

(i) Under both sentences of Article 36

6.60   As in the *Thetford v. Fiamma* case,[21] the Court in *Warner Brothers* proceeded to look at whether the contested rules constituted an arbitrary discrimination in the sense of the second sentence of Article 36 E.C. The main importance of the latter case therefore lies in the fact that the Court went significantly further in its scrutiny of the existence of the intellectual property right under Article 36 E.C. Having established that the Danish legislation did not operate an arbitrary discrimination in intra-Community trade, the Court proceeded to look into the reasons for the existence of the right. In other words, it carried out a justification test under the first sentence of Article 36 E.C. One might contend that this is a rather peculiar approach to Article 36 E.C., namely first looking at whether the exceptions to the rule apply before establishing that the rule itself is applicable. It is nevertheless important to note that it is one of the rare cases in which the Court scrutinised the existence of an intellectual property right under both sentences of Article 36 E.C.

(ii) In terms of function intellectual property rights

6.61   Contrary to the approach taken concerning licences of right,[22] the Court in *Warner Brothers* no longer looked at the justification of the contested rules

---

[19] See L. Defalque, "Copyright – free movement of goods and territoriality: recent developments" [1989] E.I.P.R. 435 at 438.

[20] Joined Cases 60 and 61/84, *Cinéthèque v. Fédération nationale de cinémas français*, Judgment of July 11, 1985: [1985] E.C.R. 2605; [1986] 1 C.M.L.R. 365, concerning the compatibility with Articles 30–36 and 59 E.C. of national law providing that no cinematographic films shown in cinemas may simultaneously be exploited in the form of video cassettes intended for sale or hire for the private use of the public before the expiry of a certain period (*i.e.* between six and 18 months to be determined by decree).

[21] See *supra*, pt. 3(2)(c).

[22] See *supra*, pt. 3(b).

under the first sentence of Article 36 E.C. in terms of the specific subject-matter of the right. The Court instead applied a three-step reasoning which resembles a functionality test.[23] As in the *Coditel* cases, which were dealt with under the rules on services,[24] the Court first clarified that the exclusive rights of both performance and reproduction are essential rights of the author which are "not called into question by the rules of the Treaty".[25] Then the Court reflected upon the importance of the newly created market for the hiring out of video-cassettes in terms of offering "a great potential as a source of revenue for the makers of films".[26] Finally, the Court held that:

> "... it is apparent that, by authorising the collection of royalties only on sales to private individuals and to persons hiring out video-cassettes, *it is impossible to guarantee to makers of films a remuneration which reflects the number of occasions on which the video-cassettes are actually hired out and which secures them a satisfactory share of the rental market.* That explains why, [...], certain national laws have recently provided specific protection of the right to hire out video-cassettes."
>
> "*Laws of that kind* are therefore clearly *justified on grounds of the protection of industrial and commercial property* pursuant to Article 36 of the Treaty."[27]

(f) Express rejection of consent theory

Having found that the existence of the intellectual property right was justified   **6.62**
under Article 36 E.C., the Court subsequently rejected the argument that the exercise of that intellectual property right should be curtailed through the application of the principle of exhaustion on the basis of the consent theory.[28] The Court held that limiting the exercise of the intellectual property right would come down to emptying the intellectual property right of its substance. It expressly stated:

> "It cannot therefore be accepted that the marketing by a film-maker of a video-cassette containing one of his works, in a Member State which does not provide specific protection for the right to hire it out, should have repercussions on the right conferred on that same film-maker by the

---

[23] On the concept of a "functionality test", see *supra*, Chap. 3, pt. 4(2)(c).

[24] See *supra*, Chap. 4, pt. 2(2)(b).

[25] Case 158/86: [1988] E.C.R. 2605; [1990] 3 C.M.L.R. 684, at para. 13. This is more in line with the Court's approach to trade marks. On this issue, see W. Rothnie, "*Hag II*: putting the common origin doctrine to sleep" [1991] E.I.P.R. 24 at 28. In his conclusion at p. 31, he writes: "the prominence accorded to the trade mark's essential function calls into question the orthodox analysis of the cases on other intellectual property rights since definitions of these have often included an element which appears to correspond to the 'essential function'. But hitherto, this has only proved important for cases involving copyright."

[26] Case 158/86: [1988] E.C.R. 2605; [1990] 3 C.M.L.R. 684, at para. 14.

[27] Case 158/86: [1988] E.C.R. 2605; [1990] 3 C.M.L.R. 684, at paras. 15 and 16 (emphasis added).

[28] It should be recalled that the Court also upheld the exercise of the right of performance in films under Article 59 E.C. in the *Coditel* cases, whereby it was expressly acknowledged that: "the right of a copyright owner and his assigns to require fees for any showing of a film is part of the *essential function* of copyright in this type of literary and artistic works", Case 62/79, *Coditel I*, Judgment of March 18, 1980: [1980] E.C.R. 881; [1981] 2 C.M.L.R. 362, at para. 14, (emphasis added). See also *supra*, Chap. 4, pt. 2(2)(b).

legislation of another Member State to restrain, in that State, the hiring-out of that video-cassette."[29]

In other words, the Court made clear that it does not suffice that there is parallel intellectual property protection and that the goods have been marketed with the intellectual property owner's consent, to come to the conclusion that the principle of exhaustion should be applied.[30] One first has to look at the reasons justifying the existence of differences in the legal protection offered and, if the existence of the rules are justified under Article 36 E.C., then the principle of exhaustion is not applicable.[31]

(g) Evaluation

6.63 It is difficult to reconcile the *Warner Brothers* judgment with the Court's ruling in the *Merck* case. In the latter, the Court allowed the effect of the non-existence of patent protection in the Member State of exportation to have severe repercussions in the Member State of importation by applying the consent theory in the absence of parallel intellectual property protection.[32] As was maintained above, the Court in so doing neglected the proper function of the patent and essentially eliminated the very possibility of obtaining a reward.[33] It was precisely the need to uphold the function of copyright and akin rights, and the possibility of the author obtaining a remuneration for his work, that led to the contrary conclusion in *Warner Brothers*. It is submitted that it was the *Merck* case, and not the *Warner Brothers* case, that was wrongfully decided.

The new approach adopted by the Court in the *Warner Brothers* case seems to be more in accordance with the overall approach to Article 36 E.C. and is therefore to be warmly welcomed. It makes it definitely clear that the existence of intellectual property protection is no longer considered as being, *per se*, exempted under Article 36 E.C. and thus is subject to scrutiny under Community law.[34] Conversely, the exercise of intellectual property rights will no longer quasi-automatically be struck down in view of achieving the single market objective but is evaluated in terms of the need to safeguard the function of intellectual property rights.

6.64 The crucial question arising is to what extent the approach adopted in the *Warner Brothers* case constitutes a precedent, if not a turning point, in the case law of the Court. In other words, it needs to be established when the Court will resort to this new approach and under what circumstances it might

---

[29] Case 158/86: [1988] E.C.R. 2605; [1990] 3 C.M.L.R. 684, at para. 18.

[30] Compare to *supra*, pt. 2(1).

[31] The Commission has taken this judgment into account when drafting its proposal "on rental and lending right and on certain rights related to copyright in the field of intellectual property", see *supra*, Chap. 3, pt. 3(2)(b)(v).

[32] See *supra*, Chap. 4, pt. 2(1)(b); and Chap. 6, pt. 2(2).

[33] See *supra*, at pt. 2(5).

[34] See also G. Friden, *op. cit.*, p. 197, where he writes: "This indicates that the existence of such rights is no longer beyond the scope of EEC law. After all, if the Court can rule on whether EEC law allows a Member State to protect the rental of a cassette, it would seem to follow that it could also decide for instance, whether a Member State may protect spare parts, rather than just complete goods, or on the amplitude of protection which is to be granted to a relatively novel invention, as opposed to an absolute novel one."

continue to invoke the traditional existence/exercise dichotomy. The Court in *Warner Brothers* for the first time examined whether, and ruled that, the existence of the intellectual property right concerned was justified not only under the second, but also under the first, sentence of Article 36 E.C. The main importance of this judgment therefore lies in the fact that the Court set a precedent by radically departing from the traditional approach to delineate between "use" and "misuse" of intellectual property rights under the free movement of goods. It should, however, be pointed out that the Court nevertheless adopted a different approach in the subsequent *Thetford v. Fiamma* and spare parts cases.[35] The latter seem to indicate that the Court may be reluctant to apply the same justification test if the outcome of the case could lead to the conclusion that the national rule cannot be justified under Article 36 E.C.

4. THE CURRENT APPROACH TO ESTABLISH "MISUSE" OF INTELLECTUAL PROPERTY RIGHTS

(1) The "traditional" approach revisited

The current evolution of the case law of the Court concerning the applicability of the rules on the free movement of goods to intellectual property rights shows that Articles 30 to 36 E.C. are finally applied in their own right and have been freed from the shackles of competition rules in the form of the existence/exercise dichotomy. Although this is to be warmly welcomed, it is nevertheless still not clear when in future cases the Court will apply merely the consent theory to the exercise of intellectual property rights[36] or the justification test with regard to the existence of these rights. At present, one can only attempt to establish some guidelines on the basis of the few indications the Court has so far given.   **6.65**

First of all, it has to be repeated that the existence/exercise dichotomy no longer necessarily applies. The premise that the conditions and procedures of intellectual property protection are a matter for the national legislator to decide, and are not subject to scrutiny under Article 36 E.C., can no longer be unconditionally upheld.[37] In particular it seems that where national intellectual property provisions discriminate against imports from other Member States, the Court will proceed to analyse whether the existence of those rules is compatible with the second sentence of Article 36 E.C. As was maintained above, this would logically imply that the Court also examines whether the rules are, prima facie, justified under the first sentence of Article 36 E.C.[38]

It is more difficult to predict which approach the Court will adopt if there is no discrimination inherent in national intellectual property law. Rather than   **6.66**

---

[35] See *infra*, Chap. 7.

[36] For examples of such cases, see *supra*, Chap. 4, and Chap. 6, pt. 2.

[37] See *supra*, pt. 3. It should be recalled that also the general principle of non-discrimination, as laid down in Article 6 E.C., applies to intellectual property law and this independent of the application of the rules on the free movement of goods. See *supra*, Chap. 2, pt. 4(1)(c)(iv).

[38] See *supra*, pt. 3(1)(b), licences of right. See also pt. 3(2), principle of relative novelty, where it is submitted that the approach of the Court was inconsistent in that it only applied a justification test under the second sentence of Article 36 E.C.

introduce positive criteria along which to distinguish the approach to be taken it is, so far, only possible to eliminate certain criteria which were held to be decisive in the past. One can state for certain that the presence of parallel intellectual property protection is not the determining factor in concluding that the principle of exhaustion will apply to curtail the exercise of intellectual property rights. This was unquestionably proved by both the *Merck* and the *Pharmon* cases.[39] However, whereas those cases led one to believe that the consent of the intellectual property owner was the determining factor in the application of the principle of exhaustion to curtail the exercise of the intellectual property right, the *Warner Brothers* case has made it clear that, even where parallel intellectual property protection exists, consent is not necessarily the decisive criterion. Although this case concerned parallel importation, and all conditions were fulfilled to apply the consent theory, the Court adopted a justification test and thus focused on the reasons for the existence of the intellectual property right.[40]

This means that in the absence of inherently discriminating rules the Court has established precedents either way. In some cases it is merely the consent test that will apply to curtail the exercise of the intellectual property right. Whereas in other cases it is the justification test that will apply to see whether the existence of the intellectual property right is compatible with Article 36 E.C. and its exercise may be upheld. The problem is that it is currently not clear on what basis the Court applies one or the other approach. It could be that in the future the justification test will be applied to uphold the full effect of national intellectual property law, whereas the consent test will be applied to curtail the effect of certain features of national intellectual property law, such as the principle of territoriality, which are considered to be incompatible with Community law.[41] It is submitted that such an approach would be fundamentally inconsistent and cannot be explained on the basis of E.C. Treaty provisions to that end.[42] At the moment, one can only take note of the fact that, up till now, the Court has not yet ruled that the existence of national intellectual property law which is not discriminatory could not be justified under Article 36 E.C.

6.67   As such, the Court has failed to give adequate and coherent criteria to conclude that one or the other approach will be used in a particular case. It is further apparent that safeguarding the specific subject-matter of the intellectual property right no longer forms the only justification for derogations on the basis of Article 36 E.C.[43] Where the Court tried to hold on to this concept

---

[39] See *supra*, pt. 2(5). This can also be deducted from the *EMI v. Patricia* case, see *supra*, pt. 2(3).

[40] See *supra*, pt. 3(3), rental and lending right, where the Court used the peculiar approach of first looking at whether the second sentence applied, before looking at whether the measure was justified under the first sentence of Article 36 E.C.

[41] In this sense, the wording used by Orf is significant: "... [the judgment] has re-emphasised the limits of the doctrine of Community-exhaustion where the essential function of copyright is affected....", see E. Orf, "*Re Warner Bros Inc. and Metronome Video Aps v. Erik Viuff Christiansen*" [1988] E.I.P.R. 309 at 310.

[42] This would also be inconsistent with the case law concerning denominations of origin, where the Court did apply the functionality test to strike down distinctly applicable national measures, see *supra*, Chap. 3, pt. 4(2)(c)(iii).

[43] On the elaboration of this concept by the Court, see *supra*, Chap. 4.

as the premise for the application of the justification test concerning patents endorsed "licences of right",[44] the concept was radically departed from in the *Warner Brothers* judgment. In the latter case the Court took the first step towards abandoning the specific subject-matter criterion in favour of a real functionality test,[45] although it remains to be seen how this will be elaborated upon in future case law.

(2) Merits and shortcomings

The implications of this evolution of the case law of the Court concerning   **6.68** intellectual property rights are multiple. The most important one is that the Court may follow different approaches to any given case.[46] This implies that legal uncertainty will continue to exist, at least until the Court clearly indicates that it does not apply one or the other approach arbitrarily or on grounds of judicial policy but rather along clearly definable and transparent criteria. Judge Everling once wrote:

> "The Court of Justice [. . .] creates its own legitimacy primarily by the internal logic and consistency of the actual results expressed in its judgments and by the significance of those results for the development of the Community legal order and the continuation of the process of integration. They acquire their own pattern only in the perspective of a whole series of judgments on given problems, in which it gradually becomes clear what the Court of Justice regards as the criteria 'justi atque injusti' in the Community."[47]

Unfortunately, this statement does not seem to be fully applicable, as yet, to the Court's case law concerning intellectual property rights.

Nowadays, it is indisputable that the Commission can challenge the com-   **6.69** patibility of national intellectual property provisions with the rules on the free movement of goods on the basis of Article 169 E.C. procedures. More importantly, it is also clear that the very existence of national intellectual property rules can, in principle, be challenged under Article 36 E.C. by Article 177 E.C. procedures. This brings the case law concerning intellectual property rights more in line with the case law concerning the other objectives mentioned in Article 36 E.C. It will be interesting to see whether the Court will go so far as to scrutinise national intellectual property law under Article 36 E.C. in the context of a case pending before it based on Articles 85 and 86 E.C. combined

---

[44] See *supra*, pt. 3(1)(b), where it is maintained that the Court had difficulties in defining and coherently applying the specific subject-matter of a patent endorsed "licences of right". See also *supra*, pt. 3(2)(a) concerning the local manufacturing clause, where it is submitted that the specific subject-matter approach was inappropriate because it is a concept which takes the existence of the intellectual property right for granted whereas the Court was precisely asked to give a ruling concerning the justification of the existence of that right.

[45] On the functionality test, see *supra*, Chap. 3, pt. 4(2)(c).

[46] For an illustration of the different approaches the Court may take to any given case, and the implications this has on the final ruling, see the analysis of the spare parts cases, *infra*, Chap. 7, pt. 4.

[47] U. Everling, "The Court of Justice as a decision-making authority" in *The Art of Governance* (Michigan Law Review ed. 1987) (Nomos Verlagsgesellshaft), pp. 156–172, at p. 171.

with Article 5 E.C.[48] The *Magill* appeal judgment, which was the first opportunity for the Court to take a clear stance on this matter, seems to be a first step – albeit a sidestep – in this direction.[49] Although the Court upheld the ruling of the Court of First Instance, which formally reiterated the existence/exercise distinction, in practice it was clearly the very existence of copyright on programme listings, rather than the straightforward exercise of it by the intellectual property owner, that was held to be incompatible with E.C. law. It is in particular to be regretted that the Court sidestepped the issue at stake in this manner for in so doing it seemingly opened the door to an unwarranted and unlimited interference by E.C. law in the field of intellectual property rights.

6.70   It should be emphasised that if the current trend, whereby the existence of intellectual property rights is scrutinised upon the fulfilment of their respective functions, is openly, coherently and effectively pursued it will not necessarily adversely affect the current situation of intellectual property owners in the E.C.; rather to the contrary. It is, of course, natural for intellectual property owners to be wary of the prospect that the existence of a nationally granted intellectual property right may be held to be incompatible with E.C. law. It should be kept in mind, though, that the introduction of the formal existence/exercise dichotomy proved not to offer any guarantee either that an intellectual property right would not live but a formal existence and be emptied of its substance through the back-door method of striking down the various ways in which it may be exercised. This is best illustrated by reference to the *Magill* cases. It is commonly accepted that national measures alleged to protect, for instance, public health whilst in fact pursuing a protectionist goal are held to be incompatible with Article 36 E.C. because they fail the justification and/or proportionality test. There seems to be no apparent reason why intellectual property law should not be subject to the same tests in order to establish whether or not contested provisions are effectively needed to safeguard the function of intellectual property rights. As for the other exceptions mentioned in Article 36 E.C., this would not entail that intellectual property law and intellectual property rights would to a large extent become redundant in practice. Rather, it would imply that the function of intellectual property rights would be fully recognised and valued in E.C. context, and shielded against abuses. If this objective were to be consistently pursued, it should not have as its only consequence that certain contested provisions of national intellectual property law could be held to be incompatible with E.C. law. As a corollary, the Court would need to thoroughly review its own case law and, as was done in the *HAG II* case, expressly reverse several controversial judgments which sometimes adversely and unjustifiably affect the rights of intellectual property owners. In this respect, the *Merck* judgment is the one that most readily comes to mind.

---

[48] See also G. Friden, *op. cit.*, p. 197, where he poses the question of whether the *Warner Brothers* ruling could be extended to cases involving Articles 5 and 85 combined, which also imply state action.
[49] On the *Magill* cases, see *supra*, Chap. 5, pt. 4(3).

PART III

THE E.C. SPARE PARTS DEBATE
A CASE STUDY

7. Compatibility of the Enforcement of Intellectual Property Rights on Spare Parts of Cars with the Rules on the Free Movement of Goods

1. PRELIMINARY REMARKS

It will be clear from the preceding chapters that there is no single obvious **7.01** solution that unconditionally settles the issue of whether or not the grant and/or enforcement of intellectual property rights is compatible with Community law. The purpose of this chapter is to illustrate the various difficulties that may arise, and the possible solutions that may be adopted, under Articles 30–36 E.C. through a detailed analysis of the spare parts cases of 1988. Attention will be given not only to the applicability of Article 36 E.C. but also to related issues liable to be invoked in any court proceedings, such as the applicability, in principle, of Articles 30 and 34 E.C. to intellectual property rights and arguments that intellectual property protection has a direct bearing on consumer protection.

Prior to the spare parts cases, the European Court of Justice had never been **7.02** confronted with the complicated issue of the legal protection of components of complex products. In essence, the spare parts cases confronted the Court with a triple legal problem. First, the Court had to consider the implications of the diversity of, and sometimes conflicting, national approaches to design protection in general, and to components of complex products in particular.[1] For instance, in the United Kingdom subsequent to the elaboration of a "spare parts exception" by the House of Lords in the *British Leyland v. Armstrong* case of 1986[2] the so-called "must-fit" and "must-match" exceptions to design protection on spare parts were introduced in the 1988 Copyright, Designs and Patents Act. Whereas this implies that in the United Kingdom no design protection will be granted for spare parts that either must fit or must match the complex product in other Member States, such as France and Germany, similar parts may, in principle, be subject to design protection. This will generally be the case if they live up to the basic requirements and provided that the design is not merely dictated by the function of the part. However, here also important discrepancies remain not only as regards the content of the specific design legislation, and the possibility of cumulation with copyright protection, but also concerning the issue of whether or not a spare part needs to fulfil the specific requirements separately from the complex product in order to qualify for protection.[3] The mere acceptance of such a situation seriously jeopardises the creation of a single European market and necessarily implies distortions to competition. A second problem results from the absence of clear criteria in the Court's prior case law to indicate whether, and when, the Community rules on the free movement of goods should prevail over the national intellectual property rights concerned. This meant that different approaches could be taken to resolve the issue either way.[4] Further, whatever solution was adopted under Articles 30–36 E.C. needed to be reconciled with the rules aimed at safeguarding free competition in the single market. The spare parts cases did not deal directly with aspects of industrial or commercial policy. Nevertheless, it was maintained that the outcome of the spare parts cases would not only affect the market power of the car manufacturers within the Community but, indirectly, would also potentially influence their competitiveness *vis-à-vis* third countries, especially Japan. In other words, it was held that the legal issues raised in the spare parts cases could hardly be dissociated from the economic and strategic importance of the automobile sector for the European Community and its Member States.

---

[1] On the diversity in protection offered for industrial designs in the Member States, see A. Firth, "Aspects of design protection in Europe" [1993] E.I.P.R. 42. This article includes "Tables of Design Protection" by country.

[2] *British Leyland Motor Corporation a.o. v. Armstrong Patents Company Limited a.o.* [1986] F.S.R. 221, H.L. The spare parts exception was introduced on the basis of the principle that a grantor cannot derogate from his grant.

[3] For instance, it seems that in France the design protection granted to the car automatically extends to the constituent body panels (see Cour d'Appel de Dijon, *Régie nationale des usines Renault v. R. Thevenaoux, Société Cass Center, O. Formento and Société Maxicar*, Judgment of January 12, 1990: [1990] R.I.P.I.A. 31). In Germany the body panels have to live up to novelty and originality requirements independently of the car but so far as the aesthetic appeal condition is concerned, it suffices that this is fulfilled when the part is incorporated into the car (see Bundesgerichtshof, *Kotflügel case*, October 16, 1986: [1987] G.R.U.R. 518, with note by Gerstenberg).

[4] See *supra*, Chap. 6.

Although the final judgments are disappointingly brief, the fact that both   **7.03**
spare parts cases were dealt with in full court proves that the issues at stake
were considered to be important. It is submitted that the most important and
delicate question posed to the Court in the spare parts cases was whether or
not design protection on spare parts of cars comes within the scope of the
exception of Article 36 E.C. to the rules on the free movement of goods. The
answer to this question, which was posed in the *CICRA and Maxicar v.
Renault* case,[5] was not only decisive for a potential approximation of national
design laws concerning components of complex products. It also set the tone
for the answers to be given in both the *Maxicar* and the *Volvo v. Veng*[6] cases
concerning the applicability of the rules on competition to the alleged anti-
competitive behaviour of the car manufacturers.[7] It should be recalled that the
latter, in turn, proved to be of a crucial importance for the *Magill* cases discussed before.[8]

2. THE *CICRA* AND *MAXICAR V. RENAULT* CASE

(1) The background

(a) Peculiarity of the case

The *CICRA and Maxicar v. Renault* case was different from the other intellec-   **7.04**
tual property cases that had been brought before the Court of Justice. The
national proceedings before the Milan court concerned a legal action initiated
by independent manufacturers claiming the annulment of certain design
rights on bodywork components for Renault cars, whereas previous cases
concerned a request by an intellectual property owner to obtain a legal injunction either against third parties who manufacture, import and sell unauthorised products, or to prevent parallel importation.[9] Furthermore, all previous
cases concerned protective rights on independent products,[10] whereas the
Maxicar case concerned components of a complex product needed for repair
purposes.

---

[5] Case 53/87, *Consorzio italiano della componentistica di ricambio per autoveicoli* (CICRA) and
Maxicar v. Renault, Judgment of October 5, 1988: [1988] E.C.R. 6039; [1990] 4 C.M.L.R.
265.
[6] Case 238/87, *AB Volvo v. Erik Veng (U.K.) Ltd*, Judgment of October 5, 1988: [1988] E.C.R.
6211; [1989] 4 C.M.L.R. 122.
[7] See *infra*, Chap. 8.
[8] See *supra*, Chap. 5, pt. 4(3).
[9] In the words of Advocate General Mischo, "It is not a case here of a proprietor of protective
rights defending his 'territory' against importers, but of independent producers attacking that
proprietor by challenging his entitlement to exercise his exclusive rights against them...", see
Case 53/87, Opinion delivered on June 21, 1988: [1988] E.C.R. 6055, pt. 7.
[10] The term "independent products" is used to denote all products that are sold separately from,
and do not have to be physically incorporated into, another product to form a complex
product. It thus includes both simple products and complex products as such, as well as
accessories. Pieces of a set which are not physically connected, such as cutlery, are considered as
simple products.

(b) Preliminary question

7.05   Although the Milan court ruled that the grant of design protection on spare parts of cars, such as the contested bodywork work components, was in conformity with Italian law it nevertheless expressed its doubt as to whether the exercise of such an exclusive right was in conformity with Articles 30–36 and 86 of the E.C. Treaty. Concerning the rules on the free movement of goods, the following question was therefore referred to the European Court of Justice:

> "Are Articles 30 to 36 of the EEC Treaty to be interpreted as prohibiting the owner of a protective right in an ornamental design which was granted in a Member State from asserting the corresponding absolute rights so as to prevent third parties from manufacturing and selling, and also exporting to another Member State, component parts, which, taken as a whole, make up the bodywork of a car which has already been put on the market, that is to say component parts intended to be sold as spare parts for that car?"

(c) Implications

7.06   The answer to that question was not only relevant from a legal point of view, it would also have significant economic repercussions for either the car manufacturers or the independent manufacturers. In the Report of the Hearing, the figure of U.S. $30,000 million turnover reached in 1984 was advanced for the total market in motorvehicle spare parts.[11] Bodywork components covered by protective rights were estimated to account for 5 per cent of the entire market of car components, taking into account their cost prices and turnover rate or, in other words, for a turnover in 1984 of approximately U.S. $1,500 million.

It is obvious that the impact of the *Maxicar* case would not be restricted to Italy but would set the tone for the compatibility of design protection on bodywork components of cars in general with Article 36 E.C. Furthermore, the outcome of the *Maxicar* case would not only bear on the market in bodywork components but would also have indirect implications for other spare parts covered by intellectual property rights.

(2) Introduction to the legal issues

(a) Measures having equivalent effect

7.07   It might at first sight be thought that the *Maxicar* case concerned a purely national situation. Independent manufacturers of spare parts in Italy sought to annul the design protection granted by Italian law on bodywork components of cars in order to be able to freely manufacture and sell those parts themselves. It was, however, specified in the preliminary question that those parts were also intended for export to other Member States so that intra-Community trade might be affected. It thus seemed that the national court assumed that the national measure concerned constituted a measure having

[11] Case 53/87: [1988] E.C.R. 6039 at 6043–6044.

equivalent effect to quantitative restrictions on export in the sense of Article 34 E.C., to which Article 36 E.C. also applies. This was important in so far as it is established case law that Article 34 E.C. only applies to measures that are distinctly applicable and favour the national production. The first question that thus arose was whether or not the grant of design rights on spare parts of cars constituted a measure having equivalent effect under Article 34 and/or Article 30 E.C.[12]

(b) Applicability of Article 36 E.C.

Having established that the measure constituted a measure having an equivalent effect, the next question arising was whether or not Article 36 E.C. applied by way of an exception to the rules on the free movement of goods in this particular case. The national court was of the opinion that the exercise of the intellectual property right appeared to be contrary to the inherent function of design rights and therefore possibly constituted an arbitrary discrimination, or a disguised restriction on trade, in the sense of the second sentence of Article 36 E.C. Two arguments were advanced to support that conclusion:

7.08

> "... the monopoly position of the proprietor of the protective right does not constitute a return for research and progress achieved in the field of aesthetics, since the design of the car as a whole (. . .) accounted for the entirety of that return. It also implies that competition is prevented in other economic sectors and leads to the charging of higher prices, and such advantages are not in harmony with the requirements of economic progress which justify industrial property rights."[13]

The preliminary question was formulated in the sense that the compatibility of the *exercise* of the right with Article 36 E.C. had to be established. However, the underlying concern seemed to be that the *existence* of design rights in certain components of complex products could not be justified, having regard to the function of the exclusive right. This raised the question of which approach the Court should take: an approach based on the specific subject-matter of the intellectual property right and the consent of the right-owner to the marketing of the product, or an approach based on the justification of the measure in the light of the function of design rights.[14] A second, but related, question that followed from the preliminary question was whether or not the possibility of obtaining a reward twice would influence the outcome of the case.[15] It is obvious that the answers given to all those questions would determine whether or not scrutiny under the rules on competition had to take the lawful existence of the exclusive rights in spare parts as a given fact.

(c) Intellectual property rights and consumer protection

It was also important to determine how this all affects the final consumer. In particular, both the car manufacturers and independent manufacturers of

7.09

---

[12] See *infra*, pt. 3.
[13] Case 53/87: [1988] E.C.R. 6039; [1990] 4 C.M.L.R. 265, Report of the Hearing.
[14] See *infra*, pt. 4.
[15] See *infra*, pt. 5.

spare parts claimed to safeguard consumers' interests through obtaining, or refusing, design protection on spare parts of cars. The central arguments to this debate were the use of design rights to enforce quality and safety standards, and the potential implications of tying-in the spare parts market to the one in cars.[16]

3. INTELLECTUAL PROPERTY RIGHTS AND MEASURES HAVING EQUIVALENT EFFECT

(1) Approach taken by the court

(a) Intellectual property cases

7.10   Considering the structure of Articles 30–36 E.C.,[17] the Court seems to have taken it for granted that intellectual property rights are measures having an effect equivalent to quantitative restrictions. It is not surprising, therefore, that its main approach was to proceed immediately with the scrutiny under Article 36 E.C. In its case law concerning intellectual property rights and free movement of goods the Court has paid little attention to the applicability of Article 30,[18] and even less so of Article 34 E.C., to the measures invoked. It is significant that there is not one case in which the Court has held that an intellectual property right did not constitute a measure having an equivalent effect.[19] This approach is severely criticised by Marenco, who has tried to demonstrate on the basis of the discrimination theory that the Court has cleared measures under Article 36 E.C. that, according to him, did not even come under Article 30 E.C.[20] It is submitted that Marenco's point of view is especially pertinent to the *Maxicar* case since he represented the Commission together with Banks.

(b) Differences of approach to Articles 30 and 34 E.C.

7.11   The Court gave the following definition of measures having an equivalent effect to quantitative restrictions in the *Dassonville* case:

> "All trading rules enacted by Member States which are capable of hindering, directly or indirectly, actually or potentially, intra-Community trade are to be considered as measures having an effect equivalent to quantitative restrictions."[21]

---

[16] See *infra*, pt. 6.

[17] See *supra*, Chap. 3, pt. 2(2). The Court's approach clearly confirms the interpretation that if intellectual property rights were not considered by the draftsmen of the Treaty to constitute measures having an equivalent effect, then their inclusion in Article 36 E.C. would not make any sense.

[18] It is especially the cases whereby the Court looked at the justification of the national measures where Article 30 E.C. was expressly dealt with. See, for instance, *supra*, Chap. 6, pt. 3.

[19] Except, perhaps, for the *Basset v. SACEM* case (Case 402/85), where the Court used a rather confusing reasoning: see *supra*, Chap. 6, pt. 3(3)(d)(i).

[20] G. Marenco, "*Pour une interpretation traditionelle de la notion de mesure d'effet équivalent à une restriction quantitative*" [1984] C.D.E. 291, especially at 346.

[21] Case 8/74, *Procureur du Roi v. Dassonville*, Judgment of July 11, 1974: [1974] E.C.R. 837; [1974] 2 C.M.L.R. 436, at para. 5.

Although this definition concerned Article 30 E.C. it would seem to be difficult to envisage a different definition for the same wording used in Article 34 E.C. Nonetheless, the Court has proceeded to apply different criteria according to whether a national measure concerns restrictions on imports or exports. Measures are only held to be contrary to Article 34 E.C. if they are to the prejudice of exports, as compared to domestic trade, whereas they can be held to be contrary to Article 30 E.C. even if they are not to the prejudice of imports as compared to domestic trade. These differences in approach have been strongly criticised in legal writings.[22] However, although the Court's approach under Articles 30 and 34 E.C. lacks formal coherence it is submitted that the Court has developed complementary, rather than mutually exclusive, approaches. This implies that a measure alleged to have an effect equivalent to quantitative restrictions can only be held to be compatible with the rules on the free movement of goods if cleared under both Articles. Conversely, it is sufficient that either Article 30 E.C. or Article 34 E.C. is infringed for a measure to be incompatible with the rules on the free movement of goods.

(2) Restrictions on exports

According to the Commission, Renault, and the French Government the preliminary question in the *Maxicar* case had to be confined to the matter of restrictions on exports in the sense of Article 34 E.C. They pointed out that the facts of the case merely concerned the manufacture and sale in Italy of goods made in Italy as well as the export to other Member States, and not the importation of unauthorised spare parts into Italy.[23]   **7.12**

The Court has consistently held that the prohibition of quantitative restrictions and measures having equivalent effect under Article 34 E.C. concern:

> "... national measures which have as their specific object or effect the restriction of patterns of export and thereby the establishment of a difference in treatment between the domestic trade of a Member State and its export trade in such a way as to provide a particular advantage for national production or for the domestic market of the State in question at the expense of the production or the trade of other Member States."[24]

For instance, in the *Delhaize* case the Court ruled that a national measure which restricted the quantity of wine that could be exported in bulk to other Member States, although no similar quantitative restrictions were imposed on sales of wine in bulk between undertakings situated within the product region, infringed Article 34 E.C. and could not be justified as a measure needed to safeguard a denomination of origin under the industrial and commercial property exception of Article 36 E.C.[25]

---

[22] For an analysis of the main criticism, see L. Gormley, *Prohibiting restrictions on trade within the EEC* (1985, North-Holland), pp. 96–111.

[23] Case 53/87: [1988] E.C.R. 6039; [1990] 4 C.M.L.R. 265, Report of the Hearing.

[24] Case 15/79, *Groenveld v. Produktschap voor vee en vlees*, Judgment of November 8, 1979, [1979] E.C.R. 3409; [1981] 1 C.M.L.R. 207, at para. 7.

[25] Case C–47/90, *Etablissements Delhaize Frères et Compagnie Le Lion SA v. Promalvin SA et AGE Bodegas Unidas SA*, Judgment of June 9, 1992: [1992] E.C.R. I-3669. For the Court's analysis under Article 36 E.C., see *supra*, Chap. 3, pt. 4(2)(c)(iii).

However, the situation in *Maxicar* was totally different in that Italian law did not provide different treatment according to the destination of the products. Both sales within Italy and exports to other Member States were prohibited in so far as they were not authorised by the holder of the design right, regardless of his nationality. No particular advantage was therefore created for the national production or the domestic market. According to the Commission, this implied that the Italian design right did not constitute a measure having an equivalent effect in the sense of Article 34 E.C. so that subsequently there was no need to examine its possible justification under Article 36 E.C.[26]

(3) The incidence of Articles 30 and 34 E.C.

(a) Examples of the application of Article 34

7.13 Although the Commission's finding is correct, if one limits the argument to Article 34 E.C., it is submitted that is incorrect to interpret the problem merely in the light of Article 34 E.C. It has to be pointed out that the Court has applied Article 34 E.C. solely to cases whereby no undue restrictions were imposed on the importation and sale of goods that had been lawfully marketed in another Member State. The Court has, for instance, held the prohibiting of exports,[27] the placing of distinctly applicable quantitative restrictions upon exports,[28] and requiring inspection documents relating specifically to domestic production intended for export to other Member States,[29] to be contrary to Article 34 E.C. These national measures clearly did not affect the importation of goods into the Member State that imposed the restrictive measure. More importantly, the Court has ruled that the following did not constitute a measure having an equivalent effect in the sense of Article 34 E.C.: prohibition for manufacturers of sausages to have in stock or to process horsemeat,[30] minimum quality standards for domestic cheese production and objective inspections,[31] prohibitions on the production of baker's wares and their transportation and delivery before a certain hour,[32] and minimum standards of enclosure for fattening calves.[33] In all those cases the national indistinctly applicable measures were aimed at regulating national production and did not prejudice the importation and sale of products coming from other Member States. Furthermore, the Court specifically mentioned that the measures

---

[26] It is interesting to note that the Commission, contrary to Renault and the German government, advanced no secondary arguments as to the possible application of Article 36 E.C. See Case 53/87: [1988] E.C.R. 6039; [1990] 4 C.M.L.R. 265, Report of the Hearing.

[27] Case 172/82, *Fabricants Raffineurs d'Huile de Graissage v. Inter-Huiles*, Judgment of March 10, 1983: [1983] E.C.R. 555; (1983) 3 C.M.L.R. 485, at para. 12.

[28] Case C–47/90, *Delhaize*: [1992] E.C.R. I-3669, at paras. 12–14.

[29] Case 53/76, *Procureur de la République v. Bouhelier*, Judgment of February 3, 1977: [1977] E.C.R. 197; [1977] 1 C.M.L.R. 436, at paras. 15–18.

[30] Case 15/79: [1979] E.C.R. 3409; [1981] 1 C.M.L.R. 207, at paras. 6–9.

[31] Case 237/82, *Jongeneel Kaas v. Netherlands*, Judgment of February 7, 1984: [1984] E.C.R. 483; [1985] 2 C.M.L.R. 53, respectively at paras. 22–23 and 25–26.

[32] Case 155/80, *Oebel*, Judgment of July 14, 1981: [1981] E.C.R. 1993; [1983] 1 C.M.L.R. 390, respectively at paras. 14–16 and 17–20.

[33] Joined Cases 141–143/81, *Holdijk*, Judgment of April 1, 1982: [1982] E.C.R. 1299; [1983] 2 C.M.L.R. 635, at para. 11.

concerned were not contrary to Articles 34 *or* 30 E.C. in the *Jongeneel Kaas* and *Oebel* cases.[34]

(b) Specific nature of intellectual property rights

The main difference between the above-mentioned cases and the *Maxicar* case   **7.14** lies in the effect that intellectual property rights, by their very nature, have on imports from other Member States. On the basis of his exclusive right the intellectual property owner may not only prohibit the domestic manufacture and sale of unauthorised goods. He may also prohibit the importation and sale of (unauthorised) goods that have been lawfully marketed in another Member State because, for instance, he either has no parallel intellectual property protection or the intellectual property protection has expired. It is significant in this respect that the Court expressly acknowledged in the *Phil Collins* case that intellectual property rights are of such a nature as to affect intra-Community trade.[35] As such, it is submitted that although the national court did not refer to possible restrictions on imports, the compatibility of the measure with Article 30 E.C. nonetheless has to be considered.

(c) The concept of "actual" and "potential" restrictions on intra-Community trade

Contrary to the Commission, Advocate General Mischo in his opinion to the   **7.15** *Maxicar* case maintained that the reference by the national court to "sales" of spare parts could be interpreted as including the prohibition on importation and marketing of parts other than those marketed by Renault. In his view this was particularly relevant since CICRA stated in its observations that it also markets spare parts that are manufactured in other Member States, such as Spain.[36] But even had CICRA not actually marketed imported spare parts, the question of the applicability of Article 30 E.C. would still have been relevant. The reason for this is that the importation of unauthorised spare parts could potentially take place. It should indeed be recalled that the Court had included both actual and potential restrictions on imports in the *Dassonville* definition of measures having an equivalent effect.

    The essential question is whether or not the national measure concerned constitutes a measure having an effect equivalent to quantitative restrictions so that it is inconceivable that this should depend upon the facts of a given case. For instance, take the hypothetical example of Renault having an exclusive right under design law in several spare parts in Member State B, and CICRA importing some unauthorised parts from Member State A to B and exporting others from B to A. If Renault enforces its intellectual property right

---

[34] Case 237/82: [1984] E.C.R. 483; [1985] 2 C.M.L.R. 53, at paras. 20 and 28. Case 155/80: [1981] E.C.R. 1993; [1983] 1 C.M.L.R. 390, at paras. 20–21.

[35] Joined Cases C 92 and 326/92, *Phil Collins*, Judgment of October 20, 1993: [1993] E.C.R. I-5145; [1993] 3 C.M.L.R. 773. On this case, in which the Court for the first time held the general principle of non-discrimination (Art. 6 E.C.) to be applicable in its own right to intellectual property rights, see *supra*, Chap. 2, pt. 4(1)(c)(iv).

[36] Case 53/87: [1988] E.C.R. 6039; [1990] 4 C.M.L.R. 265, Opinion of Advocate General Mischo, delivered on June 21, 1988, [1988] E.C.R. 6055, at paras. 13–14.

in B against the imports and sales of parts coming from A, this would clearly be a measure having equivalent effect in the sense of Article 30 E.C. so that the Article 36 E.C. exception would need to be considered. The fact that the intellectual property right is invoked to prohibit sales in B and exports to A cannot logically lead to the opposite conclusion, namely that the same intellectual property right is not a measure having an equivalent effect so that Article 36 E.C. should not even be invoked.

It is thus submitted that the same intellectual property right cannot be simultaneously compatible with, and contrary to, the rules on the free movement of goods depending on whether it is invoked to prevent exports or imports.[37] This finding does not exclude the fact, as the Court ruled in *Oosthoek's Uitgeversmaatschappij*,[38] that it is possible for a measure not to be contrary to Article 34 E.C. in the absence of a protectionist effect, even though it is incompatible with Article 30 E.C., so that it has to be justified on the basis of either mandatory requirements or Article 36 E.C. in order to be upheld.[39]

(4) Restrictions on imports

(a) Discrimination theory

(i) Concept

7.16   As mentioned above, the Commission was clearly of the opinion that Article 30 E.C. did not apply in the given case whereas Advocate General Mischo had no difficulty in accepting the contrary view.[40] The reason for this difference is most likely of a conceptual nature. The Court is generally criticised for not having applied Article 34 E.C. to non-discriminatory measures. The agents for the Commission in the *Maxicar* case, namely Giuliano Marenco and Karen Banks, voiced criticism of the Court's case law for having applied Article 30 E.C. to non-discriminatory measures and in particular for always considering intellectual property rights to come within the ambit of Article 30

---

[37] Beier also argues for a uniform interpretation under Articles 30–36 E.C., although he holds on to the use/misuse distinction to curtail intellectual property rights. With regard to the *Maxicar* case, he writes that the issue of design protection on spare parts: "...could not be made dependent upon whether the accused manufacturers produced their products for the Italian market, for the Common market or for the World market. Questions such as protectability, validity, scope of protection and infringement must be decided by applying the same legal standards regardless of whether the national, European or international constellation of facts are at stake": F.-K. Beier, "Industrial property and the free movement of goods in the internal market" [1990] I.I.C. 131 at 151.

[38] See Case 286/81, *Oosthoek's Uitgeversmaatschappij*, Judgment of December 15, 1982: [1982] E.C.R. 4575; [1983] 3 C.M.L.R. 428. In this case, the Court held that legislation that merely imposes marketing conditions within the Netherlands, without affecting the sale of goods intended for exportation, was not contrary to Article 34 E.C. However, the Court proceeded to state that such a measure is contrary to Article 30 E.C. since it restricts the volume of imports, although in this particular case this could be justified on the basis of consumer protection and fair trading.

[39] It should be pointed out that because the *Oosthoek* judgment concerned marketing conditions, it would most likely be reversed by the subsequent *Keck* judgment (see *infra*, pt. (4)(b)). However, other grounds would make it feasible for the Court to come to a similar conclusion, such as national rules regulating the components to be used in a product.

[40] See *supra*, at pts. 3(2) and 3(3) respectively.

E.C.[41] According to Marenco and Banks, only those provisions of intellectual property law which are expressly or inherently discriminatory are contrary to Article 30 and thus subject to scrutiny under Article 36 E.C.[42] The important factor is thus to establish whether or not the intellectual property right was granted in a non-discriminatory manner (for instance no different treatment on the basis of nationality) and subsequently applied in a non-discriminatory manner. It is obviously correct to state that discriminatory measures come under Article 30 E.C.[43] However, it is submitted that this does not apply vice versa, for measures do not necessarily have to be discriminatory in order to be contrary to Article 30 E.C.

(ii) Principle of exhaustion: a response to discrimination?

Marenco and Banks considered the prohibition on parallel imports to be contrary to Article 30 E.C. because of the discrimination inherent in the principle of national exhaustion.[44] The application of the latter differs according to the place where the product was first brought on the market. Although this can be argued theoretically, it should be noted that the Court's concern cannot merely be to eliminate discrimination inherent in national intellectual property law because not all national intellectual property laws incorporate the principle of exhaustion. In the United Kingdom, for instance, patent law is governed by the doctrine of implied licence. If the Court's aim was only to eliminate the discrimination inherent in the principle of national exhaustion in a Member State of importation then, it is submitted, it would not have introduced the principle of Community exhaustion. It should be emphasised in this respect that the latter is applicable regardless of the provisions embodied in national intellectual property law. The mere elimination of the discriminatory features of the principle of national exhaustion would, to the contrary, have entailed that different rules, though no longer discriminatory, would apply in various Member States and to various types of intellectual property rights.[45] It is obvious that such a situation would still have created distortions of intra-Community trade. The latter have been removed through the elaboration of the Community principle of exhaustion which applies in a uniform manner to all Member States.

7.17

(iii) Indistinctly applicable measures

The discrimination theory in essence holds that if imports are not subject to difficulties, other than those imposed on domestic production, then the

7.18

---

[41] G. Marenco, K. Banks, "Intellectual property and the Community rules on free movement: discrimination unearthed" (1990) 15 E.L.Rev. 224. See also G. Marenco, *op. cit.*.

[42] G. Marenco, K. Banks, *op. cit.*, p. 241.

[43] See, for instance, *supra*, Chap. 6, pt. 3(1), where the Court had no difficulty in finding that provisions on compulsory licences that discriminated against imports from other Member States were contrary to Article 30 E.C.

[44] G. Marenco, K. Banks, *op. cit.*, pp. 242–248.

[45] See also *supra*, Chap. 4, pt. 1(1)(c). Similarly, see N. Koch, "Article 30 and the exercise of industrial property rights to block imports" [1986] Fordham Corp. L. Inst. 605 at 612–615. At p. 613, he writes: "... not only did the Court not widen national exhaustion rules, but it used a concept of industrial property which is not known to all of the Member States. A holder of parallel patents granted throughout the Community would be faced with at least two different doctrines, one of exhaustion, the other one of the implied licence...."

measure concerned is compatible with Article 30 E.C. In the light of this reasoning, the fact that the importation of unauthorised spare parts that have been lawfully marketed in other Member States can be prohibited on the basis of an intellectual property right is not incompatible with Article 30 E.C. because similar parts could not be manufactured and marketed domestically either. Consequently, Article 36 E.C. does not need to be invoked. It should be pointed out, though, that the two situations referred to are not similar. The product is lawfully marketed in other Member States in the absence of intellectual property protection whereas all unauthorised marketing is automatically unlawful in the Member State of importation. This would seem to call for a distinctive solution in order to be compatible with the principle of non-discrimination.

7.19   The Court, by implication, rejected the discrimination theory in the *EMI v. Patricia* and *Keurkoop* cases.[46] It held that the sale of unauthorised goods that had been lawfully produced in another Member State, respectively after the expiry and in the absence of parallel intellectual property protection, could be prohibited on the basis of the intellectual property right in the Member State of importation. The Court came to this conclusion on the grounds that this was compatible with Article 36 E.C., subject to its second sentence, thus by implication acknowledging that the intellectual property rights concerned constituted measures having equivalent effect. More importantly, the Court has expressly held in the *Warner Brothers* case that the application of a national rule irrespective of the origin of the protected product comes under Article 30 E.C. if it indirectly affects trade.[47] It should be recalled that the Court ruled that the right to prohibit the hiring out of video-cassettes in a Member States is liable to influence the trade in video-cassettes in that state and hence indirectly affects intra-Community trade. As such not only measures which are imposed at the border, but also indistinctly applicable internal measures which clearly were not discriminatory, were held to have an effect equivalent to quantitative restrictions needing justification under Article 36 E.C.[48]

(b) Impact of the Keck judgment

7.20   The question arises of whether this approach to intellectual property rights is still valid after the recent *Keck* judgment. In the latter case, the Court expressly re-examined and clarified its case law on what constitutes a measure having an equivalent effect to quantitative restrictions under Article 30 E.C.[49]

---

[46] Case 341/87, *EMI Electrola v. Patricia Im-und Export and others*, Judgment of January 21, 1989: [1989] E.C.R. 79; [1989] 2 C.M.L.R. 413. See also *supra*, Chap. 6, pt. 2(3). Case 144/81, *Keurkoop v. Nancy Kean Gifts*, Judgment of September 14, 1982: [1982] E.C.R. 2853; [1983] 2 C.M.L.R. 47. See also *supra*, Chap. 4, pt. 2(4)(b) and Chap. 6, pt. 3(2)(b).

[47] Case 158/86, *Warner Brothers v. Erik Viuff*, Judgment of May 17, 1988: [1988] E.C.R. 2605; [1990] 3 C.M.L.R. 684. See also *supra*, Chap. 6, pt. 3(3).

[48] Marenco and Banks acknowledge that this ruling implies that the Court has expressly refuted the discrimination theory, although they emphasise that the reasoning of the Court is not always consistent. See G. Marenco, K. Banks, *op. cit.*, p. 241.

[49] Joined Cases C 267 and 268/91, *Criminal proceedings against Bernard Keck and Daniel Mithouard*, Judgment of November 24, 1993: [1993] E.C.R. I-6097.

The Court, in line with the *Dassonville* ruling, confirmed the applicability of Article 30 E.C. to national rules laying down requirements to be met by goods imported from other Member States (such as requirements as to designation, form, size, weight, composition, presentation, labelling and packaging), even if those rules apply without distinction to both imported and domestic products. However, contrary to its established case law, the Court held that national *sales arrangements* that apply to all traders operating within the national territory do not come under Article 30 E.C., on condition that "they affect in the same manner, in law and in fact, the marketing of domestic products and of those from other Member States".[50] It thus seems as though the Court has finally followed up Advocate General Van Gerven's contention that Article 30 E.C. should only be applicable to those national measures that endanger the interpenetration of national markets.[51] It should be pointed out in this respect that intellectual property rights, by virtue of their inherent exclusive nature combined with the principle of territoriality, are particularly apt to close down national markets to goods that have been lawfully put on the market of another Member State.[52] This was expressly acknowledged by the Court in the *Phil Collins* case.[53] In principle, the *Keck* ruling therefore does not seem to affect the prior case law on the applicability of Article 30 E.C. to the importation and sale of intellectual property protected products.

It is more or less certain that the Court did not introduce a discrimination criterion in *Keck*.[54] Uncertainty nonetheless remains as to which prior judgments are overruled by the latter.[55] It was pointed out in legal writings that this is largely due to the legal uncertainty introduced by the concept of "sales arrangements".[56] With respect to intellectual property rights in particular, the question arises of whether the Court would follow the approach it adopted in *Warner Brothers* if it had to rule on a similar case today.[57] It could be that in the light of the *Keck* ruling the Court would hold similar national rules not to be incompatible with Article 30 E.C. It should be kept in mind, though, that a peculiarity of the *Warner Brothers* case was that it concerned national requirements on *hiring*. It seems that the *Keck* ruling, which only expressly

7.21

[50] Joined Cases C 267 and 268/91: [1993] E.C.R. I-6097, at para. 16. Similarly, see Case C–292/92, *Hünermund*, Judgment of December 15, 1993: [1993] E.C.R. I-6787.

[51] Joined Cases C 267 and 268/91: [1993] E.C.R. I-6097, Second conclusion of Advocate General Van Gerven, delivered on April 28, 1993, at para. 8. See also the opinion of Advocate General Tesauro delivered on October 27, 1993 in the subsequent *Hünermund* case, Case C–292/92: [1993] E.C.R. I-6787. The latter was also clearly taken into account by the Court when ruling in the *Keck* case.

[52] See *supra*, pt. 3(b).

[53] On this case see *supra*, Chap. 2, pt. 4(1)(c)(iv).

[54] See for instance L. Gormley, "Reasoning renounced? The remarkable judgment in *Keck & Mithouard*" [1994] *European Business Law Review* 63.

[55] See, for instance, L. Gormley, *op. cit.*; D. Chalmers, "Repackaging the internal market – The ramifications of the *Keck* judgment" (1994) 19 E.L.Rev. 385.

[56] See for instance N. Reich, "The November revolution of the European Court of Justice: *Keck, Meng* and *Audi*" (1994) 31 C.M.L.Rev. 459 especially at 410–411; D. Waelbroeck, "*L'Arrêt Keck et Mithouard: les conséquences pratiques*" [1994] J.T.E. 161; A. Mattera, "*De l'arrêt 'Dassonville' à l'arrêt 'Keck': l'obscure clarté d'un jurisprudence riche en principes novateurs et en contradictions*" [1994] *Revue du Marché Unique Européen* 117. In defence of the *Keck* ruling, see R. Joliet, "*La libre circulation des marchandises: l'arrêt Keck et Mithouard et les nouvelles orientations de la jurisprudence*" [1994] J.T.E. 145.

[57] See also *supra*, Chap. 6, pt. 3(3)(c).

mentions *sales* arrangements, can therefore not be transposed to it unconditionally.

(5) Finding in the *Maxicar* case

7.22   The Court, not surprisingly, did not deviate from its earlier case law on the applicability of Article 30 E.C. to intellectual property rights in the *Maxicar* case which was decided prior to the *Keck* case. It avoided clarifying the incidence between Articles 30 and 34 E.C. by reinterpreting the facts, following Advocate General Mischo's opinion, in the sense that independent manufacturers of spare parts sought to protect themselves from infringement proceedings intended to prevent them from manufacturing for the purposes of sales on the internal market or for export, as well as from importing unauthorised spare parts from other Member States.[58] In line with the *EMI* and *Keurkoop* cases[59] the Court immediately proceeded with the analysis under Article 36 E.C. thereby impliedly rejecting the Commission's view, and once again setting the discrimination theory aside.

4. ARTICLE 36: JUSTIFICATION OR CONSENT FOR COMPONENTS OF COMPLEX PRODUCTS?

(1) Three possible approaches

7.23   As mentioned above, from the wording of the preliminary question it appears that the national court asked whether the *exercise* of the design right on spare parts of cars was compatible with Article 36 E.C., whereas the underlying reason was to question the compatibility of the *existence* of the design right with Article 36 E.C.[60] The national court was particularly concerned with the fact that, in its view, the enforcement of design protection on body panels of cars infringed the inherent function of design rights.[61] It therefore wondered whether this might not be contrary to the second sentence of Article 36 E.C.

The wording of the preliminary question made it relatively easy for the Court to choose which approach it would take to the case. On the basis of its earlier case law the Court had three options.[62] It could invoke the existence/exercise dichotomy[63] and subsequently proceed to apply the consent theory in order to establish whether or not the exercise of the intellectual property right should be upheld ("consent approach").[64] Or, the Court could take the opposite approach, namely to invoke case law whereby it put the existence/exercise dichotomy aside and to examine whether or not the national measure

---

[58] Case 53/87: [1988] E.C.R. 6039; [1990] 4 C.M.L.R. 265, at para. 9. See also G. Friden, "Recent developments in EEC intellectual property law: the distinction between existence and exercise revisited" (1989) 26 C.M.L.Rev. 193 at 206, where he points out that the Court declined to distinguish between Articles 30 and 34 E.C. in the *Maxicar* case.
[59] See *supra*, pt. (4)(iii).
[60] See *supra*, pt. 2(2).
[61] On the function of design rights, see *supra*, Chap. 2, pt. 3(5).
[62] On the diversity of criteria used by the Court, see *supra*, Chap. 6.
[63] On the origin of the existence/exercise dichotomy, see *supra*, Chap. 3, pt. 4(2).
[64] On the consent approach, see *supra*, Chap. 4 as well as Chap. 6, pt. 2.

conferring intellectual property rights on components of complex products was justified under both the first and the second sentence of Article 36 E.C. ("justification approach").[65] Or, the Court could choose to apply a half-way-house solution namely to carry out a justification test under the second sentence of Article 36 E.C. whilst upholding the existence/exercise dichotomy under the first sentence of Article 36 E.C. ("marginal appraisal approach").[66] As illustrated below, the choice of approach was not only of theoretical importance, for the nature of the approach adopted was to determine the outcome of the case.

(2) The consent approach

(a) Application

The facts of the case obviously did not concern parallel imports so that the Court could not merely apply the consent theory to hold that Renault's design right was exhausted due to the first marketing with his consent.[67] In theory, the easiest approach would have consisted of reversing the reasoning of the exhaustion doctrine as was done, *inter alia*, in the *EMI* case.[68] This would have led to the conclusion that, since the spare parts were marketed without Renault's consent, its design right was not exhausted and consequently the infringement of its exclusive right could be prohibited. However, the latter approach would not really give an answer to the questions posed by the national court.   **7.24**

(b) Implications of existence/exercise dichotomy

The premise to this approach which was proposed by Renault and the German Government is, of course, that the existence/exercise dichotomy is kept intact. The preliminary question, however, invoked the question of the compatibility of a certain feature of Italian design law, namely its applicability to components of complex products, with Community law. This is an issue of a similar kind to the one previously posed concerning design rights in the *Keurkoop* case. In the latter it was asked whether the principle of first-to-file, which implied that the person filing the design and obtaining the exclusive right is not necessarily the designer, combined with the principle of relative novelty comes within the industrial and commercial property exception of Article 36 E.C.[69] The underlying concern in both cases was that the design right was not granted in conformity with the function of design protection.   **7.25**

It should be recalled that in the *Keurkoop* case, the Court failed to review the national law from the point of view of its justification but merely held:

---

[65] See for instance the approach adopted in the *Warner Brothers* case, see *supra*, Chap. 6, pt. 3(3).

[66] See, for instance, the approach adopted in the *Thetford* case, see *supra*, Chap. 6, pt. 3(2)(c).

[67] On the principle of exhaustion in the case law of the Court, see *supra*, Chap. 4, pt. 1. However, see also the *Warner Brothers* case, where the Court did not apply the principle of exhaustion although it concerned parallel imports, *supra*, Chap. 6, pt. 3(3).

[68] See *supra*, Chap. 6, pt. 2(3).

[69] Case 144/81: [1982] E.C.R. 2853; [1983] 2 C.M.L.R. 47, See also *supra*, Chap. 4, pt. 2(4)(b) and Chap. 6, pt. 3(2)(b).

> "...that in the present state of Community law and in the absence of Community standardisation or of a harmonisation of laws the determination of the conditions and procedures under which protection of designs is granted is a matter for national rules...."[70]

In the *Maxicar* case the Court could, in theory, use similar reasoning and hold that the conditions and procedures to obtain design protection, including whether or not the protection extends to components of complex products, are to be determined solely by national law and cannot be curtailed by Community law.[71] In so doing the Court would thus once again avoid answering the implied question of whether an intellectual property right has to be granted in accordance with its function to come under Article 36 E.C. Furthermore, it would ignore also the detrimental effect of the diversity of national design laws on the establishment of the Common Market.

7.26   It should be emphasised that the Court specified in the *Keurkoop* case that the existence/exercise dichotomy prevailed "in the present state of Community law". It should be pointed out that in between the *Keurkoop* case of 1982 and the *Maxicar* case of 1988 the case law of the Court had evolved considerably. The Court gradually seemed to accept the fact that the existence of certain features of intellectual property rights might not be justified under Article 36 E.C.,[72] whereas furthermore it no longer refrained to hold discriminatory intellectual property provisions to be incompatible with Article 6 E.C.[73]

(c) Shortcomings of specific subject-matter approach

7.27   In the *Keurkoop* case the Court held the existence of the intellectual property right to be unaffected by Community law. However, in its answer to the question of whether imports from other Member States could be prohibited, it proceeded to state that the exercise of the exclusive right may be curtailed, particularly if it constitutes a disguised restriction on trade. This was held to be the case if the design was invoked to prohibit the importation of goods that were marketed in another Member State with the consent of the design holder, or if there was a collusion in the sense of Article 85 E.C.[74] This is in conformity with the case law of the Court concerning the exhaustion doctrine which holds that derogations from the free movement of goods are only acceptable to the extent that they are necessary to safeguard the specific subject-matter of the intellectual property right invoked.[75] The Court did not define the specific subject-matter of designs in the *Keurkoop* case even though it impliedly followed Advocate General Reischl's opinion in that it consists in the right to first market the product.[76]

---

[70] Case 144/81: [1982] E.C.R. 2853; [1983] 2 C.M.L.R. 47, at para. 18.
[71] This was indeed the approach taken by the Court under the first sentence of Article 36 E.C. in the *Maxicar* case, see *infra*, pt. 4(c).
[72] See especially *supra*, Chap. 6, pt. 3.
[73] See the *Phil Collins* case, *supra*, Chap. 2, pt. 4(1)(c)(iv).
[74] For the reasons underlying these examples, see *supra* Chap. 4, pt. 2(4)(b).
[75] See *supra*, Chap. 4, pt. 1(1)(e).
[76] See *supra* Chap. 4, pt. 2(4)(b).

It was submitted before that the application of the consent theory to determine whether or not an intellectual property right is exhausted was formulated in the context of curtailing the detrimental effect posed by the principle of territoriality to the free movement of goods, all the other potentially detrimental features of intellectual property law being disregarded.[77] It is obvious that such an approach does not really answer the preliminary question and does not correspond to the specific facts of the *Maxicar* case.[78] In other words, the consent theory should not apply because the *Maxicar* case did not concern the compatibility of the effect of the principle of territoriality with the rules on the free movement of goods.[79] It clearly invoked the issue of whether the consequences of the scope of design protection offered in Italy, namely extending not only to a complex product but also to its individual components, is compatible with Articles 30–36 E.C. This is a typical example of cases to which the Court has recently applied the justification test rather than the consent test.[80]

(3) The justification approach

(a) Application

The contrary, and it is submitted correct, approach would have consisted in putting the existence/exercise dichotomy aside and examining whether and when the grant of design rights for components of complex products could be justified under Article 36 E.C. This would have been in line with the *Warner Brothers* case which was decided a couple of months earlier.[81] It should be recalled that in the latter case the Court applied a justification test under both the first and second sentences of Article 36 E.C. It thereby expressly put the consent theory based on the specific subject-matter approach aside.   **7.28**

(b) The existence/exercise dichotomy rejected

Advocate General Mischo, in his opinion on the *Maxicar* case, acknowledged the fact that the national court did not inquire about the compatibility of the exercise of the design right with the specific subject-matter of designs but, rather, was concerned with the lack of justification for the exclusive rights in terms of the function of design rights.[82] He pointed out, in line with his   **7.29**

---

[77] See *supra*, Chap. 6, pt. 1.
[78] See *supra*, pt. 2(1)(a), where the difference between the *Maxicar* case and the other cases concerning intellectual property rights, so far brought to the attention of the Court, is pointed out.
[79] Similarly, see R. Franceschelli, "*Modelli ornamentali di parte di carrozzeria di automobili ed abuso di posizione dominante*" (1988) II Riv.Dir.Ind. 175 at 181.
[80] See *supra*, Chap. 6, for a classification of cases that have been dealt with on the basis of either the consent test or the justification test.
[81] Case 158/86, *Warner Brothers v. Erik Viuff Christiansen*, Judgment of May 17, 1988: [1988] E.C.R. 2605; [1990] 3 C.M.L.R. 684. See *supra*, Chap. 6, pt. 3(3).
[82] Case 53/87: [1988] E.C.R. 6039; [1990] 4 C.M.L.R. 265, at para. 19.

observations in the *Thetford* case,[83] that a specific problem arises if an intellectual property owner makes normal use of an intellectual property right that is improperly granted under national law. As to the competence of the European Court of Justice to deal with such a matter, he unequivocally stated:

> "I consider that it is clear, or at least has been since the *Warner Brothers* judgment, that in such a case the Court is entitled to consider whether the legislation in question may be regarded as justified on the ground of protection of industrial and commercial property within the meaning of Article 36. [...]"
>
> "There is, therefore, *nothing to prevent* the Court from similarly considering whether legislation which allows the prohibition of imports of unauthorised copies of bodywork components is justified on such grounds, and whether it constitutes arbitrary discrimination or a disguised restriction on trade between Member States."[84]

(c) A functionality test

7.30   The Court did not expressly refer to the function of the rental right which was alleged to be incompatible with Article 36 E.C. in the *Warner Brothers* case. Nonetheless, the Court impliedly took the function into account by ruling that the measure was justified because it legitimately guaranteed a remuneration for the author upon each hiring-out of the protected work.[85] Also, in the *Maxicar* case the crucial question was whether or not granting exclusive rights in bodywork components of cars was necessary to safeguard the function of design rights.[86] The national court had advanced the view that it was not because the return for research and progress in the field of aesthetics was already accounted for by the sale of the complex product, *i.e.* the car, and because it led to the exclusion of competition in other economic sectors.[87]

Advocate General Mischo came to the contrary conclusion that exclusive protection on components of complex products was indeed in conformity with the function of design rights. However, with respect, he based his argument on a wrong premise. Referring to the *Centrafarm* and *Pharmon* judgments,[88] he maintained that the Court attributes to industrial and commercial property rights the function of obtaining a reward for the inventor's creative effort.[89] The main flaw in this reasoning is that the Advocate General failed to

---

[83] Case 35/87, *Thetford v. Fiamma*, Judgment of June 30, 1988: [1988] E.C.R. 3585; [1988] 3 C.M.L.R. 549. In his opinion to this case, concerning patents based on the principle of relative novelty, Advocate General Mischo pointed out that the exercise of an intellectual property right might be contrary to Article 36 E.C. simply because the patent was granted in circumstances indicative of a protectionist intention. See also *supra*, Chap. 6, pt. 3(2).

[84] Case 53/87: [1988] E.C.R. 6039; [1990] 4 C.M.L.R. 265, at paras. 21 and 22 (emphasis added).

[85] See *supra*, Chap. 6, pt. 3(3).

[86] On the function of design rights, see *supra*, Chap. 2, pt. 3(5).

[87] See also *supra*, pt. 2(2)(c).

[88] Case 15/74, *Centrafarm v. Sterling Drug*, Judgment of October 31, 1974: [1974] E.C.R. 1147; [1974] 2 C.M.L.R. 480. Case 19/84, *Pharmon v. Hoechst*, Judgment of July 9, 1985: [1985] E.C.R. 2281; [1985] 3 C.M.L.R. 775. See *supra*, Chap. 4, pt. 2(1)(a) and Chap. 6, pt. 2(4) respectively.

[89] Case 53/87: [1988] E.C.R. 6039; [1990] 4 C.M.L.R. 265, at paras. 27 and 32.

point out that the Court had, correctly, held in the *Merck* judgment that an intellectual property right merely provides the *possibility* of obtaining a reward without the safeguard that this reward will always be achieved.[90] As such, he subsequently failed to examine which conditions need to be fulfilled in respect of design protection in order to safeguard the possibility of obtaining a reward for the creative effort. To the contrary, he focused his attention on the reward itself. He rejected the argument based on the possibility of obtaining a reward twice by maintaining that national intellectual property law that allows the apportionment of the return between the complex product and its components does not exceed the limits of industrial and commercial property protection. He further held that cases whereby a double reward is effectively obtained are subject to Article 86 E.C.[91]

Advocate General Mischo suggested that the Court should not express   **7.31** itself on the need to protect bodywork components of cars but should merely hold that, in general, the law concerned was justified under the first sentence of Article 36 E.C., subject to the second sentence. It is submitted below that a more detailed analysis would most likely have led to the opposite conclusion, namely that design protection on bodywork components of cars exceeds the specific function of design rights.[92] The importance of his opinion on the *Maxicar* case therefore lies in the fact that he acknowledged that it would have been logical, and in particular in the express statement that the Court had the competence, to look at the justification of the intellectual property law concerned.

(4) The "marginal appraisal" approach

(a) Application by the Court in Maxicar

The third approach which the Court could, and did, take in the *Maxicar* case   **7.32** is the least consistent one because it embodied features of both the consent and the justification approach. First, the Court reiterated the existence/exercise dichotomy in the sense of the *Keurkoop* judgment under the first sentence of Article 36 E.C., stating that the determination of the conditions and procedures under which the protection is granted is a matter for national rules.[93] The Court subsequently examined whether the granting, and thus the existence, of design rights in components of complex products is compatible with the second sentence of Article 36 E.C. As such, only the "sharp edges" of national design law, namely inherently discriminatory or protectionist features of the law, and the way in which the exclusive right was exercised, could be held to be incompatible with Article 36 E.C.[94]

---

[90] Case 187/80, *Merck v. Stephar*, Judgment of July 14, 1981; [1981] E.C.R. 2063; [1981] 3 C.M.L.R. 463. See also *supra*, Chap. 4, pt. 2(1)(b)(iii), and Chap. 6, at pts. 2(2) and 2(5), where it is submitted that the Court in the *Merck* case subsequently failed to safeguard the function of intellectual property rights effectively through focusing on the specific subject-matter of the right and the consent theory.

[91] Case 53/87: [1988] E.C.R. 6039; [1990] 4 C.M.L.R. 265, at para. 31.

[92] See *infra*, pt. 5.

[93] For the implications of this statement, see *supra*, pt. 4(2)(b).

[94] See also *supra*, Chap. 6, pt. 3(2), where it is submitted that nothing in the E.C. Treaty justifies the approach whereby the existence of the right may only be curtailed under the second sentence of Article 36 E.C., whereas only the exercise might be curtailed under its first sentence.

(b) Underlying rationale?

7.33   This was basically the same approach as was followed in the *Thetford* case of June 1988.[95] In that case the issue was raised of whether a patent granted on the basis of the principle of relative novelty came under the scope of Article 36 E.C. There is, however, no obvious reason why the Court did not also adopt the justification approach under the first sentence of Article 36 E.C. in both the *Thetford* and *Maxicar* cases, as it had done in the earlier *Warner Brothers* case,[96] particularly as the latter was also the approach suggested by Advocate General Mischo.[97] A possible explanation for the Court's refusal to look at whether the contested features of the intellectual property law were justified, with reference to the function of the intellectual property right concerned in the *Maxicar* and the *Thetford* cases, could be that this approach might have led to the finding that those features were incompatible with the first sentence of Article 36 E.C. It was pointed out before that up till now the Court has never ruled that non-discriminatory intellectual property rights could not be justified under Article 36 E.C. It was also submitted that it would be fundamentally inconsistent to use the justification test merely to uphold national intellectual property law, and to use the consent test to curtail the effect of undesirable features of the law.[98]

(c) No justification under the first sentence of Article 36

7.34   Considering the significant legal and economic importance of the *Maxicar* case[99] it is surprising that the Court dealt extremely briefly, not to say superficially, with the issues raised under Article 36 E.C. In particular, under the first sentence of Article 36 E.C. the Court failed to examine the central issue, namely the fact that the design rights were contested because they applied to both the components of complex products, needed only for repair purposes, and the complex product as such. In this respect, the Court merely stated:

> "It is for the national legislature to determine which products qualify for protection, *even if they form part of a unit already protected as such.*"[1]

(d) Justification under the second sentence of Article 36

7.35   As mentioned above, the justification test was limited to an examination of whether or not the grant of the design right constituted an arbitrary discrimination or a disguised restriction on trade between the Member States.[2] In other words, the design rights would only fall foul of Article 36 E.C. if they

---

[95] Case 35/87: [1988] E.C.R. 3585; [1988] 3 C.M.L.R. 549. See *supra*, Chap. 6, pt. 3(2)(c).
[96] See also G. Marenco, and K. Banks, *op. cit.*, at p. 255. Also Friden remarks that it is extremely difficult to reconcile the *Maxicar* and *Thetford* rulings with the approach taken in the *Warner Brothers* case. See G. Friden, *op. cit.*, at p. 206.
[97] See *supra*, at pt. 4(3).
[98] See *supra*, Chap. 6, pt. 4.
[99] See *supra*, at pt. 2(1)(c).
[1] Case 53/87: [1988] E.C.R. 6039; [1990] 4 C.M.L.R. 265, at para. 10 (emphasis added).
[2] See *supra*, at pt. (a).

were unduly discriminatory,[3] which it is clear from the analysis under Articles 30 and 34 E.C. they are not,[4] or granted on the basis of a protectionist intention. Contrary to what the national court seemed to assume, whether or not the function of design rights is affected is thereby irrelevant because this would imply an examination under the first sentence of Article 36 E.C.[5] Thus the obvious conclusion of the Court's marginal appraisal of the design law under the second sentence of Article 36 E.C. was that:

> "... it need merely be stated, [...], that the exclusive right granted by the national legislation to the proprietors of protective rights in respect of ornamental models for car bodywork components may be enforced, without distinction, both against those persons who manufacture spare parts within the national territory and against those who import them from other Member States, and that such legislation is not intended to favour national products at the expense of products originating in other Member States."[6]

It is noteworthy that the Court, in the *Thetford* case, held that the principle of relative novelty did not constitute a disguised restriction on intra-Community trade because its aim was merely to foster creative activity through giving a reward for the rediscovery of old inventions.[7] In the *Maxicar* case the Court did not state what the aim of the design law giving protection to spare parts is, precisely, but merely pointed out that it is not intended to have a protectionist effect.

(e) Specific subject-matter approach

With regard to the possible misuse of the design right by the intellectual property owner, the Court essentially reiterated its prior case law concerning the need to safeguard the specific subject-matter of intellectual property rights. It was in the *Maxicar* judgment that the Court for the first time gave an express definition of the specific subject-matter of design rights:

7.36

> "... the authority of a proprietor of a protective right in respect of an ornamental model to oppose the manufacture by third parties, for the purpose of sale on the internal market or export, of products incorporating the design or to prevent the import of such products manufactured without its consent in other Member States constitutes the *substance* of his exclusive right."[8]

---

[3] On the incompatibility of discriminatory features of intellectual property law with Article 36 E.C., see *supra*, Chap. 6, pt. 3(1). See especially pt. 3(1)(a)(vi) where it is held that the Court does not distinguish between discriminatory measures, that could possibly be justified under Article 36 E.C., and arbitrary discriminatory measures. To the contrary it seems to assume that all discriminatory intellectual property measures fall foul of Article 36 E.C.

[4] See *supra*, at pt. 3.

[5] See *supra*, at pt. 2(2) and pt. 4(1), where it is stated that the national court advanced the view that the use of the design right contrary to its inherent function might be contrary to the second sentence of Article 36 E.C.

[6] Case 53/87: [1988] E.C.R. 6039; [1990] 4 C.M.L.R. 265, at para. 12.

[7] See *supra*, Chap. 6, pt. 3(2).

[8] Case 53/87: [1988] E.C.R. 6039; [1990] 4 C.M.L.R. 265, at para. 11 (emphasis added).

As such, the Court responded to the specific facts of the case by introducing a kind of reversed consent theory.[9] Whereas the Court has generally held that the specific subject-matter of intellectual property rights is the right to first market the product by the intellectual property owner, or with his consent, the Court now seems to acknowledge that intellectual property rights are essentially prohibitive rights rather than positive rights. In the *Volvo* case it was stated even more emphatically that:

"... the right of the proprietor of a protected design to prevent third parties from manufacturing and selling or importing, without its consent, products incorporating the design constitutes the *very subject-matter* of his exclusive right."[10]

(f) Functionality test impliedly rejected

7.37   Contrary to the approach already adopted with regard to trade marks and performance rights,[11] the Court did not define, in the spare parts cases, the specific subject-matter of design rights with reference to the specific function of the intellectual property right concerned. As such, the Court in the *Maxicar* case did not examine whether or not the "use" of the exclusive right concerning both the spare parts and the car as a whole is necessary to safeguard the function of design rights. It merely applied the reversed consent theory to the spare parts as though they were independent products in their own right, rather than components of complex products, and as though the only threat to the free movement of goods was posed by a possible enforcement of the principle of territoriality.[12] The Court even rejected an examination of the function of design rights by stating that:

"To prevent the application of the national legislation in such circumstances [*i.e.* if the specific subject-matter is fulfilled] would therefore be tantamount to challenging the very existence of that right."[13]

It cannot go unnoticed that the Court omitted the usual reference to the objective of giving the possibility of obtaining a reward in its definition of the specific subject-matter of design rights in the spare parts cases. It was submitted above, with respect to independent products, that a refinement of the reward theory might have led to more acceptable and consistent judgments than a straightforward application of the consent theory.[14] At least partially, the first theory takes the function of intellectual property rights into account. It is obvious that under the reward theory the fact that the case concerned design protection on components of complex products that also benefit from design protection would have been highly relevant. In particular, the question would have arisen of whether, and when, the alleged possibility of obtaining a reward twice can be justified by the function of design rights.[15]

[9] See also *supra*, Chap. 4, pt. 2(4)(c).
[10] Case 238/87: [1988] E.C.R. 6211; [1989] 4 C.M.L.R. 122, at para. 8 (emphasis added).
[11] See *supra*, Chap. 4, respectively pts. 2(3) and 2(2)(b).
[12] On this issue, see also *supra*, at pt. 4(2).
[13] Case 53/87: [1988] E.C.R. 6039; [1990] 4 C.M.L.R. 265, at para. 11 (explanation in brackets added).
[14] See *supra*, Chap. 6, pt. 2(5).
[15] On the issue of "double" reward, see *infra*, at pt. 5.

5. THE CONCEPT OF "REWARD" AND THE FUNCTION OF INTELLECTUAL PROPERTY RIGHTS

(1) Return on investment

It is, to say the least, surprising that the Court did not once use the word 7.38
"reward" in its findings under the rules on the free movement of goods in the
Maxicar case. The alleged possibility and/or need to obtain a double reward
were the central arguments advanced by the parties in favour, or against,
upholding exclusive design rights in spare parts of cars. The latter had been
extensively dealt with by Advocate General Mischo. A possible explanation
for this omission is that the Court deliberately refrained from engaging in a
discussion about the proper function of design rights so as to avoid the possible consequences this might entail.[16]

One can discern two basic sets of arguments concerning the issue of the
return on investment through granting design rights on spare parts of cars that
were brought to the attention of the Court. The first set of arguments, which
will not be dealt with here, focused mainly on the economic repercussions of
granting exclusive rights in the ancillary market of spare parts of cars on the
market for new cars. The second set of arguments concerned the legal aspects
of granting design protection for components of complex products, and in
particular on spare parts of cars. The objective of safeguarding the inherent
function of design rights, and especially the return on investment, thereby
played a central role.

(2) Complex products and the function of intellectual property rights

(a) Legal issues raised in Maxicar

The key issue raised by the national court in the *Maxicar* case was whether or 7.39
not the protective design rights could be enforced both on the car and on the
spare parts sold subsequently without infringing the inherent function of
design rights. This single question raised three sub-questions which each call
for a separate answer. First, the validity of granting design protection for
spare parts of cars in general was challenged. Secondly, the issue was raised of
whether a designer may only obtain the reward once on the complex product
after which his intellectual property right is exhausted, whether he may
amortise the research and development costs over the complex product and
the components, or whether he may obtain a double reward. Finally, it needed
to be established how this all fits in with the function of design rights.

(b) Function of design rights: two essential criteria

The inherent function of industrial design rights under Community law could 7.40
be described as follows: "granting a temporary exclusive right on an industrial design or model so as to provide the possibility of obtaining a return for

[16] See also *supra*, at pt. 4(4)(2).

217

investment made, and progress achieved, in the field of aesthetics in order to stimulate overall research and development of aesthetic features of technical or functional products."[17] The latter incorporates two essential criteria which have to be fulfilled cumulatively. First, there has to be "progress in the field of aesthetics". This would imply that in order to qualify for intellectual property protection, in the sense of Article 36 E.C., the design has to be new and/or original even though it does not necessarily have to have aesthetic or artistic merit.[18] Spare parts of cars that live up to those requirements, the appraisal of which is a matter for the national court, would thus, in principle, come under the design exception of Article 36 E.C. in the same way as the complex product itself. However, this finding is subject to the fulfilment of the second criterion mentioned above. Namely, it needs to be established that "the exclusive right is granted to the industrial design or model to provide the possibility of obtaining a return for the investment made in the field of aesthetics". Whether or not the grant of design rights on both the spare parts and the car was necessary to fulfil this condition was the central issue in the debates of the *Maxicar* case.

(c) Factual appraisal of requirements for intellectual property protection

7.41 Maxicar and the Consorzio maintained in the *Maxicar* case that the form of a bodywork spare part does not constitute an intellectual creation capable of design protection. It was argued that it does not have an aesthetic value of its own and has not been designed individually, but merely forms a part of a model designed in its entirety.[19] This argument obviously calls for an examination of the creative and aesthetic merit of a given product. The factual appraisal of the fulfilment of the requirements posed for intellectual property protection does not, in principle, come within the scope of competence of the European Court of Justice, in particular having regard to the division of competence under Article 177 E.C. proceedings.[20] The Court could have referred this issue back to the national court by stating that intellectual property rights, whether granted for components or complex products, have to be granted in accordance with their function in order to come under Article 36 E.C. The factual appraisal of whether or not spare parts of cars qualify in terms of "investment made and progress achieved in the field of aesthetics" is then a matter for the national court to determine.

---

[17] For a more elaborate analysis of the function of design rights, see *supra*, Chap. 2, pt. 3(5).

[18] It could be argued that this aspect of the function of design rights was not fulfilled in the *Keurkoop* case, on the grounds that the principles of first-to-file and relative novelty combined do not constitute a possible return for investment made in the field of aesthetics. On this case, see *supra*, Chap. 4, pt. 2(4)(b) and Chap. 6, pt. 3(2)(b).

[19] Case 53/87: [1988] E.C.R. 6039, Report of the Hearing, at 6048.

[20] On the division of competence under Article 177 procedures, see also *supra*, Chap. 4, pt. 1(2) (d). There are cases, however, in which this distinction is less obvious. See, for instance, Case C–315/92, *Clinique*: [1994] E.C.R. I-317, where the Court, contrary to the opinion of the Advocate General, made a factual appraisal as to whether the name of a cosmetic product was liable to mislead the consumer.

(d) The "double reward" and "apportionment of reward" arguments

The national court, Maxicar and the Consorzio seemed to be of the opinion **7.42** that the sale of the car already accounted for the reward on the overall design of bodywork components of cars. It was therefore maintained that the intellectual property right should be held to be "exhausted" in so far as the subsequent sales of spare parts is concerned.[21] They pointed out that the additional grant of intellectual property rights on the bodywork components would entail that a double reward could be obtained in return for one and the same creative effort. In their view, this result is not in accordance with the function of design law. Advocate General Mischo was of the contrary opinion that granting design protection to both the complex product and its constituent components did not imply granting a "double reward". In his view, the national law merely "allowed a car manufacturer to apportion that return or amortisation between the price of the vehicle as a whole, on the one hand, and the price of the spare parts, on the other".[22]

It is submitted that both approaches were incorrect in that they both imply that the reward is merely a return on the actual costs made to design a particular product and hence is quantifiable. This is illustrated by the use of concepts such as "double reward" and "apportionment of reward", which rely heavily on the acceptance that a "just" reward for the creative effort concerned can be established in the first place. Such an approach neglects the main objective of design law which is to stimulate investment into research and development of new designs. The latter will only be fully achieved if there is the prospect that the return made on a successful design may be substantial enough to compensate for potentially less successful, or unsuccessful, designs. This implies that the interpretation of the concept "reward" should not be based on an *ex post* analysis of the real costs related to the development of a particular design.[23]

The "reward" concept under industrial design law is, in principle, strin- **7.43** gently linked with the appraisal of the final consumer as to the added value the design confers on the functional product. In other words, the reward achieved will be dependent on whether, and to what extent, the consumer is willing to buy, or even to pay a higher price for, the product embodying the protected design as compared to similar products that do not embody the design.[24] This

---

[21] It is apparent that "exhaustion" should be understood in its original meaning, namely the exhaustion due to the first use of the exclusive right with the consent of the intellectual property owner, and not in the meaning given to it by the Court of Justice, namely exhaustion due to the first marketing of a protected product by the intellectual property owner, or with his consent. On this difference, see *supra*, Chap. 6, pt. 2(5).

[22] Case 53/87: [1988] E.C.R. 6039; [1990] 4 C.M.L.R. 265, at para. 31. See also *supra*, at pt. 4(3)(c), where it is maintained that the Advocate General, through focusing on the reward itself, ignored the *Merck* judgment of the Court.

[23] See also V. Korah, "No duty to license independent repairers to make spare parts: The *Renault, Volvo* and *Bayer & Hennecke* cases" [1988] E.I.P.R. 381 at 383. She writes: "Economists analyse transaction costs *ex ante* – what incentive is required to induce investment. Such lawyers as are not used to economic analysis often analyse *ex post* – now that this investment has paid off and the costs have been recovered, there is no need for a further reward." However, she merely raises this issue in relation to the Court's finding under Article 86 E.C., namely the abuse of a dominant position through charging "unfair" prices. See also *infra*, Chap. 8, pt. 4(4)(b).

[24] See also *supra*, Chap. 2, pt. 3(5).

means that design protection merely provides the conditions necessary to confer the "possibility" of obtaining "a" reward. It does not determine what constitutes a just reward or that a reward should always be obtained. It is interesting to note the similarity between this finding and the Court's approach to the reward function of patents in the *Merck* case.[25] However, as was pointed out before, the Court in its *Merck* judgment failed to subsequently examine whether the conditions needed to confer the possibility of obtaining a reward had also been fulfilled.[26] It merely continued to apply the consent theory on the basis of the need to safeguard the specific subject-matter of patents, thereby diverting patent law from its inherent function.

(3) The concept "reward" in context

(a) Difference between patents and industrial designs

7.44 Patent law confers an exclusive right on a new product (or process) that meets the stringent conditions for patentability. The level of reward that can possibly be obtained is dependent on whether or not substitutable products are on, or may enter, the market which do not infringe the patent and with which the protected product has to compete. This means that, in the absence of substitutable products, the patent confers a legal monopoly on a product. However, whether or not monopoly prices can also be charged largely depends on the value of the functional product as perceived by potential customers.[27]

The objective of design law is, to the contrary, not to confer an exclusive let alone a monopoly right on a product, but merely to grant exclusivity in a new and/or original design. The level of reward that can possibly be obtained is dependent on the appraisal by potential customers of the added value the design confers on a functional product, in comparison to another functional product that does not incorporate the protected design.[28] The underlying condition for the fulfilment of the function of design rights is therefore that there are, or can be, competing products on the market. In other words, that the design is not an imperative feature of the product. It is obvious that, in the absence of alternative ways of designing a product, the grant of design protection comes down to the grant of an exclusive right in a product. This entails that instead of presenting a stimulus to competition between products, competition would be totally inhibited.[29] Design protection would then no longer confer a reward for the added value of the design but would relate to the

---

[25] Case 187/80: [1981] E.C.R. 2063; [1981] 3 C.M.L.R. 463. See also *supra*, Chap. 4, pt. 2(1)(b), and Chap. 6, pt. 2(2).

[26] See especially *supra*, Chap. 6, pt. 2(5).

[27] See *supra*, Chap. 2, pt. 3(2).

[28] See also *supra*, Chap. 2, pt. 3(5).

[29] On the necessary balance between competition and design rights, see also The Confederation of British Industry, "Design right: designed wrong" (February 1988), pt. 1, where it is held that: "the balance between encouraging innovative design and promoting competition is a difficult but crucial one. Design protection is itself a vital driver of enterprise and competition, encouraging innovation and thereby stimulating enterprising companies and increasing consumer choice. At the same time there are circumstances where protection can offer a manufacturer a monopoly advantage which could inhibit competition. This situation has arisen particularly in the provision of spare parts, most notably for motor vehicles."

functional product itself in the same way as patents do. However, it should be recalled that design protection does not require the same stringent conditions for protectability as patent law does.

(b) Difference between complex products and components

(i) Distinction between cars and spare parts

In so far as the market in new cars is concerned, the development of new designs of cars is an important factor of non-price competition between different brands. The grant of design rights makes it possible to give added value to the car by excluding the use of the design by competitors without, however, also excluding the possibility of competitors marketing cars with different designs. The choice of the car purchaser reflects his perception of both the added value conferred by the car design and the functional product, *i.e.* the "basic features" of the car. Design rights in cars thus fulfil their essential function.

7.45

The same does not always hold true in so far as spare parts of cars are concerned. Spare parts are indispensable components of the car which, if they break down, need to be repaired and often replaced in order to restore the car to its original function or appearance.[30] The only other option is to buy a new car which, of course, involves a much higher cost and thus cannot be maintained as an overall viable alternative. Most car owners are therefore, at one time or another, confronted with the necessity of buying replacement parts for the specific type of car they have purchased. Their choice of all subsequently purchased spare parts is thus limited by their initial choice when purchasing the car. It is nonetheless submitted that in the debate about the legitimacy of enforcing design protection on replacement parts of cars a distinction needs to be made between two types of spare parts.

(ii) Further distinction as to the type of spare parts

First, there are those parts for which the design is not an imperative feature to restore the car to its original function or appearance. This means that competing spare parts can be marketed which do not incorporate the design. It is obvious that in this case the design confers added value to the functional aspect of the spare part and thus is liable to be protected by design rights in the same way as the car itself.

7.46

Secondly, there are those parts such as bodywork components, for which the design *is* imperative to restore the car to its original function or appearance. Generally speaking, these are parts that come under the "must-fit" and "must-match" exception to design protection in the United Kingdom.[31] Since a car owner *has* to purchase the replacement part in order to restore the car, and since the spare part necessarily *has* to have a certain design, granting exclusive protection to this design would be tantamount to granting an exclusive right on the spare part concerned. The enforcement of

---

[30] This is the major difference from a set of matching single products. For instance, the loss of a knife in a cutlery set does not mean that the other knives and forks can no longer be used.

[31] See *supra*, at pt. 1.

design protection on these parts would, as a corollary, entail the exclusion of all potential competitors in the market. It could thus be said that design protection would be exceeding its function in that the conferment of an exclusive right on a design comes down to granting a monopoly right on a product for which, subsequently, monopoly prices can be charged. In other words, in this case design protection no longer fulfils its inherent function, which is to give the possibility of reward for the added value that the design confers on the functional product, in order to stimulate investment in the field of aesthetics. The reason for this is simply that the design does not confer added value to the functional product but is intrinsically linked to the function of the spare part itself.[32]

(iii) The principle of proportionality

7.47 Moreover, it should be pointed out that the grant of design rights in bodywork components is not indispensable to allowing for the recovery of the investment made for aesthetic development. The sale of the new car also accounts for the added value the overall design confers to a functional product.[33] It seems that it would not only be difficult to justify in terms of the function of design rights but that, furthermore, it would be contrary to the principle of proportionality to uphold design rights which exceed the function of industrial designs and which are not even necessary to provide the possibility of obtaining a reward for creative effort.

(4) Evaluation

7.48 It is submitted that the problem is neither whether or not the spare parts are "worthy of protection", nor whether or not the actual costs of the elaboration of the design have been achieved or exceeded. The crucial issue is whether or not design protection creates the conditions necessary to provide the possibility of a reward being given for the added value a design confers on a functional product. It could thus be argued that design protection exceeds its function if it grants exclusive rights in a product and allows a reward which no longer stands in relation to the added value the design confers on a functional product. The latter is the case in so far as design protection in bodywork components of cars is concerned.

It is therefore submitted that the application of a justification test under the first sentence of Article 36 E.C., whereby due regard is given to the inherent function of design rights, would most likely have led to a different conclusion. In particular, the finding of the Court might have been that granting design protection to bodywork components of cars is not in accordance with the

---

[32] It is interesting to note that this was also acknowledged by M. Franzosi, who represented Renault before the Court in the *Maxicar* case, at a conference organised by the CUERPI in June 1988. See the commentary by M. Franzosi, in CUERPI, *La protection des créations d'esthétique industrielle dans le cadre de la CEE: objectif 1992* (1988), pp. 67–69.

[33] In his reaction to the *British Leyland* judgment of the House of Lords (see *supra* at pt. 1), Mr Don Plaster, Chairman of the Industrial Copyright Reform Association, said: "Those who complain that research and development will suffer as a result [of the *BL* Judgment] should surely review their costing policies. R and D costs should be amortised by sales resulting from new designs, not subsidised by the sales of spare parts in which, in many cases, R and D costs should have been amortised long ago": see *Financial Times*, March 6, 1986.

objective of safeguarding the protection of industrial and commercial property. However, the Court did not engage in discussion about the justification for, and function of, design rights in the *Maxicar* case. It merely upheld the existence/exercise dichotomy under the first sentence of Article 36 E.C.[34] In so doing, the Court passed the difficult issue of finding ways to curtail the potential detrimental effects ensuing from granting design protection on a product, and not merely on a design, to its analysis under Article 86 E.C.[35]

6. CONSUMER PROTECTION AND THE FUNCTION OF INTELLECTUAL PROPERTY RIGHTS

(1) Legal issues raised in *Maxicar*

As mentioned before, in the *Maxicar* case both the car manufacturers and independent manufacturers claimed to be safeguarding the interests of consumers by obtaining, or challenging, design protection for bodywork components of cars.[36] Neither the Court nor the Advocate General in their findings under Article 36 E.C. referred expressly to the effect that granting design protection to bodywork components of cars has on the consumer, *i.e.* on the car owner. Nevertheless, it is submitted that there is a causal effect which is far from negligible and therefore merits mention.

    7.49

Basically two sets of arguments were put forward in the *Maxicar* proceedings which directly invoked consumers' interests. The first issue concerned the alleged indispensable relationship between design protection and quality/safety considerations. Renault maintained that spare parts manufactured by independent manufacturers are of a lower quality than those sold by car manufacturers. The refusal to grant design protection for spare parts, which in this particular case ensured a monopoly position, would therefore be tantamount to jeopardising the consumer's interests.[37] In other words, the argument goes that design protection on bodywork components is needed to safeguard the quality of the products and the safety of the consumers.[38] The second matter was the impact that design protection for bodywork components has on the choice of, and the price to be paid by, consumers for those parts due to the ensuing tie-in of spare parts upon purchasing a car.

(2) Intellectual property rights and quality/safety considerations

(a) Distinction between safety and quality concerns

Whether or not spare parts manufactured by independent concerns are, in fact, of a lower quality cannot be answered unconditionally in the negative or

    7.50

---

[34] See *supra*, pt. 4(4).
[35] On the Court's approach under Article 86 E.C., see *infra*, Chap. 8.
[36] See *supra*, at pt. 2(2)(c).
[37] Case 53/87: [1988] E.C.R. 6039, Report of the Hearing, at p. 6046.
[38] This view is shared by Bonet, who maintains that the grant of design protection to bodywork components is the *only* way to safeguard consumer protection. See G. Bonet, "*Les créations d'esthétiques industrielle au regard des règles de libre circulation et de libre concurrence dans le Marché Commun*" in CUERPI, *La protection des créations d'esthétiques industrielle dans le cadre de la CEE: objectif 1992* (1988), pp. 45–63 at 51.

in the positive but has to be established on a case-by-case basis. For example, as the Consorzio and Maxicar pointed out, already several so-called spurious (or non-approved) spare parts are manufactured by the same manufacturers that also supply the car manufacturers. They may therefore be expected to be of the same quality.[39] But in the hypothesis that the independent manufacturers' spare parts were of a lower quality,[40] it would still remain to be established how this actually affects the consumers' interests.

Joerges illustrates the complexity of the concept of "consumers' interests" specifically with regard to the car and spare parts sector as it relates to different groups of consumers in terms of income and social stratification. He nonetheless convincingly argues that a distinction could, and should, be made between indispensable safety controls and mere quality interests. Whereas the latter, in his view, should be left to market mechanisms he pleads for the regulation of safety. This is defined as:

> "...that realm of consumer policy which must not discriminate between consumer groups, but instead whether by specified safety standards or by mandatory rules of liability, ensures or tries to ensure minimum standards irrespective of the cost to consumers, enterprises or garages."[41]

In other words, minimum safety norms should be established for, and respected by, all. Quality norms that exceed these standards should be left to market mechanisms and, in particular, to the consumer's willingness, or not, to pay a higher price for a higher level of quality. For instance, the owner of a second-hand car might not be willing to invest money in a spare part of high quality. He should, nevertheless, be held to comply with the minimum safety norms which will necessarily be reflected in the cost of the spare part. The question is whether intellectual property protection may be invoked as a means of enforcing minimum safety norms.

(b) Intellectual property rights and safety concerns

7.51   It obviously is not the purpose of intellectual property law to provide a monopoly over a product so that quality standards can be enforced. This also holds true if the quality standards include safety standards which, as submitted above, should be subject to regulation and uniform application.

The Court has consistently rejected the use of the industrial and commercial property exception of Article 36 E.C. to protect the public against the risks arising from faulty products. For instance, in the *Centrafarm v. Sterling Drug*

---

[39] Case 53/87: [1988] E.C.R. 6039, Report of the Hearing, at 6045.

[40] It should be emphasised that this is merely an argument and not a statement. Surveys show that some spare parts are indeed of a lower quality, whereas others are of an equal or superior quality. See, for instance, B. Jarvis, "Cheap and nasty", *Commercial Motor* (September 20, 1986), pp.51–52; P. Albert, "*L'étrange duel: pièces d'origine ou parallèles?*" *Fergabel Revue* (July/August 1987), pp.13–15.

[41] See C. Joerges, "Selective distribution schemes in the motor-car sector: European competition policy, consumer interests and the draft regulation on the application of Article 85(3) of the Treaty to certain categories of motor-vehicle distribution and servicing agreements" in *EC competition policy and the consumer interest* (M. Goyens ed. 1985) (Bruylant), pp. 187–236 at pp. 189–190.

case the Court rejected the use of patent law to safeguard the public against defective pharmaceutical products in the following terms:

> "...the measures necessary to achieve this must be such as may properly be adopted in the field of health control, and *must not constitute a misuse of the rules concerning industrial and commercial property.*
>
> Moreover, the specific considerations underlying the protection of industrial and commercial property *are distinct* from the considerations underlying the protection of the public and any responsibilities which that may imply."[42]

This implies that safety control cannot be invoked as a justification to uphold design protection, or any other intellectual property rights, on spare parts of cars under Article 36 E.C. It is interesting to recall in this respect that the Court of First Instance held in the *Hilti* case that the need for safety control could not be invoked as a justification for abusive behaviour by an undertaking in a dominant position under Article 86 E.C.[43] The issue of safeguarding safety interests has to be dealt with on its own terms. More precisely, it has to be regulated in a way which sets out objective minimum standards that apply to all spare parts, whether protected by design rights or not, and regardless of whether they are supplied by the car manufacturer or manufactured by others.[44] This implies that safety regulations should emanate from and be controlled by an independent, preferably public, authority.[45] In this respect, it is worthwhile noting that the E.C. has issued product safety regulations which need to be complied with.

(c) Intellectual property rights and quality concerns

Apart from safety considerations, Renault held that the poor quality of spare parts produced by independent manufacturers might also damage the reputation of the car manufacturers because the consumer does not always know which spare parts are used to repair his car. The argument based on consumer expectations and goodwill is particularly relevant for customers that have their car repaired in approved workshops. It is apparent, though, that the most appropriate response to this argument is that the consumer should be

7.52

---

[42] Case 15/74, *Centrafarm v. Sterling Drug*, Judgment of October 31, 1974: [1974] E.C.R. 1147; [1974] 2 C.M.L.R. 480, at paras. 28 and 29, (emphasis added). On this case, see also *supra*, Chap. 4, pt. 2(1)(a).

[43] See *supra*, Chap. 5, pt. 4(2)(b)(iii).

[44] It is again interesting to note that M. Franzosi, though he represented Renault before the Court, countered the view advanced by Prof. Bonet that design protection is necessary to safeguard the safety of consumers. See M. Franzosi, *op. cit.*, at p. 67.

[45] This is in line with the opinion given by Advocate General Trabucchi in the *Centrafarm* case. He held: "If a certain parallel importer disregards the provisions in the country concerned governing the sale of pharmaceutical products, or at least, behaves in such a way as to compromise or endanger the protection of public health, this will, (...), justify the *competent authorities* in intervening to remove the danger. And, by the same token, there may even be justification for *restrictive measures* directed to that end. But this will take place *independently of the protection of a private party on the basis of an exclusive right associated with a patent* or trade mark and will, [...], in no event justify the use of such rights to prevent third parties from importing products, *whatever their nature.*" Case 15/74: [1974] E.C.R. 1147; [1974] 2 C.M.L.R. 480, at para. 9 (emphasis added).

duly informed about, and possibly have the choice of, the origin of the parts used for repair.[46] A major problem is that the workshops do not always pass on the (price) advantages of using spurious parts to their customers and hence are wary of informing their customers about the use of such parts. Living up to quality expectations and providing adequate information to consumers are, nonetheless, problems which are not specifically related to, and should not be solved through, the enforcement of exclusive design protection in order to obtain a monopoly situation over the spare parts concerned. As for safety standards, it is a problem that is posed regardless of whether or not the spare parts can be protected by design rights. The Commission had already taken this issue into account when drafting its first block exemption for selective distribution agreements in the car and after sales market.[47] The latter provides that authorised dealers should be free to purchase spare parts of an equal or superior quality from sources other than the car manufacturer but may be contractually obliged to inform the customer about the use of such parts.[48] It is obvious, however, that this solution becomes irrelevant for those parts that become captive parts through the enforcement of design rights.

(3) Complex products and consumer tie-in

(a) Underlying rationale

7.53   The strategy of the car manufacturers is to keep down the price of new cars by passing on (part of) the production costs in subsequent sales of spare parts.[49] A necessary condition in order to pursue this policy is that the car manufacturers obtain a monopoly position on certain spare parts through the exclusion of all potential competitors. It was illustrated above that a monopoly position can be obtained through enforcing exclusive design rights on certain parts, such as bodywork components, which necessarily have to have a certain shape in order to restore the car to its original function and appearance.[50] In other words, the enforcement of design protection on such parts entails the exclusion of spurious parts from the market so that bodywork components become captive parts.

(b) Consequences of granting exclusivity

7.54   The granting and the enforcement of intellectual property rights on bodywork components of cars results in a monopoly position for the car manufacturer

---

[46] See also C. Joerges, *op. cit.*, at p. 215, where he writes: "This is the only solution which also makes allowance for those customers who want to put up with a spare part of inferior quality, but who also attach importance to the expert know-how provided by appointed workshops. This proposal does not affect the manufacturer's interests, because a customer ordering repairs can, when necessary, identify the outside supplier."

[47] Regulation 123/85, [1985] O.J. L15/16. On this block exemption, see also *infra*, Chap. 9, pt. 3(2).

[48] Arts. 3, 4° and 4(1)8 of Regulation 123/85. On this solution, see J. Dubois, "*Cas d'application: la distribution automobile dans le marché commun: le point de vue de la Commission Européenne*" in *Droit des consommateurs* (J. Pizzio ed. 1987) (Story Scientia), pp. 91–97 at p. 93.

[49] See also *infra*, Chap. 8, pt. 3(2)(a)(i).

[50] See *supra*, at pt. 5(3)(b)(ii).

with the consequence that car owners are tied in. Having freely chosen to purchase a certain type of car, the latter are no longer free to choose the way in which to have their car repaired. This implies that they do not pay a certain price for a spare part having regard to its functional characteristics and the added value the design confers. They are constrained to pay the price demanded by the supplier of the authorised products.

Maxicar and CICRA pointed out that allowing this situation to occur through the use of design protection would entail several detrimental consequences for the car owner.[51] First, a monopoly position means that monopoly prices can be charged. The price of spare parts could thus be increased up to the point at which car owners refrain from effecting further repairs. This might be an indirect method of prematurely eliminating certain types of older vehicles from the market in favour of the purchase of new vehicles. Secondly, conferring an exclusive right implies that potential competitors can be excluded from the market even though the intellectual property owner may not necessarily supply all possible spare parts himself. This is the case in respect of corrosion panels which are welded to the existing component instead of the latter being replaced in cases of rust.[52] Likewise, there are parts that could be sold separately, whereas the car manufacturers only sell whole units such as car doors. The non-availability of such smaller parts would thus lead to an increase in the price of the repairs.

(c) Relation between Articles 36 and 86

The prejudicial consequences for consumers are thus stringently linked with **7.55** the exclusion of competitors from the spare parts market, and the tie-in of the spare parts market to the car market. This is, however, merely the result of enforcing design rights in bodywork components of cars, the shape of which is imperative to restore the car to its original appearance. As will be seen below, in the *Maxicar* and *Volvo* cases the Court has tried to smooth out these detrimental effects through applying the rules on competition, and in particular Article 86 E.C., to the behaviour of the intellectual property owners.[53] With respect, it is submitted that this approach was wrong in that these consequences clearly ensue from the grant of design protection to bodywork components of cars. It was maintained above that, where no alternative designs are feasible, the grant of exclusive design protection is not in accordance with the inherent function of design rights.[54] It would therefore have been more consistent to state that the very grant of design rights in bodywork

---

[51] Case 53/87: [1988] E.C.R. 6039, Report of the Hearing, at 6044.
[52] In this respect, it is interesting to note that the U.K. Monopolies and Mergers Commission held that the refusal by Ford to grant licences to manufacture and sell replacement body parts in the U.K. was anti-competitive and against the public interest, mainly because it tended to keep up prices and stifle innovation. The latter was illustrated by the fact that it was the independent manufacturers that introduced the less expensive corrosion panels on the market, whereas it was held that: "we can only speculate whether, if the independents' competition had not existed, such panels would ever have been introduced by Ford." See MMC, *Ford Motor Company Limited*, Cmnd. 9437 (February 1985) see especially p. 43, pt. 6.58.
[53] See *infra*, Chap. 8.
[54] See *supra*, at pt. 5(3)(b)(ii).

components was not justified in terms of the need to safeguard the protection of industrial and commercial property in the sense of Article 36 E.C.

7.56   The fact that the Court refrained from pursuing the analysis in terms of the function of intellectual property rights in the spare parts cases has, furthermore, had significant consequences for the approach adopted in the *Magill* cases.[55] In the latter cases the so-called exceptionally anti-competitive circumstances similarly ensued from the grant of copyright protection in facts, instead of in an original form of expression, rather than from the abuse of his copyright by the intellectual property owner. In line with the spare parts cases, the Court formally upheld the existence/exercise dichotomy whilst striking down the allegedly abusive behaviour of the intellectual property owner under Article 86 E.C. Further, the Court of First Instance and the Court of Justice expressly based the reasoning developed in *Magill* on the *Volvo* judgment which, in turn, was decided on the basis of Article 86 E.C. alone. It will be illustrated in the next chapter that there are certain important similarities between the two cases. However, comparing the *Volvo* and *Magill* cases as regards their outcome also exposes certain fundamental dissimilarities, if not contradictions, in the reasoning of the Court. The latter is difficult to explain unless the Court adopted the underlying, but not substantiated, premise that spare parts of cars were worthy of protection whereas programme listings were not.

---

[55] On the *Magill* case, see *supra*, Chap. 5, pt. 4(3).

8. The E.C. "Intellectual Property Rights – Antitrust Debate" Concerning Spare Parts for Cars

1. PRELIMINARY REMARKS

The refusal of the European Court of Justice to look at whether or not the **8.01** grant of design protection to bodywork components of cars was justified in terms of the need to safeguard the function of design rights under Article 36 E.C.,[1] had considerable consequences for the subsequent consideration of the car manufacturers' behaviour under the rules on competition, and especially under Article 86 E.C. From the analysis of the earlier cases brought before the Court, concerning the application of Article 86 E.C. to intellectual property rights, it became apparent that if the enforcement of intellectual property rights is held not to be lawful under Article 36 E.C. then it cannot become lawful under Article 86 E.C.[2] This straightforward rule might have been applicable in the spare parts cases had the Court taken a justification approach to the grant of design rights in bodywork components of cars under Article 36 E.C.[3]

The adoption by the Court of what has been called the "marginal appraisal" approach in the *Maxicar* case has led to it upholding both the existence and the exercise of the design rights concerned under Article 36 E.C.[4] This finding is also highly relevant in the context of the application of the competition rules. In its findings under Article 86 E.C. the Court has consistently held that if the existence and the exercise are held to be lawful under Article 36 E.C., then an additional element will be needed for the exercise of the intellectual property right to be contrary to Article 86 E.C.[5] The main issue under the competition rules the Court had to deal with in the *CICRA and Maxicar v. Renault*[6] and *Volvo v. Veng*[7] cases was thus whether this additional element could consist of the fact that exclusive design rights were

---

[1] See *supra*, Chap. 7.
[2] See *supra*, Chap. 5, pt. 2(3).
[3] See *supra*, Chap. 7, pt. 4(3).
[4] See *supra*, Chap. 7, pt. 4(4).
[5] See *supra*, Chap. 5, pt. 2(3)(c).
[6] Case 53/87, *CICRA and Maxicar v. Renault*, Judgment of October 5, 1988: [1988] E.C.R. 6039; [1990] 4 C.M.L.R. 265.
[7] Case 238/87, *AB Volvo v. Erik Veng (UK) Ltd*, Judgment of October 5, 1988: [1988] E.C.R. 6211; [1989] 4 C.M.L.R. 122.

invoked to eliminate competition in the after-sales market of replacement parts.

8.02   As seen before, the Court of First Instance acknowledged in the *Tetra Pak* case that the additional element for the finding of an abuse could be the factual background against which the acquisition of an intellectual property right took place.[8] Furthermore, the Court of Justice upheld the ruling of the CFI in the *Hilti* case that the use of intellectual property rights to eliminate competition in a related market in unprotected accessories and, in the *Magill* cases, that the use of copyright to prevent the creation of a derivative market in a new product, constituted an abuse of a dominant position.[9] It is particularly significant that the CFI, in the *Magill* cases, expressly based its findings on the need to safeguard the essential function of copyright.[10] It held, in essence, that the use of intellectual property rights beyond what is necessary to fulfil the essential function of the exclusive right is manifestly contrary to Article 86 E.C. However, the Court on appeal did not reiterate this reasoning but pointed to the exceptional circumstances of the case, thereby referring to the prior *Volvo* judgment. Having failed to examine whether the function of design rights was fulfilled under Article 36 E.C. it is not surprising that the Court, in the latter case, subsequently also failed to examine whether the use of those exclusive rights was necessary to safeguard the inherent function of design rights.

8.03   What constitutes the exact balance between the two apparently conflicting systems of free competition and intellectual property rights has been the topic of much debate.[11] In so far as the European Community is concerned, the Court clarified in the *Continental Can* case that safeguarding an effective competitive structure in the Common Market is both in the consumers' interests and is an essential objective of the Treaty. In the words of the Court:

> "... if Article 3(f) provides for the institution of a system ensuring that competition in the Common Market is not distorted, *then it requires a fortiori that competition must not be eliminated*."
>
> "As may further be seen from letters (c) and (d) of Article 86(2), the provision is not only aimed at practices which may cause damage to consumers directly, *but also at those which are detrimental to them through their impact on an effective competitive structure*, such as is mentioned in Article 3(f) of the Treaty."[12]

Intellectual property rights, which are inherently exclusive rights, are particularly apt to affect the competitive market structure. It should be emphasised, however, that they have a specific function to fulfil so that they should not easily be discarded. Intellectual property rights constitute a legitimate temporary restraint on competition in order to stimulate innovation and development be it in the technical, aesthetic, or cultural field.[13] It is therefore

---

[8] See *supra*, Chap. 5, pt. 5(3)(b).
[9] See *supra*, Chap. 5, pt. 4.
[10] See specifically *supra*, Chap. 5, pt. 4(3)(b)(iii).
[11] See *supra*, Chap. 2.
[12] Case 6/72, *Europemballage and Continental Can v. Commission*, Judgment of February 21, 1973: [1973] E.C.R. 215; [1973] C.M.L.R. 199, at paras. 24 and 26 respectively (emphasis added).
[13] See also *supra*, Chap. 2, pt. 3(1).

submitted that they should be fully upheld under the rules on competition if and when they are enforced in such a manner as is needed to fulfil the objectives for which the exclusive right was granted. It seems that any other approach would be tantamount either to legalising potential abuses of intellectual property rights aimed at circumventing the rules on competition or, conversely, to opening the door to unwarranted interference by the latter in the normal exercise of intellectual property rights.

2. THE SPARE PARTS CASES

(1) The background

(a) Peculiarities of the cases

Both the factual background and the legal issues raised were different in the 8.04 *Volvo* and the *Maxicar* cases. The *Maxicar* case concerned a claim by the independent manufacturers for the annulment of design rights in bodywork components that had been granted to the car manufacturer.[14] The *Volvo* case concerned proceedings initiated by a car manufacturer against an independent manufacturer on the grounds of the alleged infringement of his design rights in bodywork components through the importation and sale of unauthorised parts.

(b) Preliminary questions

(i) CICRA and Maxicar v. Renault

As mentioned before, the Italian court in the *Maxicar* case ruled that design 8.05 rights in bodywork components of cars were in conformity with Italian law. It nevertheless wondered whether or not the exercise of such an exclusive right, which appears to be contrary to the inherent function of the intellectual property right concerned, was in conformity with Articles 30 and 86 E.C.[15] Concerning specifically the rules on competition, the following question was referred to the European Court of Justice:

> "Is or is not Article 86 of the EEC Treaty applicable so as to prohibit the abuse of the dominant position held by each car manufacturer in the market for spare parts for cars of its manufacture which consists in pursuing, by means of registering protective rights, the aim of eliminating competition from independent manufacturers of spare parts?"[16]

In other words, the national court sought an answer to the question of whether obtaining, and subsequently enforcing, exclusive design protection

---

[14] See *supra*, Chap. 7, pt. 2(1)(a).
[15] See *supra*, Chap. 7, pt. 2(1)(b).
[16] Case 53/87: [1988] E.C.R. 6039; [1990] 4 C.M.L.R. 265.

could in the given circumstances amount to an abusive manner of eliminating competition which is contrary to Article 86 E.C.

(ii) *Volvo v. Veng*

8.06   Similarly, in the *Volvo* case Veng initially denied having infringed a design right by importing and selling unauthorised parts by challenging the validity of Volvo's design rights in the Volvo 200 series front wing. However, Veng subsequently seemed to accept the validity of the exclusive right and undertook to abandon all allegations of abuse under Article 86 E.C. except for the alleged abuse of a dominant position resulting from Volvo's refusal to grant a licence under the registered design. As such, the United Kingdom court referred the following questions to the European Court of Justice:

> "(1) If a substantial car manufacturer holds registered designs which, under the law of a Member State, confer on it the sole and exclusive right to make and import replacement body panels required to effect repair of the body of a car of its manufacture (if such body panels are not replaceable by body panels of any other design), is such a manufacturer, by reason of such sole and exclusive rights, in a dominant position within the meaning of Article 86 of the EEC Treaty with respect to such replacement parts?
>
> (2) Is it prima facie an abuse of such dominant position for such a manufacturer to refuse to license others to supply such body panels, even where they are willing to pay a reasonable royalty for all articles sold under the licence (such royalty to represent an award which is just and equitable having regard to the merits of the design and all the surrounding circumstances, and to be determined by arbitration or in such other manner as the national court shall direct)?
>
> (3) Is such abuse likely to affect trade between Member States within the meaning of Article 86 by reason of the fact that the intending licensee is thereby prevented from importing the body panels from a second Member State?"[17]

In other words, the national court's questions in the *Volvo* case were complementary to the question posed in the *Maxicar* case. On the assumption that the registered design could in principle be used to eliminate competition under Community law, the United Kingdom court sought to know whether the refusal to license design rights in bodywork components of cars, whereby a just and equitable royalty would be paid, nevertheless amounted to an abuse of a dominant position.

(2) Introduction to the legal issues

8.07   It should be recalled that Article 86 E.C. only applies when three conditions are cumulatively fulfilled.[18] The undertaking alleged to behave anti-competitively has to occupy a dominant position in the relevant market, this dominant

[17] Case 238/87: [1988] E.C.R. 6211; [1989] 4 C.M.L.R. 122.
[18] See also *supra*, Chap. 5, pt. 2(3).

position has to be abused, and trade between Member States has to be affected by the abusive behaviour.

(a) Dominant position

The Italian court in the *Maxicar* case assumed that Renault occupied a domi-   **8.08**
nant position in the spare parts market, considering that it is the company that consumers approach when they need to replace a bodywork component.[19] The United Kingdom court in the *Volvo* case thought that Volvo might be in a dominant position concerning replacement parts by reason of the conferment of sole and exclusive rights. The first issue which thus needed to be considered under Article 86 E.C., even though the Court did not expressly deal with it, was whether or not car manufacturers occupied a dominant position in the relevant market. The crucial question thereby was how the relevant market, and especially the relevant product market, should be determined.[20] This was rendered more difficult by reason of the fact that spare parts are components of complex products. Theoretically, one could envisage the relevant market being either the market in both the car and the spare parts needed to repair that car or, as the national courts suggested, the market in replacement parts needed to repair a given brand of car. Having established the relevant market, one then needed to examine whether or not the car manufacturers also held a dominant position in that market, and which role intellectual property rights thereby fulfilled.[21] Although the Court has consistently held that the confer-ment of intellectual property rights does not automatically imply that the intellectual property owner also has a dominant position on the market,[22] never before had it been confronted with the question of whether an intellec-tual property owner may abuse the system of intellectual property rights in order to obtain a dominant position.

(b) Abuse of a dominant position

Assuming that the car manufacturers did occupy a dominant position in the   **8.09**
relevant market, the Italian court asked whether the enforcement of design rights in bodywork components of cars constituted an abuse. In contrast, the United Kingdom court asked whether the refusal to grant a licence on reason-able terms amounted to an abuse. As mentioned before, the Court had con-sistently held that an additional element to the normal exercise of intellectual property rights is needed to establish abusive behaviour under Article 86 E.C.[23] The answer to what constituted an abuse by the holder of design rights depended largely on whether the function, or the specific subject-matter, of design rights was to be taken into account.[24] If the function was taken into account, then only anti-competitive behaviour which was not in accordance with the objectives of design legislation would be struck down. If, to the

---

[19] Case 53/87: [1988] E.C.R. 6039, Report of the Hearing, at 6041.
[20] See *infra*, at pt. 3.
[21] See *infra*, at pt. 3(3).
[22] See Case 102/77, *Hoffman-La Roche, supra*, Chap. 5, pt. 2(3)(b).
[23] See *supra*, at pt. 1, and Chap. 5, pt. 2(3)(c).
[24] See *infra*, at pt. 4(3).

contrary, the specific subject-matter test was applied, as the Court did in the spare parts cases, then it was more difficult to draw a line between acceptable and abusive behaviour. This is illustrated below, by an analysis of the three examples of abusive behaviour by holders of design rights in bodywork components of cars as advanced by the Court.[25]

(c) Effect on intra-Community trade

8.10   A further requirement for Article 86 E.C. to apply was that it should be established whether or not the abuse of the dominant position affected intra-Community trade.[26] In this respect two approaches could be adopted, namely the structural test or the "pattern of trade" test. The outcome of these tests for replacement parts of automobile vehicles was largely dependent on what, precisely, was held to constitute abusive behaviour by the car manufacturers.

3. THE CONCEPT "DOMINANT POSITION"

(1) The relevant market concept

8.11   In order to examine whether or not one or more undertakings hold a dominant position in the sense of Article 86 E.C., as well as the role intellectual property rights thereby potentially fulfil, it needs to be established in which market this alleged dominant position occurs. This implies that both the relevant geographical and the relevant product market need to be defined. It was in particular the latter that gave rise to controversy in the spare parts cases.

(a) The relevant geographical market

8.12   Article 86 E.C. expressly states that the dominant position should relate to the Common Market or a substantial part thereof. This does not imply that an undertaking needs to hold a dominant position in more than one Member State for Article 86 E.C. to apply. The Court has consistently held that the market of one Member State may constitute a substantial part of the Common Market in the sense of Article 86 E.C.[27] The debate in the spare parts cases did not deal with the definition of the relevant geographical market. Veng's statement that the relevant geographical market in the *Volvo* case was constituted by the United Kingdom market does not seem to have been challenged.[28]

---

[25] See *infra*, at pt. 4(4).

[26] See *infra*, at pt. 5.

[27] See, for instance, Case 322/81, *Michelin v. Commission*, Judgment of November 9, 1983: [1983] E.C.R. 3461; [1985] 1 C.M.L.R. 282, at para. 28. In the *Magill* cases, the CFI found that the relevant geographical market constituted by Ireland and Northern Ireland was a substantial part of the common market, see for instance Case T–69/89, *RTE v. Commission*, Judgment of July 10, 1991: [1991] E.C.R. II-485; [1991] 4 C.M.L.R. 586, at para. 64. See *supra*, Chap. 5, pt. 4(3).

[28] See Case 238/87: [1988] E.C.R. 6211, Report of the Hearing, at 6216.

(b) The relevant product market

(i) The concept

The Court has consistently given the following interpretation of the concept   **8.13**
of "relevant product market" in the sense of Article 86:

> "... for the purposes of investigating the possibly dominant position of
> an undertaking on a given market, the possibilities of competition must
> be judged in the context of the market comprising the totality of the prod-
> ucts which, with respect to their characteristics, are particularly suitable
> for satisfying constant needs and are only to a limited extent interchange-
> able with other products".[29]

As Frazer points out, the relevant product market concept thus refers to
those products that "form part of a group with characteristics which separate
them in an economically sensible way from all other products".[30] This implies
that they are necessarily interchangeable, but not necessarily homogeneous,
and are not substantially interchangeable with products outside the group.

(ii) The criteria

The Court has upheld different criteria to determine the relevant product mar-   **8.14**
ket.[31] One criterion is the substitutability of the products on the demand-side,
thus interchangeability from the consumers' point of view.[32] The extent to
which consumers consider products to be interchangeable is often determined
through the use of the cross-elasticity test. In other words, regard is had to the
willingness of consumers to turn to another product if the price is increased,
although this might be dependent on a time-factor.[33] Another criterion, which
is sometimes used in addition to the first,[34] is the substitutability of the products on the supply side. This test implies that due regard should be given to

---

[29] Case 322/81: [1983] E.C.R. 3461; [1985] 1 C.M.L.R. 282, at para. 37. See, for instance, also
Case 31/80, *L'Oréal v. De Nieuwe AMCK*, Judgment of December 11, 1980; [1980] E.C.R.
3775; [1981] 2 C.M.L.R. 235, at para. 25.

[30] See T. Frazer, *Monopoly, competition and the law: The regulation of business activity in
Britain, Europe and America* (1988, Wheatsheaf Books), pp. 14–15.

[31] There are numerous articles that give an analysis of the criteria used by the Court, see for
instance F. Fishwick, "Definition of monopoly power in the antitrust policies of the United
Kingdom and the European Community" [1989] Antitrust Bull. 451; L. Gyselen, N. Kyriazis,
"Article 86 EEC: the monopoly power measurements issue revisited" (1986) 11 E.L.Rev. 134.

[32] See for instance Case 85/76, *Hoffman-La Roche v. Commission*, Judgment of February 13,
1979: [1979] E.C.R. 461; [1979] 3 C.M.L.R. 211; Case 27/76, *United Brands v. Commission*,
Judgment of February 14, 1978: [1978] E.C.R. 207; [1978] 1 C.M.L.R. 429.

[33] See for instance Case 27/76: [1978] E.C.R. 207; [1978] 1 C.M.L.R. 429, at paras. 34 and 35,
where the Court made the following, by now famous, statement: "It follows from all these
considerations that a very large number of consumers having a constant need for bananas are
not noticeably or even appreciably enticed away from the consumption of this product by the
arrival of other fresh fruit on the market and that even the personal peak periods only affect it
for a limited period of time and to a very limited extent from the point of view of
substitutability. Consequently the banana market is a market which is sufficiently distinct from
the other fresh fruit market".

[34] See for instance Case 322/81: [1983] E.C.R. 3461; [1985] 1 C.M.L.R. 282, especially at para.
37 where the Court held: "... an examination limited to the objective characteristics of the
relevant products cannot be sufficient: the competitive conditions and the structure of supply
and demand on the market must also be taken into consideration." The Court found that there
was neither interchangeability between car tyres and tyres for heavy vehicles from the demand
side, nor cross-elasticity on the supply-side.

entry barriers, such as intellectual property rights, which may prohibit potential competitors entering the market.[35]

(2) The relevant product market for spare parts of cars

8.15 It is apparent that the wider the definition of the product market, the less it is probable that a dominant position will be held to exist, and vice versa.[36] The definition of the relevant product market was, therefore, a crucial issue for the review under Article 86 E.C. in the spare parts cases. Consumer interests, and especially consumer demand, played a crucial role in the arguments of both sides. According to the car manufacturers, replacement parts cannot be considered as being separate from the market in new cars because they offer a "package deal" to their customers. So they argued that the market in the complex products and their components should be regarded as one and the same. This view was countered by the independent manufacturers who claimed that the market in replacement parts responds to needs different to the market in new vehicles. The latter therefore maintained that there are separate markets in replacement parts specific to each brand of car.

(a) One global market for cars and spare parts

(i) The "package deal" approach

8.16 The relevant product market is not the market in replacement parts, according to the car manufacturers. Rather, it covers the highly competitive market in cars and/or maintenance and repair work. The argument goes that the consumer takes the price of spare parts and repair work into account when purchasing a car so that he does not envisage the replacement parts as constituting a separate market in which interchangeable products should be offered and competition should prevail.[37] This viewpoint is based on the concept of the car manufacturers that they offer a "package" to the potential purchaser of a car which consists not only of the new car but also of pre-sales, and especially after-sales, services such as guarantee and repair work. They therefore assume that the buyer of a new car has properly evaluated and also adhered to this package deal through the act of purchasing a car of a given brand rather than another, and will in the future purchase a car of a different brand if this package proves inadequate or excessively expensive. This package theory is also

---

[35] See for instance Case 6/72: [1973] E.C.R. 215; [1973] C.M.L.R. 199, especially at para. 33 where the Court held: "In order to be regarded as constituting a distinct market, the products in question must be individualised, not only by the mere fact that they are used for packing certain products, but by particular characteristics of production which make them specifically suitable for this purpose. Consequently, a dominant position on the market for light metal containers for meat and fish cannot be decisive, as long as it has not been proved that competitors from other sectors of the market for light metal containers are not in a position to enter this market, by simple adaptation, with sufficient strength to create a serious counterweight."

[36] Similarly, see G. Friden, "Recent developments in EEC intellectual property law: the distinction between existence and exercise revisited" (1989) 26 C.M.L.Rev. 193 at 209.

[37] This view is shared, for instance, by Bonet. See G. Bonet, "*Les créations d'esthétique industrielle au regard des règles de libre circulation et de libre concurrence dans le Marché Comun*", in *La protection des créations d'esthétique industrielle dans le cadre de la CEE: objectif 1992* (1988, CUERPI), pp. 45–64 at pp. 61–62.

invoked to justify the strategy of passing on production costs from the car to the captive replacement parts in order to keep the prices of new vehicles down and thus to enhance the competitive position of European car manufacturers.[38]

There seems to be a serious flaw in this reasoning. If the premise is that the potential purchasers can, and do, evaluate the price they will eventually pay for the whole package of any given brand then, surely, decreasing the price of the new cars and subsequently recovering production costs on the spare parts would not enhance sales of new cars. The problem is that it is impossible to know, when buying a car, how much the total package will cost. When purchasing a new car the alert consumer might take into account the estimated cost of captive replacement parts for the number of years he intends to use the car to determine the price he is willing to pay for the car. But he does not know with certainty how much the replacement parts will cost at the time the repair is needed. Also, he cannot possibly foresee how often he will need to replace a part due to either accident or breakdown, nor which parts he will need to replace. It is therefore submitted that the strategy of the car manufacturers which consists of charging competitive prices for the first sale, *i.e.* the car, and higher prices for the spare parts later on, is based on the understanding that the average consumer does not think of, and anyhow cannot possibly calculate, the cost of replacing parts when buying the car. The latter will therefore be tempted by the price/quality ratio of the car itself. In the absence of competition, monopoly prices could thus be charged to every buyer of spare parts later on. In so far as this tie-in is concerned, the interests of consumers and car manufacturers are apparently in conflict.[39]

(ii) Interchangeability on demand-side

It seems that this strategy is further based on the understanding that most car **8.17**
owners intend to keep the car running for several years. Due to the substantial price difference between the car and the spare parts, at least a majority of the consumers do not consider the purchase of a new car, which constitutes a considerable investment, to be a viable alternative to repairing a relatively new car. Having regard to the price of a new car, it is clear that the prices for spare parts would have to be raised very substantially in order to make repairs economically unjustifiable in comparison to the market value of a relatively new car.[40] It may therefore be inferred from the very idea of a package deal that the car manufacturers impliedly acknowledge the fact that the purchase of a new car is not an overall viable alternative to repairing the car. This means

---

[38] See *supra*, Chap. 7, pt. 6(3)(a).

[39] See also T. Scharpe, "Comments on Christian Joerges' paper on selective distribution in the car sector" in *EC competition policy and the consumer interest* (M. Goyens ed. 1985) (Bruylant), pp. 249–263 at p. 261, where he illustrates by reference to motor spare parts that the neo-classical theory that a monopoly price can only be charged once so that a tie-in is unexceptional does not necessarily hold true. He concludes: "Radical uncertainty about the cost of running a motor car exist; consumers can therefore be exploited [...] The tie-in serves to increase the manufacturers' profits."

[40] However, see *supra*, Chap. 7, pt. 6(3)(b), where it is held that substantially raising the price of spare parts might be a means of prematurely eliminating older types of vehicles, with a low market value, from the market in favour of the purchase of new vehicles.

that spare parts cannot be substituted by cars so far as the average consumer is concerned, and should therefore constitute a separate market for the purpose of examination under Article 86 E.C.

8.18   It is submitted in this respect that the spare parts issue is fundamentally different from the *Alsatel v. Novasam* case. In the latter, the Court held the relevant market to be the domestic market in telephone installations in general and not the separate market in the rental and maintenance of telephone equipment as the Commission maintained.[41] The Court came to this conclusion on the grounds that the consumer had the initial choice between either a rental and maintenance contract or the purchasing of the same equipment, so that these options could be considered to be interchangeable. This outweighed the fact that consumers who had initially opted for a rental and maintenance contract were subsequently dependent for the duration of the contract. The main difference to the spare parts issue is that the matters of maintenance and repairs in the car sector are not linked to a rental contract (which does not confer ownership) but to the purchase of the car. Under the package theory the customer does not necessarily choose to be but is, nevertheless, tied in in respect of the subsequent purchase of spare parts. That a consumer who wants to buy a motorised vehicle does not have this initial choice between having repairs and maintenance carried out, or not, is a typical feature of a complex consumer durable. He initially buys the complex product and is subsequently dependent on repair and maintenance in order to keep the complex product functioning.

The Court had held in the *Hugin* case[42] that in order to establish the relevant market for components of complex products it has to be established whether there are alternatives for their repair and maintenance from the consumers' point of view.[43] As seen before, the purchase of a new car is not, overall, interchangeable with repair and maintenance so that the after-sales market and in particular the market in replacement parts is to be considered as a market distinct from the market in motorvehicles.

(iii) Consumer needs and demand

8.19   The second major flaw in the definition of the relevant product market on the basis of the package theory, is that it does not take the necessities and demands of different categories of consumers into account in terms of income and social stratification. It is certain that the package deal would cost relatively

---

[41] Case 247/86, *Alsatel v. Novasam*, Judgment of October 5, 1988: [1988] E.C.R. 5987; [1990] 4 C.M.L.R. 434, at para. 17.

[42] Case 22/78, *Hugin v. Commission*, Judgment of May 31, 1979: [1979] E.C.R. 1869; [1979] 3 C.M.L.R. 345. See *infra*, at pt. (b)(ii).

[43] Korah seemingly failed to acknowledge the significance of the difference between the "maintenance" factor in the choice between rental/maintenance or sale, on the one hand, and the compulsory relationship between the complex product and its components/maintenance, on the other. She wrote that in the *Alsatel v. Novasam* case, "the Community Court considered at paragraph 17 that the relevant market should include sale as well as hire. This contradicts the *Hugin* judgment, as those who had already hired Alsatel equipment remained dependent on it, even if new users could buy telephone equipment elsewhere". See V. Korah, "No duty to license independent repairers to make spare parts: the *Renault*, *Volvo* and *Bayer & Hennecke* cases" [1988] E.I.P.R. 381 at 382, n. 8.

less to those consumers that regularly replace their cars as compared to users of older cars. In a way it could even be said that the price of their new car would be subsidised by the repairs effected by the users of older vehicles as, naturally, the latter break down more often. The package deal would even be less tenable when taking solely the interests of owners of second-hand cars into consideration because they would pay the higher price for spare parts without benefiting from the corresponding decrease in the price for the vehicle. In other words, including after-sales services in a package deal and eliminating competition with regard to spare parts would definitely not respond to the needs and demand of a substantial part of consumers.[44]

Nonetheless, it cannot be ignored that some consumers do take the availability and the quality of after-sales services into account when purchasing their cars. They might also turn to another brand if the package proves to be inadequate or excessively expensive. The question is whether the fact that the package deal offered by car manufacturers is perceived by some consumers as a good marketing strategy should imply that all consumers should therefore also be obliged to have their cars subsequently repaired in an authorised workshop. That the package theory is not universally accepted is best illustrated by the opposition from the consumers organisations, in particular the BEUC, to the inclusion of the after-sales market in the block exemption concerning selective distribution in the car sector.[45]

(iv) Findings of the Court

The Court did not expressly define the relevant product market in the spare parts cases. Prior case law indicated, however, that the Court is not inclined to readily accept the argument that the alleged fierce competition in the motor vehicle market suffices to prevent competition in related markets. For instance, the Court in the *General Motors* and *British Leyland* cases concerning type approval of motorvehicles[46] rejected the argument that the relevant product market was the one in the sales of new vehicles. To the contrary, it held that it was the separate and ancillary market in services which are in practice indispensable for dealers who wish to sell in a specific geographical area the vehicles manufactured by the said car manufacturers.[47]

8.20

---

[44] See also C. Joerges, "Selective distribution schemes in the motor-car sector: European competition policy, consumer interests and the draft regulation on the application of Article 85(3) of the Treaty to certain categories of motor-vehicle distribution and servicing agreements" in *EC competition policy and the consumer interest* (M. Goyens ed. 1985) (Bruylant), pp. 187–236 at pp. 197 where he writes: "Promotional efforts to sell new cars and encourage customers' loyalty by specialised service networks only effect a small percentage of consumers, namely those who can afford to buy new cars and/or want to avoid the hazards of the used car market. In contrast, the after-sales market must respond to the specific needs of low income consumers."

[45] See for instance the following paper by a member of the BEUC, B. Schmitz, "*Le point de vue des consommateurs*" in *Droit des consommateurs* (J. Pizzio ed. 1987) (Story Scientia), pp. 104–111, especially at pp. 109–110. Specifically on Block Exemption 123/85 for selective car distribution, see *infra*, Chap. 9, pt. 3(2).

[46] Case 26/75, *General Motors v. Commission*, Judgment of November 13, 1975: [1975] E.C.R. 1367; [1976] 1 C.M.L.R. 95; Case 226/84, *British Leyland v. Commission*, Judgment of November 11, 1986: [1986] E.C.R. 3263; [1987] 1 C.M.L.R. 184.

[47] See especially Case 226/84: [1986] E.C.R. 3263; [1987] 1 C.M.L.R. 184, at para. 5.

(b) A market in spare parts specific to a brand

(i) Rejection of the package deal

8.21   Advocate General Mischo in his opinion on both the *Maxicar* and the *Volvo* cases expressly rejected the definition of relevant product market based on the package theory. He stated:

> "There is no doubt that certain purchasers of cars, before making their choice, also obtain information as to the price of spare parts, and that factor may influence their decision. It is also certain that the owner of a vehicle of a particular shape may, when deciding to change a car, buy one of another make because the spare parts for the first car proved, in his opinion, excessively expensive. If the time factor is also taken into account, the competition prevailing in the new-car market thus also includes an element of competition regarding spare parts.
>
> The fact nevertheless remains that the owner of a vehicle who, at a given moment, decides to repair the bodywork of his vehicle rather than change model is obliged to purchase (either directly, if he repairs the car himself, or indirectly through a garage in the manufacturer's network or through an independent repairer) a body panel which is identical in shape to the original part. Consequently, *for the owners of a vehicle of a particular make the 'relevant market' is the market made up of the body panels sold by the manufacturer of the vehicle and of the components which, being copies, are capable of being substituted for them.*"[48]

This implies that for the determination of the relevant product market it does not suffice to establish whether there are substitutable goods in respect of the complex product, or whether there is a long or medium term cross-elasticity with alternative "packages" that are offered by other car manufacturers. Rather, it needs to be established that there is a specific consumer demand for spare parts of cars and examined whether bodywork components can be substituted by other products.

(ii) The Court's ruling in the *Hugin* case

8.22   This finding is fully in line with the approach taken by the Court concerning the application of Article 86 E.C. to components of complex products in the *Hugin* case.[49] The latter concerned the refusal by Hugin to supply spare parts for cash registers of its own make to independent companies. Surprisingly enough, Advocate General Mischo did not refer to this case in the car spare

---

[48] See Case 53/87: [1988] E.C.R. 6039; [1990] 4 C.M.L.R. 265, and Case 238/87: [1988] E.C.R. 6211; [1989] 4 C.M.L.R. 122, Opinion of Advocate General Mischo delivered on June 21, 1988, respectively at paras. 47–48 and 7–8 (emphasis added). On this basis, Advocate General Mischo also rejected other theoretically possible definitions of the relevant product market, such as the market in spare parts in general or the market that has grown around the manufacture and maintenance of motorvehicles.

[49] Case 22/78: [1979] E.C.R. 1869; [1979] 3 C.M.L.R. 345. On the importance of this case, see for instance J. Verstrynge, "*Het begrip 'relevante markt' in het EEG mededingingsrecht: de stand na het Hugin arrest*" [1980] S.E.W. 400.

parts cases even though it had been invoked by CICRA and Maxicar.[50] The Court in *Hugin* held that the existence of a market for Hugin spare parts at the level of independent undertakings which specialise in the maintenance and repair of cash registers, in the reconditioning of used machines, and in the sale of used machines and renting out of machines, separate from the market in cash registers was sufficient to define the relevant market as being the market in spare parts. This market was further narrowly defined as the market specifically in Hugin spare parts. The reason given for this was that those parts are not interchangeable with spare parts for cash registers of other makes, and thus are subject to a specific demand.[51]

(iii) Differences from the *Hugin* case

The *Hugin* judgment thus seems to confirm the validity of Advocate General Mischo's finding with regard to the relevant product market in the car spare parts cases. It has to be pointed out, though, that there are two important differences between the *Maxicar* and the *Volvo* cases on the one hand, and the *Hugin* case on the other hand.
    First, the structure of the supply of spare parts is not the same. Only Hugin manufactured, and was thus able to supply, the spare parts concerned in the *Hugin* case. In the car spare parts cases, independent undertakings manufactured (*Maxicar*), or wanted to manufacture under licence (*Veng*), similar spare parts so that they constituted an alternative source of supply. This is an additional argument in support of the finding that the supply of spare parts for cars is a specific market separate from the market in new cars.[52]
    Secondly, the determination of categories of potential clients, and thus the demand structure, is different. The Court had held in the *Hugin* case that considering the technical nature of cash registers, the user is not himself a purchaser of the spare parts concerned but avails himself either of Hugin after-sales services or of independent undertakings specialised in repair and maintenance work.[53] This had been criticised for at least two reasons. It was pointed out that the Court had failed to examine whether there were possible substitutes on the demand side for independent undertakings and, more importantly, had neglected the indirect demand for spare parts by owners of

8.23

---

[50] Case 53/87: [1988] E.C.R. 6039, Report of the Hearing, at 6051. See also G. Friden, *op. cit.*, p. 208, where he writes that the Advocate General "conspicuously" avoided any reference to *Hugin*. Plaisant and Daverat in 1983 advanced the contrary view that the *Hugin* case could have no bearing on the issue of spare parts exclusivity in the car sector, see R. Plaisant, G. Daverat, "*La distribution des pièces détachées pour automobiles et les lois contre les pratiques restrictives*" [1983] R.T.D.C. 147 at 169.

[51] Case 22/78: [1979] E.C.R. 1869; [1979] 3 C.M.L.R. 345, at para. 7. At para. 8, the Court unequivocally stated: "Consequently the market thus constituted by Hugin spare parts required by independent undertakings must be regarded as the relevant market for the purposes of the application of Article 86 to the facts of the case."

[52] Compare with the *Hilti* case (Case T–30/89), where the Court of First Instance held that the existence of independent producers making only Hilti-compatible nails was proof of the fact that there was a specific market for those nails. See *supra*, Chap. 5, pt. 4(b)(ii).

[53] Case 22/78: [1979] E.C.R. 1869; [1979] 3 C.M.L.R. 345, at para. 6.

Hugin cash registers.[54] This argument is not relevant to the car spare parts cases. As Advocate General Mischo in the latter cases correctly pointed out, it is indisputable that car users not only purchase spare parts indirectly through a garage in the manufacturer's network, or through an independent repairer, but also directly in order to repair cars themselves.[55] If it sufficed in the *Hugin* case that there were independent undertakings specialised in maintenance and repair work who acquired spare parts to establish that there was a separate market, then this should be all the more so if there is a specific demand for spare parts not only indirectly from consumers and directly from independent undertakings, but also from consumers directly.[56] The latter view is not incompatible with the finding of the Court in the *Hugin* judgment. In the *Hilti* appeal judgment the Court expressly followed Advocate General Jacob's opinion which clarified that:

> "...Hugin is not to be interpreted as laying down any rule to the effect that, for a separate market to exist in spare parts or other components, the purchasers of the spare parts must be distinct from the purchasers of the equipment for which they are intended."[57]

(iv) Definition with respect to a brand

8.24   It was submitted specifically with regard to bodywork components of cars that their shape is imperative to restore the car to its original appearance.[58] As in the *Hugin* case this implies that bodywork components for cars of different brands cannot be interchanged. As seen before, however, a distinction from the *Hugin* case is that there are alternative sources of supply in the market. Advocate General Mischo therefore correctly pointed out, in the car spare

---

[54] See especially C. Baden Fuller, "Article 86 EEC: Economic analysis of the existence of a dominant position" (1979) 4 E.L.Rev. 423 at 426. He points out that the independent undertakings could have shifted their activity to the repair and maintenance of other brands of cash registers, so that substitutability existed on the demand side from the point of view of independent undertakings. At p. 427, he thus puts forward the view that the Court should have defined the relevant market as "spare parts required by those who are owners of Hugin machines", which would have included, but not been limited to, those repairers of Hugin cash registers. Similarly, see also V. Korah, "Concept of a dominant position within the meaning of Article 86" (1980) 17 C.M.L.Rev. 395 at 403 where she writes: "The limitation of the demand side of the market to those who were currently buying spares, bypasses those who were most dependent on Hugin for spare parts: the shops that had bought its machines."

[55] Franceschelli, to the contrary, maintains that car owners exclusively avail themselves of the services of specialised repairers and, thus, never repair their cars themselves so that their demand for spare parts, in line with the *Hugin* case, should not be taken into account. See R. Franceschelli, "*Modelli ornamentali di parti di carrozeria di automobili ed abuso di posizione dominante*" (1988) II Riv.Dir.Ind. 175 at 183.

[56] On the specific needs and demands of car owners, and on the fact that for consumers cars are not fully interchangeable for spare parts, see also *supra*, pt. (2)(a)(i). Compare with the *Magill* cases (Cases T–76/89, T–70/89, T–69/89), where the CFI defined the relevant product market as the market in advanced weekly listings because there was a specific, constant and regular potential demand for this product. See *supra*, Chap. 5, pt. 4(3)(b)(ii).

[57] Opinion of Advocate General Jacobs delivered on November 10, 1993, at para. 18, as expressly referred to by the Court in Case C–53/92 P, *Hilti v. Commission (appeal)*, Judgment of March 2, 1994: [1994] E.C.R. I-667; [1994] 1 C.M.L.R. 590, at para. 15. On this case, see also *supra*, Chap. 5, pt. 4(2)(c).

[58] See *supra*, Chap. 7, pt. 5(3)(b)(iii).

parts cases, that the relevant product market had to be restricted to those body panels sold by the manufacturer of the vehicle *as well as copies made thereof*.[59]

The Court's ruling in the *Hugin* case had also been criticised because it defined the relevant market with respect to a brand instead of a product. It was pointed out in legal writings that the Court thus failed to consider whether alternative sources of supply, for instance copies made by independent undertakings, were feasible or whether barriers to entry such as design protection existed.[60] It is often overlooked in this respect that Advocate General Reischl in his opinion on the *Hugin* case established that there were important barriers to entry.[61] It is particularly significant that he held that it was not necessary to examine whether or not there were, in fact, legal barriers such as design rights to prevent the manufacture of competing spare parts because:

> "the impression may be gained that the existing doubts and the threat of considerable penalties make the attempts to manufacture Hugin spare parts appear too hazardous."[62]

If one could challenge whether uncertainty about the existence of design protection was a sufficient deterrent to constitute a barrier to entry in the *Hugin* case, the same would not hold true for the car spare parts cases. In the latter it was precisely the enforcement of design rights that was challenged.[63] It should be emphasised in this respect that the enforcement of design rights in the bodywork components leads to a legal monopoly through the elimination of competition from independent manufacturers of bodywork components and through constituting such a barrier to entry on the supply side.[64] After the judgments of the Court in the *Maxicar* and *Volvo* cases, which upheld these design rights under Community law, this means that the relevant market will in future most probably be restricted to the bodywork components of a given brand, as in the *Hugin* case, simply because copies will be excluded from the market.

(3) Relation between intellectual property rights and dominant position

(a) Dominant position in the absence of intellectual property rights

Having defined the relevant product market as the market in bodywork components for cars sold by the car manufacturer as well as copies thereof, the next question arising is whether the car manufacturers also occupied a dominant position on that market.

8.25

---

[59] Compare to the subsequent *Hilti* case where the CFI for similar reasons defined the relevant product market as the one in Hilti-compatible nails. See *supra*, Chap. 5, pt. 4(b)(ii).

[60] See C. Baden Fuller, *op. cit.*, p. 426 and pp. 431–432.

[61] Case 22/78: [1979] E.C.R. 1869; [1979] 3 C.M.L.R. 345, Opinion of Advocate General Reischl delivered on May 22, 1979.

[62] *id.*, at para. 2.

[63] That intellectual property rights are barriers to entry is not at all disputed by economists. To the contrary, they are held to be a classic example thereof. See, for instance, D. Price, "Abuse of a dominant position – the tale of nails, milk cartons, and TV guides" [1990] E.C.L.R. 80–90 at 85. See also V. Korah, *op. cit.*, (1988), p. 381.

[64] This was also the situation in the *Magill* cases, see also *supra*, Chap. 5, pt. 4(3).

(i) The concept

8.26   The Court has repeatedly given the following definition and explanation concerning the concept of dominant position:

> "The dominant position [. . .] relates to a position of economic strength enjoyed by an undertaking which enables it to prevent effective competition being maintained on the relevant market by affording it the power to behave independently of its competitors, its customers, and ultimately of the consumers.
>
> Such a position does not preclude some competition, which it does where there is a monopoly or a quasi-monopoly, but enables the undertaking which profits by it, if not to determine, at least to have an appreciable influence on the conditions under which that competition will develop, and in any case to act largely in disregard of it so long as such conduct does not operate to its detriment."[65]

(ii) New versus second-hand products

8.27   The issue of whether or not second-hand parts constitute an additional source of supply, which has to be taken into account to determine if a dominant position occurs, was not expressly raised in the car spare parts cases. It is interesting to point out, though, that the Court did not hold the second-hand market to be a sufficient alternative source of supply in the *Hugin* case.[66] Perhaps more importantly, the Court held in the *Michelin* case that the market in renovated tyres is but a secondary market which depends on the supply and prices of new tyres. It therefore held that the undertaking holding a dominant position in new tyres was in a privileged competitive position and could "conduct itself with greater independence on the market than would be possible for a retreading undertaking".[67] Even though this analysis specifically related to vehicle tyres, it is submitted that it most likely set the tone for the relationship between the new and the second-hand market for products under Article 86 E.C. in general.

(iii) Market in new products

8.28   Thus it needed to be established whether the car manufacturers could behave, to an appreciable extent, independently of independent manufacturers in the market for bodywork components for their cars. The Court has consistently held that very large market shares as compared with the next largest market shares of competitors, the technological lead over competitors, the existence of highly developed sales networks as well as the absence of potential competition, are relevant factors to determine the existence of a dominant position.[68] This necessarily calls for a case-by-case approach.

---

[65] Case 85/76: [1979] E.C.R. 461; [1979] 3 C.M.L.R. 211, at paras. 38 and 39. See also for instance Case 31/80: [1980] E.C.R. 3775; [1981] 2 C.M.L.R. 235, at para. 26; Case 322/81: [1983] E.C.R. 3461; [1985] 1 C.M.L.R. 282, at paras. 37 and 48.

[66] See Case 22/78: [1979] E.C.R. 1869; [1979] 3 C.M.L.R. 345, at para. 9.

[67] Case 322/81: [1983] E.C.R. 3461; [1985] 1 C.M.L.R. 282, at para. 51.

[68] See, for instance, Case 85/76: [1979] E.C.R. 461; [1979] 3 C.M.L.R. 211, at para. 48. For an analysis of the Court's approach, see V. Korah, "Concept of a dominant position within the meaning of Article 86" (1980) 17 C.M.L.Rev. 395.

It was argued in the *Maxicar* case that Renault held a market share of about 80–85 per cent in respect of body panels.[69] Neither the Commission nor the Advocate General had any difficulty in finding that, even disregarding the additional economic strength conferred by design protection, the car manufacturers occupied a dominant position in the relevant market. This was held to be the case because the existence and reputation of the manufacturers' close-knit selective distribution network as compared with the lesser known products and locations of independent manufacturers,[70] and especially the car manufacturers' system of guarantee which is dependent on the use of original parts,[71] induce consumers to obtain spare parts supplied by the car manufacturer rather than spurious parts. This entails a large market share in bodywork components for the car manufacturers.

(b) The impact of intellectual property rights on the dominant position

It is logical that if the car manufacturers already occupy a dominant position in the market for bodywork components for their cars without design protection this will be all the more so when design protection, which confers market power, is obtained and enforced. The question is, nevertheless, whether there is a relationship between the enforcement of intellectual property rights and the finding of a dominant position.

8.29

(i) The basic rule

As seen previously, the Court has consistently held that the mere enforcement of intellectual property rights to exclude competitors from the market is not necessarily tantamount to conferring a dominant position in the sense of Article 86 E.C.[72] Conversely, the Court has never stated that intellectual property protection is an obstacle to establishing a dominant position.[73] It therefore seems that the enforcement of intellectual property rights may, in certain circumstances, contribute to the finding of a dominant position.

8.30

---

[69] Case 53/87: [1988] E.C.R. 6039, Report of the Hearing, at 6044.

[70] See especially the Opinion of Advocate General Mischo on Case 238/87: [1988] E.C.R. 6211; [1989] 4 C.M.L.R. 122, at para. 11 and on Case 53/87: [1988] E.C.R. 6039; [1990] 4 C.M.L.R. 265, at para. 51, where he held that the parts produced by independent manufacturers "do not enjoy the prestige associated with the 'original part' label and the places where they can be obtained are less known". For an analysis of market power as conferred by a strong established brand, see N. Parr, M. Hughes, "The relevance of consumer brands and advertising in competition inquiries" [1993] E.C.L.R. 157. In n. 35, they point out that "even if consumers loyalty and advertising do not create barriers to entry *per se*, they may do so combined with barriers at the manufacturing and/or distribution level". On the impact of the selective distribution network on the spare parts market, see also *infra*, Chap. 9, pt. 3(2)(d).

[71] See, for instance, the arguments of the Commission in the *Maxicar* case, Case 53/87: [1988] E.C.R. 6039, Report of the Hearing, at 6052–6053. See also the Opinion of Advocate General Mischo on Case 238/87: [1988] E.C.R. 6211; [1989] 4 C.M.L.R. 122, at para. 11 and in Case 53/87: [1988] E.C.R. 6039; [1990] 4 C.M.L.R. 265, at para. 51, where he held that "at a time when manufacturers offer anti-rust guarantees of up to six years, that fact is not without significance".

[72] See for instance Case 40/70, *Sirena v. Eda*, Judgment of February 18, 1971: [1971] E.C.R. 69; [1971] C.M.L.R. 260, at para. 16. See *supra*, Chap. 5, pt. 2(3)(a).

[73] See also the ruling of the CFI and the Court in the subsequent *Magill* cases, *supra*, Chap. 5, pt. 4(3)(b), where a similar issue was raised.

(ii) Exclusivity conferred by national law

8.31   The Court has consistently held, concerning Article 86 E.C. in general, that:

> "The fact that the absence of competition or its restriction on the relevant market is brought about or encouraged by provisions laid down by national law in no way precludes the application of Article 86."[74]

With regard to intellectual property rights in particular, the Court has clarified that it is necessary to examine whether the intellectual property owner can impede the maintenance of effective competition in a substantial part of the relevant market.[75] This means that intellectual property rights are neither an indication of, nor an obstacle to, the finding of a dominant position. But this does not imply that the enforcement of intellectual property rights may not influence the finding of a dominant position. This is best illustrated by the *Magill* cases, in which the plaintiffs were held to be in a dominant position not because of, but rather as a consequence of, their copyright on advance weekly listings of TV programmes.[76]

(iii) Intellectual property rights and position of economic strength

8.32   The enforcement of intellectual property rights in most cases does not significantly affect the definition of the relevant product market. Competitors are not necessarily excluded from the market so that the opportunity to manufacture interchangeable products remains. This is typical for those intellectual property rights whose objective is not so much to confer an exclusive right on a product, but merely on the form in which an idea is expressed (copyright),[77] or on the shape or configuration of an industrial product (design rights),[78] or on the use of distinctive signs (trade marks).[79] This means that the enforcement of those intellectual property rights will not automatically entail the finding of a dominant position. That will depend on the extent to which the intellectual property owner can also prevent the maintenance of effective competition in the relevant market. Take, for instance, design protection on cars or on spare parts the shape of which is not imperative to restore the car to

---

[74] Case 311/84, *Telemarketing*, Judgment of October 3, 1985: [1985] E.C.R. 3261; [1986] 2 C.M.L.R. 558, at para. 16. On the applicability of Article 86 E.C. to monopolies conferred by national law other than intellectual property rights, see C.-D. Ehlermann, "Managing monopolies: the role of the State in controlling market dominance in the European Community" [1993] E.C.L.R. 61.

[75] See, for instance, Case 78/70, *Deutsche Grammophon Gesellschaft*, Judgment of June 8, 1971: [1971] E.C.R. 487; [1971] C.M.L.R. 631, at para. 17. Case 51/75, *EMI v. CBS*, Judgment of June 15, 1976: [1976] E.C.R. 811; [1976] 2 C.M.L.R. 235, at para. 36. See also *supra*, Chap. 5, pt. 2(3)(b).

[76] See *supra*, Chap. 5, pt. 4(3).

[77] See *supra*, Chap. 2, pt. 3(3). See also I. Forrester, "Software licensing in the light of current E.C. competition law considerations" [1992] E.C.L.R. 5 at 5–6. At p. 6, he points out that when the expression and the idea merge, the merger doctrine is applicable which implies that copyright cannot be enforced against unauthorised use by others.

[78] See *supra*, Chap. 2, pt. 3(5).

[79] See *supra*, Chap. 2, pt. 3(4). In this sense, it is submitted that Subiotto was not accurate in maintaining that copyright and design rights confer temporary exclusive rights on a product, although it is correct that the Court has interpreted intellectual property rights in this way. See R. Subiotto, *op. cit.*, p. 237.

its original function or appearance. To assess the impact of the design rights on the establishment of a dominant position, one needs to consider to what extent the exclusive right confers additional economic strength upon the intellectual property owner in comparison to his competitors.

There are nevertheless other, and it is submitted exceptional, cases in which the enforcement of intellectual property rights fundamentally affects the definition of the relevant market. This will be so if an exclusive right is granted in relation to a product for which no non-infringing substitutes exist. In other words, the conferring of an intellectual property right in those cases comes down to the grant of a legal monopoly in the relevant market because all competitors can be lawfully excluded. This is a situation which is most likely to occur with regard to patents as the objective of the latter is to confer an exclusive right on a new product or process. It should nevertheless be emphasised that the finding of a monopoly position in relation to patents is not quasi-automatic. This is subject to the existence, or possible entry, of other products into the market that could be used for the same purpose and are regarded as being interchangeable by the consumers.[80]

(iv) Peculiarity of the *Magill* and spare parts cases

The Court had been confronted with these two straightforward types of intellectual property cases under Article 86 E.C. prior to the *Maxicar* and *Volvo* cases. The peculiarity of the car spare parts cases, as with the *Magill* cases, lies in the fact that they concerned intellectual property rights which belonged in the first group mentioned above, but contained features detrimental to competition typical of the second group.

8.33

It should be recalled that in the *Magill* cases the grant and enforcement of copyright in facts, namely weekly advance listings for TV programmes, led to the finding of a monopoly position by the copyright holders in the relevant product market. The latter was restrictively defined as the market in their own listings because these could not be substituted by other information in so far as the final consumers were concerned. It was submitted above that this was the consequence of granting copyright in mere facts, rather than in the form in which an idea is expressed which is the objective of copyright.[81]

It was similarly pointed out previously that the enforcement of design rights in bodywork components of cars, the shape of which is considered by consumers to be imperative in order to restore the car to its original appearance, will necessarily lead to the exclusion of competitors from the market. The relevant market will therefore, in future, be restricted to the bodywork components of a given brand simply because interchangeable copies will be excluded from the market.[82] As both the Commission and Advocate General Mischo impliedly acknowledged, this means that the enforcement of design rights in bodywork components of cars implies a shift from a mere dominant position for the car manufacturers to a monopoly position. In the words of Advocate General Mischo:

[80] See also *supra*, Chap. 2, pt. 3(2).
[81] See *supra*, Chap. 5, pt. 4(3).
[82] See *supra*, pt. (2)(b)(iv).

> "...in the present case, the industrial property rights relate to body pan-
> els for a motor vehicle and the only products which can be substituted for
> them are products having exactly the same shape as the parts produced
> by the manufacturer. As the Commission rightly pointed out, in the cir-
> cumstances of this case no substitutable goods exist which do not
> encroach upon the registered rights of the manufacturer. Accordingly, as
> soon as the proprietor exercises his rights deriving from his registered
> design and substitutable parts can no longer be produced, there is no
> doubt that the manufacturer holds a dominant position in the market in
> the spare parts for which he registered his design and which is, in the last
> analysis, the 'relevant market' in the present case."[83]

Also in this case the monopoly position was clearly the consequence of the
grant and subsequent enforcement of design rights in a product which could
not be substituted by others, rather than on a shape or configuration which is
the objective of design rights.

In other words, the *Maxicar*, *Volvo* and *Magill* cases had in common that
exclusive rights were granted and enforced on a product in disregard of the
essential functions of copyright and design rights respectively. It could therefore be said that it was the abuse of intellectual property rights in terms of their
function that necessarily entailed the finding not only of a dominant, but even
a monopoly, position in the relevant market.

(v) Approach adopted by the Court

8.34 The Court did not expressly state that the car manufacturers occupied a dominant position in the spare parts cases, although this could be inferred from the
judgment. Neither did it offer any guidance as to how the relevant market for
components of complex products, such as bodywork components for cars,
should be determined. Instead, the Court answered the crucial questions
posed by the national courts. In the *Maxicar* case this was whether obtaining
and subsequently enforcing exclusive design rights in bodywork components
of cars amounted to an abusive way of eliminating competition; in the *Volvo*
case whether the refusal to license the design right on reasonable terms
amounted to an abuse of a dominant position.[84]

4. THE "ABUSE" OF A DOMINANT POSITION

(1) Use, misuse and abuse of intellectual property rights

8.35 The Court has consistently held that the "normal" exercise of an intellectual
property right which is lawful under Article 36 E.C. is not contrary to Article
86 E.C. if the exclusive right has not been used as an instrument for the abuse
of such a position.[85] This would seem to imply that the examination under

[83] Opinion of Advocate General Mischo on Case 238/87: [1988] E.C.R. 6211; [1989] 4 C.M.L.R.
122, at para. 14. See also his opinion on Case 53/87: [1988] E.C.R. 6039; [1990] 4 C.M.L.R.
265, at para. 54.
[84] See also *supra*, at pt. 2(1).
[85] Case 102/77, *Hoffmann-La Roche*, see *supra*, Chap. 5, pt. 2(3)(c).

Article 86 E.C. is dependent on prior examination under Article 36 E.C. It was shown above that having regard to its prior case law, the Court in the *Maxicar* case could, under Article 36 E.C., choose between either upholding design rights in bodywork components of cars or to declare them to be incompatible with Community law.[86] In this respect it was submitted that the intellectual property rights could have been held not to be in accordance with the inherent function of design rights. The conclusion could therefore have been that there was a "misuse" of intellectual property rights because the contested practice was difficult to justify in terms of the need to safeguard the protection of industrial and commercial property in the sense of Article 36 E.C.[87] It is apparent that under the latter approach the question of the compatibility of the enforcement of design rights in bodywork components with Article 86 E.C. would have become superfluous. The reason for this is that the potential detrimental effects resulting from the monopoly position on the competitive market structure in general, and for the consumers in particular, would not have occurred.[88]

The Court, however, did not adopt the justification test in the *Maxicar* case. It held that the grant and enforcement of design rights in bodywork components of cars was compatible with Article 36 E.C. This means that it needed to be established whether, and to what extent, the detrimental effects that are likely to occur may be curtailed under Article 86 E.C. In other words, the question arose of when the enforcement of intellectual property rights in components of complex products by an undertaking holding a dominant position on the market would be held to be abusive.

(2) The concept of "abuse"

The Court has consistently given the following definition of the concept of "abuse": **8.36**

> "The concept of abuse is an objective concept relating to the behaviour of an undertaking in a dominant position which is such as to influence the structure of a market where, as a result of the very presence of the undertaking in question, the degree of competition is weakened and through recourse to methods which, different from those which condition normal competition in products or services on the basis of transactions of commercial operators, has the effect of hindering the maintenance of the degree of competition still existing in the market or the growth of that competition."[89]

---

[86] See *supra*, Chap. 7, pt. 4.
[87] See *supra*, Chap. 7, pt. 5(3).
[88] See also *supra*, Chap. 7, pt. 6(3)(c).
[89] Case C–62/86, *Akzo v. Commission*, Judgment of July 3, 1991, [1991] E.C.R. I-3359; [1993] 5 C.M.L.R. 215, at para. 69. On the Commission's approach in this case, which stressed the importance of maintaining a competitive market structure, see P. Smith, "The Wolf in Wolf's clothing: the problem with predatory pricing" (1989) 14 E.L.Rev. 209. On the relationship between abusive behaviour and dominant position, see P. Vogelenzang, "Abuse of a dominant position in Article 86: the problem of causality and some applications" (1976) 13 C.M.L.Rev. 61.

Furthermore, the Court expressly acknowledged in the *AKZO* case that the elimination of competitors "by using methods other than those which come within the scope of competition on the basis of quality" is prohibited by Article 86 E.C.[90]

(3) Abusive behaviour by intellectual property owners

(a) The basic rule

8.37   The enforcement of intellectual property rights is particularly apt to affect the competitive market structure because third parties may be excluded from a part of the market to which they would have free access in the absence of intellectual property protection.[91] It has already been pointed out in this respect that if the exercise of the exclusive right is covered by the specific sub-ject-matter of the intellectual property right, the behaviour will not be auto-matically lawful or unlawful under the rules on competition. Rather, an additional element will be needed to hold that the intellectual property owner has made a use of his intellectual property right which amounts to an abuse of a dominant position under Article 86 E.C.[92] It should be recalled that the Court held in the car spare parts cases that the very subject-matter of design rights is constituted by "the right of the proprietor of a protected design to prevent third parties from manufacturing and selling or importing, without its consent, products incorporating the design".[93] It is therefore important to examine which "additional element" to the normal use of design rights in the sense Article 36 E.C. is needed for it to be held that there has been an abusive behaviour by the car manufacturers under Article 86 E.C.[94]

It is interesting to recall the Court of First Instance's judgment in the *Tetra Pak* case in this respect.[95] The CFI held that the acquisition of an exclusive patent licence from a competing firm by an undertaking which already occu-pied a dominant position in that market amounted to an abuse.[96] Although the CFI acknowledged that an additional element to the acquisition of the patent licence was needed to establish abusive behaviour, it held that this additional element lay in the detrimental effect of the latter on the competitive

---

[90] Case C–62/86: [1991] E.C.R. I-3359; [1993] 5 C.M.L.R. 215, at para. 70. On the abusive behaviour through the elimination of competition, see for instance also Joined Cases 6 and 7/73, *Commercial Solvents*, Judgment of March 6, 1974: [1974] E.C.R. 223; [1974] 1 C.M.L.R. 309, at para. 25. On this case, see J. Bentil, "Control of abuse of monopoly power in EEC business law: a commentary on the *Commercial Solvents* case" (1975) 12 C.M.L.Rev. 59.

[91] See also *supra*, Chap. 2, pt. 2(1).

[92] On the need for an additional element, see also *supra*, Chap. 5, pt. 2(3)(c).

[93] See, for instance, Case 238/87: [1988] E.C.R. 6211; [1989] 4 C.M.L.R. 122, at para. 8. See also *supra*, Chap. 4, pt. 2(4)(c) and Chap. 7, pt. 4(4).

[94] See also Advocate General Mischo, who wrote that the mere acquisition and exercise of intellectual property rights do not constitute an abuse of a dominant position but that "a further element is required". See his opinion on Case 53/87: [1988] E.C.R. 6039; [1990] 4 C.M.L.R. 265, at para. 59. And on Case 238/87: [1988] E.C.R. 6211; [1989] 4 C.M.L.R. 122, at para. 21.

[95] Case T–51/89, *Tetra Pak Rausing SA v. Commission*, Judgment of July 10, 1990: [1990] E.C.R. II-309; [1991] 4 C.M.L.R. 334.

[96] See *supra*, Chap. 5, pt. 5(3)(b).

market structure because consequently all competition was eliminated.[97] As in the *Magill* cases, the question arose in the car spare parts cases of whether a similar reasoning could be applied if the undertaking alleged to abuse its dominant position is not a licensee but the owner of the exclusive intellectual property right.

(b) Abuse in relation to the function of intellectual property rights

The Italian court pointed out that all competition was eliminated through the **8.38** grant and subsequent enforcement of design rights in bodywork components of cars. Because, in its view, this appeared to be contrary to the function of design rights it assumed that the latter could be a sufficient additional element to establish abusive behaviour under Article 86 E.C.[98]

(i) Underlying rationale

The Italian court's question was most likely based on the understanding that a **8.39** balance needed to be maintained between conflicting legitimate objectives of both Community competition rules and national design rights. The competition rules are aimed at safeguarding an effective competitive structure in the Common Market.[99] Intellectual property rights on the other hand confer temporary exclusive rights and are thus apt to affect the latter. It is therefore necessary to determine how these two potentially conflicting systems of rules should interact.[1] It was submitted before that a possible approach could consist in examining whether the restraint on competition posed by the enforcement of intellectual property rights is in accordance with the objective for which those exclusive rights are granted or whether, to the contrary, the system of intellectual property rights is (ab)used to gain undue market power.[2] It was pointed out in this respect that the use of design rights in accordance with their function does not exclude competitors from the market[3] and should thus be upheld under the rules on competition. Conversely the use of design rights, which clearly exceed their function in that they confer a monopoly on a product and in this specific case moreover tie in consumers in the after-sales market for cars, clearly affects the competitive structure in a way which is not intended by design law and should thus be struck down under the rules on competition.

(ii) An example: the *Magill* cases

The latter was also the approach taken by the Court of First Instance in the **8.40** *Magill* cases.[4] It is significant in this respect that even though the European

---

[97] On this issue, see J. Daltrop, J. Ferry, "The relationship between Articles 85 and 86: *Tetra Pak* (T–51/89)" [1991] E.I.P.R. 31; H. James, "*Tetra Pak*: exemption and abuse of dominant position" [1990] E.C.L.R. 267. At p. 269, she writes: "an interesting feature of the judgment is an emerging principle whereby a dominant undertaking has a special responsibility not to allow its conduct to impair genuine competition."

[98] Case 53/87: [1988] E.C.R. 6039, Report of the Hearing, at 6041–6042.

[99] Case 6/72: [1973] E.C.R. 215; [1973] C.M.L.R. 199, see *supra*, pt. 1.

[1] On the patent-antitrust debate, see also *supra*, Chap. 2, pt. 3(2).

[2] On the functionality test as applied to the rules on competition, see *supra*, Chap. 3, pt. 4(2)(c).

[3] On the inherent function of design rights, see *supra*, Chap. 2, pt. 3(5) and Chap. 7, pt. 5(3).

[4] See *supra*, Chap. 5, pt. 4(3)(b).

Court of Justice on appeal did not expressly reiterate the findings of the CFI in terms of the function of intellectual property rights, it fully upheld the judgment by the latter.[5] The CFI held, in essence, that the behaviour by copyright holders which consisted in invoking their exclusive right to prohibit others from producing a new product for which there was a potential consumer demand in an ancillary market, exceeded the function of copyright and was therefore contrary to Article 86 E.C. Or in other words, the exercise of copyright in a manner which did not correspond to its essential function was held to amount to an abusive exercise which was "manifestly" contrary to Article 86 E.C.[6]

(c) Abuse in relation to the specific subject-matter of intellectual property rights

8.41 A major problem in applying a similar justification test under Article 86 E.C. in the earlier car spare parts cases lay in the fact that the Court did not apply the justification approach under Article 36 E.C.[7] It is therefore not surprising that the need to safeguard the function of design rights was equally disregarded under the rules on competition. Instead, the Court adopted what could be called the specific subject-matter approach.

(i) Specific subject-matter approach

8.42 It is significant that the Court in the *Volvo* case, which merely concerned Article 86 E.C., first of all reiterated its findings under Article 36 E.C. in the *Maxicar* case.[8] In particular, it was recalled that the existence of design rights is a matter for the national legislator whereas the exercise of design rights, which consists in prohibiting the unauthorised use of protected designs, comes under the specific subject-matter of design rights.[9]

— Refusal to license

8.43 A fundamental question, which was also of crucial importance in the subsequent *Magill* cases, was whether or not the refusal to grant a licence on reasonable terms was in accordance with the specific subject-matter of intellectual property rights. Advocate General Mischo pointed out in this respect that the Court had already held in the *Pharmon v. Hoechst* case that to prohibit the importation of goods marketed under compulsory licences, regardless of whether a reasonable royalty was paid, would deprive the proprietor of

---

[5] See *supra*, Chap. 5, pt. 4(3)(c).
[6] See also J. Smith, "Television guides: the European Court doesn't know 'there's so much in it'", [1992] E.C.L.R. 135 at 137, where he points out that the CFI considered the use of copyright as a tool of abuse under Article 86 E.C.
[7] On the need for the elaboration of a coherent "functionality test" under both Articles 36 and 86 EEC, see also *supra*, Chap. 3, pt. 4(2)(c).
[8] For an analysis of the Court's approach under Article 36 E.C. in the *Maxicar* case, see *supra*, Chap. 7, pt. 4(4).
[9] Case 238/87: [1988] E.C.R. 6211; [1989] 4 C.M.L.R. 122, at paras. 7 and 8.

the substance of his right.[10] The Court subsequently held in the *Volvo* case that:

> "It follows that an obligation imposed upon the proprietor of a protected design to grant third parties, even in return for a reasonable royalty, a licence for the supply of products incorporating the design would lead to the proprietor thereof being deprived of the substance of his exclusive right, and that a refusal to grant such a licence cannot in itself constitute an abuse of a dominant position."[11]

—Enforcement of intellectual property rights to eliminate competition

In line with Advocate General Mischo's approach,[12] the Court in the car spare parts cases did not consider the possible abuse of design rights, in the sense that their function was exceeded, to be relevant for the findings under Article 86 E.C. This is clearly illustrated by the following statement in the *Maxicar* judgment:

8.44

> "It should be noted from the outset that the mere fact of securing the benefit of an exclusive right granted by law, the effect of which is to enable the manufacture and sale of protected products by unauthorised third parties to be prevented, cannot be regarded as an abusive method of eliminating competition."[13]

The result of this approach is that the Court, in principle, accepted that through the use of design rights the competitive structure in the after-sales market for bodywork components could be appreciably altered in the sense that all competition could be eliminated and a legal monopoly position conferred on the car manufacturers. Consequently, this entailed that consumers could be tied-in with all the potential negative consequences for car owners as explained above.[14]

—Comparison with the *Magill* cases

The approach adopted in the car spare parts cases stands in sharp contrast to the approach adopted by the Court in the subsequent *Magill* appeal judgment: this in spite of the fact that the Court in the latter expressly referred to the first, and that in both the existence/exercise dichotomy was reiterated.[15]

8.45

---

[10] On the reasoning of the Advocate General, Case 238/87: [1988] E.C.R. 6211; [1989] 4 C.M.L.R. 122, especially at para. 22–27. For an analysis of the *Pharmon v. Hoechst* case (Case 19/84), which concerned the effect of compulsory licences on the principle of exhaustion, see *supra*, Chap. 6, pt. 2(4).

[11] Case 238/87: [1988] E.C.R. 6211; [1989] 4 C.M.L.R. 122, at para. 8. It is interesting to note that the Commission, in the *Maxicar* case, "wondered" whether the refusal to grant licences might not be held to be contrary to Article 86 E.C., so that not all competition in the spare parts market would be eliminated. See Case 53/87: [1988] E.C.R. 6039, Report of the Hearing, at 6053.

[12] Advocate General Mischo held: "The elimination of that competition is the necessary consequence of an industrial property right *in respect of a product* which can have no other form than that which was endowed upon it by its creator, the proprietor of the exclusive right", thereby failing to acknowledge that design rights do not have the objective to grant an exclusive right on a product, but merely on its shape or configuration. See his opinion on Case 53/87: [1988] E.C.R. 6039; [1990] 4 C.M.L.R. 265, at para. 60 (emphasis added).

[13] Case 53/87: [1988] E.C.R. 6039; [1990] 4 C.M.L.R. 265, at para. 15.

[14] See *supra*, Chap. 7, pt. 6(3).

[15] See also *supra*, Chap. 5, pt. 4(3)(c).

Although the Court endeavoured to establish a link between the car spare parts and the *Magill* cases, both the approaches adopted and the conclusions reached are diametrically opposed. In the spare parts cases the Court expressly refrained from taking the specific anti-competitive circumstances of the cases into account. The Court thereby took as a premise that the refusal to licence is an essential right of the intellectual property owner which should be fully upheld in order not to empty the nationally granted intellectual property right of its substance. It was further expressly held that the enforcement of intellectual property rights does not amount to an abusive manner of eliminating competition. The fact that, potentially, all competition in the market for bodywork components could be eliminated did not seem to be relevant in this respect. In the *Magill* appeal case the contrary view prevailed. The Court first examined the specific anti-competitive circumstances of the case. These essentially consisted of the prevention of the appearance of a new product in the market for which there was a potential consumer demand and in the fact that a secondary market was reserved for the intellectual property owners by the exclusion of all competition from that market. The Court therefore concluded that the refusal to license amounted to an abuse of a dominant position so that compulsory licences could be imposed by the Commission to remedy this situation. In other words, in this case the Court allowed the intellectual property right to be emptied of its substance in order to safeguard the competitive market structure.

A comparison of the spare parts and the *Magill* cases thus gives rise to legal uncertainty. The Court, in the latter, failed to clearly indicate when, in future, the fact that the enforcement of intellectual property rights leads to the exclusion of all competition from the market will be held to outweigh the need to safeguard the substance of intellectual property rights. Although an explanation could be that the Court in the *Magill* case endorsed the reasoning of the CFI that the enforcement of copyright was not in accordance with the function of the intellectual property rights and should therefore not be upheld, it did not openly state this as such. Therefore, there are apparently precedents either way now to determine whether or not the exclusion of competition from the market by the enforcement of intellectual property rights and the refusal to license intellectual property rights is compatible with Article 86 E.C.

(ii) Examples of abusive behaviour

8.46   Contrary to the approach adopted by the CFI in the *Magill* cases, the Court in the spare parts cases thus impliedly rejected the contention that the use of design rights in a manner which clearly goes beyond their function may constitute the additional element for the finding of an abuse. The Court therefore faced the difficult task of determining how the detrimental effects on competition, and in particular on consumers, could be curtailed by virtue of the rules on competition. This implied that the Court had to establish what could be the element, additional to the use of design rights in accordance with their specific subject-matter, needed for a finding of abusive behaviour by the holder of the legal monopoly.[16] The Court did not state unequivocally what precisely this additional element is. On the basis of the examples already mentioned in Article 86 E.C., the Court merely gave examples of situations which are manifestly detrimental to consumers' interests and may be indicative of abusive behaviour. The occurrence of the latter was left for the national courts to find.[17] The only guidelines given by the Court to the national courts concerning the application of Article 86 E.C. to the enforcement of design rights in bodywork components of cars by the car manufacturers in both the *Maxicar* and *Volvo* cases, were as follows:

> "Exercise of the exclusive right *may* be prohibited by Article 86 if it gives rise to *certain abusive conduct* on the part of an undertaking occupying a dominant position *such as* an arbitrary refusal to deliver spare parts to independent repairers, the fixing of prices for spare parts at an unfair level or a decision no longer to produce spare parts for a particular model even though many cars of that model remain in circulation, provided that such conduct is liable to affect trade between Member States."[18]

(4) Analysis of the examples of abusive behaviour given by the Court

(a) Arbitrary refusal to sell to independent repairers

The first example of abusive behaviour given by the Court, which is clearly inspired by Article 86(c) E.C., is the arbitrary refusal by the car manufacturers to deliver bodywork components of cars to independent repairers.

8.47

(i) Refusal to sell versus refusal to license

If the arbitrary refusal to sell spare parts to independent repairers may amount to an abuse under Article 86, from the *Volvo* judgment it seemed that the same would not hold true in so far as the arbitrary refusal to give an intellectual property licence to the latter was concerned. As seen above, the Court expressly held that the refusal to grant a licence is in conformity with the specific subject-matter of intellectual property rights and does not, as such, constitute abusive behaviour under Article 86 E.C.[19] The CFI came to a contrary conclusion in the *Magill* cases which, it is important to emphasise, were fully upheld by the Court on appeal. It should be recalled that the CFI held that the finding of abusive behaviour based on the refusal to grant a copyright licence was "borne out" of the *Volvo* judgment.[20] It was thereby apparently disregarded that the Court in the *Volvo* case referred only to the refusal to supply

8.48

---

[16] See also T. Vinje, "*Magill*: its impact on the information technology industry" [1992] E.I.P.R. 397 at 399. He writes that in the *Volvo* case "the difficulties of applying the existence/exercise doctrine, especially in Article 86 cases, became particularly apparent", and that the Court "appears to have acknowledged the limits of the 'specific subject-matter' concept".

[17] See also G. Friden, *op. cit.*, p. 210, where he writes that one should not read too much into these examples because "the Court probably felt obliged, after having given an example of what was not abusive conduct, to give a few examples of what would be considered as abusive".

[18] Case 53/87: [1988] E.C.R. 6039; [1990] 4 C.M.L.R. 265, at para. 16 (emphasis added). Similarly, see Case 238/87: [1988] E.C.R. 6211; [1989] 4 C.M.L.R. 122, at para. 9.

[19] See *supra*, at pt. 3(c)(i).

[20] See *supra*, Chap. 5, pt. 4(3)(b).

physical goods manufactured by the car manufacturers. The latter did not seem to imply that the car manufacturers could also be obliged to share their design rights with independent manufacturers.[21] In other words, it seemed to follow from the *Volvo* case that the car manufacturers could invoke their design rights to remain the only manufacturers and sources of supply of body-work components under Article 86 E.C., whereas they could not arbitrarily refuse to supply those body panels to independent repairers. As Reindl pointed out, in the absence of the latter prohibition the intellectual property owners would have been able to extend their manufacturing monopoly which resulted from the design right to the derivative market of automobile mainten-ance.[22] The crucial question, however, is whether this fundamental distinction between the refusal to supply intellectual property protected products and the refusal to grant intellectual property licences, in so far as the application of Article 86 E.C. is concerned, is still of any importance after the ruling in the *Magill* cases.

(ii) "Arbitrary" versus "bare" refusal to supply

8.49   From the wording used by the Court in the *Volvo* case it was apparent that the bare refusal to supply bodywork components of cars to independent repairers would not suffice to conclude that there was abusive behaviour in the sense of Article 86 E.C.[23] The Court specified that this would only be the case if the refusal was "arbitrary". Korah convincingly illustrated that it would be diffi-cult in practice to evaluate whether or not the refusal to supply bodywork components of cars to independent repairers is "arbitrary". She pointed out that car manufacturers can always plead they have an objective interest in stimulating the development of their own distribution network and in safe-guarding the reputation of their brand.[24]

(iii) Impact of block exemption on selective car distribution

8.50   It should not be disregarded in this respect that the after-sales, and thus also the spare parts, market has been included in the scope of the block exemption for selective distribution agreements in the motorvehicle sector.[25] Both the "selective" and the "exclusive" features of the distribution network, which are held to be compatible with Article 85 E.C., could be invoked by the car

---

[21] See also R. Subiotto, "The right to deal with whom one pleases under EEC competition law: a small contribution to a necessary debate" [1992] E.C.L.R. 234 at 241; J. Flynn, "Intellectual property and anti-trust: EC attitudes" [1992] E.I.P.R. 49 at 53.

[22] See A. Reindl, "The magic of *Magill*: TV program guides as a limit of copyright law?" [1993] I.I.C. 60 at 75.

[23] Similarly, see C. Vadja, "The application of Community competition law to the distribution of computer products and parts" [1992] E.C.L.R. 110 at 116; I. Forrester, *op. cit.*, p. 17.

[24] See V. Korah, "No duty to license independent repairers to make spare parts: the *Renault*, *Volvo* and *Bayer & Hennecke* cases" [1988] E.I.P.R. 381 at 382. She raises the following questions: "Is a refusal to supply body panels to an independent repairer arbitrary if it is costly to test his ability to fit the parts properly, and the car producer wants to maintain the reputation of his brand without incurring that cost by supplying only his franchised dealers whose skills and stock of tools and parts he controls? Is it more arbitrary if the brand owner wants to ensure sufficient turnover for his network of appointed dealers in order to persuade them to make the necessary investment in personnel, equipment and spares?"

[25] On Regulation 123/85 and the new block exemption, see *infra*, Chap. 9, pt. 3(2).

manufacturers to "objectively" justify the refusal to supply bodywork components of cars to independent repairers. The selective car distribution system is based on quantitative rather than qualitative criteria.[26] Nonetheless, the Commission motivated the exclusion of wholesalers not belonging to the authorised network on the basis that this is essential to maintain the system of rapid availability of spare parts originating from the motorvehicle manufacturer.[27] It appears to be conceptually difficult to maintain that there is an objective justification for excluding independent repairers as potential resellers of bodywork components from the selective distribution network whereas the same exclusion would be held to be arbitrary, and thus abusive, under Article 86 E.C.

This still leaves open the possibility of car manufacturers supplying independent manufacturers with bodywork components not for resale but rather specifically for repair purposes. The latter seems to be the situation envisaged by the Court in the *Volvo* case. However, the block exemption expressly allows for the following contractual obligations to be imposed on the supplier of spare parts, *i.e.* the car manufacturer: to supply only the contracting party within a given territory and to refrain from selling the contract goods to final consumers (which in this context most likely includes independent repairers) or providing them with servicing for the contract goods.[28] This does not prejudice the supply of spare parts by appointed dealers. In this respect, it is held in the block exemption that an obligation may be imposed on a dealer to supply spare parts to a reseller "only where they are for the purpose of repair or maintenance of a motor vehicle by the reseller".[29] This implies that a dealer may be contractually obliged to supply bodywork components of cars to independent repairers only for repair purposes and not for further sale. It should be pointed out, however, that the block exemption does not give any guarantees concerning the conditions of resale and does not deal with the refusal by dealers to sell to independent repairers or final customers.[30]

Attention should on the other hand also be drawn to the *Tetra Pak* judgment.[31] It should be emphasised that fulfilment of the conditions under a block exemption does not confer immunity as to a possible application of Article 86 E.C. A national court could therefore, in certain circumstances, find the refusal to supply independent repairers by the car manufacturers to be arbitrary despite arguments based on the need to live up to obligations contracted under selective distribution agreements.   **8.51**

(iv) Affirmative action obligation

It was pointed out in legal writings that an additional factor of uncertainty for national courts lay in the fact that the European Court of Justice, prior to the *Volvo* case, had only held the refusal by a dominant undertaking to supply   **8.52**

---

[26] On the importance of this distinction, see *infra*, Chap. 9, pt. 3(1).
[27] See also *infra*, Chap. 9, pt. 3(2).
[28] Articles 1 and 2 of both Regulation 123/85 and the new block exemption.
[29] See Articles 3 and 10(b) of both Regulation 123/85 and the new block exemption.
[30] See also B. Schmitz, "*Le point de vue des consommateurs*" in *Droit des consommateurs* (J. Pizzio ed. 1987) (Story Scientia), pp. 104–111 at p. 110.
[31] Case T–51/89: [1990] E.C.R. II-309; [1991] 4 C.M.L.R. 334, for the relationship between Articles 85 and 86 E.C. as explained in the *Tetra Pak* case, see *supra*, Chap. 5, pt. 5(3).

already existing customers to be contrary to Article 86 E.C.[32] This kind of argument appears to have become largely redundant as the Court went much further in the *Magill* case by holding that the refusal to license, and not merely to supply, third parties may amount to an abuse under Article 86 E.C.[33] The Court had already, however, prior to the spare parts cases imposed the obligation to deal with third parties in particular with respect to the provision of services by a copyright collecting society. In the *GUL* case, the Court ruled as follows:

> "Such a refusal by an undertaking having a *de facto* monopoly to provide its services for all those who may be in need of them but who do not come within a category of persons defined by the undertaking on the basis of nationality or residence must be regarded as an abuse of a dominant position within the meaning of Article 86 of the Treaty."[34]

A similar reasoning could, by analogy, most likely be applied to products. However, this does not solve the above-mentioned problem which arises from the spare parts ruling, namely to determine when the refusal to supply spare parts for repair purposes may also be held to be arbitrary.

(b) Setting unfair prices

8.53   The second example of abusive behaviour given by the Court, which is mentioned in Article 86(a) E.C., is the fixing of prices for bodywork components of cars at an unfair level. A problem of interpretation arises with regard to the meaning of "unfair prices" similarly to the concept of "arbitrary refusal" in the first example.

(i) The concept of "unfair prices" and criteria

8.54   The Court explained in the *United Brands* case that the concept of unfair prices under Article 86 E.C. relates to the trading benefits an undertaking in a dominant position reaps which it would not have reaped if there had been normal and sufficiently effective competition in the market.[35] The Court further held that the excess benefit in relation to the economic value of the product could be determined objectively. For instance, a comparison between the selling price and the production cost or a comparison with the selling price of competing products can be made.[36]

(ii) Clarification with regard to intellectual property rights

8.55   A practical problem arises where the excess benefit has to be determined not only in relation to the economic value of the product, but also having regard to the reward the proprietor of an intellectual property right may obtain for his

---

[32] See R. Subiotto, *op. cit.*, at pp. 234–237; V. Korah, *op. cit.*, p. 382. They point out that the Court had never imposed the obligation to deal with third parties.

[33] See *supra*, Chap. 5, pt. 4(3)(c).

[34] Case 7/82, *GUL v. Commission*, Judgment of March 2, 1983: [1983] E.C.R. 483; [1983] 3 C.M.L.R. 645, at para. 56.

[35] Case 27/76: [1978] E.C.R. 207; [1978] 1 C.M.L.R. 429, at para. 249.

[36] Case 27/76: [1978] E.C.R. 207; [1978] 1 C.M.L.R. 429, at paras. 250–253.

investment in research and development. It is not surprising, therefore, that the Court reiterated its established case law concerning the concept of "unfair prices" with regard to intellectual property rights in the *Maxicar* case.[37] It was stated as follows:

> "With reference [...] to the difference in prices between components sold by the manufacturer and those sold by the independent producers, it should be noted [...] that a higher price for the former than for the latter does not necessarily constitute an abuse, since the proprietor of protective rights in respect of an ornamental design may lawfully call for a return on the amounts which he has invested in order to perfect the protected design."[38]

This clearly means that a national court cannot merely compare the prices of the car manufacturers with those of the independent manufacturers to determine whether or not there is abusive behaviour. In this respect Veng maintained in the *Volvo* case that the price of the car manufacturers is almost twice the price demanded by independent manufacturers for the same bodywork component. It is apparent, however, that it is also impossible for a national court to determine what should constitute a "just reward" for the creative effort when trying to reconstruct the fair price that could be demanded for a protected product on the basis of its economic value. It would theoretically be possible for a national court to take the actual cost of the investment made to develop a particular bodywork component into account when determining what constitutes a "fair price". But it could not possibly calculate what reward is needed to induce further investment, which is a major objective of design law.[39]

(iii) "Fair prices" and intellectual property rights

It was submitted before that a "just" reward for design rights cannot be calcu- **8.56** lated or quantified at any given time. It is usually determined by the willingness of the consumers to pay for the added value the design confers on a product compared with another product that does not incorporate the protected design.[40] This is based on the understanding that design rights are used in conformity with their function and do not lead to the elimination of the

---

[37] On the prior case law of the Court concerning intellectual property rights whereby the example of abusive behaviour through the imposition of unfair prices was given, see *supra*, Chap. 5, pt. 2(3)(d).

[38] Case 53/87: [1988] E.C.R. 6039; [1990] 4 C.M.L.R. 265, at para. 17.

[39] See *supra*, Chap. 2, pt. 3(5). See also pt. 3(2) where it is held that economists have tried repeatedly, though without success, to find a method to calculate the just reward conferred by patents. See also G. Friden, *op. cit.*, p. 211, where he writes: "It represents not the possibility to charge 'reasonable' prices and obtain 'reasonable' profits, but rather the possibility, for the holder of an exclusive right, to charge whatever the market will pay, one of the main justifications being the need to give the innovator an incentive to bear the risk of innovation, which he might refuse to do if only promised a 'reasonable' profit." Korah to the contrary maintains that "the concept of costs can be reconciled with providing incentives to investment, provided that factors for the risk of failure and delay in obtaining a return are included in the costs that can be recovered before prices are considered unreasonable", see V. Korah, *op. cit.*, (1988), p. 383. However, she does not indicate how the risk factors could, or should, be calculated.

[40] On the concept of "reward", see *supra*, Chap. 7, pt. 5(3).

competitive market structure. Once all competition is removed by the enforcement of design rights and monopoly prices can be charged in a tied-in market, as may be the result of the Court's ruling in *Maxicar* and *Volvo*, it becomes virtually impossible to determine how much benefit the right-owner reaps that he would not have obtained if there had been normal and sufficiently effective competition in that market.[41] It is further submitted that the task of a national court to determine what constitutes a fair price for bodywork components of cars would become even more difficult if it had to take into consideration that body panels are components of complex products on which, probably, part of the "just" reward for the design effort had already been recovered through the sale of the car itself. The latter approach was rather laconically suggested by Advocate General Mischo in the *Maxicar* case.[42] In other words, it is maintained that the concept of unfair prices in relation to intellectual property protected products is unworkable because it is based on the untenable presumption that a "just" reward can be calculated for the innovative effort. This conclusion, which already imposes itself in relation to simple or to complex products, is all the more relevant in relation to components of the latter.

(c) Prematurely terminating production whilst many cars are still in circulation

8.57   The Court's third example of abusive behaviour, namely prematurely terminating production of body panels whilst many cars are still in circulation, is based on Article 86(b) E.C.[43] According to Korah, this example is unlikely to give rise to difficulties.[44] The argument goes that if the car manufacturer no longer produces the body panels himself then it is unlikely that he will enforce his design rights to prohibit the making of those parts by independent manufacturers. This appraisal disregards the fact that the car manufacturers may, at a certain stage, actually want to prevent all production of body panels by both terminating production themselves and enforcing their exclusive rights against independent manufacturers in order to induce owners of older cars to buy new cars.[45] Selling new cars is, after all, the car manufacturers' primary objective.

---

[41] See also V. Korah, *op. cit.*, (1988), p. 382, where she writes: "...I am concerned by the very concept of unfair prices in the absence of a competitive market".

[42] See his opinion on Case 53/87: [1988] E.C.R. 6039; [1990] 4 C.M.L.R. 265, at para. 63 where he writes: "As regards the bodywork components sold as spare parts the problem displays an unusual aspect in so far as part of that expenditure has probably already been recovered from the sale of new cars. It is therefore necessary, when fixing the prices of spare parts, to take due account of that factor. It is the responsibility of the national court hearing the main proceedings to establish whether or not that has been done."

[43] See also A. Françon, "*Propriété littéraire et artistique*" [1992] R.T.D.C. 372 at 373–374.

[44] V. Korah, *op. cit.*, p. 383.

[45] By way of analogy to the CFI's finding in the *Magill* cases, it is interesting to note that Vinje argues that whilst this third example in the spare parts cases expressly refers to "the right holder's decision not to produce parts itself, it clearly implied that the right holder's refusal to license others to produce the parts would under some circumstances constitute an abuse", see T. Vinje, *op. cit.*, p. 400.

(i) Problems of a conceptual nature

The problems the national court are likely to encounter when applying this 8.58
example are once again of a conceptual nature. The first issue is the appraisal
of the concept of "prematurely" in relation to the number of cars that are still
in circulation. The Court did not state that production of body panels had to
continue as long as there were still cars of a given model on the market, but
merely that the termination of production may be abusive if there are still
"many" cars in circulation. This apparently extends beyond the termination
of the production of the specific car itself but does not limit the production of
spare parts in time, for instance to 10 or 15 years after the last new car is sold.
It seems that it will depend on the market, including the market in second-
hand cars, to determine for each specific type of car how long spare parts will
have to be provided by the car manufacturers.

As a corollary, the national court in a particular case will have to determine,
more or less exactly, how many "many" cars is. In other words the question
arises of what number of cars have to be in circulation for the termination of
production of bodywork components to be abusive. The national court could
simply take the number of cars in circulation (for instance it might be held to
suffice that 50 cars are still on the market), or the percentage the car represents
of the total of comparable types cars of a given brand on the market (for
instance 2 per cent of all Renault passenger cars), or the percentage the car
concerned represents of the total cars of a given Member State (for instance
1 per cent of all passenger cars in circulation). It thus seems that each national
court might set a different level and base its finding of abuse on different
approaches. It goes without saying that this is a situation which does not
enhance legal certainty for the car manufacturers.

(ii) Back-door solution

It should further be pointed out that there is a back-door solution in order to 8.59
avoid a finding of abusive behaviour on the grounds of having prematurely
terminated production of spare parts. The car manufacturers could obtain the
same result through setting the prices of bodywork components for cars at
such a level that for the owner of an older car it becomes economically unjustifiable, having regard to the market value of the car, to have the car repaired
rather than buy a new car.[46] Such an approach, which consists in artificially
putting off consumer demand for spare parts of older vehicles rather than
terminating their production and supply, would apparently not be covered by
this third example. It was mentioned before that it would be equally difficult
for a national court to come to the finding that the price is unfair and thus that
the car manufacturer, in so doing, behaves abusively.[47]

---

[46] See also *supra*, Chap. 7, pt. 6(3).
[47] See *supra*, at pt. (b).

5. The Concept of "Affecting Trade Between Member States"

(1) Clarification of the concept

8.60   The question remains, of course, of whether abusive behaviour by car manufacturers of the type mentioned above, and on a relevant market which is
geographically limited to the territory of one Member State, may be held to
affect intra-Community trade so that Community law should apply rather
than national law. In this regard, the Court has given the following
clarification:

> "...It must be stated that when the holder of a dominant position
> obstructs access to the market by competitors it makes no difference
> whether such conduct is confined to a single Member State as long as it is
> capable of affecting the patterns of trade and competition on the com-
> mon market
>   It must also be remembered that Article 86 EEC does not require it to
> be proved that the abusive conduct has in fact appreciably affected trade
> between Member States but that it is capable of having that effect."[48]

The Court reiterated in the *Magill* appeal judgment that it suffices to establish that abusive conduct is capable of having a substantial effect on intra-
Community trade so that it was not necessary for the CFI to establish that the
latter also had that effect in practice.[49]

(2) The criteria

8.61   The Court has traditionally used the two following tests to establish whether
or not intra-Community trade was actually or potentially affected by abusive
behaviour: the "pattern of trade", and the structural or "pattern of competition" tests. The "pattern of trade" test consists of examining whether
normal trade between Member States is diverted by virtue of the abusive
behaviour.[50] The structural test, on the other hand, is not so much aimed at
establishing whether the normal pattern of trade is diverted as to whether the
effective competitive market structure is affected by the abusive behaviour. As
the Court held in the *United Brands* case:

> "...if the occupier of a dominant position, established in the Common
> Market, aims at eliminating a competitor who is also established in the
> Common Market, it is immaterial whether this behaviour relates to trade
> between Member States once it has been shown that such elimination
> will have repercussions on the patterns of competition in the Common
> Market."[51]

---

[48] Case 322/81: [1983] E.C.R. 3461; [1985] 1 C.M.L.R. 282, at paras. 103 and 104.
[49] Joined Cases C 241 and 242/91 P: [1995] E.C.R. I–743; [1995] 4 C.M.L.R. 718, at para. 69.
[50] This was the test applied, for instance, in the *Hilti* case, see *supra*, Chap. 5, pt. 4(2)(b)(iii).
[51] Case 27/76: [1978] E.C.R. 207; [1978] 1 C.M.L.R. 429, at para. 201.

It thus suffices that either the normal pattern of trade or the normal pattern of competition is altered by the abusive behaviour for it to have an appreciable effect on intra-Community trade.

(3) Normal pattern of trade in the absence of intellectual property rights

(a) Spare parts for cash registers

In the *Hugin* case the Court held that Hugin's conduct, which consisted in the **8.62** refusal to supply spare parts to independent repairers, did not affect trade between Member States because it did not have the effect of diverting trade in spare parts from its normal channels.[52] The Court came to this conclusion on the basis that there was no market for spare parts of cash registers which extended beyond the territory of each Member State due to the relatively insignificant value of the spare parts not rendering them a commodity of commercial interest in intra-Community trade. This was confirmed by the fact that the commercial activities of repairers of Hugin cash registers were confined to the territory of one Member State at the most. The fact that the latter sought to purchase spare parts in other Member States was held to be the direct result of the alleged abusive behaviour and not the normal pattern of trade.

(b) Spare parts for cars

The main difference between spare parts for cash registers and spare parts for **8.63** cars is that the latter do represent a commodity of commercial value in intra-Community trade. The existence of a normal pattern of intra-Community trade in bodywork components of cars is best illustrated by the factual background to both the *Maxicar* and the *Volvo* case. The *Volvo* case arose from the fact that Veng imported the contested bodywork components into the United Kingdom from Denmark and Italy. In the *Maxicar* case it was the prohibition on the manufacture and export of the contested body panels to other Member States that was challenged. Further, Maxicar maintained that some of those parts were imported into Italy from Spain.

(4) Enforcement of intellectual property rights to eliminate competitors

(a) The impact

It was maintained above that the enforcement of design rights in bodywork **8.64** components of cars, the shape of which is imperative to restore the cars to their original appearance, significantly alters the competitive market structure in that all competitors are eliminated from the market.[53] Concurrently, the exclusion of competitors means that the normal pattern of intra-Community trade, as described above, is affected. It should also be recalled in

---

[52] Case 22/78: [1979] E.C.R. 1869; [1979] 3 C.M.L.R. 345, at paras. 25–26. On this case, see also *supra*, at pt. 2(b).
[53] See *supra*, at pt. 3(3)(b).

this respect that design rights constitute measures having an equivalent effect to quantitative restrictions so that the importation of products that were lawfully marketed in another Member State may be prohibited.[54]

(b) The condition: relation to abusive behaviour

8.65 This finding did not, in itself, suffice to trigger the application of Article 86 E.C. in the car spare parts cases. The concept of effect on trade between Member States specifically relates to the alleged abusive behaviour of the undertaking occupying a dominant position in the market. As seen before, the elimination of competition by the enforcement of intellectual property rights was held not to constitute an abuse of a dominant position in the spare parts cases.[55] It is submitted that if the enforcement of design rights in bodywork components of cars had been held to be abusive because it exceeded the function of design rights,[56] then it is apparent that intra-Community trade would also have been held to be affected in the car spare parts cases. The latter is unequivocally confirmed by the finding in the *Magill* cases. The CFI had held that abusive behaviour consisting in the enforcement of copyright which led to the exclusion of competitors on the market "undeniably" affected intra-Community trade.[57] The Court on appeal fully upheld this judgment. It ruled:

> "In this case, the Court of First Instance found that the applicant had excluded all potential competitors on the geographical market consisting in one Member State (Ireland) and part of another Member State (Northern Ireland) and thus modified the structure of competition on that market, thereby affecting potential commercial exchanges between Ireland and the United Kingdom. From this the Court of First Instance drew the proper conclusion that the condition that trade between Member States must be affected has been satisfied."[58]

(5) Structural test and consumer interests

8.66 The Court has consistently held that the maintenance of an effective competitive structure follows from Article 3(g) E.C. (formerly Article 3(f) E.C.) and is further in consumers' interests.[59] In the *Hoffmann-La Roche* case, the Court thus clarified that:

---

[54] See *supra*, Chap. 7, pt. 3(4).

[55] See *supra*, at pt. 4(3)(c).

[56] On this hypothesis, see *supra*, at pt. 4(3)(b).

[57] See, for instance, Case T–69/89: [1991] E.C.R. II-485; [1991] 4 C.M.L.R. 586, where it is held at para. 77 that: "The applicant's refusal to authorize interested third parties to publish its weekly listings [through invoking its copyright] had decisive repercussions on the structure of competition in the field of television magazines in the territory of Ireland and Northern Ireland. Through its licensing policy which prevented, *inter alia*, Magill from publishing a general television magazine to be marketed in both Ireland and Northern Ireland, the applicant not only eliminated a competing undertaking from the market for television guides but also excluded any potential competition from that market, thus in effect maintaining the partitioning of the markets represented by Ireland and Northern Ireland respectively. The conduct in question was therefore undeniably capable of affecting trade between Member States", (brackets added). On the *Magill* cases, see *supra*, Chap. 5, pt. 4(3).

[58] Joined Cases C 241 and 242/91 P: [1995] E.C.R. I-743; [1995] 4 C.M.L.R 718, at para. 70.

[59] Case 6/72: [1973] E.C.R. 215; [1973] C.M.L.R. 199, see *supra*, at pt. 1.

"By prohibiting the abuse of a dominant position within the market in so far as it may affect trade between Member States, Article 86 therefore covers not only abuse which may directly prejudice consumers but also abuse which indirectly prejudices them by impairing the effective competitive structure as envisaged by Article 3(f) of the Treaty."[60]

Consequently, the Court of First Instance additionally held in the *Magill* cases that evidence of the effect of enforcing copyright in advance weekly TV listings on the potential flow of trade was found in the specific consumer demand for a comprehensive TV guide.[61] The main difference from the *Magill* cases was that in the *Maxicar* and *Volvo* cases the abusive behaviour was not held to be the enforcement of design rights in bodywork components of cars, but the refusal to supply spare parts, demanding unfair prices, or prematurely terminating production.[62] In other words, the pattern of competition, or the structural test, could not be applied to those cases simply because behaviour which consisted of eliminating the effective competitive market structure was not held to be abusive. This also implied that actual, or potential, consumer demand for spurious parts was irrelevant in determining whether or not the potential or actual pattern of trade was appreciably affected. This again is diametrically opposed to the *Magill* cases as in the latter potential consumer demand played a crucial role throughout the consideration of Article 86 E.C. **8.67**

(6) Pattern of trade test

Contrary to the *Magill* cases, whether or not alleged abusive behaviour by the car manufacturers affected intra-Community trade thus had to be determined solely on the basis of the pattern of trade test. This test could, furthermore, only be applied with regard to the normal pattern of trade of the car manufacturers' own bodywork components. This meant that Article 86 E.C. would only apply if a car manufacturer's abusive behaviour, as mentioned above, resulted or might result in a deflection of intra-Community trade in his own products. **8.68**

In the light of the *Hugin* judgment it seems unlikely that this condition would be fulfilled if an independent repairer sought to obtain spare parts in another Member State because the car manufacturer arbitrarily refused to supply him with spare parts. It might be held that this is the direct result of the alleged abusive behaviour and does not constitute the normal pattern of trade.[63] As the Court held in the *Hugin* case: **8.69**

"In the present case Liptons turned to Hugin subsidiaries and distributors in certain other Member States precisely because Hugin's restrictive policy prevented it from satisfying its spare parts requirements through normal commercial channels. Its attempts to obtain spare parts in the other Member States can therefore not be regarded as an indication of the

[60] Case 85/76: [1979] E.C.R. 461; [1979] 3 C.M.L.R. 211, at para. 125.
[61] See, for instance, Case T–69/89: [1991] E.C.R. II-485; [1991] 4 C.M.L.R. 586, at para. 77. On the *Magill* cases, see *supra* Chap. 5, pt. 4(3).
[62] See *supra*, pt. (3)(c)(ii) and pt. (4).
[63] For the ruling of the Court in the *Hugin* case, see *supra*, at pt. (3)(a).

existence, whether actual or potential, of a normal pattern of trade between the Member States in spare parts. In other words, if Liptons had been able to obtain spare parts from a Hugin subsidiary in another Member State it would have been because Hugin was willing to sell those parts outside its own distribution network. In such a case, however, it would be customary for Liptons to apply to the Hugin subsidiary in its own country rather than to a subsidiary in another Member State."[64]

Having regard to the existence of close-knit distribution networks for motor vehicles and their spare parts it is not surprising, therefore, that in the *Volvo* case Advocate General Mischo merely put forward the view that it should be left to the national court:

"to investigate whether the undertaking abusing its dominant position imports the parts in question from one Member State into another Member States."[65]

He did not refer to the possible importation of those goods by third parties.

6. EVALUATION

8.70   The conclusion which puts itself forward is that by not taking the function of design rights into account, the Court has opened the door to an almost unrestricted (ab)use of those exclusive rights to circumvent the rules on competition in the market for bodywork components of cars by car manufacturers. Having upheld, under Article 36 E.C. in the *Maxicar* case,[66] the existence and the exercise of design rights in bodywork components of cars the shape of which is imperative to restore the car to its original appearance, the Court subsequently failed to find adequate means to curtail the detrimental effects on competition, and on consumers, under the rules on competition in both the *Maxicar* and *Volvo* cases. The examples of possible abusive behaviour, in the sense of Article 86 E.C., given by the Court raise more practical questions than they give answers to.[67] First of all, they give rise to difficulties of a conceptual nature. When they are effectively applied it will be difficult to maintain that such abusive conduct also appreciably affects intra-Community trade.[68] It is therefore submitted that it can be expected that potential abusive behaviour of car manufacturers in the market for bodywork components, even if it goes manifestly against the interests of consumers and free competition, is not likely to be effectively curtailed by virtue of Article 86 E.C.

8.71   The virtual non-applicability of Article 86 E.C. to the cases concerned essentially ensues from the fact that the Court has allowed the grant, and subsequent use of design rights, to amount to the elimination of inter-brand com-

---

[64] Case 22/78: [1979] E.C.R. 1869; [1979] 3 C.M.L.R. 345, at para. 24.
[65] See his opinion on Case 238/87: [1988] E.C.R. 6211; [1989] 4 C.M.L.R. 122, at para. 39. He did not deal with this question in the *Maxicar* case.
[66] See *supra*, Chap. 7.
[67] See *supra*, at pt. 4(4).
[68] See *supra*, at pt. 5.

petition in the market for bodywork components of cars, whereas it is the objective of both the rules on competition and design rights to enhance inter-brand competition. In other words, through rejecting the very hypothesis that the system of design rights might be abused to obtain a legal monopoly in the market, the Court could not possibly strike a balance between the need to safeguard exclusive design rights on the one hand, and the need to safeguard an effective competitive market structure in the common market on the other. The reason for this is simply because the elimination of the latter counter-balance was accepted from the start.

The spare parts cases stand in sharp contrast to both the approach and conclusion adopted in the subsequent *Magill* case. By not expressly referring to the function of copyright in its appeal judgment, the Court in the latter cases seems to have opened the door to an almost unrestricted interference by competition rules in the normal use of intellectual property rights.[69] It seems that in this case the Court only looked at the anti-competitive effects of the enforcement of intellectual property rights. In other words, it was apparently the counterbalance consisting of the need to safeguard the system of intellec-tual property protection that was eliminated from the start.

Specifically concerning the market for bodywork components of cars, the detrimental impact of the *Maxicar* and *Volvo* judgments on competition and consumer interests does not merely lie in the fact that inter-brand competition can be eliminated. It also has to be considered in the light of the acceptance of selective distribution agreements for cars and replacement parts under Article 85 E.C.[70] The latter implies that restrictions on intra-brand competition are also imposed in the market for bodywork components of cars so that, as is illustrated in the next chapter, a perfect legal monopoly may occur. **8.72**

[69] See *supra*, Chap. 5, pt. 4(3)(c).
[70] See *infra*, Chap. 9, pt. 3(2).

9. The Impact of the Enforcement of Intellectual Property Rights on Competition Policy Objectives: Legal Issues and Possible Solutions

1. PRELIMINARY REMARKS

A typical feature of the automobile industry is the development of close-knit **9.01** selective and exclusive distribution networks throughout the European Community. As mentioned in the previous chapter, the Commission issued a block exemption specifically with regard to selective distribution agreements in the motorvehicle sector. The purpose of this chapter is to examine the effect of the outcome of the spare parts cases on the Commission's automobile policy under Article 85 E.C., and vice versa. In particular, the enforcement of intellectual property rights seems to be a way to circumvent the prohibition on inserting exclusivity clauses concerning spare parts in selective distribution agreements. Whereas the latter is contrary to the block exemption the former is not, as such, prohibited although it clearly goes against the objectives of the exemption. This does not imply that the impact of this practice on the competitive market structure cannot influence the finding by the Commission of the well-foundedness of vertical restraints in selective distribution agreements. The question therefore arises of what kind of action the Commission could undertake in a case in which the competition policy objectives are jeopardised by the enforcement of intellectual property rights, and in particular design rights in spare parts of cars.

2. E.C. COMPETITION POLICY OBJECTIVES

E.C. competition policy traditionally responds to three fundamental objec- **9.02** tives which have been defined by the Commission as follows: contributing to an open and unified Common Market,[1] preserving a competitive market structure, and maintaining a degree of fairness in the market including safeguarding the position of small- and medium-sized enterprises (SMES) and consumers' interests.[2] It should be emphasised that, contrary to United States

---

[1] According to Korah, "in competition cases,..., integration has been elevated by the Commission and the Court as a goal in itself, more important than efficiency": see V. Korah, "EEC competition policy – Legal form or economic efficiency" [1986] *Current Legal Problems* 85 at 91.
[2] See 9th Report on Competition Policy 1979, Luxembourg, 1980, at pp. 9–10.

antitrust policy, competition policy in the E.C. is not exclusively or even mainly concerned with efficiency.[3] It was only in its Report on Competition Policy of 1991, with the completion of the single market in sight, that the Commission expressly stated that the link between competition and economic efficiency is generally recognised throughout the world and may benefit the consumer.[4] This does not imply, though, that to strive for efficiency has become the first, let alone the sole, priority of E.C. competition policy. In its subsequent Report on Competition Policy of 1992, the Commission explained that:

> "The policy priorities detailed in previous reports remain unchanged; in particular, competition policy seeks to contribute to the achievement of a genuine frontier-free area, and to economical and social cohesion, by throwing open markets which might otherwise be protected by exclusive rights, restrictive practices, the abuse of dominant positions, or State aids."[5]

For instance, in relation to regulated sectors and state aid, it was specified that to strive for economic efficiency is not a goal in itself but has to be balanced against the need to take the social dimension into account and to maintain a universal service.[6]

3. COMPETITION POLICY PRIOR TO THE SPARE PARTS CASES

(1) Selective distribution agreements

(a) Introduction to economic theory on vertical restraints

9.03 There is no agreement among economists as to whether, and when, vertical restraints should be allowed or prohibited. Whereas some economists advocate a very strict *per se* illegality for all vertical restrictions, certain Chicago School economists advocate a *per se* legalisation of all vertical restraints.[7] Most mainstream and neo-Chicago economists agree on the need to apply the more pragmatic rule of reason test to see whether the restrictions concerned are pro- or anti-competitive, although they disagree as to whether there should be a more or a less interventionist policy, respectively. The difference in view between mainstream and neo-Chicago economists stems from a different perception of the objectives of antitrust policy. According to the Chicago school the sole objective of antitrust policy is to promote economic

---

[3] See also B. Hawk, "The American (antitrust) revolution: lessons for the EEC?" [1988] E.C.L.R. 53 at 54–62, where he sets out the differences between U.S. and E.C. competition policy goals and analyses the (limited) influence of the Chicago School of economic thought on E.C. competition policy-making. For a critical view of E.C. competition policy objectives, see also V. Korah, "From legal form toward economic efficiency – Article 85(1) of the EEC Treaty in contrast to U.S. antitrust" [1990] Antitrust Bull. 1009.
[4] See XXIst Report on Competition Policy 1991, Luxembourg, 1992, at p. 11.
[5] See XXIInd Report on Competition Policy 1992, Luxembourg, 1993, at p. 13.
[6] See XXIInd Report on Competition Policy 1992, Luxembourg, 1993, at p. 14.
[7] For a detailed overview of the different economic approaches to vertical restraints, see D. Audretsch, "Divergent views in antitrust economics" [1988] Antitrust Bull. 135 at 156–159.

efficiency. For other economists the objective is much wider and includes political and social values, such as distributive equity and fairness.[8]

In the United States, Chicago School adherents in particular often success- **9.04** fully invoke the free-rider argument in support of the necessity for allowing vertical restraints for products which require pre-sales and/or after-sales services, such as cars.[9] It is best illustrated, by way of the following schoolbook example, that it is difficult to ignore the practical implications that the prohibition of territorial restrictions in dealer agreements would have as far as pre-sales services are concerned. Assume that retailers A and B both deal in the same product, car X. Retailer A offers pre-sale services to the customers, in accordance with the prestige of the car. For instance, he informs potential customers of the characteristics of car X and takes them for a test drive. These services will inevitably be reflected in A's selling price. In the absence of territorial restrictions retailer B could, in principle, establish his business round the corner from A. Being a free-rider, B tells his customers to obtain all the information from A and return to B to buy car X from him at a lower price than A. As such, A is incurring costs for which he is not compensated as he does not sell car X in the end. A would inevitably be forced to stop providing pre-sale services and would have to start selling at similar prices to B in order to stay in the market. Only if both retailers were contractually obliged to sell car X at the same price could this non-price competition go on in the absence of territorial restrictions. The essence of the theory is thus that, in the absence of territorial restrictions and price-fixing, a free-rider might profit from the pre-sales services provided by another dealer to sell the car himself at a lower price. This practice would lead to the abandonment of certain pre-sales services due to the inability of the provider of the services to charge consumers upon providing the service, or to recover the cost in the selling price of the car.[10]

A similar reasoning has also been applied to illustrate the need for selective distribution due to the close link between the sale of a new motorvehicle and after-sales services. The hypothesis is that the approved dealer is contractually bound to offer a certain amount of after-sales services, the cost of which will be reflected in the price of the car, whereas the car can also be distributed through non-approved dealers. The latter, being free-riders, do not provide the after-sales services themselves and are thus able to sell the car at a lower price. The theory goes that in order to remain competitive in the new car market, the approved dealers would thus be obliged to reduce the after-sales services they offer.[11] However, the after-sales argument seems to be far less convincing than the pre-sales argument, because it is difficult to see why, unless for marketing reasons, the approved dealers could not simply charge

---

[8] See, for instance, T. Frazer, *Monopoly, competition & the law – the regulation of business activity in Britain, Europe and America* (1988, Wheatsheaf Books), pp. 1–3.

[9] For an economic analysis of vertical restraints in terms of the free-rider argument, see for instance L. White, "Vertical restraints in antitrust law: a coherent model" [1981] Antitrust Bull. 327. For an assessment of the influence of Chicago School in the U.S., see B. Hawk, *op. cit.*

[10] On the Chicago School free-riders rationale in relation to pre-sales services, see also V. Korah, *op. cit.*, pp. 86–87.

[11] See W. Möschel, "*La distribution sélective d'automobiles en droit européen de la concurrence*" [1991] R.T.D.C. 1 at 11–12.

for the after-sales services when they are provided rather than incorporating their cost in the price of the car.

9.05   The main objection to the various approaches taken by the neo-Chicagoans is that vertical restrictions on intra-brand competition are exclusively considered in the context of any given firm's strive for efficiency. Efficiency is thereby held to be tantamount to consumer welfare whereas the occurrence of monopolistic behaviour, such as the raising of prices, is to a large extent rejected or held to be irrelevant.[12] This, at first sight paradoxical, finding is to be explained by the fact that the term "consumer welfare" does not refer to the welfare of consumers as commonly understood. The definition of consumers is extended to include monopolists and cartels, so that consumer welfare is not held to be prejudiced by the transfer of wealth from the (genuine) consumer to firms with market power through the imposition of higher prices.[13]

Although Chicago School adherents accept that antitrust law can apply to horizontal collusion and cartels, whether or not inter-brand competition exists at the level of the manufacturer only receives marginal attention when dealing with vertical restraints. This is best illustrated by the following statement by White, who is rather moderate in that he is in favour of a rule of reason approach:

> "...if the manufacturer is a monopolist, the vertical restraints cannot increase the likelihood of collusion at that level and hence are harmless; *only if they somehow build up the barriers to entry and thus cement his monopoly position are they potentially harmful*. Similarly, studies of market structures at the retailing level are useful only if they give some indication of the likelihood of the retailers becoming a vehicle for manufacturer collusion."[14]

Or, in other words, according to this theory the absence of inter-brand competition is not relevant to determine whether or not intra-brand competition can be restricted, unless it can be established that the intra-brand restrictions are a means of restricting inter-brand competition.

(b) Selective distribution and Article 85

9.06   The Chicago School doctrine has not had the same impact in the E.C. as in the United States, considering that to strive for efficiency is not the sole, or even main, objective of E.C. competition policy.[15] It should be recalled in this respect that the European Court of Justice already held in the *Consten Grundig* case of 1966 that not only horizontal restrictions but also vertical restraints come under the scope of the rules on competition.[16] It is, nonetheless, generally accepted that certain vertical restraints may be written into certain types of selective distribution agreements. In the *Metro* case, the Court

---

[12] This is particulary striking when reading the following article: R. Posner, "The Chicago School of antitrust analysis" [1978/79] *University of Pennsylvania Law Review* 925.
[13] See R. Lande, "The rise and (coming) fall of efficiency as the ruler of antitrust" [1988] Antitrust Bull. 429 especially at 434–435.
[14] L. White, *op. cit.*, p. 344 (emphasis in original text).
[15] See *supra*, at pt. 2.
[16] Joined Cases 56 and 58/64, *Consten and Grundig v. Commission*, Judgment of July 13, 1966: [1966] E.C.R. 229; [1966] C.M.L.R. 418. See also *supra*, Chap. 5, pt. 3(2)(b).

held that if resellers are chosen on the basis of objective criteria of a qualitative nature, then the agreement might not even be caught by Article 85(1) E.C.[17] Conversely, it was expressly stated in the *L'Oréal* case that, in principle, Article 85(1) E.C. applies if the selective distribution agreements are based on quantitative criteria so that in this case the conditions stipulated in Article 85(3) E.C. have to be fulfilled in order to qualify for an exemption.[18]

(c) Selective distribution in the automobile sector

Considering that an automobile is a highly complex consumer product with a relatively long life-time requiring after-sales service, the Commission had taken the view early on that selective and exclusive distribution agreements in this sector could, under certain conditions, be exempted under Article 85(3) E.C.[19] The reason for resorting to Article 85(3) E.C. lay in the fact that those selective distribution systems are based on quantitative, rather than qualitative, criteria so that they indisputably come under the scope of Article 85(1) E.C.[20] Establishing a selective distribution system is the quasi-general rule in the motorvehicle sector. It is not surprising, therefore, that the Commission was faced with numerous demands for individual exemptions so that in 1984 Regulation 123/85 was issued on the application of Article 85(3) of the Treaty to certain categories of motorvehicle distribution and servicing agreements.[21] In view of the fact that the latter is due to expire on June 30, 1995 it will be replaced by a new regulation. The new block exemption, which was adopted by the Commission on April 26, 1995, is largely based on Regulation 123/85.[22] Certain amendments have been made in order to strengthen the position of the dealers *vis-à-vis* the car manufacturers, to improve the market access of spare parts of independent manufacturers, and to increase consumers' choice. It should also be pointed out that the blacklist has been substantially extended.[23]

9.07

(2) A block exemption for selective distribution in the automobile sector

(a) Peculiarity of the block exemption

Neither the finding of the compatibility of selective distribution agreements with the Community rules on competition,[24] nor the issuing of block

9.08

---

[17] Case 26/76, *Metro v. Commission*, Judgment of October 25, 1977: [1977] E.C.R. 1875; [1978] 2 C.M.L.R. 1.

[18] Case 31/80, *NV L'Oréal and SA L'Oréal v. PVBA De Nieuwe AMCK*, Judgment of December 11, 1980: [1980] E.C.R. 3775; [1981] 2 C.M.L.R. 235, at para. 17.

[19] See the *BMW* Decision of December 13, 1974: [1975] O.J. L29/1; [1975] 1 C.M.L.R. D44.

[20] See Case 31/80, *L'Oréal v. De Nieuwe AMCK*: [1980] E.C.R. 3775; [1981] 2 C.M.L.R. 235. See also W. Möschel, *op. cit.*, p. 8.

[21] Commission Regulation 123/85 of December 12, 1984: [1985] O.J. L15/16. On the "*raison d'être*" of this block exemption, see the following article written by the person who conceived the regulation: K. Stöver, "*Les règlements d'exemption catégorielle relatifs à la distribution des voitures et aux stations-service*" in M. Collard, a.o., *op. cit.*, pp. 181–204, especially at p. 187.

[22] IP/95/420, April 26, 1995. For the text of the draft proposal, see [1994] O.J. C379/16.

[23] For the extended blacklist, see Article 6 of the new block exemption.

[24] On the Community approach to selective distribution, see, for instance, P. Cesarini, "*Les systèmes de distribution sélective en droit communautaire de la concurrence*" [1992] *Revue du Marché Unique Européen* 81.

exemptions, are peculiar under Community law. Regulation 123/85 was, nonetheless, very special in that it was the first time that a group exemption was issued with regard to selective distribution.[25] The peculiarity resides in the fact that the Court in its case law on selective distribution agreements seems to have attached a great importance to the coexistence of a variety of distribution channels in order to fulfil the requirements of the various categories of consumers. For instance, in the *Metro* case, the Court expressly held that:

> "In the sector covering the production of high quality and technically advanced consumer durables, where a relatively small number of large and medium-scale producers offer a varied range of items which, or so consumers may consider, are readily interchangeable, the structure of the market does not preclude the existence of a variety of channels of distribution adapted to the peculiar characteristics of the various producers and to the requirements of the various categories of consumers.
> ...the Commission must ensure that this structural rigidity is not reinforced, as might happen if there were an increase in the number of selective distribution networks for marketing the same product."[26]

The issuing of a block exemption for selective distribution agreements, in a market in which selective distribution networks are the quasi-general rule, thus seemed to point to an underlying sectoral competition policy concerning the application of Article 85 E.C. An innovative feature of the new block exemption in this respect is that it is provided that multi-dealerships should be allowed although it may be stipulated that competing motorvehicles of different brands should be sold in separate sales premises under separate management and should not give rise to confusion.[27] The Commission points out that these conditions guarantee "exclusivity of distribution of each make in each place of sale".[28]

(b) Justification in terms of efficiency

9.09 The Commission justifies the restrictions on competition caused by the selective and exclusive nature of the agreements principally by invoking the need to establish a specialised after-sales service for the product concerned. In the words of the Commission:

> "The exclusive and selective distribution clauses can be regarded as indispensable measures of rationalisation in the motorvehicle industry because motorvehicles are consumer durables which at both regular and irregular intervals require expert maintenance and repair, not always in the same place. Motor vehicle manufacturers cooperate with the selected dealers and repairers in order to provide specialised servicing for the product. On grounds of capacity and efficiency alone, such a form of

---

[25] See B. Schmitz, "*Le point de vue des consommateurs*", in *Droit des consommateurs* (J. Pizzio ed. 1987) (Story Scientia), pp. 104–111 at p. 105.
[26] Case 26/76, *Metro v. Commission*, Judgment of October 25, 1977: [1977] E.C.R. 1875; [1978] 2 C.M.L.R. 1; respectively at pts. 20 and 22.
[27] See Article 3(3) and 3(5) of the new block exemption.
[28] See point 7 of the preamble to the new block exemption.

cooperation cannot be extended to an unlimited number of dealers and repairers. The linking of servicing and distribution must be regarded as more efficient than a separation between a distribution organisation for new vehicles on the one hand and a servicing organisation which would also distribute spare parts on the other...."[29]

It therefore seemed at first sight that the Commission adhered to the so-called "package deal theory". This implied that the sale of a new car and the after-sales services, including spare parts but not accessories, had to be considered as a single package offered by the car manufacturers to the consumers for the latter's benefit.[30] The inclusion of after-sales services in the group exemption for selective distribution in the motorvehicle sector has been strongly contested. Considering the underlying justification for the block exemption, it is paradoxical that it is consumers' organisations that have pointed out that the market structure for after-sales services is much more lively and responsive to different consumer needs than the market for the sale of new cars.[31] In particular, attention was drawn to the fact that the extension of the exclusivity clauses to spare parts would, in practice, mean that the consumer would be "tied in" once he had purchased a car.

(c) "Safety valves" in the consumers' interest

(i) Underlying rationale

The Commission had underlined the importance of safeguarding consumers' interests in its notice concerning Regulation 123/85.[32] It maintained that European consumers must derive a fair share of the benefits which flow from the distribution and servicing agreements. This is a condition which is expressly laid down in Article 85(3) E.C. The Commission acknowledged that the package deal offered by car manufacturers may contain certain advantages for consumers, such as specialised servicing. The car manufacturers' contention that enforcing the package deal is tantamount to protecting consumers' overall interests was, nevertheless, rejected. In the words of the Commission:

9.10

> "...the European consumers' basic rights include above all the right to buy a motorvehicle and to have it maintained or repaired wherever prices and quality are most advantageous to him."[33]

Certain "safety valves" were therefore introduced in the block exemption in order to safeguard these basic rights of the European consumers.

---

[29] See point 4 of the preamble to both Regulation 123/85 and the new block exemption.
[30] Similarly, see P. Crockford, "Trucks, parts and summing up", paper presented at the SMMT conference, London, March 5, 1985, at p. 5. On the "package deal" in the motorvehicle sector, see also *supra*, Chap. 8, pt. 3(2)(a).
[31] See for instance B. Schmitz, "Free movement of motorvehicles and spare parts in view of 1992; the consumer experience with Regulation 123/85", paper presented at a Conference in Sienna, July 8/9, 1988, at p. 1; B. Schmitz, "*Le point de vue des consommateurs*" in *Droit des consommateurs* (J. Pizzio ed. 1987) (Story Scientia), pp. 104–111 at p. 109.
[32] Commission Notice concerning Regulation 123/85 of December 12, 1984 on the application of Article 85(3) of the Treaty to certain categories of motorvehicle distribution and servicing agreements: [1985] O.J. C17/4.
[33] Commission Notice, *op. cit.*, at pt. 1.

(ii) The safety valves

9.11 With regard to the sale of new motorvehicles, the Commission held that dealer-to-dealer sales and purchases by consumers and intermediaries in other Member States should not be prohibited or obstructed.[34] It should be pointed out that the regulation also provides that there should be no substantial price differences maintained between the Member States so that, eventually, the incentive to buy cars in other Member States should be significantly reduced.[35] In the new block exemption it is also provided that multi-dealership should be allowed for, but only on such terms as guarantee the exclusive nature of the distribution system.[36]

9.12 In order to safeguard the basic consumer right to have his motorvehicle maintained and repaired wherever prices and quality are most advantageous, the Commission went much further in that it prohibited the extension of the exclusive purchasing and distribution clauses to the spare parts sector. Unlike new cars, which are virtually exclusively distributed through the authorised distribution network, the consumer can obtain spare parts from a variety of sources which respond to different consumer needs. Surveys have shown that low income consumers and users of older and second-hand cars make use of after-sales services offered by non-franchised garages, specialised workshops or do-it-yourself outlets, whereas the franchised network is turned to especially during the first five years of a car's lifetime.[37] In order to perpetuate the specificity of the after-sales market structure, the main idea expressed in the block exemption is that the selective and exclusive distribution and servicing network should not be foreclosed to spare parts produced by independent manufacturers; also, independent garages should be able to obtain spare parts for repair purposes. In other words, the Commission acknowledged that the spare parts sector is a related, but distinct, market to the market in motorvehicles,[38] in which as much inter-brand competition as possible should prevail in the consumer's interest.[39]

(iii) Inter-brand versus intra-brand competition for cars and spare parts

9.13 With regard to the markets in both motorvehicles and spare parts, the rationale of the block exemption is that certain intra-brand restrictions may be tol-

---

[34] See, in particular, Article 10, point 2 of Regulation 123/85, where it is held that such a practice may lead to the withdrawal of the block exemption. This is not repeated in the new block exemption because in the latter similar provisions are blacklisted in Article 6(7).

[35] See Article 10, point 3 of Regulation 123/85(now Article 8, point 3 in the new block exemption), as well as the figures of what is acceptable as advanced in point II of the Notice on Regulation 123/85. For different studies on the remaining price differentials see, for instance, the MMC Report on New Motor Cars, Cm. 1808 (1992), at pp. 119–148.

[36] See *supra*, at pt. (b).

[37] See C. Joerges, "The Commission Regulation 123/85 on automobile distribution and servicing agreements: competition policy objectives and their implications for the consumer interest" in Joerges, Hiller, Holzcheck, Micklitz, *Vertriebspraktiken im Automobil-ersatzteilsektor* (1985, Verlag Peter Lang), pp. 353–386 at p. 364. This article gives a comprehensive and critical analysis of the block exemption concerning spare parts from the consumers' point of view.

[38] Similarly, see F. Jeantet, R. Kovar, "*Les accords de distribution et de service des véhicules automobiles et l'article 85 du traité CEE: Etude du projet de règlement de la Commission des Communautés Européennes*" [1983] R.T.D.E. 547 at 573, although they do not agree with this point of view.

[39] This was also the conclusion reached by the U.K. Monopolies and Mergers Commission in its 1982 Car Parts Report, H.C. 318, HMSO, London, 1982.

erated because inter-brand competition prevails. This is illustrated by the fact that it is held in the preamble to the block exemption that the conditions necessary for effective competition may be taken to exist as regards the products set out in Article 1.[40] The latter expressly mentions both motorvehicles and spare parts. Furthermore, it may be inferred from Article 10(1) of the block exemption that the continued existence of inter-brand competition is a *conditio sine qua non* in so far as the exemption of intra-brand restrictions is concerned. It is stipulated that the benefit of the block exemption may be withdrawn in the case that goods "are not subject to competition from products considered by consumers as similar by reason of their characteristics, price and intended use".

Although the objective of safeguarding a competitive market structure is the same for both markets in cars and spare parts, there is an important difference between these two markets which explains the divergent rules applicable to these two sectors, as expressed in the block exemption. Even in the context of a market which is characterised by structural rigidity, the exemption of exclusivity clauses as far as new cars are concerned does not lead to the elimination of inter-brand competition between cars. This explains why only intra-brand restriction are blacklisted in relation to cars. Conversely, there is a real danger that unconditionally extending exclusivity to spare parts would lead to the elimination of inter-brand competition in this ancillary market. The obvious reason is that when a certain brand of car has been purchased, spare parts will subsequently need to be purchased that fit this car. In order to safeguard the same kind of competitive market structure as exists for cars in the spare parts market, it is therefore necessary not only to blacklist certain types of intra-brand restrictions, but above all clauses which might restrict inter-brand competition.   **9.14**

(d) Safeguarding a competitive spare parts market

(i) No tie-in of spare parts

Article 3, pt. 4 of both Regulation 123/85 and the new block exemption allow for the imposition of a limited non-competition clause upon the authorised dealer with regard to spare parts of cars. The latter may only be contractually obliged not to sell, or use for repair purposes, competing spare parts which do not match the quality of the parts supplied by the car manufacturer. Or in other words, it was apparent from Regulation 123/85 that the dealer must be free to obtain and use spare parts from third parties which match or exceed the quality of the parts supplied by the car manufacturer.[41] The new block exemption goes somewhat further in this respect. In order to improve market access for competing spare parts which match or exceed the quality of those supplied by the car manufacturer, the following clauses are now expressly black-listed: **9.15**

> "the supplier restricts the dealer's freedom, provided for in Article 3, point 4, to obtain from a third undertaking of his choice spare parts which compete with contract goods and which match their quality; or

[40] See point 25 of the preamble to Regulation 123/85 and point 30 of the preamble to the new block exemption.
[41] See also point 8 of the preamble to Regulation 123/85.

the manufacturer directly or indirectly restricts the freedom of spare-part manufacturers or distributors to supply such products to resellers of their choice, including those which are undertakings within the distribution system, in so far as such spare parts match the quality of contract goods; or

the manufacturer directly or indirectly restricts the freedom of spare-parts manufacturers to place effectively and in an easily visible manner their trade mark or logo on parts supplied for the initial assembly or for the repair or maintenance of contract goods or corresponding goods...."[42]

The main limitations to this rule consist in the obligation to inform customers about the use of spare parts from other sources[43] and the obligation to use genuine, or in other words approved, parts for guarantee work.[44]

9.16   Even though the new block exemption attempts to offer better market access to spare parts of independent manufacturers, it should be emphasised that this "safety valve" can only apply if there are spurious, or in other words non-approved, parts on the market. For those spare parts that are only distributed through the manufacturer's own distribution network, *i.e.* the so-called captive parts, the dealer will necessarily have to turn to the car manufacturer as the sole supplier. Also, a much-debated and controversial question is how to establish when a spurious part is of an equal or superior quality to a genuine part.[45] In some cases this becomes superfluous because the spurious parts have the same commercial origin as the genuine, or OEM (original equipment manufacture), parts and are thus likely to be of the same quality. This situation occurs where the car manufacturer does not manufacture the spare parts himself but merely attaches his trade mark to parts purchased from the same independent component manufacturer who also supplies the market under a different trade mark.[46] According to recital 8 of the preamble to both Regulation 123/85 and the new block exemption, the dealer must be free to use those spurious spare parts.

Besides these limitations inherent in the specificity of the spare part concerned, another restriction may arise from the very nature of the relationship between the car manufacturer and his dealers. It has been pointed out that although Regulation 123/85 aimed at providing some security and independence to dealers, their relationship with the car manufacturer is so unequal that even when their interests diverge the dealer is unlikely to behave to a large

---

[42] See Article 6, pts. 9 to 11 of the new block exemption.
[43] See also J. Dubois, "*Cas d'application: la distribution automobile dans le marché commun: le point de vue de la Commission*" in *Droit des consommateurs* (J. Pizzio ed. 1987) (Story Scientia), pp. 91–97 at p. 93.
[44] See Article 4, pt. 1(7), (8) and (9) of both Regulation 123/85 and the new block exemption.
[45] See, for instance, J. Davidow, "EEC proposed competition rules for motorvehicle distribution: an American perspective" [1983] Antitrust Bull. 863 at 878, where he points out that it is not clear who will have the burden of proof.
[46] See also P. Groves, "Motor vehicle distribution: the block exemption" [1987] E.C.L.R. 77 at 79.

extent independently of the car manufacturer.[47] It is doubtful whether continuing endeavours to strengthen the position of dealers in the new block exemption will significantly alter this finding in practice.

(ii) Supply of spare parts for repair purposes

It was mentioned above that certain spare parts, the so-called captive parts, are distributed exclusively through the car manufacturers' distribution network. One class of captive spare parts are constituted by slow-moving parts. These are not usually manufactured by independent manufacturers due to their low turnover rate which make large investments, for instance installing a production chain, uneconomical. A second class of captive parts consists of either slow- or fast-moving parts on which the car manufacturer has a monopoly right, for instance by virtue of patent protection. **9.17**

The fact that the car manufacturer has a supply monopoly with regard to these captive parts does not necessarily mean that he also manufactures those parts. Increasingly often the production of those parts is outsourced to independent suppliers who may be contractually obliged to supply the car manufacturer exclusively or to assign related intellectual property rights to the latter. Whether or not he manufactures the parts himself, the car manufacturer is thus the pivot in the supply chain in captive parts.

Articles 1 and 2 of both Regulation 123/85 and the new block exemption acknowledge the right of the car manufacturer to distribute genuine, thus including captive, parts exclusively through the selective distribution network. The Commission justifies this in the following terms: **9.18**

> "It should be possible to bar wholesalers not belonging to the distribution system from reselling parts originating from motorvehicle manufacturers. It may be supposed that the system of rapid availability of spare parts across the whole contract programme, including those with a low turnover, which is beneficial to the consumer, could not be obtained without obligatory recourse to the authorised network."[48]

To avoid tying-in consumers, and to safeguard the possibility of having repair work effected outside the approved network, Article 3, point 10(b) stipulates that the dealer may not be contractually prohibited from supplying spare parts to third parties for the purpose of repair or maintenance work.[49] However, as already pointed out in relation to Regulation 123/85, this does not offer guarantees as to the conditions under which the dealers may supply those parts.[50]

---

[47] See especially H. Beale, "Car distribution contracts and block exemption Regulation 123/85", paper presented at the Giessen-Warwick Colloquium, November 1987, at pp. 7–10. At p. 10 he writes: "I am sceptical as to whether a relationship which is structurally so unequal (because of the differences in size if nothing else) can ever be changed significantly by controls which govern only part of the relationship."

[48] See point 6 of the preamble to both Regulation 123/85 and the new block exemption.

[49] See also point 5 of the preamble to both Regulation 123/85 and the new block exemption.

[50] See B. Schmitz, *op. cit.* (1987), p. 110. See also *supra*, Chap. 8, pt. 4(4)(a)(iii).

4. THE IMPACT OF THE SPARE PARTS CASES ON THE COMPETITION POLICY OBJECTIVES

(1) The spare parts cases in context

9.19   It is apparent from the block exemptions that the specificity of the spare markets market, with its variety of supply channels living up to diverging consumer interests and responding to economic and commercial realities different from the market in motorvehicles has, to a certain extent, been taken into account in formulating a competition policy specific to the automobile sector. Since the early 1980s, it seems that the car manufacturers have been increasingly reluctant to tolerate inter-brand competition in the related market in spare parts by seeking to enforce intellectual property rights. There are various reasons for this. Whereas the motorvehicle sector has suffered from a substantial brake on continued growth, and is increasingly put under strain in a changing international competitive environment,[51] the parts and accessories sector has steadily emerged as an important market in its own right.[52] In other words, whereas the car market has been subject to a decrease in profit margins, the spare parts market has increasingly gained in economic importance and has become highly lucrative. The car manufacturers, and the various independent manufacturers for that matter, thus obviously have a commercial interest in trying to increase their share of that market. Furthermore, car manufacturers could, by virtue of Block Exemption 123/85, no longer safeguard their market share in spare parts, and especially fast-moving parts, through inserting exclusive purchasing clauses in respect of spare parts in selective distribution agreements with their dealers.[53] One solution consisted in increasing the duration of guarantee work solely in relation to genuine parts and on condition that genuine parts should be used. However, motorvehicle manufacturers have also sought to circumvent the ban on exclusivity clauses concerning spare parts in their dealer contracts through the enforce-

---

[51] Unlike the Japanese industry the European motorvehicle industry has, since the 1973 oil crisis, suffered from a substantial brake on continued growth which has resulted in cyclical, rather than the previous regular annual expansion. Japanese motorvehicle manufacturers not only increased their market share in third markets at the expense of European producers, but also steadily increased their share in the Community market either through direct exports or through the establishment of transplant industries in the Community and in particular in the United Kingdom. On July 31, 1991 the E.C. and Japan reached an agreement whereby the latter undertook to voluntarily restrain its automobile exports to the E.C. until the end of 1999.

[52] Whereas in 1988 this sector already accounted for a turnover of around 65 billion ECUs, and employed about 0.6 million people, in 1991 it employed around 1 million people – or in other words more or less the same number as the motorvehicle industry – and accounted for a turnover estimated at almost 100 billion ECUs – or half the turnover of the motorvehicle industry. See E.C. Commission, *Panorama of E.C. industry 1990* and *Panorama of E.C. industry 1993* (Luxembourg, NACE 353), pp. 13–14 and 11–17 respectively. These figures should probably even be higher because the NACE data excludes, for example, most of the electronics and electrical components.

[53] See *supra*, at pt. 3(2)(d). It should be pointed out that the U.K. Monopolies and Mergers Commission recommended in 1982 that exclusivity clauses relating to the supply of spare parts should be excluded from all franchising contracts in order to provide for the possibility of independent manufacturers supplying spare parts to approved dealers of the distribution network. See the MMC, "Car Parts: a report on the matter of the existence or the possible existence of a complex monopoly position in relation to the wholesale supply of motor car parts in the United Kingdom" (1982, H.C. 318) in particular at pp. 38–40.

ment of intellectual property rights, and in particular design rights, in certain spare parts.[54] Body panels in particular were envisaged, as the latter constitute an important item of production by independent manufacturers.

Intellectual property rights are one of the factors that can turn a spare part   **9.20** into a captive part so that a supply monopoly may be obtained, whereas it should be recalled that the block exemption allows for exclusivity in relation to captive parts.[55] The enforcement of intellectual property rights in spare parts of cars may therefore have the same practical result as writing an exclusivity clause into a selective distribution agreement. Its effect may even go beyond in that all inter-brand competition may be eliminated. This would seriously affect the market structure in spare parts and significantly reduce consumers' choice as to where, and on which conditions, they have their cars repaired. Although this result is manifestly contrary to the objectives set forth by the Commission in the block exemption for car distribution agreements it is not, as such, prohibited by the latter. It should be emphasised that Article 85 E.C. is not applicable to the unilateral enforcement of intellectual property rights.[56] Through the enforcement of intellectual property rights the focus is shifted from fulfilling the objectives of the automobile policy to fulfilling the objectives of intellectual property law. The key question, therefore, is no longer whether or not exclusivity clauses can contractually be imposed on dealers under Article 85 E.C. but, rather, whether or not it is lawful to unilaterally enforce intellectual property rights on replacement parts for motor-vehicles under Article 86 E.C.

The Court has on two occasions been confronted with this crucial question with regard to the car manufacturers' practice of enforcing design rights on bodywork components of cars. It should be recalled that in the *CICRA and Maxicar v. Renault* case,[57] the national court questioned whether reliance on design rights to eliminate all competition in the market for spare parts was in conformity with Articles 36 and 86 E.C.[58] The *Volvo v. Veng* case,[59] which was ruled on the same day, was complementary to the *Maxicar* case. Here the issue raised was whether the car manufacturer could lawfully maintain his

---

[54] For instance subsequent to the MMC 1982 Car Parts Report, the Ford Motor Company radically changed its strategy in that it initiated legal action against U.K. independent manufacturers and importers of body panels for Ford cars invoking alleged infringement of its copyright and refusing to grant licences. This behaviour was held to be anti-competitive by the MMC in its 1985 Ford Motor Company Report (Cmnd. 9437) because it tended to keep up prices and to stifle innovation. It was pointed out that Ford's new strategy "was viewed as an attempt to foreclose a market by destroying the competition, rather than simply a decision by one company to exercise its legal rights": see T. Burke, A. Genn-Bash, B. Haines, *Competition in theory and practice* (2nd ed., 1991, Routledge), p. 171.

[55] See *supra*, at pt. 3(2)(d)(ii).

[56] See *supra*, Chap. 5, pt. 2(2).

[57] Case 53/87, *Consorzio italiano della componentistica di ricambio per autoveicoli and Maxicar v. Régie nationale des usines Renault*, Judgment of October 5, 1988: [1988] E.C.R. 6039; [1990] 4 C.M.L.R. 265.

[58] See *supra*, Chaps. 7 and 8 respectively.

[59] Case 238/87, *AB Volvo v. Erik Veng (U.K.) Ltd*, Judgment of October 5, 1988: [1988] E.C.R. 6211; [1989] 4 C.M.L.R. 122.

supply monopoly by refusing to grant licences on reasonable terms to independent manufacturers without infringing Article 86 E.C.[60] As was seen before, the Court gave a positive, albeit qualified, answer to both questions.[61] It should be mentioned that the spare parts picture under Community law could have been completed had the French courts been willing to pose a preliminary question to the Court of Justice in the *Renault v. Maxicar* case.[62] This third, and missing, panel of the spare parts triptych raised the issue of whether the simultaneous action for the seizure of spurious spare parts by car manufacturers, all of whom were holders of design rights, could constitute a concerted practice in the sense of Article 85 E.C. It was pointed out by the defendants that this behaviour frustrated the objectives of Regulation 123/85. The latter argument was of no relevance, however, in the two spare parts cases brought before the Court under Article 86 E.C.

(2) The impact of the spare parts cases

(a) Obtaining a supply monopoly

9.21   It is apparent that as far as the market for bodywork components is concerned, the rationale of tolerating certain restrictions on intra-brand competition on the assumption that effective inter-brand competition prevails[63] was seriously jeopardised by the acceptance of the enforcement of design rights in the *Maxicar* and *Volvo* cases.[64] The Commission's idea when drafting Article 3, point 4 of Regulation 123/85 was that prohibiting the insertion of a non-competition clause with respect to spare parts of an equal or superior quality in selective distribution contracts would ensure the perpetuation of effective inter-brand competition in the spare parts market.[65] The outcome of the spare parts cases have proved that it was premature to foster this expectation.

In both the *Maxicar* and *Volvo* cases, the Court upheld the car manufacturers' practice of enforcing design rights in bodywork components of cars under both the rules on the free movement of goods and the rules on competition. It should be recalled that the Court came to this conclusion without taking the function of design rights into account and despite the fact that this practice may entail the elimination of all inter-brand competition for the parts concerned.[66] By invoking design protection on parts which necessarily have to be identical to restore the car to its original appearance, car manufacturers thus succeeded in eliminating spurious parts from the market, simultaneously obtaining a legal supply monopoly for their bodywork components. Logically, this implies that, with regard to the bodywork components concerned, the prohibition on exclusive purchasing clauses in selective distribution agree-

---

[60] See *supra*, Chap. 8.
[61] See *supra*, Chap. 8, pt. 4(3)(c).
[62] Cour d'Appel de Dijon, *Régie nationale des usines Renault v. R. Thevenoux, Société Cass Center, O. Formento and Société Maxicar*, Judgment of January 12, 1990: [1990] R.I.P.I.A. 31.
[63] See *supra*, at pt. 3(2)(c)(iii).
[64] See *supra*, Chaps. 7 and 8.
[65] See *supra*, at pt. 3(2)(d)(i).
[66] See *supra*, Chap. 8, pt. 4(3).

ments became redundant. Furthermore, those parts became captive and might therefore be distributed exclusively through the car manufacturer's distribution network.

(b) Right to exclusive and selective distribution

(i) The rule

It should be recalled that the block exemption allows for exclusivity and selectivity with regard to parts supplied by the motorvehicle manufacturer, including captive spare parts.[67] Intra-brand competition in relation to these spare parts may be prohibited on more or less the same terms as apply to cars. In so far as captive spare parts are concerned, the block exemption had already made possible the occurrence of a legal monopoly for car manufacturers under Article 85(3) E.C. Contractual restrictions on intra-brand competition were thereby accepted even in the absence of inter-brand competition. The fact that the Court upheld the enforcement of design rights in bodywork components of cars in the spare parts cases under Article 86 E.C. not merely perpetuated this situation, but extended it to parts that traditionally were considered as spurious parts. In other words, rather than merely acknowledging the fact that no inter-brand competition existed in relation to certain parts, the Court went far beyond that in that it accepted the practice of eliminating existing competitors from the market. Admittedly, it is difficult to succesfully invoke vested rights and legitimate expectations against claims based on the protection of intellectual property rights. However, as was pointed out before, the Court failed to establish whether or not the enforcement of design rights in bodywork components of cars was at all in accordance with their functions.[68] The spare parts cases thus seemingly set a precedent for the unlimited invoking of intellectual property protection with the sole aim of excluding competitors from the market. The *Magill* cases put an unequivocal end to any further speculation in this respect.[69] It is to be regretted that the Court, in the latter cases, did not convincingly indicate where precisely the borderline between normal use and abuse of intellectual property rights is to be drawn under Article 86 E.C.

9.22

(ii) The exception: supply for repair purposes

The limitation imposed by the block exemption, in the sense that the supply of spare parts to resellers may not be contractually prohibited if the spare parts are purchased for their own use in effecting repairs or maintenance, is particularly relevant to captive spare parts.[70] It is apparent that otherwise independent repairers would not have access to those parts whereas competing parts might be eliminated from the market. The result would be that the consumer would necessarily have to avail himself of the services of the approved network. The spare parts cases will most likely have lowered the expectations of those who found the purchasing-for-repair-purposes exception to have

9.23

---

[67] See *supra*, at pt. 3(2)(c)(ii).
[68] See *supra*, Chaps. 7 and 8.
[69] On the *Magill* cases, see *supra*, Chap. 5, pt. 4(3).
[70] See *supra*, at pt. 3(2)(d)(ii).

several shortcomings. For instance, it has been pointed out that the block exemption offers no guarantee as to the conditions under which the parts will be sold, if they will be sold at all, for repair purposes by dealers. The hope was therefore expressed that, despite the exemption of exclusivity clauses in distribution contracts, the car manufacturers themselves would be held to be under an obligation to supply captive spare parts to independent repairers.[71] The argument that the refusal to supply would amount to an abuse of a dominant position under Article 86 E.C. has become difficult to maintain after the spare parts cases. It should be recalled that the Court held in the *Volvo* case that only an *arbitrary* refusal to sell spare parts to independent repairers might constitute an infringement of Article 86 E.C. This would seem to imply that a bare refusal to supply spare parts for repair purposes by the car manufacturers would not be incompatible with Article 86 E.C.[72]

(c) Evaluation

9.24   Through the enforcement of design rights in bodywork components of cars, the objectives set forth in the block exemption for selective car distribution with regard to spare parts have been seriously jeopardised. Most striking, when combining the spare parts cases with the block exemption, is the finding that the car manufacturer obtains a perfect legal monopoly on what was previously a competitive good. This is the result of the fact that the spare parts cases allow for the elimination of inter-brand competition under Article 86 E.C., whereas the block exemption already exempted restrictions on intra-brand competition under Article 85(3) E.C. As a consequence, the competitive and lively market structure in spare parts will most likely be substantially affected. Simultaneously, it is also liable to jeopardise the rationale underlying the safety valves inserted in the block exemption, namely to safeguard the consumer's basic right to have the car repaired wherever price and quality are most advantageous to him.[73] In other words, the enforcement of design rights in bodywork components of cars is manifestly contrary to the competition policy objectives set forth by the Commission. However, even if it leads to the elimination of all competition from the market, the unilateral enforcement of intellectual property rights is not contrary to Article 85 E.C. whereas in the spare parts cases, contrary to the subsequent *Magill* case, such behaviour was upheld by the Court under Article 86 E.C. The question remains of whether it is, nevertheless, still possible for the Commission to undertake some kind of action in order to safeguard the competition policy objectives.

[71] See, for instance, C. Joerges, "The Commission Regulation 123/85 on automobile distribution and servicing agreements: competition policy objectives and their implications for the consumer interest", in Joerges, Hiller, Holzeck, Micklitz, *Vertriebspraktiken im Automobilersatzteilsektor* (1985, Verlag Peter Lang), pp. 353–386 at pp. 377–379, where he points to the incoherence between Regulation 123/85 and the tone of the *Hugin* decision in this respect.
[72] On this issue, see *supra*, Chap. 8, pt. 4(4)(a).
[73] See *supra*, at pt. 3(2)(c)(i).

5. POSSIBLE SCOPE OF ACTION FOR THE E.C. COMMISSION

(1) The rules on competition

The fact that the Court held in the spare parts cases that the enforcement of 9.25
design rights in bodywork components of cars is not contrary to Articles
30–36 E.C. or Article 86 E.C., whereas this practice is not as such prohibited
by the block exemption for selective car distribution, does not imply that the
Commission is devoid of all means of action to try to restore competition in
the spare parts market. Although the Commission obviously does not have
the competence to alter the ruling of the Court in the spare parts cases, it does
have the task of ensuring that the objectives of E.C. competition policy in
general, and those put forward in the block exemption in particular, are
observed by undertakings.

(a) Revoking the benefit of the block exemption

Article 10 of the block exemption for selective car distribution expressly pro- 9.26
vides that the Commission may withdraw the benefit of the application of the
block exemption if it finds that an agreement, although formally in accordance with the regulation, nevertheless has effects which are incompatible with
Article 85(3) E.C. In particular, this possibility exists if:

> "the contract goods are not subject to competition from products con-
> sidered by consumers as similar by reason of their characteristics, price
> and intended use."[74]

In essence this means that whereas the Commission cannot prevent the application of intellectual property rights to eliminate competition in the market
for spare parts it can, nevertheless, re-examine the status of dealer contracts
which restrict intra-brand competition in cases where inter-brand competition has been eliminated by virtue of the enforcement of intellectual property
rights.

In this respect, it is important to note that although the possible revoking of
the application of the block exemption may act as a deterrent, it by no means
restores inter-brand competition. At the most, the Commission may determine that if inter-brand competition has been eliminated with regard to what
were previously spurious spare parts, then the general exemption for restrictions on intra-brand competition contained in the block exemption can no
longer be justified. It should be recalled that the rationale of the block exemption is that certain restrictions on intra-brand competition may be tolerated
because inter-brand competition is held to exist.[75] It would apparently need to
be re-considered whether the conditions of Article 85(3) E.C. are still fulfilled
subsequent to the enforcement of intellectual property rights if this entails the

---

[74] See Article 10, pt. 1 of Regulation 123/85 and Article 8, pt. 1 of the new block exemption. In this
respect see also *supra*, at pt. 3(2)(c)(iii). On the general possibility of revoking, see J. Dubois,
"*La distribution automobile dans le marché commun: le point de vue de la Commission
Européenne*" in *Droit des Consommateurs* (J. Pizzio ed. 1987) (Story Scientia), pp. 91–97, at
p. 96.
[75] See *supra*, at pt. 3(2)(c)(iii).

exclusion of all competition from the market. However, it is obvious that for this kind of analysis many elements need to be taken into account, such as the impact of specific clauses in individual agreements against a well-defined competitive background.

(b) Imposing compulsory licences

(i) Regulation 17

9.27 A more controversial issue is whether, and when, the Commission may impose compulsory licences with respect to intellectual property rights under Regulation 17.[76] The Court expressly acknowledged this possibility for the first time in the *Magill* appeal case.[77] Advocate General Mischo maintained in the *Volvo* case that the Commission, on the basis of Article 3 of Regulation 17, could impose compulsory licences to bring a possible abuse of a dominant position with regard to intellectual property rights to an end.[78] Article 3 of Regulation 17 provides that the Commission can, by way of a decision, order undertakings to bring an infringement of Article 86 E.C. to an end. Although the Court decided differently in the *Magill* case, it was pointed out in legal writings that this seemed to exclude the possibility of the Commission directly intervening through the granting of obligatory licences to third parties.[79] The same result could, nonetheless, also be achieved indirectly. The possibility of the Commission imposing fines upon finding an infringement might be a sufficient deterrent to bring the alleged anti-competitive behaviour to an end.[80] If not, the Commission could also impose a recognisance, or periodic penalty payments, upon non-termination of the infringement.[81]

(ii) The consequences

9.28 One consequence of the imposition of compulsory licences, whether directly or indirectly, under Regulation 17 is that it puts an affirmative action obligation upon intellectual property owners. The further question arises of what the consequences of the compulsory licence will be in terms of the exhaustion of intellectual property rights, having regard to the Court's prior case law in that respect.

—Affirmative action obligation

9.29 In both the *Volvo* and the *Magill* cases the alleged anti-competitive behaviour consisted of the refusal to grant intellectual property licences on reasonable terms to third parties. In other words, the issue of the applicability of Article 86 E.C. arose because the dominant undertaking failed to take action. Terminating the alleged infringement of Article 86 E.C. would thus entail a positive

---

[76] Regulation 17, [1962] O.J. L13/204, as modified by Regulations 59, ([1962] O.J. 1655), 118/63 ([1963] O.J. 2696), 2822/71 ([1971] O.J. L285/49).

[77] See *supra*, Chap. 5, pt. 4(3)(c).

[78] See his opinion on Case 238/87: [1988] E.C.R. 6211; [1989] 4 C.M.L.R. 122, at para. 31.

[79] See, for instance, J.-J. Burst, R. Kovar, "*Les licences imposées et le droit communautaire*" [1990] C.D.E. 249 at 268.

[80] On the competence of the Commission to impose fines, see Article 15 of Regulation 17.

[81] On the competence of the Commission to impose a recognisance, see Article 16 of Regulation 17.

action by the undertaking concerned in the sense that the exclusivity resulting from intellectual property protection would need to be shared with third parties. This is different from mainstream cases where the anti-competitive behaviour consists in a positive action which has to be terminated or made undone.

The approach taken by the Court to this issue in the *Magill* case seems to be radically opposed to the one adopted in the earlier *Volvo* case. In the *Volvo* case, the Court held that the refusal to license is not, of itself, contrary to Article 86 E.C. It was further held that the imposition of the obligation to license would lead to the proprietor of the intellectual property right being deprived of the substance of his exclusive right.[82] In the light of these clarifications it seemed rather doubtful if the Commission could impose a positive action upon undertakings, particularly in relation to the exercise of their exclusive intellectual property rights.[83] The ruling of the CFI in the *Magill* cases nevertheless impliedly acknowledged this possibility.[84] The latter approach was upheld by the Court on appeal.[85] It was thereby expressly stated that also in relation to the exercise of intellectual property rights the application made by the Commission of Article 3 of Regulation 17 may include "an order to do certain things which, unlawfully, have not been done...".[86] In other words, compulsory intellectual property licences may be imposed by the Commission if this is the only means of bringing an infringement under Article 86 E.C. to an end. The crucial question remains, however, of when the Court will in future hold the refusal to license either not to constitute an infringement, as in the *Volvo* case or, to the contrary, to be abusive as in *Magill*. If there is no finding of abusive behaviour, the question of whether or not compulsory licences should be imposed in order to remedy the infringement of Article 86 E.C. obviously does not even arise.

—Exhaustion of intellectual property rights

The second issue is what impact the imposition of compulsory licences 9.30
will have on the application of the rules on the free movement of goods. In

---

[82] See *supra*, Chap. 8, pt. 4(3)(c).

[83] See also A. Reindl, *op. cit.*, at pp. 77–80, where he argues that although there might be a justification for the "essential facilities" doctrine, which implies that the obligation to share access to an essential facility might be imposed on an undertaking controlling this facility, the *Maxicar* and *Volvo* cases show that this will not be accepted by the Court if the undertaking concerned holds exclusive intellectual property rights. It is significant that the Commission, prior to the car spare parts cases, thought that the refusal to license independent undertakings, which leads to the total elimination of competition in the market for bodywork components of cars, might constitute an abuse of a dominant position in the sense of Article 86 E.C. On those grounds it opened an investigation under the rules on competition in the *Ford* case. Subsequent to the coming into force of the 1988 U.K. Act, which excluded bodywork components from design and copyright protection but allowed for a transitional period of protection for existing designs of 15 years, Ford gave a formal undertaking to the Commission to limit the enforcement of its exclusive right to a maximum of five years (see IP (90) 4 as well as the XXth Report on Competition Policy 1990, pp. 108–109, at pt. 112). However, the *Maxicar* and *Volvo* cases had, in the meantime, been decided in the sense that the enforcement of design rights and the subsequent elimination of competition were not in themselves contrary to Article 86 E.C. The Commission nonetheless pointed out that it wanted to ensure that consumers are not dependent on one source of supply for spare parts.

[84] See *supra*, Chap. 5, pt. 4(3)(b).

[85] See *supra*, Chap. 5, pt. 4(3)(c).

[86] Joined Cases C 241 and 242/91 P: [1995] E.C.R. I–743; [1995] 4 C.M.L.R. 718, at para. 90.

particular, the question arises of what will be the consequences in terms of the exhaustion of intellectual property rights. This question does not arise only with respect to compulsory licences that may apparently be directly imposed by the Commission subsequent to the *Magill* case. If the same result is achieved indirectly through the imposition of fines and recognisances by the Commission in order to force intellectual property owners to grant licences, would not this also constitute compulsory licences for the application of the principle of exhaustion? If it were held that the licence has not really been given with the intellectual property owner's consent, then it seems that the *Pharmon v. Hoechst* ruling could be held to be applicable in respect of the free movement of intellectual property protected goods.[87] Applied to the spare parts cases, this would imply that parallel imports of goods manufactured by independent manufacturers under such a licence could be prohibited by the car manufacturers, so that the activity of the independent manufacturers could be confined to the market of one Member State. Needless to say, this prospect would make the possibility of manufacturing bodywork components for cars less attractive to independent manufacturers because it would obviously prevent them from benefiting from the same economies of scale as the car manufacturers.

(2) Legislative initiative: proposals on the legal protection of industrial designs

(a) Preliminary remarks

9.31   Another possibility for the Commission to take action consists of using its prerogative to propose E.C. harmonisation measures in relation to intellectual property rights. Other than the application of the rules on competition, which merely curtail the exercise of intellectual property rights, this form of action may have a direct effect on the conditions and requirements that need to be fulfilled for the conferment of intellectual property protection. In other words, if they are also adopted by the Council, these measures may affect and determine the very existence of intellectual property rights.

9.32   The Commission is currently trying to elaborate a system of Community Designs modelled on the approach adopted concerning the Community Trademark,[88] namely introducing both a directive to approximate national design laws and a regulation introducing the Community Design based on a Community-wide territoriality principle.[89] The Green Paper of June 1991 was a first initiative in this sense and at the Hearing of the Commission on the Green Paper in Brussels, February 25 and 26, 1992 some amendments to the text were proposed.[90] This resulted in the proposals currently tabled on a Council Regulation on the Community Design and a Directive on the Legal Protection of Designs.[91] It is significant that the Commission specifically

---

[87] Case 19/84, *Pharmon v. Hoechst*, Judgment of July 9, 1985: [1985] E.C.R. 2281; [1985] 3 C.M.L.R. 775. For an analysis, see *supra*, Chap. 6, pt. 2(4).

[88] See *supra*, Chap. 3, pt. 3(2)(b)(ii).

[89] See also *supra*, Chap. 3, pt. 3(2)(b)(iv).

[90] Green Paper on the Legal Protection of Industrial Design (III/F/5131/91, June 1991).

[91] Respectively COM (93) 342 final and COM (93) 344 final, both of December 3, 1993; respectively [1994] O.J. C29/20 and [1993] O.J. C345/14.

endeavoured to smooth out the differences which currently exist in the Member States concerning design protection on spare parts of cars, whilst giving due regard to the other Community policies. The draftsman of the Green Paper, B. Posner, wrote:

> "One of the hot issues of design protection in the last years has been the protection of components of spare parts. I take it that I do not need to recall the history and the battles which have been fought in the U.K. on the protection of exhaust pipes and the like. The Commission has been following this discussion since the mid eighties and it was quite clear to me from the outset that we would have to find a compromise solution which was coherent with Commission policies in other areas."[92]

This compromise solution proposed by the Commission in the Green Paper was merely to exclude "interconnections" from Community design protection. However, the spare parts debate proved to be the most controversial issue during the hearing,[93] and finally led the Commission to insert a repair clause in its current proposals.

(b) Main features

As mentioned above, the aim of the Commission's proposals is to introduce a directive to approximate national design laws, as well as a regulation providing a system of Community-wide design protection. This implies that in principle national design law, although in an approximated form concerning substantive features of the protection, will coexist alongside the Community design. The objective of the harmonisation of national design laws is to introduce common rules covering some, but not all, of the designs currently in force in the Member States.[94] For instance, the Community design will not affect the United Kingdom system of unregistered design protection.[95] Harmonisation also implies that the national territoriality principle is left intact so that this will not totally remedy the obstacles posed to the free circulation of goods.[96] Similarly, the introduction of a Community design based on a "Community territoriality principle" will not in itself solve the problems posed concerning the relationship between competition rules and intellectual property rights. Regard must therefore be had to the type of protection which is envisaged in the proposals in order to assess the changes that they will bring about.

9.33

In so far as the Community design is concerned, two different forms of legal protection would be available, namely an Unregistered Community Design

9.34

---

[92] B. Posner, "The Community Design: purpose and scope of the Green Paper on the legal protection of industrial design" in F. Gotzen (ed.), *op. cit.*, pp. 1–11, at p. 10.

[93] See COM (93) 342 final, pt. 7.3.

[94] See P. Groves, "Don't be vague: towards an international system for design registration" [1992] *European Business Law Review* 230 at 231, where he maintains that this implies that "those left over may be protected, or not, as the Member State wishes".

[95] See B. Posner, *op. cit.*, p. 5. The reason given for this is that in the U.K., copyright will hardly ever be applicable to industrial designs so that the unregistered design system can be assimilated to the copyright protection offered in the other Member States. To remove the U.K. system of unregistered design protection as it currently exists would mean that only registered designs could be protected.

[96] See *supra*, Chap. 3, pt. 3(3).

and a Registered Community Design. The conditions for obtaining one or the other would be the same. The major difference between the two types of protection lies in the nature of the rights they confer. The Unregistered Community Design would be, as the name suggests, a design right which requires no formalities. It would be granted for a limited period of time (the Commission tentatively proposes three years) and offer protection against unauthorised reproduction. The term of protection would start with the first disclosure of the design to the public.[97] The Registered Community Design, on the other hand, would, as the name suggests, be subject to registration and valid for up to 25 years on the basis of a five-year renewal term. The protection granted here would be much wider in scope since it would confer genuine exclusive rights on the design holder.[98]

(c) Relation to competition

(i) Underlying rationale

9.35   The Commission underlines the balance between intellectual property protection and competition policy objectives which is already inherent in the functions of the former, and of design protection in particular.[99] It is pointed out that:

> "Intellectual property rights confer upon the right holder exclusive rights. Given the objectives of intellectual and industrial property rights as regards the investment in innovation and creativity, this aspect of intellectual property does not normally give rise to misgivings from a competition policy point of view provided that the rights are exercised in an equitable manner and provided that competition in the market place is not stultified by the creation of monopolies in generic products.
>
> The Regulation is fully in conformity with these guidelines. Design protection does not monopolise given products, but protects the individual appearance given to a products by its designer. Protection of the design of a watch does not hamper competition in the watch market."[1]

(ii) Exceptions to design protection

9.36   In the proposals it is foreseen that design protection may be granted to both functional and aesthetic designs. In order to ensure that the grant of design protection does not lead to the creation of a monopoly on a generic product, designs which are dictated solely by their technical function have been excluded from the scope of protection by virtue of Article 9(1) Draft Regulation. This exception to design protection is also provided for in most national design law.

9.37   Article 9(2) Draft Regulation goes a step further for it provides a general exception to design protection where the product concerned is an interconnecting part of another product. It goes without saying that this is a very

---

[97] Article 20 Draft Regulation, COM (93) 342 final.
[98] See Article 21 of the proposed regulation.
[99] See also *supra*, Chap. 2, pt. 3.
[1] See the preamble to the Explanatory Memorandum to COM (93) 342 final, pts. 9.1 and 9.2.

important exception as far as spare parts of cars are concerned.[2] It is not surprising that it was drafted with the United Kingdom debates on spare parts very much in mind. The way in which the provision is drafted is very restrictive in its definition of "interconnections". It is stated that:

"A Community Design shall not subsist in a design to the extent that it must necessarily be reproduced in their exact form and dimensions in order to permit the product to which the design is applied to be mechanically assembled or connected with another product."[3]

The purpose is to safeguard the interoperability of products and to prevent the creation of captive markets by conferring a monopoly on the shape and dimension of interconnections. Modular products do not, however, come under this exception and may thus be subject to design protection.[4]

(iii) The repair clause

A peculiarity of components of complex products is that they may need to have a certain design, not because this is dictated by a technical function or in order to safeguard interoperability, but in order to match the design of the complex product. The above-mentioned exceptions therefore do not always suffice to prevent the creation of captive markets or monopolies from arising by virtue of the enforcement of design rights. The market for spare parts for motorvehicles is a prime example in this respect. This was also acknowledged by the Commission, which wrote: **9.38**

"In very rare cases a design protection sweeping in scope as the Community Design may have secondary unwanted effects as regards exclusion or limitation of competition in the market place. This is true in particular for costly, long lasting complex products such as motorvehicles, where design protection of the design relating to the individual parts of which the complex product is composed could create a truly captive market in spare parts."[5]

Considering the wide-spread criticism, especially by consumers organisations and independent manufacturers of spare parts of cars, of the absence of any reference to this problem in its first draft, the Commission inserted the so-called "repair clause" in its final proposals. The objective is to allow for the use of spurious spare parts, the shape of which is imperative to restore the car to its original appearance, exclusively for repair purposes and after three years from the first marketing of the spare part by the car manufacturers. The new Article 23 of the Draft Regulation reads as follows:

---

[2] This issue was not dealt with in the Max Planck draft on which the proposals of the Commission are largely based, much to the regret of Professor Cornish who wrote: "The only major issue that goes unresolved in the plan, but which cannot sensibly be avoided, is the spare parts question: when the form of a replacement part is dictated by 'must-fit' or 'must-match' considerations, should the right to exclude copying really be available?": W.R. Cornish, "Designs Again" [1991] E.I.P.R. 3 at 3.

[3] Article 9(2) Draft Regulation, COM (93) 342 final.

[4] See Article 9(3) Draft Regulation.

[5] Explanatory Memorandum to the Draft Regulation, COM (93) 342 final, pt. 9.3.

"The rights conferred by a Registered Community Design shall not be exercised against third parties who, after three years from the first putting on the market of a product incorporating the design or to which the design is applied, use the design under Article 21, provided that:

(a) the product incorporating the design or to which the design is applied is a part of a complex product upon whose appearance the protected design is dependent;

(b) the purpose of such a use is to permit the repair of the complex product so as to restore its original appearance; and

(c) the public is not misled as to the origin of the product used for repair."[6]

The Commission explains that the purpose is "to avoid the creation of captive markets in certain spare parts".[7] Or, in other words, to prevent the long-term tie-in of consumers through the elimination of all competition, especially in the market for bodywork components of cars, which would provide a monopoly position for the car manufacturers even after the expiry of the design protection. The Commission points out that it would, for practical reasons, most likely not be worthwhile for independent manufacturers of those spare parts to enter the market after the expiry of the full term of design protection.

(iv) Evaluation of the repair clause

9.39 Although the repair clause thus resembles a "must-match" exception, it is submitted that the underlying rationale is diametrically opposed. The "must-match" exception can be explained in terms of the function of design protection.[8] Designs are not meant to create a monopoly in generic products but are essentially a factor of non-price competition. If a part has to have a certain shape to restore the car to its original appearance, then the design obviously does not confer an added value to the spare part so that it should not benefit from exclusive protection. The premise to the repair clause is, to the contrary, that the design holder's right is impinged upon so that the exception should be restrictively interpreted.[9] The Commission merely presents the issue as a compromise between respecting the legitimate claims of a design holder and the need to safeguard competition in the market for replacement parts. The compromise lies in that the design holder may exercise his exclusive right for three years after which competition will be free. Yet it is apparent that the Commission is not really concerned with the imperatives of design legislation. The real issue seems to be to draw a balance between the claims of consumer organisations and independent manufacturers of spare parts, on the one hand, and the claims for protection by the motorvehicle industry on the other. It is therefore not surprising that the repair clause is highly controversial since it seems to be based on arbitrary criteria inspired merely by competition policy concerns, and does not live up to the expectations of either party. It

[6] Article 23 of the Draft Regulation, COM (93) 342 final; Article 14 of the Draft Directive, COM (93) 344 final.
[7] COM (93) 342 final, p. 20.
[8] On the functions inherent to design protection, see *supra*, Chap. 2, pt. 3(5).
[9] See the explanation given by the Commission, COM (93) 342 final, at p. 20.

is significant in this respect that Commissioner Bangemann has already stated that the three-year term of protection for car manufacturers as currently proposed is not sufficient, not because of the need to safeguard the function of design protection, but because industrial designs are among our best weapons to defend our share of the market ("... *nos meilleurs armes pour défendre nos parts de marché*").[10]

(d) Relationship to other forms of intellectual property protection

It is, of course, not sufficient to look at the implications the Community design system will have on its own. Consideration should be given equally to the extent to which parallel national intellectual property protection will remain possible. The following questions are of crucial importance: will national design law coexist and will double protection, especially the cumulation of copyright and design law, be possible? **9.40**

(i) National design protection

The Commission has no clear vision as yet of whether or not national design protection should continue to coexist with the Community design in the long run. Therefore, a pragmatic approach is advocated until enough experience is acquired with the new system.[11] This approach consists in maintaining parallel national design protection on condition that a sufficient level of harmonisation takes place so as not to jeopardise the system of Community design. It is to achieve this end that the Commission has tabled a proposal for a directive on the approximation of national design law alongside the proposal for a Community Design Regulation. **9.41**

There is a double reason underlying the harmonisation directive. The first, and most obvious one, is to render national design laws more uniform so that the competitive position of potential design holders will not differ from one Member State to another.[12] The second reason is directly linked to the introduction of the Community design. Namely, national design laws not only need to be harmonised among themselves, but they also have to be rendered compatible with the Community design system as far as their substantive features are concerned.[13] If this were not so, preference would be given to more favourable national protection to the detriment of the Community design instrument.

A different question is the one of cumulation with national design protection. Does a designer have to choose between national or Community design protection or can he obtain both? In the Green Paper proposals, the Commission excluded the cumulation of both kinds of registered design **9.42**

---

[10] Speech of Commissioner Bangemann at a Conference in Turin on November 9, 1993 on "Turin meets the future of the European car" as reported in *Agence Europe* (No. 6106, November 13, 1993), p. 9.
[11] Green Paper, Explanatory Memorandum, Chap. 10; COM (93) 344 final, pt. 1.3.
[12] Green Paper, Explanatory Memorandum, pt. 10.3.2. To use the words of the Commission, "harmonisation is required to avoid distortion of competition within the internal market".
[13] *id.*, pt. 10.3.1. In COM (93) 344 final, pt. 1.4., it is held that "this proposals for a Directive on the legal protection of designs is an essential accompaniment to the Regulation on the Community Design".

protection, on the basis that their legal effect is the same.[14] As such, it was initially specified that a registered Community design would render previously existing national registered designs ineffective. This has, however, been abandoned in the final proposals which allow for full cumulation of both national and Community registered designs.[15]

(ii) Patents, utility models and trade marks

9.43   Besides the coexistence of national design protection, another important factor is whether or not other forms of national intellectual property protection can be cumulated with the Community design. In so far as patents, utility models and trade marks are concerned, it is provided that double protection will be possible as long as the design concerned lives up to the requirements imposed by the different systems.[16] It should be pointed out, in this respect, that patents and utility models may thus be obtained on designs that are dictated solely by their function in as much as the conditions required for that type of intellectual property protection are fulfilled.

(iii) Copyright

9.44   More important is the question of whether Community design protection can be cumulated with national copyright protection. The approach taken to this problem varies considerably from one Member State to another. The Commission has opted for making the possibility of double protection a matter of principle whilst leaving it up to the Member States to determine the extent and the conditions, including the definition of the concept "originality", for obtaining copyright protection.[17] However, certain conditions which are currently in force in certain Member States are expressly mentioned as conditions which could no longer be imposed once the Community system enters into force. For instance, copyright protection should be granted regardless of whether "the design can be dissociated from the products to which it is applied or intended to be applied".[18] However, it should be mentioned that the Commission does not exclude the possibility of harmonising the copyright notion of "originality" relating to industrial designs, in future, in a similar way as has been done for computer programs.[19]

Making the granting of copyright in designs compulsory would, in the light of the objective expressed in the Green Paper to render the legal protection on industrial designs more uniform throughout the Community, logically imply

[14] id., pt. 10.4.1.
[15] See the new Article 99 of the Draft Regulation and the explanation given on p. 42 of COM (93) 342 final.
[16] Article 100 Draft Regulation and Article 18 Draft Directive. Civil liability and unfair competition rules are also mentioned.
[17] See B. Posner, op. cit., at p. 4, where he explains that "the Commission fears that an attempt to harmonise this issue – which by many Member States is felt being a delicate and difficult one touching upon fundamental copyright policies – could delay or even jeopardize the whole design project. For this reason alone a postponement is suggested".
[18] Article 100(2) Draft Regulation and Article 18(1) Draft Directive, respectively COM (93) 342 final and COM (93) 344 final. This clearly aims at removing the Italian requirement of scindibilità. See also B. Posner, op. cit., p. 4, where he confirms that it is the Italian system of single protection and some peculiarities of the U.K. and Irish systems that are envisaged.
[19] Green Paper, Explanatory Memorandum, pt. 11.3.6. On the legal protection of computer programs, see supra, Chap. 3, pt. 3(2)(b).

that copyright legislation is itself at least to some extent harmonised so as not to create distortions of competition within the internal market and not to jeopardise the principle of free movement of goods, or the objectives put forward in the Green Paper. However, it is clear that the mere insertion of Article 100 Draft Regulation, and Article 18 Draft Directive, in design legislation will not suffice to achieve this end. Up till now the Commission has not taken a coherent approach towards harmonisation of national copyright laws but rather has dealt with the matter on a sectoral basis.[20] The most important measure taken so far in this respect is the Council Directive to harmonise the term of protection of copyright and certain related rights. The standard duration of protection for literary or artistic works, within the meaning of Article 2 of the Berne Convention, is fixed at 70 years after the death of the author or 70 years after the work is lawfully made public in the case of collective works or works created by a legal person. According to Article 2(7) Berne Convention (Paris Act), it is up to the legislator of the countries of the Union to include industrial designs and models in the scope of protection.[21] However, as seen above, copyright protection will probably have to be granted in industrial designs by virtue of the Commission's proposals. As such, it seems that through the combination of both the directive on copyright duration and the proposal on industrial design rights, Member States will not only be invited to offer copyright protection on industrial designs but will further have to extend the duration of protection beyond what is currently provided for in most Member States.[22]

9.45 Besides the introduction of the principle of cumulation of design and copyright protection, the proposal further alters the existing conditions on which such a double protection was granted to designs having another country of origin. As seen above, Article 2(7) of the Berne Convention expressly mentions that in such a case of double copyright/design protection, a reciprocity requirement may be imposed. The Commission, however, maintained that this is contrary to the principle of non-discrimination in Community law and substituted this with the requirement of national treatment.[23] As such, Article 100(3) Draft Regulation introduces the following obligation:

> "Each Member State shall admit to the protection under its law of copyright a design protected by a Community Design which fulfils the conditions required by such a law, even if in another Member State which is the country of origin of the design, the latter does not fulfil the conditions for protection under the law of copyright of that state."[24]

[20] See *supra*, Chap. 3, pt. 3(2)((b)(iv).

[21] On the Berne Convention, see *supra*, Chap. 2, pt. 4(1).

[22] Currently, only Germany offers copyright protection for 70 years *post mortem auctores* (pma). The other Member States have adopted the minimum term of protection provided for in the Berne Convention, namely 50 years pma, with the exception of Spain who has a standard term of protection of 60 years pma. For a comparative list, see COM (92) 33 final of 23 March 1992, p. 45.

[23] Green Paper, Explanatory Memorandum, pt. 11.3.3. See also A. Firth, "Aspects of design protection in Europe" [1993] E.I.P.R. 42 at 43, where she writes that Article 2 (7) Berne Convention "...enables those countries which do use copyright protection for protecting industrial designs to discriminate between foreign designs according to the kind of protection available in the country of origin".

[24] COM (93) 342 final. Similarly, see Article 18(2) Draft Directive, COM (93) 344 final.

This is fully in accordance with the ruling which the Court in the meantime adopted in the *Phil Collins* case.[25]

(e) Evaluation

9.46   The protection to be granted to components of complex products is the most controversial issue the Commission has had to deal with in its proposals. It is also this issue which is most likely to jeopardise the acceptance of the proposals, as they stand now, by the European Parliament and the Council. The basic principle is that components of complex products, such as spare parts of cars, can fully benefit from design protection if, individually, they fulfil the requirements for this. This rule is subject, however, to certain exceptions which are particularly relevant to the spare parts controversy. In order to benefit from design protection, the design of the spare part may not be dictated by its technical function. Furthermore, a "must-fit" exception in the form of the exclusion of interconnection was accepted from the start. Conversely, it was never the intention of the Commission to insert a "must-match" exception as is currently in force in the United Kingdom. Instead, a repair clause has been introduced in the final proposals which is intended specifically for, but which will most likely not be limited to, the motorvehicle and related industries. This clause, which limits the exercise of design rights in spare parts, the shape of which is imperative to restore the car to its original appearance, to three years, is highly controversial. In theory, it acknowledges the existence, or grant, of the exclusive right whereas the limitation of its full exercise, or enforcement, to a three-year term of protection seems to be based on arbitrary criteria rather than by imperatives of design protection.

9.47   When, and if, the Community design system enters into force as it is conceived now by the Commission, design protection on spare parts of cars will have to be made possible in all Member States on the condition that the individual spare part concerned can be individually marketed, lives up to the requirements for design protection, and provided the "must-fit" exception does not apply to it. Furthermore, the cumulation of copyright and design protection will become the general principle. This means a radical change concerning the legal systems currently in force in the different Member States. It may therefore be doubted if the approximation directive will be readily adopted by the Council. Just to give some examples, this would imply that the United Kingdom would have to reconsider the recently introduced, and much debated, "must-match" exception.[26] France, as well as the other Member States, would have to introduce the "must-fit" exception. Italy would have to radically revise its system of single protection.[27] Considering the close link

---

[25] See *supra*, Chap. 2, pt. 4(1)(c)(iv).

[26] Comparing the current system of design protection in the United Kingdom to the Green Paper proposal, Armitage writes: "There are some important differences which are not obviously for the better." The three differences he focuses upon are: (1) extending registered designs protection to functional designs; (2) a novelty-test referring to knowledge of Community circles rather than to publication in the U.K.; (3) offering unregistered designs protection for a period of three years. See E. Armitage, "Community Designs" [1992] E.I.P.R. 3.

[27] On the proposal tabled in Italy in order to bring Italian design law more into line with the E.C. Commission's proposals, see M. Cimoli, "Towards a new Italian design law" [1993] E.I.P.R. 425. He points out that although the principle of *scindibilità* would be formally abolished, doubts remain as to the practical impact of these formal changes.

between the "Community Design Regulation" and the directive with regard to the substantive features of the protection proposed, it may be expected that the regulation will not be adopted before the approximation directive so as not to jeopardise the envisaged objectives. But even when the Commission's proposals, as they stand now or in an amended version, come into force, the design rights derived from the Community Design system will still need to be applied with due regard to the principle of free movement of goods, because of the coexistence of national design legislation and the cumulation with copyright protection. Due regard will also need to be given to the rules on competition especially as the Community design, despite the stated objectives to the contrary, confers a legal monopoly in certain cases.

PART IV

CONCLUSION

10. General Conclusion

Distinguishing between the use and abuse of intellectual property rights in Community law is not an easy exercise. Clearly there is a difficulty in reconciling the current evolution, whereby intellectual property rights are increasingly used to gain market dominance, with the traditional perception of intellectual property rights as non-economic barriers to trade expressed in Article 36 of the E.C. Treaty.[1] This difficulty is further enhanced by the fact that the granting of intellectual property protection is to a large extent still governed by national law. The scope of protection offered may therefore vary greatly from one Member State to another so that different competitive conditions may prevail. One could, nonetheless, conceive of essentially three ways to deal with the detrimental effects arising from the potential abuse of the system of intellectual property rights in Community context: legislative action, application of the rules on competition, and scrutiny of the existence of intellectual property rights under Article 36 E.C. by the European Court of Justice. Whilst each of these solutions has its merit, each also has its major shortcomings, particularly if considered under the current state of Community law. An alternative solution therefore seems to impose itself.

10.01

---

[1] On Article 36 E.C., see *supra*, Chap. 3, pt. 2(2).

• SOLUTION 1: LEGISLATIVE ACTION

10.02 Legislative action is by far to be preferred over the other two solutions, particularly because it confers a certain degree of legal certainty and transparency which is currently lacking. The issuing of comprehensive harmonisation measures in the field of intellectual property protection makes it possible to render the conditions and procedures for obtaining intellectual property rights more or less uniform throughout the Community.[2] Distortions posed to intra-Community trade due to differing competitive conditions may thus be eliminated. Also, harmonisation measures may lay down exceptions to protectability in order to prevent unwarranted anti-competitive effects, such as monopolies on generic products, from arising. Similarly, it may also be determined what use the intellectual property owner may lawfully make of his exclusive right.

10.03 Harmonisation of intellectual property laws does not imply, however, that the rules on competition become totally redundant. The latter will continue to apply whenever the enforcement of the exclusive right gives rise to certain exceptional and unforeseen anti-competitive effects, such as tie-ins. Similarly, harmonisation does not totally eliminate the effect of the principle of territoriality in the intra-Community context. It is of course possible, and this is the current practice, to write the principle of exhaustion of intellectual property rights into harmonisation measures.[3] This then implies that the intellectual property owner may no longer invoke his intellectual property rights in a Member State in order to prohibit the importation of products that were first put on the Community market by himself or with his consent. Conversely, he may still invoke his exclusive right on the basis of Article 36 E.C. to prohibit the importation of products that were lawfully marketed in another Member State by a third party in the absence of parallel intellectual property protection. Such a situation is most likely to arise in cases in which intellectual property protection is not applied for, or the registration has not been duly renewed, in all Member States. The only way to eliminate the obstacles posed to intra-Community trade by the principle of territoriality inherent in intellectual property rights is to extend the latter principle to the whole territory of the Community. This calls for a unification of intellectual property rights in the sense that national intellectual property rights are replaced by Community intellectual property rights.[4] Only then would Article 36 E.C. become redundant with respect to intellectual property rights and one could truly speak of a single market in so far as intellectual property protected products are concerned.

10.04 A major problem is raised by the fact that the Member States are traditionally reluctant to transfer their sovereignty on the matter to the Community by virtue of harmonisation measures or unification of intellectual property rights. This was once again clearly illustrated by the controversy surrounding the conclusion of the TRIPS-Agreement.[5] In particular it was the fact that the TRIPS-Agreement also implied harmonisation of intellectual property laws

[2] On E.C. harmonisation, see *supra*, Chap. 3, pt. 3.
[3] On the principle of Community exhaustion, see *supra*, Chap. 4, pt. 1.
[4] See *supra*, Chap. 3, pt. 3(3).
[5] On the TRIPS-Agreement, see *supra*, Chap. 2, pt. 4(2).

within the Community that led to the claim of the joint competence of the Community and the Member States. The opposition of Member States to exclusive E.C. competence to conclude the TRIPS-Agreement does not mean that harmonisation, or even unification, of intellectual property law is totally inconceivable in the Community context. It should be recalled that some harmonisation measures have already been adopted, whereas the Community trade mark was introduced alongside national trade marks.[6] However, as the Court pointed out in Opinion 1/94:

> "Suffice it to say... that the harmonisation achieved within the Community in certain areas covered by TRIPs is only partial and that, in other areas, no harmonisation has been envisaged."[7]

Pending full harmonisation or unification of intellectual property rights the outcome of the issue of the use or abuse of intellectual property rights is almost entirely dependent on the approach taken by the Court to intellectual property rights under the rules on competition and free movement of goods.

• SOLUTION 2: APPLICATION OF THE RULES ON COMPETITION

In the absence of harmonisation measures, intellectual property rights are granted according to the procedures and conditions laid down by national law. This raises the fundamental issue of whether, and to what extent, Community law may interfere with the exclusive rights thus conferred. It could be argued that an exclusive right which is granted by national law should not be taken away by Community law but, to the contrary, should be fully upheld both in substance and in legal effect. Or in other words, in the absence of harmonisation measures Community law should leave national intellectual property rights untouched. Such a view would obviously be tantamount to giving a blank cheque to intellectual property owners and would, potentially, open the door to widespread anti-competitive behaviour. It is therefore generally acknowledged by both lawyers and economists that competition rules have a role to play, at least in order to counter flagrant abuses of the exclusive right.[8] The main issue under discussion is therefore not so much whether, but rather to what extent, the rules on competition should apply to intellectual property rights.   **10.05**

The rules on competition are directed towards undertakings in order to curtail anti-competitive behaviour in the market place.[9] This implies that Articles 85 and 86 E.C. are concerned with the manner in which intellectual property rights are enforced rather than with the procedures and conditions under which the latter were granted by national law. This was confirmed by the Court in the early competition cases in which intellectual property rights were invoked.[10] The Court introduced the distinction between, on the one hand, the   **10.06**

---

[6] For an overview of the harmonisation measures, see *supra*, Chap. 3, pt. 3(2).
[7] Opinion 1/94, November 15, 1994, [1994] E.C.R. I–5267 para. 103.
[8] See *supra*, Chap. 2, pt. 3(2)(c).
[9] See *supra*, Chap. 3, pt. 2(4)(b).
[10] See *supra*, Chap. 3, pt. 4(2).

existence of intellectual property rights which is to be left unaffected by the rules on competition and, on the other hand, the exercise of them which may be curtailed under Articles 85 and 86 E.C. The existence/exercise dichotomy thus appears to safeguard the nationally granted exclusive right. A major problem, however, is raised by the fact that this formal distinction is difficult to draw in practice because the existence of an intellectual property right is essentially constituted by the various ways in which the exclusive right may be exercised. Both the early *Consten Grundig* and the recent *Magill* cases are clear illustrations that the existence of an intellectual property right may be formally upheld whilst being emptied of its substance through the back door act of striking down the exercise of the exclusive right.[11]

For intellectual property owners it is therefore of crucial importance to know on what basis the exercise of their exclusive rights will be considered to be a normal use left unaffected by the rules on competition, or an abuse which may be struck down. In this respect the Court has consistently held that the exercise of intellectual property rights is not *of itself* contrary to Article 85 E.C. in the absence of agreements or concerted practices, nor to Article 86 E.C. in the absence of an abuse of a dominant position. In all other circumstances the rules on competition potentially come into play.[12]

10.07   Intellectual property rights allow temporary restraints on competition in order to enhance competition in the long run.[13] It could therefore be argued that there is no fundamental conflict between these exclusive rights and competition policy objectives because the balance between the two is already inherent in the very system of intellectual property rights. The normal exercise of exclusive rights should therefore be fully upheld in spite of the fact that competition may be impinged upon when considered from the short-term perspective. Only those restraints on competition which are not inherent in, or necessary to safeguard the function of, intellectual property rights should thus be curtailed by the rules on competition. In particular, tie-ins of unprotected products and clauses in licensing agreements which unduly restrict the licensee's freedom *vis-à-vis* the licensor readily come to mind in this respect.

At least on the face of it the Court seems to share this view. The general rule is that the clauses in agreements relating to the essence of an intellectual property right will not run foul of Article 85(1) E.C., whereas there needs to be an additional element to the normal use of the exclusive right in accordance with its specific subject-matter for Article 86 E.C. to apply.[14] Although this seems to be a plausible approach which formally distinguishes between normal use and abuse, nevertheless a closer look reveals major shortcomings. In particular it is to be regretted that the approach so far adopted by the Court does not eliminate the legal uncertainty prevailing in the market place in so far as the enforcement of intellectual property rights is concerned. This is largely due to the fact that the Court has refrained from clearly defining the concepts it has introduced to delineate between use and abuse. Instead, a case by case approach has been adopted.

[11] See *supra*, respectively Chap. 3, pt. 4(2) and Chap. 5, pt. 4(3).
[12] See *supra*, Chap. 5, pt. 2.
[13] See *supra*, Chap. 2, pt. 3(6).
[14] See *supra*, Chap. 5, pt. 2.

The uncertainty about the concept of the "essence" of intellectual property **10.08** rights which is not contrary to Article 85(1) E.C. initially led the Commission to adopt what seemed to be a trial and error strategy concerning patent licences.[15] It is significant in this respect to recall that the Commission acknowledged, in its Fourth Report on Competition Policy of 1975, that it faced problems of definition exposed by the Court in the distinction between the existence and exercise of intellectual property rights. Subsequently, the approach to be taken to patent licences under Article 85 E.C. was gradually clarified, by virtue of examples given in case law, whereas eventually some degree of legal certainty for patent holders was introduced by virtue of the block exemption for patent licences. It should be pointed out, though, that a coherent and workable definition of what constitutes the essence of the various types of intellectual property rights is still lacking today.

Similarly, under Article 86 E.C. a major problem is raised by uncertainty **10.09** relating to the concept of the "additional element" which triggers Article 86 E.C. The Court has consistently held that the normal use of an intellectual property right in accordance with its specific subject-matter does not, of itself, fall within Article 86 E.C.[16] The concept of "specific subject-matter" is generally defined under the rules on the free movement of goods as being the exclusive right to manufacture and put protected products into circulation for the first time, either directly or by the grant of licences, as well as to oppose infringements.[17] No definition is given of the additional element required for Article 86 E.C. to apply. The following crucial question therefore arises: is it necessary for there to be anti-competitive behaviour extraneous to the specific subject-matter of intellectual property rights, or could the specific circumstances of a case trigger Article 86 E.C. even though the use made of the exclusive right is in accordance with its specific subject-matter?

In the *Maxicar* and *Volvo* cases the Court apparently gave a positive reply to the first question.[18] Neither the specific circumstances of the case nor the exceptionally anti-competitive effects of the enforcement of design rights in bodywork components of cars carried much weight in the analysis under Article 86 E.C. The fact that intellectual property rights were enforced in components of complex products relating to the after-sales market, with the elimination of all competition and consumer tie-ins as a consequence, thereby did not seem to matter. On the contrary, the Court expressly stated that the enforcement of intellectual property rights to prevent the unauthorised manufacture and sale by third parties cannot be regarded as an abusive method of eliminating competition. It was furthermore held that the refusal to grant licences on reasonable terms cannot in itself constitute an abuse of a dominant position. Instead, the following examples of abusive behaviour in terms of Article 86 E.C. were given, all of which are extraneous to the specific subject-matter concept: arbitrary refusal to deliver spare parts to independent repairers, fixing unfair prices, and termination of production even though many cars are still in circulation. In other words, the spare parts cases seemed

---

[15] See *supra*, Chap. 5, pt. 3.
[16] See *supra*, Chap. 5, pt. 2(3).
[17] See *supra*, Chap. 4, pt. 2.
[18] See *supra*, Chap. 8, pt. 4.

to indicate that the additional element needed for Article 86 E.C. to apply is constituted by anti-competitive behaviour which is not covered by the specific subject-matter concept.

The subsequent *Magill* cases[19] proved that it was somewhat premature to foster the expectation that the relationship between intellectual property rights and Article 86 E.C. had been unequivocally clarified by the spare parts cases. Even though the Court expressly referred to the ruling in the prior *Volvo* case both the approach taken and the conclusions adopted in *Magill* were, in fact, radically opposed. As in the spare parts cases, there was no anti-competitive behaviour in *Magill* extraneous to the specific subject-matter of copyright. All the broadcasting companies did was to refuse to grant licences and to enforce their nationally granted copyright on programme listings in order to prevent the unauthorised use thereof by third parties. In the light of the outcome of the spare parts cases it seemed reasonable to expect that in so doing they did not infringe Article 86 E.C. The Court, however, took a different view and emphasised the exceptional circumstances of the case. In particular, the fact that all competition was eliminated and consumer demand for a comprehensive weekly TV guide frustrated by the enforcement of the copyright led to the conclusion that Article 86 E.C. applied to this specific case. Furthermore, it was held that in order to remedy the infringement of Article 86 E.C. an affirmative action in the form of compulsory licences could be imposed on the copyright holders.[20] It is significant to recall in this respect that the Court itself pointed out in the *Volvo* case that imposing the obligation to license on an intellectual property owner would be tantamount to depriving him of the substance of his exclusive right.[21] Despite the fact that the existence/exercise dichotomy was expressly reiterated it is apparent that safeguarding the substance of the copyright was not a priority of the Court in *Magill*.

10.10   It is to be regretted that the Court did not elaborate upon the analysis in terms of the function of intellectual property rights as initiated by the Court of First Instance in *Magill*. The latter in essence held that an exercise of copyright which exceeds its function may be contrary to Article 86 E.C.[22] The merit of such an approach is that it calls for a preliminary analysis in terms of the balance between exclusive rights and competition which is already inherent in the different types of intellectual property rights. This would imply that the rules on competition may curtail the exercise made of the exclusive right only if the restraints on competition cannot be justified in terms of the function of the intellectual property right invoked. It is submitted that this is to be preferred to both the rather untransparent, if not arbitrary, concept of "exceptional circumstances" and the transposition of the doctrine of essential facilities to intellectual property rights.[23] It could be said that the Court has already impliedly opened the door to the introduction of the latter doctrine in

---

[19] See *supra*, Chap. 5, pt. 4(3).

[20] On this issue, see also *supra*, Chap. 9, pt. 4(1)(b).

[21] See *supra*, Chap. 8, pt. 4(3)(c).

[22] See *supra*, Chap. 5, pt. 5(3)(b).

[23] On the doctrine of essential facilities see, for instance, D. Glasl, "Essential facilities doctrine in E.C. anti-trust law: a contribution to the current debate" [1994] E.C.L.R. 306. In his view, *Magill* does not contribute to this doctrine "because the intellectual property concerned cannot be classified as an essential facility" (p. 311).

the *Magill* case. This would imply that intangible property protected by exclusive rights may be assimilated to an essential facility to which third parties need to have access in order to be able to compete. The major shortcoming of such an approach is that it neglects the fact that the relationship between restraints on competition and access to intellectual creation by third parties is already inherent in the system of intellectual property protection. No additional restraints on intellectual property owners need to be introduced in order to safeguard competition; it suffices to reinforce the restrictions inherent in the different types of intellectual property rights. Take, for instance, patent and copyright protection. Patent protection confers exclusivity on a new product or process and may under exceptional circumstances lead to a monopoly position in the market-place.[24] As a counterbalance stringent conditions for protectability are imposed, the exclusive right is limited in time to, usually, a maximum of 20 years and the invention is duly publicised. Furthermore the possibility of imposing compulsory licences, as well as the conditions under which they could be imposed, is already provided for in most national laws. Conversely, copyright protection does not confer a monopoly on ideas or facts but merely offers protection against the unauthorised reproduction of the original manner in which an idea is expressed.[25] This is the so-called idea/expression dichotomy underlying copyright. It is therefore generally acknowledged that when the idea and expression merge, in the sense that there is no alternative way to express the same idea, then copyright may not be invoked. Otherwise, a monopoly could be secured over ideas or basic information with the consequence that competition and innovation could be stifled for 50 years and, in the E.C., even 70 years after the death of the author. There is therefore no need to have recourse to the essential facilities doctrine to explain the outcome of the *Magill* case. It may simply be that the Court impliedly agreed with the Court of First Instance that the enforcement of copyright on programme listings exceeded the function of copyright in that it transgressed the idea/expression dichotomy.

If it is not totally clear whether or not the Court impliedly reasoned in terms **10.11** of the function of copyright in the *Magill* case, it is apparent that the function of design rights was not at all taken into consideration in the spare parts cases. Whereas the former case may at least be explained in terms of the function of copyright, the latter cases present fundamental inconsistencies and lead to paradoxical results when taking the objectives of design protection into account.[26] In particular, the need to uphold design rights under the rules on competition was invoked to justify the encroachment on the competition policy objective to safeguard a competitive market structure in spare parts for cars. It should be pointed out that, contrary to patents which may give rise to monopolies, design protection is not meant to confer exclusivity on a product but merely on the original manner in which a product is shaped.[27] As such it is an important factor in stimulating non-price competition and increasing consumers' choice. It seems to be difficult to justify the elimination of all

[24] See *supra*, Chap. 2, pt. 3(2).
[25] See *supra*, Chap. 2, pt. 3(3).
[26] See *supra*, Chap. 8, pt. 4(3)(b).
[27] See *supra*, Chap. 2, pt. 3(5).

inter-brand competition in the market for bodywork components of cars in terms of the need to safeguard the function of design rights as instead of being a factor of non-price competition it may be used to eliminate all competition from the market. Conversely, the Court held in the spare parts cases that the fixing of unfair prices could amount to an abuse under Article 86 E.C. The possibility of obtaining whatever reward the market will pay is, however, essential to fulfil both the reward and the incentive functions inherent in design protection. The level of reward is usually determined by the willingness of consumers to buy, or perhaps even pay a higher price for, a product incorporating the design rather than another. In the absence of competition it seems to be hardly possible for a judge to determine what constitutes a just or fair reward which is needed to induce further investment, and consequently what constitutes an unfair price that may amount to an abuse under Article 86 E.C.[28] It is therefore submitted that it is fundamentally contradictory to first formally uphold the design right and subsequently to prevent it from fulfilling its main functions, as the Court suggests.

10.12   The outcome of the spare parts cases in essence implies that whereas a potential abuse of design protection in terms of its inherent objectives may be considered as a normal use under the rules on competition, a normal use in terms of its inherent function may amount to an abuse under Article 86 E.C. In *Magill* the Court did not expressly overrule the approach taken in the spare parts cases but, on the contrary, expressly referred to the *Volvo* case.[29] This finding makes it particularly difficult to understand on what criteria the distinction between the normal use and the abuse of a dominant position by the holder of intellectual property rights is currently based. A comparison of the spare parts and the *Magill* cases shows that the additional element required for Article 86 E.C. to apply will in some cases necessitate anti-competitive behaviour extraneous to the specific subject-matter of intellectual property rights, whereas in other cases it may suffice to point to the exceptional circumstances of the case. The result is that it is currently impossible to predict for certain when intellectual property owners holding a dominant position on the market will be held to have infringed Article 86 E.C. simply by enforcing their nationally granted exclusive rights.

The impression may thus be created that the Court considered spare parts for cars to be worthy, and programme listing to be unworthy, of protection. However, the central issue is not whether or not certain products are worthy of protection but rather to what extent intellectual property rights may be curtailed under Community law. Over the past decade there has been an increasing awareness of the fact that the exercise of intellectual property rights may be abusive simply because the exclusive right was abusively granted. In other words, the normal use of an abusively granted exclusive right is equated with abusive behaviour of the intellectual property owner. This finding obviously calls the existence/exercise dichotomy into question, not in the least because it is prejudicial to intellectual property owners in at least two respects. Whilst the legitimate expectation is created that they will

[28] See *supra*, Chap. 8, pt. 4(4)(b).
[29] See *supra*, Chap. 5, pt. 4(3)(c).

be able to enforce their exclusive rights, the latter may subsequently be emptied of its substance and lead a solely formal existence. Long- or medium-term marketing or research strategies in which intellectual property rights play a crucial role are therefore based on precarious grounds. Furthermore, if an infringement of the rules on competition is established then fines may be imposed on the intellectual property owner. In other words, intellectual property owners may be penalised because their exclusive right was abusively granted. In order to remedy the prejudicial effects for the intellectual property owners it would seem more logical to do away with the existence/exercise dichotomy altogether and thus to review intellectual property measures on their compatibility with Community law. At least this would have as its merit that intellectual property owners are no longer held to be responsible, and penalised, for intellectual property rights which were in fact abusively granted. This result could perhaps be achieved by reviewing intellectual property rights under the rules on competition combined with Article 5 E.C. It is submitted, however, that the proper approach consists in subjecting the existence of intellectual property rights to scrutiny under Article 36 E.C.

• SOLUTION 3: SCRUTINY OF THE EXISTENCE OF INTELLECTUAL PROPERTY RIGHTS

The main responsibility for shielding intellectual property rights from potential abuses obviously lies with the legislator and with the courts that interpret and apply intellectual property laws. Economic actors in the market seek in the first place to protect their commercial interests so that it cannot be held against them if they attempt, and are successful, in exploiting the system of intellectual property protection to the full. However, intellectual property protection does not serve only the interest of economic actors on the market. Due to its importance for economic progress, intellectual property protection is a means of creating favourable circumstances to stimulate national economic growth and to attract foreign industries and technologies. This implies that there may be a potential convergence between the interests of the economic actors and the legislator in extending the scope of intellectual property protection for economic purposes. The following statement by Commissioner Bangemann is an illustrative example thereof. In support of the European car manufacturers' view that design protection of spare parts for cars needed for repair purposes should be extended beyond the three years currently proposed by the Commission,[30] it is reported that he stated that industrial designs are among "... *nos meilleurs armes pour défendre nos parts de marchés*" (... our best weapons to defend our shares of the market).[31]   **10.13**

Without going so far as maintaining that this is a common practice, considerations of a commercial, or even protectionist, nature may nevertheless   **10.14**

---

[30] On the so-called "repair clause" in the proposals on the Community Design, see *supra*, Chap. 9, pt. 4(2)(c).
[31] Speech given by M. Bangemann at the conference "Turin meets the future of the European car" held in Turin on November 9, 1993, as reported in *Agence Europe* (No. 6106, November 13, 1993), at p. 9.

have a certain influence on the way in which national intellectual property legislation is drafted. This poses a problem in that most national courts in the Community, except United Kingdom courts, in principle merely have the competence to interpret those laws and to apply them to the given facts. As such, they usually do not call the well-foundedness of certain provisions of intellectual property laws into question. National courts merely examine an intellectual property right on its conformity with the requirements stipulated in the law, without analysing whether or not the repercussions on competition are in accordance with the objective of the intellectual property right invoked. In other words, whether or not there is an abuse of the exclusive right is exclusively determined with respect to formal requirements and conditions and not by the inherent functions of the exclusive right concerned. This does not imply that a national court may not be aware of the fact that an exclusive right granted in conformity with national intellectual property legislation may, nevertheless, be difficult to justify in terms of the function of that right. It was precisely this apparent paradox, which was evidenced in the spare parts debate, that led the Italian national court to pose a preliminary question in the *Maxicar* case as to the compatibility of this practice with Community law.[32]

10.15   The mere existence of national intellectual property rights conferred on the basis of the principle of territoriality is already difficult to reconcile with the objective of establishing a common market. It is apparent that this problem becomes even greater if national exclusive rights may be conferred that do not necessarily meet the objectives of the intellectual property right invoked. Although it appears far-fetched, it is not at all inconceivable that the extension of the scope of intellectual property protection may be used as a means of circumventing the prohibition on the maintenance of measures having an effect equivalent to quantitative restrictions or the full applicability of the rules on competition in order to protect or favour national industries. This is all the more relevant in view of the fact that, with the establishment of the internal market, the mandatory requirements derogation and the exceptions laid down in Article 36 E.C. obviously gain even more in importance. In other words, it is submitted that the more the Community objective to create a single market prevails, both in law and in fact, the stronger will be the incentive to use derogation measures. In principle the Court counters the latter practice by examining whether or not an alleged derogation measure is justified and proportional in view of the need to safeguard the higher interest invoked.[33] It should be emphasised that it is only in relation to intellectual property rights that the Court has been reluctant to scrutinise the national measure concerned on its justification in order to curtail possible abuses under the rules on the free movement of goods. It is significant that the Court has never held a specific intellectual property measure, except in respect of denominations of origin, not to come under the concept of "industrial and commercial property" as mentioned in the first sentence of Article 36 E.C.

10.16   The reluctance of the Court to examine intellectual property measures upon their compatibility with Article 36 E.C. may possibly be explained by its

[32] See *supra*, Chap. 7.
[33] See *supra*, Chap. 3, pt. 2(2).

concern not to put the whole system of intellectual property protection in the balance. However, the latter is precisely the result of current case law on the rules on competition. What is certain is that it cannot be formally explained by the division of competence between the E.C. and its Member States under either Article 36 E.C. or Article 177 E.C. It should be pointed out that the Court has not refrained from reviewing the well-foundedness of national measures alleged to come under the other exceptions mentioned in Article 36 E.C. in preliminary procedures.[34] A more reasonable explanation therefore might be that the Court's approach specific to intellectual property rights stems from a chronological confusion. The first intellectual property cases the Court dealt with concerned the application of the rules on competition which are not directed at the Member States but apply to the anti-competitive behaviour of undertakings. It is in this context that the Court quite logically introduced the reasoning that, whereas the existence of the intellectual property right should not be affected, the exercise made by the owner of the exclusive right could, nevertheless, be curtailed by the rules on competition. It is rather surprising to find that the existence/exercise dichotomy was later on merely transposed to cases concerning the free movement of goods.[35] The latter rules are directed at Member States and not at the anti-competitive behaviour of undertakings so that, in principle, the reverse reasoning should have applied. It would have been logical for the Court to examine whether the existence of the right could be justified, and thus upheld, under Article 36 E.C. rather than curtail the exercise of it by undertakings. The mere transposition of the existence/exercise dichotomy to the rules on the free movement of goods implied that this distinction became the criterion by which to delineate between the competence of the E.C. and its Member States in so far as *all* matters of intellectual property rights were concerned, and not only in view of the application of the rules on competition. In other words, it introduced a kind of *per se* exemption for all intellectual property measures under Article 36 E.C. It thus became irrelevant whether or not the national measure was justified and necessary to fulfil the essential objectives of intellectual property protection for it to be upheld under Community law.

10.17 In order to limit the detrimental impact of certain features of intellectual property law on the establishment of the Common Market, the Court instead applied the rules on the free movement of goods to the way in which the owner of an exclusive right makes use of that right. The principle of Community exhaustion was thus introduced to curtail the prejudicial effect of the principle of territoriality, inherent to all intellectual property rights, on the establishment of a single market without national frontiers.[36] The fact that the Court was thereby more concerned with extending the single market concept to protected products than with safeguarding the essential function of intellectual property rights is clearly illustrated by the elaboration of the concept of the "specific subject-matter" of the exclusive right.[37] It is on the basis of this concept that the Court distinguishes between what constitutes a normal use

[34] See *supra*, Chap. 4, pt. 1(2)(d).
[35] See *supra*, Chap. 3, pt. 4.
[36] See *supra*, Chap. 4, pt. 1.
[37] See *supra*, Chap. 4, pt. 2.

and a misuse of national intellectual property rights under the rules on the free movement of goods, whilst it is often also invoked under Article 86 E.C. The specific subject-matter concept has been more or less uniformly developed for all types of intellectual property rights on the basis of what seems to be a straightforward application of the consent theory.[38] In essence, it means that if within the E.C. the protected goods have been brought on to the market by the intellectual property owner, or with his consent, then the principle of exhaustion quasi-automatically applies. Whether or not the right-owner could make use of a parallel intellectual property right in the Member State of first marketing, or whether national measures such as price regulation, interfered with the way in which he could enforce his exclusive right is thereby disregarded. Whilst the traditional case law thus seems to be consistent when formally compared, it presents important discrepancies and inconsistencies when a closer analysis in terms of the functions of intellectual property protection and the impact for intellectual property owners is made. A comparison of the *Pharmon* and *Merck* cases is an illustrative example thereof.[39] The most striking result of the case law of the Court is that an intellectual property owner may benefit from having his exclusive right exploited under compulsory licences rather than marketing his products himself in the absence of parallel protection. In the latter case his exclusive right in the Member State of importation will be held to be exhausted whereas in the former case it will not. Except for trade marks and performance rights,[40] it seems to be totally irrelevant to the Court whether or not intellectual property protection has fulfilled its function in any given case, as long as the free flow of protected goods within the Community is to the fullest guaranteed. In other words, whereas the existence of the exclusive right is formally upheld under the rules on the free movement of goods it may nevertheless be severely undermined in practice.

10.18   Some recent cases have highlighted the fact that intellectual property rights may no longer be regarded merely as barriers to trade. In particular, cases concerning obligatory licences and the principle of relative novelty made clear that the detrimental effect on intra-Community trade and competition may be due not only to the principle of territoriality but may also arise from the national conditions or procedures under which the intellectual property right is granted.[41] As such, the existence/exercise dichotomy came under strain with the newly gained awareness of the fact that the exercise of intellectual property rights may be contrary to Community law simply because the exclusive right was granted in circumstances indicative of a protectionist intention. A typical example is that of a patent granted on an ordinary football in order to obtain a monopoly for national manufacturers which, under the Court's traditional approach, could not be curtailed under Community law. The problem in coming to terms with this kind of situation was therefore of a dual nature.

First, the *per se* legality of all national measures granting intellectual property rights, ensuing from the existence/exercise dichotomy, could no longer be

---

[38] On the consent theory see, in particular, *supra*, Chap. 6, pt. 2.
[39] See *supra*, Chap. 6, pt. 2(5).
[40] See *supra*, Chap. 4, pts. 2(3) and 2(2)(b) respectively.
[41] See *supra*, Chap. 6, pt. 3(3).

taken for granted. The apparent shortcomings in its traditional approach thus led the Court to deviate in more recent cases from its traditional case law under the rules on the free movement of goods. It began to review national measures upon their justification under the second sentence of Article 36 E.C. whilst continuing to apply the existence/exercise dichotomy under the first sentence of Article 36 E.C. This "marginal appraisal" approach seems to be inconsistent both in view of the structure of Article 36 and in view of its efficacy to counter abusively granted exclusive rights. Although there is one important precedent, the *Warner Brothers* case, in which the Court did apply a justification test under both sentences of Article 36 E.C.[42]

Secondly, adequate criteria needed to be established to curtail potential abuses of the system of intellectual property rights whilst maintaining a proper balance with the principle of free movement of goods and competition. Except for denominations of origin,[43] the Court's scrutiny of intellectual property law has, up till now, either led to it upholding the compatibility of the national measure with Article 36 E.C. or has merely led to the finding of incompatibility with the second sentence of Article 36 E.C.[44] It thus seems that the Court's main concern is whether or not the measure concerned is discriminatory or openly protectionist, rather than whether it is in accordance with the function of intellectual property protection. In the absence of inherently discriminatory rules it is not clear, currently, which approach the Court will adopt in the future. It would nonetheless be fundamentally inconsistent to apply the justification approach merely to uphold the full effect of national law and to resort to the traditional existence/exercise dichotomy to strike down certain features of intellectual property law which are held to be incompatible with Community objectives. However, if any real importance were to be given to the justification approach in terms of safeguarding the function of intellectual property rights, then it is submitted that the Court would need to closely examine, and possibly radically revise, its existing case law on the exhaustion of rights. Whilst the *HAG II* case already provides an important precedent in this respect,[45] we are currently still awaiting *Merck II*.[46]

The spare parts cases have the doubtful merit of emphasising the inability of **10.19** Community law in its present state to come to terms with the essence of intellectual property rights. It was apparent from the proceedings in the *Maxicar* case that the national court specifically questioned whether a national intellectual property right that is granted in conformity with national law, but nevertheless does not seem to be justified in terms of the function of the exclusive right concerned, may be upheld under the first sentence of Article 36 E.C.[47] In particular, the national court pointed out that design rights were enforced on components of complex products the reward for which was already accounted for through the sale of the car, and the result of which was the exclusion of competition in other economic sectors. In other words, the

[42] See *supra*, Chap. 6, pt. 3(3).
[43] See *supra*, Chap. 3, pt. 4(2)(c).
[44] See *supra*, Chap. 6, pt. 4.
[45] See *supra*, Chap. 3, pt. 2(3)(c).
[46] On the *Merck* case, see *supra*, Chap. 3, pt. 2(1)(b) and Chap. 6, pt. 2(5).
[47] See *supra*, Chap. 7, pt. 2.

national court clearly invited the Court to elaborate upon the justification approach and to give guidelines as to what constitutes an abuse of the system of intellectual property protection which will not be permitted under Community law. This was also the understanding by Advocate General Mischo who, in his opinion in the case, acknowledged that the national court was concerned with the lack of justification in terms of the function of design rights and not with the compatibility of the exercise of design rights with the specific subject-matter of designs.[48] He unequivocally held that nothing prevented the Court from considering whether such legislation, which allows for the prohibition of imports of unauthorised copies of bodywork components of cars, is justified both in the terms of the function of design rights and under the second sentence of Article 36 E.C. This approach would obviously call for a Community definition of the function of design protection. In this respect, it is significant that the Court did already give a definition of what constitutes the function of denomination of origins as understood under the commercial and industrial property exception mentioned in Article 36 E.C. in the *Delhaize* case,[49] so that nothing seemed to prevent the application of similar reasoning in the *Maxicar* case. Nevertheless, the Court followed Advocate General Mischo only in so far as the analysis under the second sentence of Article 36 E.C. was concerned. With regard to the crucial question, namely whether or not design legislation that might not be justified in terms of the function of designs comes under the first sentence of Article 36 E.C., the Court merely reinforced the existence/exercise dichotomy. It reiterated that it is up to the national legislator to determine the conditions and procedures on the basis of which designs rights are granted, even if it concerns components of complex products.[50] In other words, the Court impliedly held that it is irrelevant for the application of the exception to the free movement of goods whether or not intellectual property rights are abusively granted with respect to the function and objectives of intellectual property law. The only abuse or misuse of intellectual property rights withheld by the Court under Articles 36 E.C. is constituted by discriminatory or overtly protectionist measures, or by the misuse made by the owner of the right in terms of frustrating the single market objective. It remains to be seen whether the Court would have adopted a similar approach had the *Magill* case been brought before it on the basis of a preliminary question posed by a national court as the latter procedure might have led to a scrutiny of the contested copyright on programme listings also in the light of Article 36 E.C.

• SOLUTION 4: AN ALTERNATIVE APPROACH

10.20   The approach currently adopted by the Court under the rules on the free movement of goods obviously opens the door to the potential use of intellectual property law for purposes other than the mere protection of intangible property. It might also prove to be detrimental to the achievement of an inter-

---

[48] See *supra*, Chap. 7, pt. 4(3).
[49] See *supra*, Chap. 3, pt. 4(2)(c).
[50] See *supra*, Chap. 7, pt. 4(4).

nal market in protected products because it not only allows for different conditions to be applied in different Member States, but for the underlying objectives to be disparate. Although the specific function of the different kinds of intellectual property rights is often invoked by the Advocates General in their opinions, the Court seems to be reluctant to apply what could be called a "functionality test" effectively to intellectual property cases.[51] Instead, the approach taken by the Court is still largely based on the existence/exercise dichotomy. At first sight it is most likely very reassuring for intellectual property owners in the Community to think that their nationally granted exclusive right will not be affected fundamentally by Community law. However, a closer look shows that it is premature to draw such a conclusion. On the one hand, the Court apparently formally refutes the hypothesis that the system of intellectual property rights may be abused in order to obtain a legal monopoly. But on the other hand, the Court does not refrain from striking down the full effect of the exclusive right under both the rules on the free movement of goods and competition. The latter may be the case even if the exclusive right was not abused but, to the contrary, was used to fulfil the inherent functions of the right concerned.

It is submitted that it is highly unsatisfactory that intellectual property rights are not subject to a prior examination upon their merit and subsequently fully upheld when granted and used in accordance with the function of the specific exclusive right. Conversely, it would be logical that in the rare cases where the grant and enforcement of intellectual property rights cannot be justified in terms of the need to safeguard the essential objectives or functions of the specific type of exclusive right invoked, they could then—and only then—be struck down under the rules on the free movement of goods and competition respectively.[52] Using the criterion of the need to safeguard the specific functions of each type of intellectual property right in order to delineate between what constitutes a normal use and what constitutes an abuse of the exclusive right would not only have the merit of providing legal certainty on the market. Above all, it is submitted that only then would the system and nature of intellectual property rights be fully valued and maintained in the Community context.

---

[51] On the functionality test, see *supra*, Chap. 3, pt. 4(2)(c).
[52] On the feasibility of a functionality test, see *supra*, Chap. 3, pt. 4(2)(c).

Selected Bibliography

I. Books and Documents

F.-K. Beier, G. Schricker (eds.), *GATT or WIPO? New ways in the international protection of intellectual property, IIC studies* (Vol. 11, 1989, VCH Verlagsgesellschaft mbH, Weinheim).

Bieber, Dehousse, Pinder, Weiler (eds.), *1992: One European market? A critical analysis of the Commission's internal market strategy* (1988, Nomos Verlagsgesellschaft).

F. Bradbury (ed.), *Technology transfer practice of international firms* (1978, Alpen aan den Rijn).

T. Burke, A. Genn-Bash, B. Haines, *Competition in theory and practice* (2nd ed., 1991, Routledge).

B.I. Cawthra, *Patent licensing in Europe* (2nd ed., 1986, Butterworth's, London).

M. Collard, P. Desaux, D. Dessard, a.o., *L'automobile et le droit européen* (1986, Editions du Jeune Barreau de Liège).

W.R. Cornish, *Intellectual property: patents, copyright, trade marks and allied rights* (2nd ed., 1989, Sweet & Maxwell).

CUERPI, *La protection des créations d'esthétique industrielle dans le cadre de la CEE*, Colloque international organisé par le centre universitaire d'enseignement et de recherche de propriété industrielle, Chateau de Sassenage, juin 17 1988.

P. Demaret, *Patent, territorial restrictions and EEC law* (1978, VCH Verlagsgesellschaft mbH).

G. Dworkin, R. Taylor, *Blackstone's guide to the Copyright, Designs & Patents Act 1988* (1989, Blackstone).

Ekedi-Samnik, *L'Organisation Mondiale de la Propriété Intellectuelle (OMPI)* (1975, Etablissements Emile Bruylant).

T. Frazer, *Monopoly, competition and the law: the regulation of business activity in Britain, Europe and America* (1988, Wheatsheaf Books).

S. Gee (ed.), *Technology transfer in industrialised countries* (1979, Sythoff & Noordhoff).

E. Goldstein, *Cases and materials on patents, trademark and copyright law* (1959, The Foundation Press).

L. Gormley, *Prohibiting restrictions on trade within the EEC: the theory and application of Articles 30–36 of the EEC Treaty* (1985, North-Holland).

F. Gotzen (ed.), *The Green Paper on the legal protection of industrial design* (1992, Story Scientia).

315

M. Goyens (ed.), *E.C. competition policy and the consumer interest*, Centre de droit de la consommation Louvain-la-Neuve, Vol. 9, Droit et Consommation, Cabay-Bruylant, 1985.

J. Groux, P. Manin, *The European Communities in the international order* (1985, European Perspectives Series, E.C. Commission).

P. Groves, *Copyright and design law: a question of balance* (1991, Graham & Trotman).

P. Hearn, *The business of industrial licensing: a practical guide to patents, know how, trade marks and industrial design* (1981, Gower).

Institut Universitaire International Luxembourg, *La place de l'Europe dans le commerce mondial* (1994, July Session Luxembourg).

Institut Universitaire International Luxembourg, *La protection de la propriété intellectuelle: Aspects juridiques européens et internationaux* (1989, July Session, Luxembourg).

Joerges, Hiller, Holzscheck, Micklitz, *Vetriebspraktiken im Automobilersatzteilsektor: ihre Auswerkungen auf die Interessen der Verbraucher*, Frankfurter Wirtschaftsrechtliche Studien, Bank 4, Verlag Peter Lang, Frankfurt am Main, 1985.

P. Kaufman, *Passing off and misappropriation*, IIC Studies, Vol. 9, VCH Verlagsgesellschaft mbH, 1986.

C.S. Kerse, *EEC antitrust procedure* (3rd ed., 1994, Sweet & Maxwell).

V. Korah, *An introductory guide to EEC competition law and practice* (5th ed., 1994, Sweet & Maxwell).

V. Korah, *Franchising and the EEC competition rules: Regulation 4087/88* (1990, European competition law monographies, Oxford).

V. Korah, *Know-how licensing agreements and the EEC competition rules: Regulation 556/89* (1989, ESC).

V. Korah, *Patent licensing and EEC competition rules: Regulation 2349/84* (1985, ESC).

S. Ladas, *Patents, trademarks, and related rights: national and international protection*, Vol. II (1975, Harvard University Press).

J. Lowe, N. Crawford, *Innovation and technology transfer for the growing firm* (1984, Oxford).

M. Maresceau (ed.), *The European Community's commercial policy after 1992: the legal dimension* (1992, Martinus Nijhoff Publishers).

Michigan Law Review Association (ed.), *The art of governance: Festschrift zu ehren von Eric Stein* (1987, Nomos Verlagsgesellschaft).

MMC (U.K. Monopolies and Mergers Commission), *Ford Motor Company Limited: A report on the policy and practice of the Ford Motor Company Ltd of not granting licences to manufacture or sell in the U.K. of certain replacement body parts for Ford vehicles*, Cmnd. 9437 (1985, HMSO).

MMC, *Car parts: A report on the matter of the existence or the possible existence of a complex monopoly situation in relation to the wholesale supply of motor car parts in the United Kingdom*, H.C. 318, (1982, HMSO).

National Bureau of Economic Research, *The rate and direction of inventive activity: economic and social factors* (1975, New York).

OECD, *Market power and the law* (1970, Paris).

J. Palmer (ed.), *The economics of patents and copyright*, Research in Law and Economics, Vol. 8. (1986, London).

M.-A. Perot-Morel, *Les principes de protection des dessins et modèles dans les pays du Marché Commun* (1968, Editions Mouton).

J.P. Pizzio (ed.), *Droit des consommateurs: sécurité, concurrence, publicité. Droit français et droit communautaire*, Vol. XIV, Droit et Consommation (1987, Story Scientia).

J.-M. Salamolard, *La licence obligatoire en matière de brevets d'invention* (1978, Geneva).

F. Scherer, *Innovation and growth – Schumpeterian perspectives* (1984, Cambridge).

F. Scherer, *Industrial market structure and economic performance* (2nd ed., 1980, Chicago).

G. Schrans, *Octrooien en octrooilicenties in het Europees mededingingsrecht* (1966, Story Scientia).

J. Schumpeter, *Capitalism, socialism and democracy* (1976, George Allen & Unwin).

Schwarze, Govaere, Hélin, Van den Bossche (eds.), *Implementing the internal market: problems and perspectives* (1990, Nomos Verlagsgesellschagt).

S. Stewart, *International copyright and neighbouring rights* (1983, Butterworths).

A. Strowel, *Droit d'auteur et copyright: divergences et convergences* (1993, Bruylant).

C. Taylor and Z. Silberstone, *The economic impact of the patent system* (1973, Cambridge).

E. Ulmer, *Intellectual property rights and the conflict of laws* (1978, Kluwer).

Van Empel, *Bescherming van de intellectuele eigendom* (1987, Kluwer).

WIPO, *Background reading material on intellectual property* (1988, WIPO).

II. Articles and Conference Papers

M. Abbey, "Exhaustion of IP rights under the EEA Agreement does not apply to third country goods" [1992] E.C.L.R. 231.

R. Adelstein, S. Peretz, "The competition of technologies in markets for ideas: copyright and fair use in evolutionary perspective" [1985] *International Review of Law and Economics* 209.

P. Albert, "*L'étrange duel: pièces d'origine ou parallèles?*" [July/August 1987] *Fergabel Revue* 13.

G. Albrechtskirchinger, "The impact of the Luxembourg Conference for the establishment of a Community patent on the law of licence agreements" [1976] I.I.C. 447.

E. Armitage, "Community designs" [1992] E.I.P.R. 3.

K. Arrow, "Economic Welfare and the allocation of resources for invention" in *The rate and direction of inventive activity* (1975, National Bureau of Economic Reseach), pp. 609–626.

D. Audretsch, "Divergent views in antitrust economics" [1988] Antitrust Bull. 135.

C. Baden Fuller, "Article 86 EEC: Economic analysis of the existence of a dominant position" (1979) 4 E.L.Rev. 423.

C. Baden Fuller, "Economic issues relating to property rights in trademarks: export bans, differential pricing, restrictions on resale and repackaging" (1981) 6 E.L.Rev. 162.

R. Barents, "New developments in measures having equivalent effect" (1981) 18 C.M.L.Rev. 271.

H. Beale, "Car distribution contracts and block exemption Regulation 123/85", paper presented at the *Giessen–Warwick Colloquium*, November 1987.

F.-K. Beier, "The future of intellectual property in Europe: Thoughts on the development of patent, utility model and industrial design law" [1991] I.I.C. 157.

F.-K. Beier, "Industrial property and the free movement of goods in the internal market" [1990] I.I.C. 131.

F.-K. Beier, "The significance of the patent system for technical, economic and social progress" [1980] I.I.C. 563.

F.-K. Beier, "The doctrine of exhaustion in EEC trademark law: scope and limits" [1979] I.I.C. 20.

F.-K. Beier, J. Strauss, "The patent system and its informational function yesterday and today" [1977] I.I.C. 387.

J. Bentil, "Control of the abuse of monopoly power in EEC business law: a commentary on the *Commercial Solvents* case" (1975) 12 C.M.L.Rev. 59.

R. Bieber, "On the mutual completion of overlapping legal systems: the case of the European Communities and the national legal orders" (1988) 13 E.L.Rev. 147.

P. Blok, "Articles 30–36 of the EEC Treaty and intellectual property rights: a Danish view" [1982] I.I.C. 729.

G. Bonet, "*Les créations d'esthétique industrielle au regard des règles de libre circulation et de libre concurrence dans le Marché Commun*" in *La protection des créations d'esthétique industrielle dans le cadre de la CEE: objectif 1992* (1988, CUERPI), pp. 45–64.

A. Brown, "Impact of patents and licences on the transfer of technology" in S. Gee (ed.), *Technology transfer in industrialised countries* (1979, Sythoff & Noordhoff), pp. 311–324.

J. Brown, G. Robert, "The European Economic Area: how important is it?" [1992] E.I.P.R. 379.

A. Brun, "*L'unification et l'harmonisation du droit des marques*", in *La protection de la propriété intellectuelle*, Institut Universitaire International Luxembourg (July Session 1989), pp. 187–216.

J.-J. Burst, R. Kovar, "*Les licences imposées et le droit communautaire*" [1990] C.D.E. 249.

B. Cawthra, "Exclusive, sole and non-exclusive rights in patent licensing agreements" [1977] I.I.C. 430.

P. Cesarini, "*Les systèmes de distribution sélective en droit communautaire de la concurrence*" [1992] *Revue du Marché Unique Européen* 81.

D. Chalmers, "Repackaging the internal market – The ramifications of the *Keck* judgment" (1994) 19 E.L.Rev. 385.

S. Cheung, "Property rights and invention" in J. Palmer (ed.), *The economics of patents and copyright* (1986), pp. 5–18.

M. Cimoli, "Towards a new Italian Design Law" [1993] E.I.P.R. 425.

J. Clark, "Towards a concept of workable competition" [1940] *American Economic Review* 241.

H. Cohen Jehoram, "Critical reflections on the economic importance of copyright" [1989] I.I.C. 485.

H. Cohen Jehoram, "The E.C. copyright directives, economics and author's rights" [1994] I.I.C. 821.

H. Cohen Jehoram, "The E.C. Green paper on the legal protection of industrial design. Half way down the right track – a view from the Benelux" [1992] E.I.P.R. 75.

A.-M. Constant, *"L'épuisement du droit à la marque: problématique et conséquences"* [1992] Ing. -Cons. 1.

W.R. Cornish, "Designs again" [1991] E.I.P.R. 3.

P. Crockford, "Trucks, parts and summing up", paper presented at *the S.M.M.T. Selective Distribution Block Exemption Seminar*, London, March 8, 1985.

J. Daltrop, J. Perry, "The relationship between Articles 85 and 86: *Tetra Pak* (T–51/89)" [1991] E.I.P.R. 31.

M. Dauses, *"Mesures d'effet équivalent à des restrictions quantitatives à la lumière de la jurisprudence de la Cour de Justice des Communautés Européennes"* [1992] R.T.D.E. 607.

J. Davidow, "EEC proposed competition rules for motor vehicle distribution: An American perspective" [1983] Antitrust Bull. 863.

L. DeBrock, "Market structure, innovation, and optimal patent life" [1985] *The Journal of Law and Economics* 223.

L. Defalque, "Copyright – free movement of goods and territoriality: recent developments" [1989] E.I.P.R. 435.

L. Defalque, *"Le concept de discrimination en matière de libre circulation des marchandises"* [1987] C.D.E. 471.

P. Demaret, "Industrial property rights, compulsory licences and the free movement of goods under Community law" [1987] I.I.C. 161.

N. De Souza, "The Commission's draft group exemption on technology transfer" [1994] E.C.L.R. 338.

A. Dietz, "The harmonization of copyight in the European Community" [1985] I.I.C. 379.

J. Dubois, *"Cas d'application: la distribution automobile dans le marche commun; le point de vue de la Commission Européenne"* in J. Pizzio (ed.), *Droit des consommateurs* (1987, Story Scientia), pp. 91–97.

G. Dworkin, J.A.L. Sterling, *"Phil Collins* and the term directive" [1994] E.I.P.R. 187.

G. Dworkin, "Authorship of films and the European Commission proposals for harmonising the term of copyright" [1993] E.I.P.R. 151.

R. Eccles, "Patentee's right to prevent importation: *Thetford Corporation v. Fiamma S.P.A.*" [1982] E.I.P.R. 26.

C.-D. Ehlermann, "Managing monopolies: the role of the state in controlling market dominance in the European Community" [1993] E.C.L.R. 61.

R. Eisenberg, "Patents and the progress of science: exclusive rights and experimental use" [1989] *The University of Chicago Law Review* 1017.

U. Everling, "The Court of Justice as a decision making authority" in Michigan Law Review Association (ed.), *The art of governance* (1987, Nomos Verlagsgesellschaft), pp. 156–172.

Ky P. Ewing Jr., "Antitrust enforcement and the patent system, similarities in the European and American approach" [1980] I.I.C. 279.

S. Farr, "Abuse of a dominant position – The *Hilti* case" [1992] E.C.L.R. 174.

J. Feenstra, S. Krawczyck, "*De Magill-arresten: de uitoefening van het auteursrecht en misbruik van machtspositie*" [1992] *Informatierecht* 43.

A. Firth, "Aspects of design protection in Europe" [1993] E.I.P.R. 42.

F. Fishwick, "Definition of monopoly power in the antitrust policies of the United Kingdom and the European Community" [1989] Antitrust Bull. 451.

J. Flynn, "Intellectual property and anti-trust: E.C. attitudes" [1992] E.I.P.R. 49.

I. Forrester, "Software licensing in the light of the current E.C. competition law considerations" [1992] E.C.L.R. 5.

R. Franceschelli, "*Modelli ornamentali di parte di carrozzeria di automobili ed abuso di posizione dominante*" (1988) II *Rivista di Diritto Industriale* 175.

A. Françon, "*Propriété littéraire et artistique*", note to the *Magill* cases, [1992] R.T.D.C. 372.

A. Françon, "*Le droit internationale de la propriété intellectuelle*" in *La protection de la propriété intellectuelle: aspects juridiques européens et internationaux* (1989, Institut Universitaire International de Luxembourg), pp. 11–78.

G. Frank, "Intellectual property rights in the European Economic Community and the Treaty of Rome – conflict or harmony" [1977] *Journal of the Patent Office Society* 274.

D. Franzone, "*Droit d'auteur et droits voisins: bilan et perspectives de l'action communautaire*" [1993] *Revue du Marché Unique Européen* 143.

M. Franzosi, "Grey market – parallel importation as a trade mark violation or an act of unfair competition" [1990] I.I.C. 194.

M. Franzosi, "Commentary" in *La protection des créations d'esthétique industrielle dans le cadre de la CEE: objectif 1992* (1988, CUERPI), pp. 67–69.

G. Friden, "Recent developments in EEC intellectual property law: the distinction between existence and exercise revisited" (1989) 26 C.M.L.Rev. 193.

H.-J. Glaesner, "*L'Article 100 A: un nouvel instrument pour la realisation du Marché Commun*" [1989] C.D.E. 615.

D. Glasl, "Essential facilities doctrine in E.C. anti-trust law: a contribution to the current debate" [1994] E.C.L.R. 306.

P. Glazener, "*Verplichte licenties in het gemeenschapsrecht*" [1992] *Intellectuele Eigendom & Reclamerecht* 10.

P. Gori, "The European patent grant system and how it ties in with revocation procedures" [1990] I.I.C. 452.

L. Gormley, "Newcastle disease and the free movement of goods – I" [1983] New L.J. 1037.

L. Gormley, "Reasoning renounced? The remarkable judgment in *Keck & Mithouard*" [1994] *European Business Law Review* 63.

L. Gormley, "Recent cases on Articles 30–36 EEC: compulsory patent licensing" (1985) 10 E.L.Rev. 447.

F. Gotzen, "*La libre circulation des produits couverts par un droit de propriété intellectuelle dans la jurisprudence de la Cour de Justice*" [1985] R.T.D.C. 467.

M. Gotzen, "*La propriété industrielle et les Articles 36 et 90 du Traité instituant la Communauté Economique Européenne*" [1958] R.T.D.C. 261.

I. Govaere, "Trade-related aspects of intellectual property rights: the E.C. dichotomy uncovered" in *La place de l'Europe dans le commerce mondiale* July Session 1994 (Institut Universitaire International Luxembourg), pp. 161–215.

I. Govaere, "Intellectual property protection and commercial policy" in M. Maresceau (ed.), *The European Community's commercial policy after 1992: the legal dimension* (1993, Martinus Nijhoff Publishers), pp. 197–222.

I. Govaere, P. Eeckhout, "On dual use goods and dualist case law: the *Aimé Richardt* judgment on export controls" (1992) 29 C.M.L.Rev. 941.

I. Govaere, "*Hag II of de ommekeer in de rechtspraak van het Europese Hof van Justitie inzake merken met een gemeenschappelijke oorsprong*" [1992] R.W. 105.

I. Govaere, "The impact of intellectual property protection on technology transfer between the E.C. and the Central and Eastern European countries" [1991] J.W.T. 57.

I. Govaere, F. Hélin, "Implementing the Internal Market: problems and perspectives" in Schwarze, Govaere, Hélin, Van den Bossche (eds.), *The 1992 Challenge at National Level* (1990, Nomos Verlagsgesellschaft), pp. 681–703.

S. Greif, "Patents and economic growth" [1987] I.I.C. 191.

P. Groves, "Don't be vague: towards an international system for design registration" [1992] *European Business Law Review* 230.

P. Groves "Motor vehicle distribution: the block exemption" [1987] E.C.L.R. 77.

D. Guy, "*Pharmon v. Hoechst* – Compulsory licences clarified" [1986] E.I.P.R. 252.

L. Gyselen, N. Kyriazis, "Article 86 EEC: the monopoly power measurement issue revisited" (1986) 11 E.L.Rev. 134.

T. Hagan, S. Henry, "Is a compulsory patent licensing statute necessary? A study of the US and foreign experience" [1976] *Patent Law Review* 285.

S. Haines, "Copyright takes the dominant position" [1994] E.I.P.R. 401.

B. Harris, "Community law and intellectual property: recent cases in the Court of Justice" (1982) 19 C.M.L.Rev. 61.

B. Hawk, "The American (antitrust) revolution: lessons for the EEC?" [1988] E.C.L.R. 53.

R. Higgins, P. Rubin, "Counterfeit goods" [1986] *Journal of Law & Economics* 211.

L. Idot, "*Le rapprochement des législations en matière de propriété intellectuelle. Bilan provisoire des travaux*" [1989] *Droit et Pratiques du Commerce International* 272.

H. James, "*Tetra Pak*: Exemption and abuse of dominant position" [1990] E.C.L.R. 267.

B. Jarvis, "Cheap and nasty" (September 20, 1986) *Commercial Motor* 51.

F.-C. Jeantet, R. Kovar, "*Les accords de distribution et de service des véhicules automobiles et l'Article 85 du Traité CEE: Etude du projet de règlement de la Commission des Communautés Européennes*" [1983] R.T.D.E. 547.

C. Joerges, "The Commission Regulation 123/85 on automobile distribution and servicing agreements: competition policy objectives and their implications for the consumer interests" in Joerges, Hiller, Holzcheck, Micklitz, *Vertriebspraktiken im Automobil-ersatzsektor* (1985, Verlag Peter Lang), pp. 353–386.

C. Joerges, "Selective distribution schemes in the motor-car sector: European competition policy, consumer interests and the draft regulation on the application of Article 85(3) of the Treaty to certain categories of motor-vehicle distribution and servicing agreements" in M. Goyens (ed.), *EC competition policy and the consumer interest* (1985, Bruylant), pp. 187–236.

J. Johannes, G. Wright, "In defense of Café Hag" (1976) 1 E.L.Rev. 230.

H. Johannes, "*La propriété industrielle et le droit d'auteur dans le droit des Communautés Européennes*" [1973] R.T.D.E. 369 and 557.

R. Joliet, "Copyright in the case-law of the Court of Justice of the European Communities" in W. Cornish (ed.), *Copyright in free and competitive markets* (1986, ESC), pp. 21–40.

R. Joliet, "*Droit de marques et libre circulation des marchandises: l'abandon de l'arrêt HAG I*" [1991] R.T.D.E. 169.

R. Joliet, "*La libre circulation des marchandises: l'arrêt Keck et Mithouard et les nouvelles orientations de la jurisprudence*" [1994] J.T.E. 145.

R. Joliet, "Patented articles and the free movement of goods within the EEC" [1975] *Current Legal Problems* 15.

U. Joos, R. Moufang, "*Report of the second Ringberg Symposium*" in Beier and Schricker (eds.), *GATT or WIPO?* (1989, VCH), pp. 1–41.

L. Kaplow, "The patent-antitrust intersection: a reappraisal" [1983–84] *Harvard Law Review* 1813.

P. Katzenberger, "General principles of the Berne and the Universal Copyright Conventions" in Beier and Schricker (eds.), *GATT or WIPO?* (1989, VCH), pp. 43–52.

E. Kitch, "Patents: monopolies or property rights?" in J. Palmer (ed.), *The economics of patents and copyright* (1986) pp. 31–49.

N. Koch, "Article 30 and the exercise of industrial property rights to block imports" [1986] Fordham Corp.L.Inst. 605.

V. Korah, "The preliminary draft of a new E.C. group exemption for technology licensing" [1994] E.I.P.R. 263.

V. Korah, "From legal form towards economic efficiency – Article 85(1) of the EEC Treaty in contrast to US antitrust" [1990] Antitrust Bull. 1009.

V. Korah, "No duty to license independent repairers to make spare parts: the *Renault, Volvo* and *Bayer & Hennecke* cases" [1988] E.I.P.R. 381.

V. Korah, "EEC competition policy – legal form or economic efficiency" [1986] *Current Legal Problems* 85.

V. Korah, "The limitations of copyright and patents by the rules for the free movement of goods in the European common market" [1982] *Case Western Reserve Journal of International Law* 7.

V. Korah, "Concept of a dominant position within the meaning of Article 86" (1980) 17 C.M.L.Rev. 395.

V. Korah, "Dividing the common market through national industrial property rights" [1972] M.L.R. 634.

G. Kunze, "Waiting for *Sirena II* – Trademark assignment in the case law of the European Court of Justice" [1991] I.I.C. 327.

A. Kur, "The Green paper's 'design approach' – what's wrong with it?" [1993] E.I.P.R. 374.

A. Kur, "The Max Planck Draft for a European Design Law" in F. Gotzen (ed.), *The Green Paper on industrial design* (1992, Story Scientia), pp. 13–26.

R. Lande, "The rise and (coming) fall of efficiency as the ruler of antitrust" [1988] Antitrust Bull. 429.

W. Landes, R. Posner, "An economic analysis of copyright law" [1989] *Journal of Legal Studies* 325.

M. Lehmann, "Property and intellectual property – property rights as restrictions on competition in furtherance of competition" [1989] I.I.C. 1.

M. Levitt, "*Delimitis* and *De Minimis*" [1994] E.C.L.R. 283.

R. Ludding, "*Groepsvrijstelling octrooilicenties*" [1985] S.E.W. 332.

N. MacFarlane, C. Wardle, J. Wilkinson, "The tension between intellectual property rights and certain provisions of E.C. law" [1994] E.I.P.R. 525.

G. Marenco, K. Banks, "Intellectual property and the Community rules on free movement of goods: discrimination unearthed" (1990) 15 E.L.Rev. 224.

G. Marenco, "*Pour une interpretation traditionelle de la notion de mesure d'effet équivalent a une restriction quantitative*" [1984] C.D.E. 291.

J. Markham, "Inventive activity: government controls and the legal environment" in *The rate and direction of inventive activity: economic and social factors* (1975, National Bureau of Economic Research), pp. 587–608.

A. Mattera, "*De l'arrêt 'Dassonville' à l'arrêt 'Keck': L'obscure clarté d'un jurisprudence riche en principes novateurs et en contradictions*" [1994] *Revue du Marché Unique Européen* 117.

A. Mattera, "*La libre circulation des oeuvres d'art à l'intérieur de la Communauté et la protection des trésors nationaux ayant une valeur artistique, historique ou archéologique*" [1993] *Revue du Marché Unique Européen* 9.

R. Merkin, "The interface between anti-trust and intellectual property" [1985] E.C.L.R. 377.

J. Mertens de Wilmar, "*Het Hof van Justitie van de Europese Gemeenschappen na de Europese Akte*" [1986] S.E.W. 615.

J. Mertens de Wilmar, "*Réflexions sur les méthodes d'interpretation de la Cour de Justice des Communautés Européennes*" [1986] C.D.E. 5.

J. Mertens de Wilmar, "*De Communautaire rechtspraak over het vrij verkeer van goederen*" [1984] R.W. 1.

J. Mertens de Wilmar, "The case-law of the Court of Justice in relation to the review of the legality of economic policy in mixed-economy systems" [1982] L.I.E.I. 1.

W. Möschel, "*La distribution sélective d'automobiles en droit européen de la concurrence*" [1991] R.T.D.C. 1.

J. Neukom, "What price the Community Patent?" [1992] E.I.P.R. 111.

E. Orf, "*Re Warner Bros Inc. and Metronome Video APS v. Erik Vuyff Christiansen*" [1988] E.I.P.R. 309.

N. Parr, M. Hughes, "The relevance of consumer brands and advertising in competition inquiries" [1993] E.C.L.R. 157.

R. Plaisant, G. Daverat, "*La distribution des pièces détachées pour automobiles et les lois contre les pratiques restrictives*" [1983] R.T.D.C. 147.

B. Posner, "The Community Design: purpose and scope of the Green Paper on the legal protection of industrial design" in F. Gotzen (ed.), *The Green Paper on the legal protection of industrial design* (1992, Story Scientia), pp. 1–11.

R. Posner, "The Chicago School of antitrust analysis" [1978/79] *University of Pennsylvania Law Review* 925.

F. Prändl, "Exhaustion of IP rights in the EEA applies to third-country goods placed on the EEA market" [1993] E.C.L.R. 43.

D. Price, "Abuse of a dominant position – the tale of nails, milk cartons, and TV guides" [1990] E.C.L.R. 80.

G. Priest, "What economists can tell lawyers about intellectual property rights" in J. Palmer (ed.), *Research in Law and Economics* (1986), pp. 19–24.

M. Quinn, N. MacGowan, "Could Article 30 impose obligations on individuals?" (1987) 12 E.L.Rev. 163.

N. Reich, "The November revolution of the European Court of Justice: *Keck, Meng* and *Audi*" (1994) 31 C.M.L.Rev. 459.

A. Reindl, "The magic of *Magill*: TV program guides as a limit of copyright law?" [1993] I.I.C. 60.

W. Rothnie, "*HAG II*: Putting the common origin doctrine to sleep" [1991] E.I.P.R. 24.

F. Savignon, "Luxembourg Conference on the Community Patent – A general report" [1976] I.I.C. 91.

A. Schäfers, "The Luxembourg Patent Convention, the best option for the internal market" [1987] *Journal of Common Market Studies* 193.

T. Schaper, "*Het 'specifiek voorwerp' van de industriële en commerciële eigendom in de EEG-rechtspraak*" [1977] *Rechtsgeleerd Magazijn Themis* 556.

T. Scharpe, "Comments on Christian Joerges' paper on selective distribution in the car sector" in M. Goyens (ed.), *EC competition policy and the consumer interest* (1985, Bruylant), pp. 249–263.

B. Schmitz, "Free movement of motor vehicles and spare parts in view of 1992: the consumer experience with Regulation 123/85", paper presented at the conference *Libera Circolazione degli Autoveicoli e dei loro Componenti nella Prospettiva del 1992*, Sienna, July 8–9, 1988.

B. Schmitz, "*Le point de vue des consommateurs*" in J. Pizzio (ed.), *Droit des consommateurs* (1987, Story Scientia), pp. 104–111.

B. Schwab, "*L'unification et l'harmonisation du droit des brevets*" in *La protection de la propriété intellectuelle*, Institut Universitaire International Luxembourg (July Session 1989), pp. 169–185.

V. Scordamaglia, "The Common Appeal Court and the future of the Community Patent following the Luxembourg Conference: Part One", (1991) I.I.C. 334.

V. Scordamaglia, "The Common Appeal Court and the future of the Community patent following the Luxembourg Conference: Part Two" [1991] I.I.C. 458.

M. Scott, "Compulsory licensing of intellectual property in international transactions" [1988] E.I.P.R. 319.

R. Seymour, "Patents and the transfer of technology" in F. Bradbury (ed.), *Technology transfer practice of international firms* (1978, Alpen Aan den Rijn), pp. 35–40.

J. Shaw, "Performing rights and Community law" (1988) 13 E.L.Rev. 45.

C. Shelley, "Abolition of the doctrine of common origin: some reflections on *Hag II* and its implications" [1991] *European Business Law Review* 87.

S. Singleton, "Intellectual property disputes: settlement agreements and ancillary licences under E.C. and U.K. competition law" [1993] E.I.P.R. 48.

T. Skinner, "The oral hearing of the *Magill* case" [1994] E.C.L.R. 103.

P. Slot, "The application of Articles 3(F), 5 and 85 to 94 EEC" (1987) 12 E.L.Rev. 179.

J. Smith, "Television guides: the European Court doesn't know 'there's so much in it'" [1992] E.C.L.R. 135.

P. Smith, "The Wolf in Wolf's clothing: the problem with predatory pricing" (1989) 14 E.L.Rev. 209.

B. Smulders, P. Glazener, "*Delimiteringsovereenkomsten en de bepalingen van het EEG-Verdrag inzake het vrij verkeer van goederen en de mededinging*" [1991] *Bijblad Industriële Eigendom* 103.

J. Staehelin, "The European Patent Organisation" [1981] *Yearbook of European Law* 333.

J. Stedman, "Patents and antitrust – the impact of varying legal doctrines" [1973] Utah L. Rev. 588.

K. Stöver, "*Les règlements d'exemption catégorielle relatifs à la distribution des voitures et aux stations-service*" in M. Collard *et al.*, *L'automobile et le droit européen* (1986, Editions du Jeune Barreau de Liège), pp. 181–204.

R. Strivens, "The E.C. Commission Green Paper on copyright" [1989] E.I.P.R. 275.

R. Subiotto, "The right to deal with whom one pleases under EEC competition law: a small contribution to a necessary debate" [1992] E.C.L.R. 234.

A. Subramanian, "The international economics of intellectual property right protection: a welfare-theoretic trade policy analysis" [1991] *World Development* 945.

J. Turner, "*Allen & Hanbury's v. Generics: Acte claire* – and wrong" [1988] E.I.P.R. 186.

L. Ubertazzi, "Copyright and the free movement of goods" [1985] I.I.C. 46.

C. Vadja, "The application of Community competition law to the distribution of computer products and parts" [1992] E.C.L.R. 110.

L. Van Aelen, "*De EEG-groepsvrijstelling voor franchise-overeenkomsten*" [1990] S.E.W. 3.

G. Van der Wal, "Article 86 EC: The limits of compulsory licensing" [1994] E.C.L.R. 230.

M. Van Kerckhove, "The Advocate General delivers his opinion on *Magill*" [1994] E.C.L.R. 276.

B. Van Voorst tot Voorst, J. Van Dam, "Europe 1992: free movement of goods in the wider context of a changing Europe" (1988) 25 C.M.L.Rev. 693.

J. Venit, "In the wake of windsurfing: Patent licensing in the common market" [1987] I.I.C. 1.

J. Venit, "EEC patent licensing revisited: the Commission's patent licence regulation" [1985] Antitrust Bull. 457.

P. Verloren van Themaat, "The contributions to the establishment of the internal market by the case-law of the Court of Justice of the European Communities" in Bieber *et al.* (eds.), *1992: One European market? A critical analysis of the Commission's internal market strategy* (1988, Nomos Verlagsgesellschaft), pp. 109–126.

P. Verloren van Themaat, "De Europese Akte" [1986] S.E.W. 478.

P. Verloren van Themaat, "*La libre circulation des marchandises après l'arrêt* 'Cassis de Dijon'" [1982] C.D.E. 123.

P. Verloren van Themaat, "*Précisions sur la portée de l'Article 36 par rapport à l'Article 85 du Traité de la CEE concernant les contrats de licence de brevets*" [1964] S.E.W. 83.

D. Vignes, "The harmonisation of national legislation and the EEC" (1990) 15 E.L.Rev. 358.

D. Vincent, "The role of patents in the transfer of technology" in F. Bradbury (ed.), *Technology transfer practice of international firms* (1978, Alpen Aan den Rijn), pp. 40–45.

T. Vinje, "*Magill*: its impact on the information technology industry" [1992] E.I.P.R. 397.

T. Vinje, "*Magill*: its impact on the information technology industry: Appendices" [1993] E.I.P.R. 71.

P. Vogelenzang, "Abuse of a dominant position in Article 86; the problem of causality and some applications" (1976) 13 C.M.L.Rev. 61.

D. Waelbroeck, "*L'arrêt* Keck et Mithouard: *les conséquences pratiques*" [1994] J.T.E. 459.

M. Waelbroeck, "Competition, integration and economic efficiency in the EEC from the point of view of the private firm" in Michigan Law Review Association (ed.), *The Art of Governance* (1987, Nomos), pp. 301–308.

J. Wallace, "Proper use of the patent misuse doctrine – an antitrust defense to patent infringement actions in need of rational reform" [1976] *Patent Law Review* 357.

W. Wallace, "Protection for designs in the United Kingdom" [1974] I.I.C. 421.

R. Whaite, "The draft technology transfer block exemption" [1994] E.I.P.R. 259.

E. White, "In search of the limits to Article 30 of the EEC Treaty" (1989) 26 C.M.L.Rev. 235.

E. White, "Case 19/84, *Pharmon BV v. Hoechst AG*" (1986) 23 C.M.L.Rev. 719.

L. White, "Vertical restraints in antitrust law: a coherent model" [1981] Antitrust Bull. 327.

J. Worthy, "Intellectual property protection after GATT" [1994] E.I.P.R. 195.

Index

(All references are to paragraph number)

Abuse of dominant position,
  derivative market, 5.49–5.50, 5.54–5.57, 5.60
  "spare parts" cases,
    arbitrary refusal to sell to repairers, 8.47–8.52
    concept, 8.36
    examples, 8.46
    generally, 8.09, 8.35
    nature,
      function theory, 8.38–8.40
      generally, 8.37
      specific subject-matter concept, 8.41–8.46
    premature termination of product production, 8.57–8.59
    unfair price setting, 8.53–8.56
    unprotected product, 5.37, 5.41, 5.44
Abuse of exercise of rights. *See also* **Competition rules**
  abusive practices,
    case law, 5.34
    copyright enforcement, 5.49, 5.54–5.57
    derivative market,
      CFI appraisal, 5.51–5.57
      Commission approach, 5.47–5.50
      ECJ appraisal, 5.58–5.67
    dominant position,
      abuse of. *See also* **Abuse of dominant position**
        derivative market, 5.49–5.50, 5.54–5.57, 5.60
        unprotected product, 5.37, 5.41, 5.44
      generally. *See also* **Dominant position**
        derivative market, 5.48, 5.52–5.53
        unprotected product, 5.36, 5.40
    product marks, 5.48, 5.57
    unprotected product,
      CFI appraisal, 5.39–5.43
      Commission approach, 5.35–5.38
      ECJ appraisal, 5.44–5.46
  approach to determining,
    generally, 5.78, 6.01
  case law, 3.36–3.49
  distinction between Articles 85 and 86,
    case law, 5.69–5.72
    CFI appraisal, 5.73–5.77
    generally, 5.68

Abuse of exercise of rights—*cont.*
  distinguished from misuse of exercise of rights, 5.01, 5.78
  functionality test, 3.44–3.48
  generally, 3.33–3.39
  licensing agreements,
    essence of rights criteria, 5.15
    patent licence policy,
      Commission approach, 5.17–5.21
      ECJ appraisal, 5.22–5.31
    technology transfer agreements, block exemption, 5.32–5.33
  principles,
    Article 85, 5.03–5.09
    Article 86, 5.10–5.14
    basic rule, 5.02
  rules establishing, 5.78
Abuse of existence of rights,
  consent theory, application of, 6.02–6.19. *See also* **Consent theory**
  generally, 6.01, 6.20
  justification test, 6.65
  obligatory licences, 6.21–6.42. *See also* **Obligatory licences**
  relative novelty, 6.43–6.52. *See also* **Novelty**
  rental and lending rights, 6.53–6.64. *See also* **Rental and lending rights**
Approximation principle,
  generally, 3.26
Article 36. *See* **Free movement of goods principle**
Article 85. *See also* **Competition**
  distinguished from Article 86,
    case law, 5.69–5.72
    CFI appraisal, 5.73–5.77
    generally, 5.68
  licensing agreements,
    essence of rights criteria, 5.15
    patent licence policy,
      Commission approach, 5.17–5.21
      ECJ appraisal, 5.22–5.31
    technology transfer agreements, block exemption, 5.32–5.33
  selective distribution agreements, and, 9.06
Article 86. *See also* **Competition**
  abusive practices,
    case law, 5.34
    copyright enforcement, 5.49, 5.54–5.57

329